Managing High-Risk Sex Offenders in the Community

Managing High-Risk Sex Offenders in the Community

Risk management, treatment and social responsibility

Edited by

Karen Harrison

WILLAN
PUBLISHING

Published by

Willan Publishing
Culmcott House
Mill Street, Uffculme
Cullompton, Devon
EX15 3AT, UK
Tel: +44(0)1884 840337
Fax: +44(0)1884 840251
e-mail: info@willanpublishing.co.uk
Website: www.willanpublishing.co.uk

Published simultaneously in the USA and Canada by

Willan Publishing
c/o ISBS, 920 NE 58th Ave, Suite 300
Portland, Oregon 97213-3786, USA
Tel: +001(0)503 287 3093
Fax: +001(0)503 280 8832
e-mail: info@isbs.com
Website: www.isbs.com

First published 2010

ISBN   978-1-84392-526-2 paperback
          978-1-84392-525-5 hardback

British Library Cataloguing-in-Publication Data

A catalogue record for this book is available from the British Library.

Project managed by Deer Park Productions, Tavistock, Devon
Typeset by GCS, Leighton Buzzard, Bedfordshire
Printed and bound by T.J. International Ltd, Padstow, Cornwall

Contents

List of tables and figures   *vii*
List of abbreviations   *ix*
Notes on contributors   *xi*
Preface   *xvii*

Part I: Introduction

1   Paedophilia: definitions and aetiology   3
    Karen Harrison, Kieran McCartan and Rachel Manning

2   High-risk sex offenders: issues of policy   18
    Mark Farmer and Ruth Mann

Part II: Risk management

3   Effective multi-agency public protection: learning from
       the research   39
    Jason Wood and Hazel Kemshall

4   The sex offender register, community notification and
       some reflections on privacy   61
    Terry Thomas

Part III: Treatment and risk reduction

5   An introduction to sex offender treatment programmes
       and their risk reduction efficacy   81
    Sarah Brown

6 The use of pharmacotherapy with high-risk sex offenders   105
   Karen Harrison

7 Restorative justice and the reintegration of high-risk
      sex offenders   133
   Anne-Marie McAlinden

Part IV: Special offender groups

8 Female sexual offenders: a special subgroup   159
   Franca Cortoni

9 Enhancing community collaboration to stop sexual
      harm by youth   174
   Joann Schladale

10 Mentally disordered sexual offenders   193
   Brad Booth

11 Intellectually disabled sexual offenders: subgroup
      profiling and recidivism after outpatient treatment   209
   Joan van Horn, Jules Mulder and Ine Kusters

Part V: Social and moral responsibilities

12 Cyber-sex offences: patterns, prevention and protection   229
   Majid Yar

13 Media constructions of, and reactions to, paedophilia
      in society   249
   Kieran McCartan

14 Dignity and dangerousness: sex offenders and the
      community – human rights in the balance?   269
   Bernadette Rainey

Index   291

List of tables and figures

Tables

3.1	Summary of the HMIC and HMIP 2005 findings	48
4.1	Registration periods for commission of designated sexual offences	64
4.2	Statements by Home Office Ministers on strengthening the register	65
4.3	'Strengthening' and 'tightening' the Sex Offender 'Register' 1997–2009	68
11.1	Sample characteristics	214

Figures

6.1	Hierarchy of medication for controlling sexually deviant behaviour	119
10.1	Rates of institutionalisation in the USA (per 100,000 adults)	194
11.1	Rearrests and recidivism rates (%) among low-risk offenders, specialists, and generalists	218

List of abbreviations

ACPO	Association of Chief Police Officers
ADHD	attention deficit hyperactivity disorder
APA	American Psychiatric Association
ASACP	Association of Sites Advocating Child Protection
ATSA	Association for the Treatment of Sexual Abuse
BIF	borderline intellectual functioning
CBT	cognitive-behavioural techniques
CEOP	Child Exploitation and Online Protection Centre
CJA	Criminal Justice Act
CJCSA	Criminal Justice and Court Services Act
CODC	Collaborative Outcome Data Committee
COSA	Circles of Support and Accountability
CPA	cyproterone acetate
CRU	Cyberspace Research Unit
CSA	child sexual abuse
CSOR	Child Sex Offender Review
DSM	*Diagnostic and Statistical Manual of Mental Disorders*
ECHR	European Convention on Human Rights
ECtHR	European Court of Human Rights
ECPAT	End Child Prostitution, Child Pornography and Trafficking of Children for Sexual Purposes
ECT	electroconvulsive therapy
FSH	follicle-stimulating hormone
GAD	generalised anxiety disorder
GnRH	gonadotrophin-releasing hormone
HMIC	Her Majesty's Inspectorate of Constabulary

HMIP	Her Majesty's Inspectorate of Probation
HRA	Human Rights Act
ICC	intraclass correlation coefficients
ID	intellectually disabled
IFR	Internet Filter Review
IM	intramuscular
INHOPE	Internet Hotline Providers in Europe
IOG	intensive outpatient group therapy
IPP	imprisonment for public protection
ISPs	Internet service providers
IWF	Internet Watch Foundation
JDS	Judicial Documentation System
LH	luteinising hormone
LHRH	luteinising hormone-releasing hormone
MAPPA	Multi-Agency Public Protection Arrangements
MAPPP	Multi-Agency Public Protection Panel
MDSO	mentally disordered sexual offender
MPA	medroxyprogesterone acetate
NCIS	National Crime Intelligence Service
NCR	not criminally responsible on account of mental disorder
ng	nanogram
NGRI	not guilty by reason of insanity
NOMS	National Offender Management Service
OASys	Offender Assessment System
OCD	obsessive compulsive disorder
PNC	Police National Computer
PSA	Police Superintendents Association
PTSD	post-traumatic stress disorder
RM2000	Risk Matrix 2000
RSS	Recognition Service System
SC	Sentencing Circles
SOA	Sexual Offences Act
SOPO	Sex Offender Prevention Order
SSRI	selective serotonin reuptake inhibitor
SVR-20	Sexual Violence Risk – 20
WAIS	Wechsler Adult Intelligence Scale

Notes on contributors

Brad Booth is a forensic psychiatrist who completed his residency training at the University of Ottawa, Canada with a special interest in sexual offenders. He then continued fellowship training at Case Western Reserve University in Cleveland, Ohio, USA. He is currently co-director of the sexual offender unit for mentally disordered offenders at the St Lawrence Correctional and Treatment Centre in Brockville, Ontario, and an assistant professor at the University of Ottawa. Dr Booth focuses on the treatment of offenders with co-morbid mental disorders and regularly assesses offenders for the courts.

Sarah Brown has considerable experience in sex offender treatment programmes and in forensic risk assessment. She is a forensic psychologist, a chartered psychologist and an Associate Fellow of the British Psychological Society. Sarah developed and is the course director of Coventry University's MSc Forensic Psychology Course, which is accredited by the British Psychology Society. She has conducted and supervised research focusing on sex offenders; for example, her doctoral research evaluated sex offender treatment programmes provided by British probation services, and she has recently supervised doctoral research on sexual grooming. Her 2005 book, *Treating Sex Offenders*, has received positive international reviews. She is also the editor of *The Journal of Sexual Aggression*.

Franca Cortoni received her PhD in clinical and forensic psychology from Queen's University at Kingston, Ontario, Canada. Since 1989, she has worked with and conducted research on male and female offenders in a variety of Canadian and Australian penitentiaries and community settings. In addition, she has provided consultancy and training services in the assessment, treatment and management of sexual offenders in Canada, Australia, the USA and the UK. Formerly with the Correctional Service Canada, Dr Cortoni is now assistant professor at the School of Criminology of the University of Montreal. She has published and made numerous presentations at national and international conferences. She is an associate editor of *The Journal of Sexual Aggression*.

Mark Farmer is head of the sex offender team in the public protection unit of the National Offender Management Service England and Wales, a post he has held since January 2007. As such, he is responsible for the development of policy and strategy with regard to the management of sex offenders in prisons and probation. Prior to that he had been employed in a variety of management roles within criminal justice organisations associated with the management and treatment of sexual offenders.

Karen Harrison is a lecturer in law at the University of Hull. She has research interests in sentencing, the use of community penalties, and dangerous offenders. She graduated from the University of Wales, Aberystwyth, with a PhD in 2003 and has also worked at Coventry University and Bristol Law School, UWE – Bristol. Her current research is focused on dangerous offenders, and she has published several articles on the use of chemical castration for high-risk sex offenders. She is an editorial board member of both *The Journal of Sexual Aggression* and *The Prison Service Journal*.

Hazel Kemshall is Professor of Community and Criminal Justice at De Montfort University, Leicester, UK. She has research interests in risk assessment, risk management, and risk policies in criminal justice and has carried out research on risk under the Economic and Social Research Council's 'Risk and Human Behaviour' programme. She has investigated the work of public protection panels for the UK Home Office, and has developed training materials for the Probation Service in England and Wales, and for social workers in Scotland. She has published numerous books and articles on risk in social care and criminal justice.

Joan van Horn took her doctoral degree in 2002, and since March 2003 she has been employed at De Waag, a Dutch forensic psychiatric outpatient treatment centre, as a senior researcher. With the assistance of master students in psychology and criminology, she has conducted several research projects, such as the evaluation of various risk assessment instruments in a sample of juvenile and adult sex and violent (intellectually disabled) offenders, recidivism among domestic violent offenders, and arsonists.

Ine Kusters has been employed at De Waag forensic centre, Utrecht, The Netherlands, as a therapist, since 1999. She gives individual and group-based treatments to (intellectually disabled) sexual and aggressive clients. In 2000, she conducted the psychological assessment of mentally disabled sexual offenders.

Ruth Mann works for the National Offender Management Service England and Wales (NOMS), in the headquarters group responsible for interventions with offenders. She is responsible for sex offender treatment policy across prison and probation services, and for research into the effectiveness of NOMS interventions. She has worked in the field of sex offender assessment and treatment for over 20 years, and has published numerous papers and chapters on this topic. She is an associate editor for *The Journal of Sexual Aggression* and recently guest-edited an edition of *The Prison Service Journal* that focused on responses to sexual offending.

Rachel Manning is a senior lecturer in social psychology at the University of the West of England – Bristol. Her research interests broadly relate to 'pro-' and 'anti-social' behaviour, and are informed by social and environmental psychology. Her research in these areas has included a historical analysis of research in social psychology, the implications of socio-spatial identities, and everyday understandings of crime-related actions. Her work is facilitated by the use of multi-method research programmes.

Anne-Marie McAlinden is a lecturer in law at Queen's University Belfast, where she previously completed her PhD. She has published widely in the area of sexual offences and is the author of *The Shaming of Sexual Offenders* (2007; Oxford: Hart). This book was awarded the British Society of Criminology Book Prize 2008.

Kieran McCartan is a senior lecturer in criminology at the University of the West of England (UWE) – Bristol. Kieran completed his first degree in psychology at Queen's University Belfast, before moving to Leicester to do an MSc in criminology at the Scarman Centre, and a PhD in the Department of Psychology. He is a multi-disciplinary researcher with an interest in criminal psychology, and has published previously on sex offenders. Prior to joining UWE in 2007 he taught psychology and criminology at the University of Leicester.

Jules Mulder is a psychotherapist and is the programme director of De Waag, the Dutch forensic centre. He has published in The Netherlands and internationally on the treatment of paedosexual offenders, relapse prevention and domestic violence.

Bernadette Rainey is a lecturer at Cardiff Law School, UK. She teaches human rights and criminal law. Her research interests include human rights and equality law, refugee law and public law. Bernadette graduated in law from Queen's University Belfast in 1993, and she was awarded a PhD in refugee law at Queen's University Belfast in 2003. Bernadette has held a research post at the law department of the University of Wales, Aberystwyth, 2000–3 and at the School of Law, Swansea University, 2003–5. Bernadette was a lecturer at Queen's University Belfast before joining Cardiff Law School in September 2006.

Joann Schladale has been working in the field of interpersonal violence and trauma since 1981. In 1991, at the University of Louisville, Kentucky, USA, she developed and coordinated the internationally acclaimed Juvenile Sexual Offender Counselor Certification Program. As the founder and executive director of Resources for Resolving Violence, Inc., Joann provides extensive consultation, programme development and evaluation, clinical supervision, and staff development and training focusing on empirically driven assessment and treatment. She is a clinical member of the American Association for Marriage and Family Therapy and the Association for Treatment of Sexual Abusers. She recently collaborated with other professionals in the field to create Community-Based Standards for Addressing Sexual Harm by Youth.

Terry Thomas is Professor of Criminal Justice Studies, School of Social Sciences, Leeds Metropolitan University, UK, and is the author of *Privacy and Social Services* (1995), *Sex Crime: Sex Offending and Society* (2005, 2nd edn), and *Criminal Records: A Database for the Criminal Justice System and Beyond* (2007). He spent six months in the USA in 2002 looking at sex offender registers and community notification while based at the University of Minnesota. In an earlier life, he worked for 12 years in local authority social services departments.

Jason Wood is currently Acting Head of Research in the Youth and Community Division at De Montfort University, Leicester, UK. He has research interests and expertise in the community management of high-risk offenders, including the effectiveness of strategies used to involve the public. In 2005, he evaluated the implementation of Multi-Agency Public Protection Arrangements (MAPPA) with Hazel Kemshall and Gill Mackenzie, for the Home Office. He also led an investigation into MAPPA work with high-risk sex offenders (with Hazel Kemshall, Mike Maguire, Kirsty Hudson and Gill Mackenzie) commissioned by the Home Secretary in 2006 for the Child Sex Offender Review.

Majid Yar is Professor of Sociology at the University of Hull, UK. Educated at the universities of York and Lancaster, he previously taught and researched at the universities of Keele, Kent and Lancaster. His research interests include the Internet and new media; cybercrime; representations of crime and deviance in popular culture; globalisation, inequalities and social harms; and criminological and social theory. He is the author of *Cybercrime and Society* (2006), co-author (with Martin O'Brien) of *Criminology: The Key Concepts* (2008), and co-editor (with Yvonne Jewkes) of *Handbook on Internet Crime* (2009).

Preface

Sex offenders and in particular paedophiles have become the 'folk devils' of modern society, with such a view of offenders being promoted by the media and to a lesser extent by the government and politicians. Although practitioners and other professionals know that 'stranger danger' is not the main cause of concern, in terms of personal safety, this information has not been widely distributed throughout the general public, much of the community believing that it is the outsider whom they need to protect their children from. This view has been promulgated by campaigns such as 'Name and Shame', which was introduced and supported by the *News of the World* and the subsequent drive for a UK Megan's Law, which was named Sarah's Law after Sarah Payne. Again, however, there is confusion, generally created by a lack of knowledge, over what Sara Payne (Sarah's mother) is campaigning for, with assumptions and postulations often taking the place of fact.

Claims regarding perceived lenient sentencing often feature prominently in the media. This creates further fear within society and, to an extent, anger at what the public perceive to be an unjust system; this is perhaps felt because of the often held, but arguably incorrect, view that community punishment is the soft option within sentencing. Errors made by the responsible authorities also feature more frequently and more prominently in headlines and breaking news, promoting further fear within society that such high-risk offenders cannot be effectively managed. While mistakes leading to the creation of further victims are highly regrettable and we should seek to ensure that such errors are avoided in future, such information is never balanced with reports of the many offenders who are successfully managed. As we all know, good news does not sell, and so society only gets to hear the bad, further creating fear and loathing within our communities, but, importantly, additionally propagating the incorrect and negative connotations and beliefs about sex offenders and how they are managed by the authorities.

The aim of this book is therefore to look at the truth behind the 'stories', with an emphasis on how sex offenders and in particular high-risk sex offenders are managed and treated within the community. While it is not assumed that all in the garden is rosy, a more considered approach will be taken, using up-to-date research, written by academics, policymakers and practitioners from England, Wales, Canada, the USA and the Netherlands, some of whom have been working in the field of sex offenders for many years. It brings together experts from psychology, criminology, law, offender treatment, sociology and psychotherapy. In short, the book evaluates the measures used, and being considered for use, in the treatment and risk management of sex offenders and ultimately questions whether such high-risk offenders can be effectively managed within the community. This is important, as the overall aim of the book is to identify methods of preventing further sexual victimisation. In addition, the book also looks at a number of specific sex offender groups and questions whether policy and practice need to change when dealing with 'different' types of offenders. Finally, it turns the spotlight on the media and more generally on us as members of society, asking what our social responsibilities are and what we need to do in order to help in the treatment and risk management of those high-risk sex offenders living within our communities.

The first drafts of many of these chapters were presented at a conference, 'Managing High-Risk Sex Offenders in the Community', held at Bristol Law School, University of the West of England (UWE) – Bristol in September 2008. The rationale for the conference, as for this book, is to add to the ongoing dialogue as research, practice, beliefs and attitudes continue to evolve; with this collection representing contemporary developments up until early 2009.

The book is divided into five sections: Introduction, Risk Management, Treatment and Risk Reduction, Special Offender Groups and Social and Moral Responsibilities. Part one of the book provides general introductory material including views from academics and practitioners/policy makers. Chapter 1 by Harrison, McCartan and Manning looks at the definitions and aetiology of sex offenders, with particular reference to paedophiles. It considers what is meant by the term 'paedophile' arguing that there are substantial differences in the use of the word depending whether it is defined using legal, sociological, biological, historical or cultural definitions. The chapter also briefly looks at the question of cause and why sex offenders offend, concluding that there is no single aetiology which they argue should be taken into account when risk treatment and management decisions are made.

Chapter 2 is written by Farmer and Mann, two experts concerned with policy making and offender treatment in England and Wales. They begin by examining the all important question of what is meant by the term high-risk offender and, equally significantly, consider whether it is a term which can be justifiably applied to sex offenders. They then examine what should be done with high-risk sex offenders focusing on the meaning of risk, risk assessment, restrictive interventions, rehabilitative responses and the challenges which offender management organisations are faced with. Using these arguments they also examine public, media and political debates around sexual offending, and the impact these have had on public policy in late modernity and the impact of the so called risk society.

The second part of the book, Risk Management, was originally meant to contain three chapters: those detailed below and another on current developments in the use of satellite tracking technology with sex offenders. This work is important because of the risk that some sex offenders pose when they are released from prison; especially those who had been given determinate sentences and thus are released from prison even if risk levels have not decreased. Satellite tracking technology can currently pinpoint the location of the tracking unit to an accuracy of between two and 10 metres, which, when compared with electronic monitoring which can only inform when an offender is not at the designated residence, is a valuable breakthrough in risk management. The Home Office has already identified sex offenders as one of four priority groups of offenders which it believes are suitable for satellite tracking technology and most would agree that this is entirely appropriate. Whilst published trials have only looked at passive and hybrid tracking, there is also the possibility of active tracking which is able to track an offender in real time and enables the responsible authorities to know where the person is 24/7. Whilst such technology is extremely expensive, it can be argued that its advantages far outweigh this and further research is thus needed to test its usability and efficiency. Unfortunately, however, it has not been possible to include the proposed chapter on satellite tracking technology with sex offenders.

The risk management part therefore opens with a chapter by Wood and Kemshall which looks at the effectiveness of agencies working in partnership through the Multi-Agency Public Protection Arrangements (MAPPA). Based on the extensive research carried out by the authors, this chapter undertakes a review of MAPPA as it has evolved over the past decade. In particular it examines what constitutes 'good practice' and how effectiveness is and could be further measured. It concludes by critically considering whether the current model of MAPPA is really the best way to ensure a balance between restriction and reintegration of high-risk sex offenders.

Chapter 4, by Thomas, continues with the theme of risk management by outlining the development and rationale for the UK sex offender register. Looking at subsequent changes to, and strengthening of, the register since its introduction in 1997, the chapter considers the more punitive direction it appears to be taking in 2009. At the same time, it acknowledges the parallel pressures being put on the Home Office to allow a right of public access to the register (community notification) to allow communities to know where 'known' sex offenders live. The Home Office has steadfastly refused to allow public access but has made concessions over 'discretionary' disclosure. Finally, the chapter concludes with some thoughts on the nature of privacy, with particular reference to offenders, and the advent of the 'surveillance society'.

Part III of the book moves on to look at the treatment and risk reduction of high-risk sex offenders, opening with Chapter 5 by Brown, which considers the use of sex offender treatment programmes. This chapter outlines the basic principles and theoretical approaches that underpin the programmes and describes the core elements of the majority of programmes used. The second part of the chapter looks at the efficacy of these programmes, briefly explaining why it is so difficult to conduct evaluation projects in the criminal justice context that provide conclusive findings of efficacy or otherwise, and then assesses what can be determined from the research evidence about sex offender treatment programme efficacy.

This is followed by Chapter 6 on the more controversial use of pharmacotherapy (chemical castration) with sex offenders. Written by Harrison, this chapter looks at what pharmacotherapy is and how it works and, importantly, it questions how effective it has been in other jurisdictions such as the USA and other European countries. The chapter comments on the introduction of drug treatment in the sex offender strategy in England and Wales and evaluates the drugs used and the referral process. In addition, it questions whether drug treatment should be part of a punishment agenda or a treatment package, and considers whether such treatment should ever be given on a mandatory basis.

Finally in Part III, McAlinden in Chapter 7 looks at the use of restorative justice in the reintegration of high-risk sex offenders. Looking at a number of restorative programmes, but focusing on Circles of Support and Accountability (COSA), this chapter argues that restorative programmes can operate as a practical means of addressing the core problems with the reintegration of sex offenders. Originating in Canada, COSA involves the development of informal networks of support and treatment that involve the offender, state, voluntary agencies and the wider community. Such programmes not only work to meet the offender's rehabilitative needs but also to allay public anxieties concerning the presence of sex offenders in our communities. The effectiveness of such programmes and their contribution to public protection are also assessed.

While Parts II and III of the book provide a plethora of information on current thinking and practice, much of this evidence is based on male, adult, mentally 'normal' offenders. In acknowledgement of the fact that sex offenders come in all shapes and sizes, Part IV of the book considers a number of special offender groups, with Cortoni opening the section by looking at females who sexually offend. As female sexual offenders increasingly come to the attention of the criminal justice system, she argues that we need to develop a better understanding of the issues related to the assessment and management of these offenders. The chapter therefore provides a review of the current knowledge in the areas of the risk, assessment and treatment needs of women who sexually offend, considering issues such as the prevalence of female sexual offending, recidivism rates, and factors relating to sexually offending behaviour among women.

Chapter 9 looks at the specific group of juveniles, focusing on how enhancing community collaboration can help to stop sexual harm by youth. Written by Schladale, a consultant practitioner working with youth who sexually offend in the USA, the chapter provides a foundation for a comprehensive, community-based response to sexual harm by youth, based on a collaborative approach. Addressing issues such as risk factors, motivation and obstacles to community collaboration, the chapter outlines how creating a standardised approach involving a shared vision, mission, core values and philosophy of care can contribute to addressing sexual harm by youth. Furthermore, the chapter describes what community collaboration looks like and highlights solutions for problem solving throughout the full length of time a youth and family are involved with systems of care.

This is followed by a consideration of mentally disordered offenders in Chapter 10, which is written by Booth. Focusing on practice in Canada, this chapter outlines the migration of mentally ill people from psychiatric hospitals to criminal justice institutions and jails, highlighting how many correctional facilities are not equipped to deal with severe mental illnesses. Concentrating on his experiences as a practitioner at the sexual offender unit for mentally disordered offenders at the St Lawrence Correctional and Treatment Centre in Brockville, Ontario, the author looks at the prevalence of mental illness among sex offenders and discusses issues such as diagnosis, treatment and the needs of specific populations. Booth argues that awareness of mentally disordered offenders needs to be increased and outlines effective treatment strategies to be used when treating such offenders.

The last chapter in Part IV, written by van Horn, Mulder and Kusters, looks at the special group of intellectually disabled (ID) sex offenders. The chapter outlines prevalence estimates of ID offenders and also identifies recidivism rates, risk factors and treatment needs. Focusing on the results of a study carried out by the authors on ID sex offenders at De Waag, a forensic psychiatric outpatient treatment centre in the Netherlands, Chapter 11 identifies subgroups of ID offenders and evaluates the effectiveness of their intensive outpatient group therapy programme. After dividing ID sex offenders into low-risk offenders, generalists and specialists, the chapter concludes with recommendations for treating this specific group of offenders.

The final part of the book deals with social and moral responsibilities, beginning with cyber-sex offences in Chapter 12. Written by Yar, this chapter surveys the patterns of Internet-based sexual offending, paying particular attention to those offenders who target and exploit children. Looking at issues such as the production and circulation of child pornography, abuses committed via electronic communication, and the use of Internet chat rooms by sex offenders to groom minors for subsequent abuse, the chapter examines the range of actual and potential preventative strategies to protect children from online sexual exploitation. These include formal and informal policing, the electronic monitoring of Internet communications, and content and safety education programmes that have been designed and directed at both young users and their parents.

Moving on from personal and parental responsibility, Chapter 13, by McCartan, looks at media constructions of and reactions to paedophilia in society. Examining the language and ideas used by the media in discussing sex offenders and paedophiles, the chapter questions how close to reality this rhetoric is. Furthermore, it discusses the social responsibilities of the media, assesses whether such responsibilities have been achieved, and finally evaluates the impact and influence such reporting has had on society's perceptions and attitudes. In conclusion, the chapter discusses how the media can more constructively discuss paedophiles, working to educate the public and to dispel common myths surrounding such offences and offenders.

The final chapter, by Rainey, looks at human rights and the balancing of dignity and dangerousness. By using examples such as indeterminate sentencing, the sex offender register, and the use of pharmacotherapy, the chapter discusses the premise that the rights of the sex offender should be balanced against community protection. Furthermore, it examines whether such a balancing exercise can undermine the fundamental rights guaranteed to everyone, through numerous human rights instruments, and in so doing whether this undermines the dignity of all, irrespective of risk or dangerousness.

As mentioned above, the overall aim of this book is to identify methods of preventing further sexual victimisation. Whether this has been achieved is for the reader to assess.

Karen Harrison
Hull

Part I

Introduction

Chapter 1

Paedophilia: definitions and aetiology

Karen Harrison, Kieran McCartan
and Rachel Manning

Introduction

Seemingly nowhere but in the realms of social science research do sex offenders enjoy such popularity. Yet in spite of the current high level of interest in this area, numerous commentators have noted the lack of cohesiveness and clarity in this field (van Dam 2001; McCartan 2008). While it might be difficult to orchestrate overall coherence in the face of what is perceived to be a pressing public safety problem, effecting consensus in issues relating to high-risk sex offenders is additionally challenging, in a variety of ways. As this book illustrates, such issues are suffused with debate, ambiguity and argument; yet we are still presented with the harm experienced by individuals at the hand of those labelled as sex offenders, and, crucially, the potential of these individuals to inflict future harm. It is the debate regarding the management and treatment of this future risk that concerns much of this volume. However, in this chapter, we wish to contextualise these issues by reflecting on some of the perceptions and understandings of sex offenders that we have available to us (as a society). Such reflection, we suggest, is requisite of us as academics and practitioners in critically evaluating the theoretical and conceptual foundations upon which issues of treatment and management are grounded.

In this chapter we therefore begin to examine the definitions and aetiology of sex offenders, although, due to limitations of space, we only present some ideas here. In so doing, we focus in particular on sexual offences against children, and paedophilia in particular. This is for a variety of reasons, not least that we must necessarily be selective in our coverage and do not attempt here a more comprehensive review of definitional issues. Focusing on this particular group of sex offenders also allows us to illustrate a number of issues that are common (in broad terms) to a range of forms of sexual offending. Moreover, the inclusion of child–adult sexual activity as central to paedophilia allows us to highlight additional factors which problematise existing debate.

Definitions of paedophilia from a multi-disciplinary perspective

Paedophilia has been previously defined as 'a severe public health problem of staggering proportions' (McDonald Wilson Bradford 2000: 248). It has thus become a high-profile media issue, increasing exponentially over the last 10 years (Greer 2002; McCartan 2004). Considering the centrality of paedophilia to modern society (McAlinden 2006a), it is easy to assume that there is clarity regarding what paedophilia is, who paedophiles are, what causes a person to demonstrate paedophilic behaviour, and what can be done to manage and treat such behaviour. While most of this book looks at the latter issues, this chapter will begin to discuss the various contemporary understandings of paedophilia, in order to illustrate some of the issues that underlie/necessarily precede management and treatment.

Despite the volume of research into paedophilia, academic and applied clarity and cohesiveness concerning definitions have not resulted (Howitt 1998; Silverman and Wilson 2002), with commentators pointing to the substantial differences (Howitt 1998) in contemporary legal, sociological and biological definitions of paedophilia. Moreover, the interrelationship between these different arenas presents further challenges – for example, in terms of the positioning of paedophilia as a criminal offence as opposed to a pathological condition (Ames and Houston 1990). Such issues are compounded by the additional range of concerns that are attendant on phenomena such as paedophilia (i.e. the nature and definitions of concepts such as child, adult and sexual). While some commentators suggest that our current understandings are better than they have ever been (van Dam 2001; Ireland and Worthington 2009), it is nonetheless instructive to examine these contemporary perceptions.

Paedophilia from a clinical perspective

One core feature of clinical perspectives (in contrast to legal and other perspectives, where the term 'child sexual abuse' (CSA) is used as a blanket term to cover all forms of CSA and child sexual offenders, Rind *et al.* 1998) is that within the clinical literature a distinction is made between paedophilia and other forms of CSA. This distinction is reflective of the range of typologies developed from clinical perspectives (for example, extrafamilial child molestation, intrafamilial child molestation, paedophilia, child molestation, hebephilia and paraphilia (for more information, see Bartol and Bartol 2008)). One of the reasons why the clinical definition of paedophilia has become somewhat ambiguous is the focus on the way that offenders are conceptualised by clinicians along a variety of different dimensions, with each individual being categorised through his or her offending behaviour, psychology, personality, personal motivations and degree of risk. For example, an individual clinically classified as a paedophile may not necessarily be classified as a child sexual molester, for he may not offend against a child (Leberg 1997; Howitt 1998), or he may not wish to harm the child, and/or he may believe that he is in love with the child (O'Carroll 1980).

The historical particularity of this endeavour to provide typologies suitable for carving up the range of behaviours involved in CSA is no better illustrated than in *The Diagnostic and Statistical Manual of Mental Disorders* (DSM). Generally speaking, from a clinical perspective, paedophilia is seen as a paraphilia (Freund 1994; American Psychiatric Association (APA) 2000). However, there is no consistent clinical definition, as conceptions constantly adapt. The DSM definition, like other typologies, focuses on the assumed homogeneous characteristics of paedophilia (Freund 1994), in spite of its recognised heterogeneous nature (Bickley and Beech 2001; Taylor and Quayle 2003). In the DSM definitions, paedophilia has ranged from being a sexual deviation and a sociopathic condition (APA 1952), to a sexual deviation classified as a non-psychotic medical disorder (APA 1968), to a paraphilia, with offenders being defined as interested only in sexual acts with prepubescent children (APA 1980) and the definition later adapted to include paedophiles who also have an interest in adult–adult sexual relations (APA 1987). More recently, this was further changed so as to define paedophilia as a sexual paraphilia, stating that the offender has to be at least 16 years of age as well as being at least five years older than the victim; that the victim is not older than 12 or 13; and that the offender has serious sexual urges/fantasies that are causing him distress or that he has acted upon (APA 2000). These constantly adapting and conflicting

5

definitions of paedophilia, as well as a lack of specificity in places (Bickley and Beech 2001), have resulted in expert opposition to the DSM classifications (Freund 1994; Feelgood and Hoyer 2008), with O'Donohue *et al.* (2000) referring to them as vague, poorly defined, and lacking reliability and validity as a tool. Such criticisms have led to calls for the DSM classification of paedophilia to be abandoned (Marshall 1997). These issues raise questions about the possibility of an agreed definition, and the resulting implications for practice. If treatment is predicated on our understanding of the phenomenon, then any such treatment is subject to similar controversy.

Paedophilia from a legal perspective

It is notable that proposed clinical typologies of paedophilia often, but not always, depend on the notion of sexual offending for their definition. However, unlike the clinical realm, it is perhaps to be expected that there is no current legal definition of paedophilia (Hansard, 14 October 1997: column WA113), especially considering that paedophilia is not in itself a criminal or illegal act. Any feasible definition tends therefore to focus on the criminal acts and behaviour involved. This consequently suggests that a paedophile is an adult who commits a sexual offence against a child. While this would appear at first glance to be fairly straightforward, albeit circular, problems concerning age and the meaning of 'child', 'adult' and 'sexual' are palpable in this context. For example, from a legal perspective, in England and Wales, a child can be someone under the age of 14 (Children Act 1989), under 16 (Child Benefit Act 2005), or under 18 (United Nations Convention on the Rights of the Child). Moreover, concepts such as child and adult are interdependent, particularly in this context.

The question thus arises regarding at what point on a spectrum of age, sexual offending additionally becomes paedophilia. Weeks (1985) points out that our concern with age in conjunction with sexual activity is ultimately a debate about the appropriate minimum age for engagement in such activity (in England and Wales this currently stands at 16). When assessing this we are really asking when we feel a child has the mental maturity, intellectual capacity and competence to make a free and reasoned decision (Waites 2005). Waites also acknowledges that this is not a straightforward question and can depend on what is held to be important. This also ties in with children's rights and at what age children should be allowed or even be entitled to participate in decisions regarding their life and behaviour (for more information on this, see Alderson 1992; Schofield and Thoburn 1996). This would suggest that a child's competence should be assessed on an individual basis, rather than using a broad-brush approach such as age. While this viewpoint has gained support in other legal areas such as medical law and the availability of assessing a child as Gillick competent,[1] this has not been followed with regard to consent to sexual activity.

The age of consent law in England and Wales would thus suggest that paedophilia, from a legal perspective, is sexual activity with a child under 16. This, however, does not align with the DSM definition discussed above. In clinical understandings, paedophilia is sexual activity with a child not older than 12 or 13. Despite this clinical interpretation, the law in this area is designed to protect vulnerable children from harm, and to a lesser extent serves to protect the child from him/herself. However, common understandings of paedophilia might, we suggest, include a 40-year-old man participating in acts of a sexual nature with a 15-year-old boy or girl – even though it is accepted that in clinical terms this might be viewed as ephebophilia. Such fine distinctions are not apparent outside psychological circles, and thus we see common understandings perhaps originating from socio-legal rather than clinical perspectives.

The most relevant legislation in this area is the Sexual Offences Act (SOA) 2003, which, although it does not use terms such as 'paedophile', 'paedophilic' or 'paedophilia', can still be useful in examining legal concerns around the phenomena of child, adult and sexual. The Act, as its name suggests, sets out a number of sexual offences, including rape, sexual assault and sexual activity with a child. For almost all offences, there needs to be a physical act coupled with an intention to commit that physical act. Some offences also require that the act be sexual. This is defined in section 78 of the Act as either sexual because of its nature, regardless of the circumstances, or, although in nature it may not be regarded as sexual, because of the circumstances or characteristics of the individual offender it is regarded as such (this has the ability to turn 'normal' behaviour into that which has a sexual undertone). Defining a person as a paedophile because he has a sexual preference for children does not, therefore, fit in with legal conceptualisations, and again highlights differences between clinical and legal approaches.

For the purposes of the SOA 2003, a child is generally regarded as an individual who is under the age of 16, mirroring the age of consent. In covering sexual activities with children, the Act includes a number of offences where the child is under 13 and some where

7

the child is under 16 (this distinction is largely because the offence is deemed more serious where the child is under 13, and thus such crimes attract higher sentencing powers). This might suggest that paedophilia from a legal perspective involves committing offences against those younger than 16, although, clearly, sexual acts directed towards children aged between 13 and 15 years of age are considered to constitute a lesser degree of harm than those directed towards children under the age of 13 – an age closer to that suggested in the DSM definition and the definition found in the Children Act 1989.

However, perhaps unsurprisingly, the Act has anomalies. For example, it extends the list of persons who can be guilty of a sexual offence committed against a child in a family (incest) and, for these offences, considers a child to be someone under 18 (sections 25–26). Similar examples can be found in relation to the offence of child pornography/indecent photographs, where the raising of consent to imagery of sexual acts until the age of 18 gives rise to the suggestion that it is more harmful for a 16-year-old to have a sexual photograph taken than to have sexual intercourse (Stevenson *et al.* 2004). Such distinctions point to a range of contemporary moral concerns around the hierarchical arrangements of harm in relation to children and sexuality, and indicate how twenty-first-century reforms focus on separating sex and sexuality from the world of children (Phoenix and Oerton 2005).

The age of the offender is also important under the Act. To commit an offence under sections 9–12 and 14–15[2] the offender must be aged 18 or over. However, section 13 of the SOA 2003 makes the offences covered in sections 9–12 additionally criminal where the offender is aged under 16. Again, we see that there is incongruence with clinical understandings, where the victim must be under 13 and the perpetrator older than 16. From a criminality viewpoint, the decision of whether or not to prosecute a child will turn on the existence of factual consent and understanding, not legal consent (Stevenson *et al.* 2004). The question remains, however, as to whether consensual sexual activity that is not prosecuted can be considered paedophilic if the victim is under 13 (the DSM age). Is it the nature of the sexual activity that we are concerned about, the age of the perceived victim, the age of the offender, or, as the DSM now focuses on, the age gap between the perceived offender and victim? Until such questions are answered, it is difficult to provide a clear and specific definition of what is and is not classed as paedophilic activity, and thus when the term is used, we need to be aware that it can mean a variety of things.

Paedophilia from a medical perspective

While it can be argued that the law does not need to define paedophilia, it is important that it facilitates the use of such terms in other social and clinical arenas where, arguably, their use is more important. While so far we have found little consensus between clinical and legal understandings, these fields become further intertwined and arguably more powerful in the regulation of individuals under mental health law. Mental health law in England and Wales is largely governed by the Mental Health Act 2007. The major change of the new Act with regard to the meaning of paedophilia is the amendment to the meaning of the term 'mental disorder'. Under the preceding 1983 Act, a person did not suffer from a mental disorder by reason of immoral conduct, promiscuity, dependence on alcohol or drugs, or sexual deviancy (Bowen 2007). The 2007 Act largely reverses the exception of sexual deviancy, giving the term 'mental disorder' a much wider meaning. Indeed, it was argued in the House of Commons that 'the amendment makes it clear that paedophilia is not within the scope of the exclusion' (Hansard, 19 June 2007: column 1326).

Commentators, including Bowen (2007), have argued that in practice the amendment will make little difference, as it was always possible under the 1983 Act to justify an individual's detention and treatment by arguing that their behaviour either caused or was caused by a mental disorder. However, it may make a huge difference to how the condition, preference or sexuality is more generally understood. While it remains the case that a person cannot be held in a mental institution solely due to his or her sexually deviant behaviour, as other tests involving appropriateness and necessity also need to be met, it does offer a means by which sexual deviants, including paedophiles, can be forcibly detained and treated under the Act. Consequently, the change in the definition of mental disorder means that definitions published by the APA can now permissibly work under English and Welsh law. Given the issues in the DSM definition as set out above, there is clearly a need for further clarification in the application of this legislation. Moreover, as some point to the far from straightforward relationship between sexual offending and mental illness (for more information on this, see Chapter 10 of this volume), the debate over criminality versus pathology is clearly as pertinent now as it has been in the past.

Aetiology of paedophilic offenders

The debate regarding criminality and pathology is inevitably tied to the question of cause, to which we now turn, albeit with some brevity. In terms of general characteristics, paedophiles (classified by DSM definitions) are a heterogeneous population, including both men and women (Howitt 1998; McCartan 2008), although it is accepted that the majority of paedophiles are men (Dobash *et al.* 1996). Other noted characteristics from research include, for example, that paedophiles tend to come from a working-class background, although this is not always the case (La Fontaine 1990), and that some, albeit not all, experienced a disorganised family system in childhood (Howitt 1998). It has been shown that paedophiles can be employed in a diverse variety of careers (Wilson and Cox 1983); that there are no concrete findings regarding their IQ, although those who abuse children are thought to have lower IQs than other offenders (Cantor *et al.* 2005); and that paedophiles can be, but are not always, of a specific age group (Whiskin 1997; Howitt 1998). Research also suggests that paedophiles tend to have higher levels of social introversion, sensitivity, loneliness and depression (Wilson and Cox 1983), with poor interrelationships and social skills (Blanchette and Coleman 2002), often leading them to feel socially isolated (Taylor 1981). Despite this, it has also been found that paedophiles can be, or often have been, married or in age-appropriate relationships (Groth and Birnbaum 1978) and are capable of complex grooming behaviours (McAlinden 2006b).

Moreover, there is no single aetiology, with paedophilia being described by different sources as a mental illness (Bagley *et al.* 1994), a mental deficiency (Blanchard *et al.* 1999), a brain deficiency (Cantor *et al.* 2008), a developmental abnormality (Lee *et al.* 2002), or the result of a cycle of abuse (Bagley *et al.* 1994; Howitt 1998). While the origin of paedophilic behaviour is difficult to isolate, why such offending commences and continues has been explained by the cycle of sexual offending behaviour (Wolf 1984, cited in Silverman and Wilson 2002) and the existence of cognitive distortions (Burn and Brown 2006). The cycle of sexual offending behaviour commences with an offender's poor self-worth, which leads to self-rejection, withdrawal, the development of fantasies, escapism, and grooming, in turn leading to sexual offending, guilt and finally acceptance of guilt. Each time the cycle restarts, the offending increases and the offender arguably becomes more dangerous. This explanation has been developed to incorporate the central use of CSA imagery (Bentovim 1993; Taylor and Quayle 2003) by paedophiles, although this has been challenged by some paedophiles themselves (O'Carroll 1980; Howitt 1998). Similarly, the suggestion that paedophiles experience cognitive distortions (for example, that the child enjoys it, that they are helping the child to develop, etc. (O'Carroll 1980; Brongersma 1984)) is also used to explain the commencement and continuation of CSA, particularly when they are reinforced through contact with other paedophiles (Taylor and Quayle 2003).

Given the discussion so far, it is probably not surprising that typical offending behaviour of paedophiles has not been identified. Predictably, they do not all offend in the same fashion, nor with the same frequency or level of intensity (Howitt 1998; La Fontaine 1990). Moreover, paedophiles do not always sexually and/or physically abuse children (Taylor and Quayle 2003; Howitt 1998), for some can achieve sexual arousal from chatting with children online, looking at child abuse imagery, or having non-contact time with children (Silverman and Wilson 2002; Taylor and Quayle 2003). Research with victims of CSA indicates that sexual intercourse is the least prevalent form of abuse, non-physical sexual abuse being more common, followed by physical sexual abuse (Dobash et al. 1996).

The lack of a single aetiology of paedophilia (Bradford 2000) makes the treatment of paedophiles a complex and difficult issue to resolve. A range of different approaches exist, including cognitive-behavioural programmes (see Chapter 5 of this volume), community care programmes such as Circles of Support and Accountability (see Chapter 7 of this volume) and drug treatments (see Chapter 6 of this volume). As one might expect, different treatments work better or worse for different offenders, and this will be discussed in the aforementioned chapters. The heterogeneity of this group thus presents problems not simply for definition, but also, ultimately, for treatment.

Addressing variation in understandings of paedophilia

Thus far, we have been faced with a variety of definitions and explanations of paedophilia. This variety stems in part from the acknowledgement that the group of people who are (at least from clinical perspectives) labelled paedophiles differ greatly from one another in a variety of ways. However, as we know, while definitions are important, as they specify the problem in need of attention, they are inherently ideological (Gough 1996). Thus, legal and clinical definitions vary according to the orientation of the disciplines themselves, although, they are also subject to their socio-historical context. We can see, for example, how clinical definitions of paedophilia have shifted over time, and how the legal notion of mental disorder under mental health legislation continues to be revised.

While we began this chapter with the claim that paedophilia is a 'public health problem of staggering proportions', it has not always and everywhere been so. As various commentators (e.g. Gough 1996; Thomas 2005) have pointed out, understandings of sexual behaviour change over time. Thus, a number of researchers in the area of paedophilia have pointed to the historical and cultural variation in our understandings of adult–child sex. For example, Green (2002) points to the work of various authors who have documented the acceptance of sexual contact between adults and children in other times and cultures, quoting Bauserman (1997), who states that 'almost every sort of sexual activity ... has been considered normal and acceptable in some society at some time' (120). In addition, a number of authors have pointed to the problems surrounding the necessary boundary between adulthood and childhood that underlies the problem of adult/child sex, particularly as childhood is a relatively new, and to a certain degree a Westernised, idea (Jenkins 1996; Cunningham 1995). Recourse to the seemingly fundamental biological marker of puberty is similarly problematic (Weeks 1985; Green 2002), with an array of exotic examples regularly mobilised to illustrate the particularity of our current understandings. These include, for example, various rites of passage involving childhood sexuality (e.g. Bauserman 1997), along with other reports of sexual activity between or involving prepubescent children. In some cases, these are perceived as beneficial for the child, rather than gratifying the adult (Green 2002). This inevitable variation can also be used to important effect in questioning the positioning of paedophilia as a mental disorder (Green 2002).

Social constructionist perspectives (see Burr 1995) may be particularly useful here, in that they allow us to approach phenomena such as paedophilia with an expectation of such variation. As noted by Stainton Rogers and Stainton Rogers (1999), areas of social policy and professional practice, such as law, medicine and social work, are in the process of being influenced by constructionist ideas. They explain how the uncertainty and incoherence that are markers of scholarship can be seen as problematic in practical contexts. However, as they further elucidate, constructionist perspectives have the potential to focus our attention on the more intractable problems that are often ignored when focusing on deviant individuals, and can contribute to a climate of change. It is by engagement at this critical level that, they suggest, we might begin to examine whose interests are being served by the creation of such moral panics – and what is being obscured. As noted by Best (1990, cited in Stainton Rogers and Stainton Rogers 1999), focusing on deviant individuals pays little attention to flaws in the social system, and controlling individuals serves to make fears of these particular threats more manageable.

The complexity highlighted in this chapter, which is inevitable from a social constructionist perspective, further problematises the issue of whether it is possible to have a one size fits all definition of paedophilia and, if it were possible, what this would mean for practice. If treatment is predicated on our understanding of the phenomenon itself, then any such treatment is subject to the same level of disagreement.

Conclusion

This chapter has provided an overview of current theoretical and evidence-based underpinnings around sex offenders, sexual offending in general, and paedophilia in particular. Although this chapter is a brief introduction to what is a complex and continually growing area (Farrington 2009), our aim has been to provide the reader with a grounding in definitions and understandings of paedophilia, some of which will be built on and developed in the reminder of the book. Given the way in which theories, research and attitudes towards sexual offending are continually adapting and vary across different contexts, we have also pointed to the potential contribution of social constructionist ideas in this area, as a means through which we might examine contemporary changes and adaptations in understandings of sexual offending – in terms of not only public opinion, but also government policy, academic research and professional practice. However, we are also mindful of responding appropriately to current constructions of paedophilia. As such, this chapter points to the need for ideas around sexual offending, in its widest conception (i.e. stalking, rape, CSA, paedophilia, etc.) and through all related aspects (i.e., aetiology, offender behaviour and personality, treatment, etc.), to be evidence based (Farrington 2009), and subject to critical reflection, rather than based upon or influenced by knee jerk reactions.

Notes

1 The phrase 'Gillick competent' derives from the case of *Gillick* v *West Norfolk and Wisbech Area Health Authority* [1986] AC 112, which involved the provision of contraceptive advice to girls under the age of 16. Victoria Gillick was a mother of five girls, who sought a ruling that none of her daughters would be prescribed or advised about birth control, while under 16, without her knowledge or consent. The case progressed to the House of Lords, where Lord Fraser laid down a number of criteria, which have since become known as the Fraser Guidelines. The guidelines centre on the child's 'maturity and intelligence to understand the nature and implications of the proposed treatment' (113) with the premise being that once this stage has been reached, the parent's right to determine matters relating to medical treatment ends.

2 Offences where the child is under 16, including sexual activity (9), causing or inciting a child to engage in sexual activity (10), engaging in sexual activity in the presence of a child (11), causing a child to watch a sexual act (12), arranging or facilitating commission of a child sex offence (14) and meeting a child following sexual grooming (15).

References

Alderson, P. (1992) 'In the Genes or in the Stars? Children's Competence to Consent', *Journal of Medical Ethics*, 18(3): 119–124.

American Psychiatric Association (APA) (1952) *Diagnostic and Statistical Manual of Mental Disorders* (DSM-I). Washington, DC: American Psychiatric Association.

American Psychiatric Association (1968) *Diagnostic and Statistical Manual of Mental Disorders* (2nd edn, DSM-II). Washington, DC: American Psychiatric Association.

American Psychiatric Association (1980) *Diagnostic and Statistical Manual of Mental Disorders* (3rd edn, DSM-III). Washington, DC: American Psychiatric Association.

American Psychiatric Association (1987) *Diagnostic and Statistical Manual of Mental Disorders* (rev. 3rd edn, DSM-III-R). Washington, DC: American Psychiatric Association.

American Psychiatric Association (2000) *Diagnostic and Statistical Manual of Mental Disorders* (rev. 4th edn, DSM-IV-R). Washington, DC: American Psychiatric Association.

Ames, M. A. and Houston, D. A. (1990) 'Legal, Social, and Biological Definitions of Pedophilia', *Archives of Sexual Behavior*, 19: 333–342.

Bagley, C., Wood, M. and Young, L. (1994) 'Victim to Abuser: Mental Health and Behavioural Sequels of Child Sexual Abuse in a Community Survey of Young Adult Males', *Child Abuse and Neglect*, 18: 683–697.

Bartol, C. R. and Bartol, A. M. (2008) *Criminal Behavior: A Psychosocial Approach* (8th edn). Englewood Cliffs, NJ: Pearson, Prentice-Hall.

Bauserman, R. (1997) 'Man–boy Sexual Relationships in a Cross-Cultural Perspective', in J. Geraci (ed.) *Dares to Speak: Historical and Contemporary Perspectives on Boy-Love*. Norfolk, UK: Gay Men's Press.

Bentovim, A. (1993) 'Why Do Adults Sexually Abuse Children? Men and Society are Mostly to Blame, but Apportioning Guilt is Difficult' (Editorial), *British Medical Journal*, 307: 144–146.

Bickley, J. and Beech, A. R. (2001) 'Classifying Child Abusers: Its Relevance to Theory and Clinical Practice', *International Journal of Offender Therapy and Comparative Criminology*, 45: 51–69.

Blanchard, R., Watson, M.S., Choy, A. *et al.* (1999) 'Paedophiles: Mental Retardation, Maternal Age, and Sexual Orientation', *Archives of Sexual Behaviour*, 28: 111-27.

Blanchette, M. C. and Coleman, G. D. (2002) 'Priest Pedophiles: Pedophiles and Ephebophiles Have No Capacity for Authentic Sexual Relationships', *America, The National Catholic Weekly*, 186(13): 18.

Bowen, P. (2007) *Blackstone's Guide to the Mental Health Act 2007*. Oxford: Oxford University Press.

Brongersma, E. (1984) 'Aggression Against Paedophiles', *International Journal of Law and Psychiatry*, 7: 79-87.

Burn, M. F. and Brown, S. (2006) 'A Review of the Cognitive Distortions in Child Sex Offenders: An Examination of the Motivations and Mechanisms that Underlie the Justification for Abuse', *Aggression and Violent Behaviour*, 11: 225–236.

Burr, V. (1995) *An Introduction to Social Construction*. London: Routledge.

Cantor, J. M., Blanchard, R., Robichaud, L. K. and Christensen, B. K. (2005) 'Quantitative Reanalysis of Aggregate Data on IQ in Sexual Offenders', *Psychological Bulletin*, 131: 555–568.

Cantor, J. M., Kabani, N., Christensen, B. K. *et al.* (2008) 'Cerebral White Matter Deficiencies in Paedophilic Men', *Journal of Psychiatric Research*, 42: 167–183.

Cunningham, H. (1995) *Child and Childhood in Western Society Since 1500*. London: Longman.

Dobash, R., Carnie, J. and Waterhouse, L. (1996) 'Child Sexual Abusers: Recognition and Response', in L. Waterhouse (ed.) *Child Abuse and Child Abusers: Protection and Prevention*. London: Jessica Kingsley.

Farrington, D. P. (2009) 'Foreword', in J. L. Ireland, C. A. Ireland and P. Birch (eds), *Violent and Sexual Offenders: Assessment, Treatment and Management*. Cullompton: Willan.

Feelgood, S. and Hoyer, J. (2008) 'Child Molester or Paedophile? Socio-Legal Versus Psychological Classification of Sexual Offenders Against Children', *Journal of Sexual Aggression*, 14: 33–43.

Freund, K. (1994) 'In Search of an Etiological Model of Pedophilia', *Sexological Review*, 2: 171–184.

Gough, D. (1996) 'The Literature on Child Abuse and the Media', *Child Abuse Review*, 5: 363–376.

Green, R. (2002) 'Is Pedophilia a Mental Disorder?', *Archives of Sexual Behavior*, 31(6): 467–471.

Greer, C. (2002) *Sex Crime and the Media: Sex Offending and the Press in a Divided Society*. Cullompton: Willan.

Groth, A. N. and Birnbaum, H. J. (1978) 'Adult Sexual Orientation and Attraction to Underage Persons', *Archives of Sexual Behavior*, 7: 175–181.

Howitt, D. (1998) *Paedophiles and Sexual Offences Against Children*. Chichester: Wiley.

Ireland, C. A. and Worthington, R. (2009) 'Treatment Approaches for Sexual Offenders', in J. L. Ireland, C. A. Ireland, and P. Birch (eds), *Violent and Sexual Offenders: Assessment, Treatment and Management*. Cullompton: Willan.

Jenkins, P. (1998) *Moral Panic: Changing Concepts of the Child Molester in Modern America*. New Haven, CT: Yale University Press.

La Fontaine, J. (1990) *Child Sexual Abuse*. Cambridge: Polity Press.

Leberg, E. (1997) *Understanding Child Molesters*. London: Sage.

Lee, J. K., Jackson, H. J. and Ward, T. (2002) 'Developmental Risk Factors for Sexual Offending', *Child Abuse and Neglect*, 26: 73–92.

Marshall, P. (1997) 'Paedophilia: Psychopathology and Theory', in D. Laws, and W. O'Donohue (eds), *Sexual Deviance*. New York: Guilford.

McAlinden, A. (2006a) 'Managing Risk: From Regulation to the Reintegration of Sexual Offenders', *Criminology and Criminal Justice*, 6: 197–218.

McAlinden, A. (2006b) 'Setting 'Em Up: Personal, Familial and Institutional Grooming in the Sexual Abuse of Children', *Social and Legal Studies*, 15: 339–362.

McCartan, K. F. (2004) '"HERE THERE BE MONSTERS"; the Public's Perception of Paedophiles with Particular Reference to Belfast and Leicester', *Medicine, Science and the Law*, 44: 327–342.

McCartan, K. F. (2008) 'Current Understandings of Paedophilia and the Resulting Crisis in Modern Society', in J. M. Caroll and M. K. Alena (eds), *Psychological Sexual Dysfunctions*. New York: Nova Publishers.

McDonald Wilson Bradford, J. (2000) 'The Treatment of Sexual Deviation Using a Pharmacological Approach', *Journal of Sex Research*, 37(3): 248–257.

O'Carroll, T. (1980) *Paedophilia: The Radical Case*. London: Peter Owen.

O'Donohue, W., Regev, L. G. and Hagstrom, A. (2000) 'Problems with the DSM–IV Diagnosis of Paedophilia', *Sexual Abuse: A Journal of Research and Treatment*, 12: 95–105.

Phoenix, J. and Oerton, S. (2005) *Illicit and Illegal: Sex, Regulation and Social Control*. Cullompton: Willan.

Rind, B., Tromovitch, P. and Bauserman, R. (1998) 'A Meta-Analytic Examination of Assumed Properties of Child Sexual Abuse Using College Samples', *Psychological Bulletin*, 124: 22–53.

Schofield, G. and Thoburn, J. (1996) *The Voice of the Child in Decision Making*. London: Institute for Public Policy Research.

Silverman, J. and Wilson, D. (2002) *Innocence Betrayed: Paedophilia, the Media and Society*. Cambridge: Polity.

Stainton Rogers, W. and Stainton Rogers, R. (1999) 'That's All Very Well, but What Use Is It?', in D. J. Nightingale and J. Cromby (eds), *Social Constructionist Psychology: A Critical Analysis of Theory and Practice*. Buckingham: Open University Press.

Stevenson, K., Davies, A. and Gunn, M. (2004) *Blackstone's Guide to The Sexual Offences Act 2003*. Oxford: Oxford University Press.

Taylor, B. (1981) *Perspectives on Paedophilia*. London: Batsford Academic and Educational.

Taylor, M. and Quayle, E. (2003) *Child Pornography: An Internet Crime*. Hove and New York: Brunner-Routledge.

Thomas, T. (2005) *Sex Crime: Sex Offending and Society* (2nd edn). Cullompton: Willan.

van Dam, C. (2001) *Identifying Child Molesters: Preventing Child Sexual Abuse by Recognizing the Patterns of the Offenders*. New York: Haworth Maltreatment and Trauma Press.

Waites, M. (2005) *The Age of Consent. Young People, Sexuality and Citizenship*. Basingstoke: Palgrave Macmillan.

Weeks, J. (1985) *Sexuality and Its Discontents. Meanings, Myths and Modern Sexualities*. London: Routledge.

Whiskin, F. E. (1997) 'The Geriatic Sex Offender', in C. D. Bryant (ed.) *Sexual Deviancy in Social Context*. New York: New Viewpoints, Franklin Watts.

Wilson, G. D. and Cox, D. N. (1983) 'Personality of Paedophile Club Members', *Personality and Individual Differences*, 4: 323–329.

Chapter 2

High-risk sex offenders: issues of policy

Mark Farmer and Ruth Mann

Introduction

High-risk sex offenders are those who by definition pose the greatest risk to the public and who require the most robust response from the criminal justice system. However, in public parlance, the term 'high-risk' has come to be synonymous with the label 'sex offender' used to describe a group of individuals feared by the public at large and beloved of tabloid headline writers. But what do we actually mean by high-risk, and is it accurate to refer to all sex offenders as such? In this chapter we will examine some of the policy issues facing those within offender management organisations who deal with such offenders.

We will begin by examining what is meant by the term 'high-risk', and consider whether it is one that can be justifiably applied to sex offenders. We then examine the various responses to sexual offending in terms of policy and practice. In particular, we focus on restrictive practices and rehabilitative practices, looking at whether such practices are supported by the theoretical and research evidence that sets out to explain and account for sexual offending. In short, we are asking what we should do with high-risk sex offenders. Using these arguments, we examine public, media and political debates about sexual offending, and the impact these have had on public policy in late modernity and the impact of the so-called risk society. We will demonstrate that practice over the past 20 years with regard to treatment and management of known sex offenders is largely in line with the extant evidence base.

Current policy on sex offender management is developed in the context of a new penology concerned particularly with management and exclusion of certain risky individuals. However, we argue that the treatment of known sex offenders is essential, but only one part of the solution to the problem of sexual crime, and that theoretical perspectives on sexual offending indicate that further attention should be paid to primary prevention; that is, dealing with the factors that appear to lead to the development of vulnerabilities for sexual offending, before those vulnerabilities emerge.

The meaning of risk

It is general orthodoxy within penology that the risk presented by offenders has dimensions of likelihood and seriousness. The likelihood dimension refers to the rate at which known offenders reoffend, and the seriousness dimension relates to the degree of harm that would be caused by reoffending if it were to take place. It is important that any assessment of risk presented by offenders should take account of these two dimensions. It is therefore pertinent to consider the degree to which research has so far been able to determine the extent of these dimensions with regard to sex offenders.

The likelihood dimension has attracted much interest from researchers and policymakers, intent on determining the extent to which reoffending is likely to occur with sex offenders under the auspices of various criminal justice agencies, in the hope that it may be possible to prioritise those agencies' resources towards the highest-risk cases. However, research into reoffending rates among sex offenders (or indeed any offenders) is confounded by the fact that it is impossible, using current methodologies, to determine whether a particular offender has in fact reoffended. While sources such as the Police National Computer can be used to determine reconviction rates, the relationship between these and true reoffending rates is largely unknown, and certainly there is evidence with sexual offences in particular that much offending goes unreported or does not result in a conviction. However, there is at present no reason to suppose that the ratio of reported to unreported offending will differ systematically from one offender subgroup to another. Probably the best we can say, therefore, is that reconviction rates serve as a proxy for reoffending rates, but that the latter will always be higher than the former.

Most studies in recent years have used reconviction rates as a measure of reoffending, sometimes taking into account accusations that have not resulted in conviction in an effort to move closer to a reoffending rate. The problem is exacerbated by the fact that the term 'sex offender' is unhelpfully used to describe a multitude of different offence types, and many of these offenders appear to reoffend at different rates (Harris and Hanson 2004). Many studies provide an average reconviction figure across offence types, although it should be borne in mind that subgroups of different offenders within these overall rates will reoffend at different rates. Notwithstanding this, the messages from research have been remarkably consistent and point to a reconviction rate possibly lower than that anticipated by much public opinion (e.g. Grubin 1998; Hood et al. 2002). This is well illustrated by a recent meta-analysis (Harris and Hanson 2004) covering some 10 individual studies that, when combined, involved 4,724 offenders. Overall, a reconviction rate of 14 per cent over 5 years, 20 per cent over 10 years, and 24 per cent over 15 years was found. Hanson emphasises that, overall, sex offenders are reconvicted at a lower rate than most other groups of offender, and that even after 15 years most sex offenders do not reoffend. Figures in England and Wales show a similar pattern. Cunliffe and Shepherd (2007) reported an overall two-year recidivism rate (from a cohort released in 2000) for all sex offender types of 32.2 per cent, with 16.9 per cent of child molesters being reconvicted. For a cohort released in 2004, the two-year recidivism rate was 26.6 per cent for all sex offenders, and 12.4 per cent for child molesters. However, these figures included any type of reoffending, and so the sexual recidivism rate will have been appreciably smaller.

Not all sex offenders are of equal risk, and so within the overall picture there are some groups of offenders who are reconvicted at an extremely low rate, whereas smaller groups of offenders are reconvicted at far higher rates. Static risk scales aim to differentiate groups with higher reconviction rates from groups with lower reconviction rates. Thornton et al. (2003), for example, reported reconviction rates across different categories of Risk Matrix 2000 (RM2000). RM2000 is an actuarial risk assessment tool that uses a number of static or relatively unchanging risk factors to subdivide groups of offenders into categories with similar reconviction rates. The reconviction rates for a group of sex offenders released from prison in 1979, when followed up for 19 years, was 8 per cent for the low-risk group, 18.1 per cent for the medium-risk group, 40.5 per cent for the high-risk group, and 60 per cent for the very-high-risk group.

As it is likely that the base rates of reconviction have changed in the intervening period, these percentage categories should not be assumed to apply to offenders today. To examine whether RM2000 remained consistently able to differentiate risk groups over time, Barnett *et al.* (forthcoming) examined a more recent cohort of sex offenders serving both prison and community sentences. Their findings were consistent with the assertion that most sex offenders do not present a high likelihood of reconviction, with some being extremely unlikely to be reconvicted but with the existence of a small subgroup who are very likely to be reconvicted.

Static risk tools such as RM2000 enable practitioners to focus on those offenders who are most likely to reoffend, and so to direct the most resources, both restrictive and rehabilitative, to them. This targeting of resources to higher-risk groups is known as the risk principle (Andrews and Bonta 2003); this is simply defined to mean that resources should follow risk, and in principle urges those responsible for managing risk to direct their resources appropriately. The reality, of course, is more complicated, as those at a low risk of reoffending might nevertheless have committed extremely serious offences, leading practitioners to feel duty bound to intervene.

Additionally, while static risk tools such as RM2000 can provide useful rules of thumb about how intense an intervention is needed, they are insensitive to changes in an offender's life. Therefore although an offender might, for example, complete a sex offender treatment programme, or undergo significant change in his life, his RM2000 score would not change despite an apparent change in likelihood of reoffending (in fact, the only real way in which an offender can reduce his risk score is by growing older). Nor does RM2000 indicate in what areas of an offender's life intervention should take place. Static actuarial tools such as this should therefore be seen as a screening device and should be supplemented by assessment of dynamic or changeable factors. Recent work looking at such factors has identified certain changeable features that appear to be related to the likelihood of reoffending, and others that appear to indicate the imminence of reoffending (Hanson *et al.* 2007). An up-to-date list of evidence-based risk factors for sexual offending is given in Mann *et al.* (2009).

A rather different picture emerges when we look at the seriousness dimension. While reconviction rates are objective and quantifiable, risk of harm is a more subjective issue, and many might argue that all sexual offences cause a high degree of harm. While it is probably reasonable to presume that the harm caused by a sexual murder is relatively higher than the harm caused by indecent exposure or voyeurism, to take examples that are more extreme, it is not so comfortable to make distinctions about the harm caused by, say, an

21

indecent assault upon a child versus the rape of an adult woman. Overall, evidence consistently points to the considerable long-term psychological damage caused to victims of child sexual abuse. Johnson (2001), for example, found that incidents of sexual abuse led to numerous harmful later outcomes for victims. In contrast to a non-abused sample, victims of sexual abuse were more likely to suffer from depression, have low self-esteem, have fewer close friends, and so on.

To sum up, then, sex offenders on the whole are relatively unlikely to be reconvicted of a further sexual offence. Within this broad picture, however, is a subgroup that are much more likely to be reconvicted. In nearly all cases, the consequences of sexual abuse are likely to be serious and long-lasting. It follows, then, that the initial answer to the question of what we should do about sex offenders is that we should do *something* in most cases. Low-risk offenders, who are apparently no more likely to offend again than an unconvicted man in the general population, probably need minimal formal treatment beyond normal supervision and monitoring, unless the risk of harm is very high (for example, as with sexual murderers). Medium- and higher-risk offenders may be still less likely to reoffend than offenders who have committed non-sexual offences, but the level of harm associated with sexual offending means that even low reconviction rates warrant a more intense response over and above normal supervision.

But it is not the case that it is better to do anything than nothing. It is quite possible that inappropriate interventions with sex offenders could at worst exacerbate their psychological problems, and at best could be ineffective and thus a waste of money. The effective treatment and management of sex offenders has become a matter of considerable public, as well as academic, debate and concern, with these issues being the main subject of this volume. To introduce such areas, we will now examine some of the major policy and legislative developments, before moving on to examine the respective cases for restrictive and rehabilitative responses to sex offenders.

Restrictive interventions

Perhaps the most significant of the many new pieces of legislation aimed at managing sex offenders was the 1997 Sex Offender Act. Of course this Act has largely been superseded by more recent legislation, but it was the first Act that required certain sex offenders to register their name and address with the police; the fact that police were in possession of data concerning sex offenders in their area often precipitated them into partnerships with local probation services aimed at managing these individuals. Although the requirement for police and probation jointly to establish arrangements for assessing and managing the risk from sex offenders was brought into law by the Criminal Justice and Court Services Act 2000; prior to this, and spurred on by the Home Office, most police areas had already by then established some form of multi-agency working with probation services and sometimes other agencies (Maguire *et al.* 2001) (for more on the development and effectiveness of Multi-Agency Public Protection Arrangements (MAPPA) in dealing with sexual offenders, see Chapter 3 of this volume). The success of MAPPA is often quoted as a beacon in the management of sex offenders in the UK. In addition, initiatives that seek to tackle sexual offending are regularly announced. Recent ones include disclosure pilots, in which carers of children can request disclosure of convictions for sexual offences of new partners, and polygraph pilots, in which new legislation has been introduced under which offenders on licence release from prison can be required to undergo regular polygraph or lie-detector tests.

One of the problems in national initiatives such as new legislation or management arrangements is the difficulty of evaluating them because of the lack of a direct control group. If legislation is implemented nationally, there can be no randomly allocated control against which to measure the effects of the policy. For example, in the USA, it has proved difficult to evaluate properly the impact of wide-ranging restrictive laws such as community notification and residency restriction. At present, evidence as to the overall effectiveness of restrictive measures is slim. Commenting on this consistent drive to increase restrictions upon sex offenders despite the lack of any evidence of effectiveness, some writers are beginning to draw attention to the dangers of neglecting, or in some cases riding roughshod over, the rights of offenders. For example, some consider that it is reasonable for a society to curtail an offender's human rights in order to prevent further offending, but that it is dangerous to expect offenders to forfeit their rights. This is because it is argued that an offender who is alienated without a stake in society will be consequently more likely to reoffend. For a debate on offenders' rights, see Ward *et al.* (2008) and also Chapter 14 of this volume.

Rehabilitative responses

Rehabilitative responses are predicated on an understanding of the aetiology of sexual offending and a recognition of the psychological (but potentially changeable) features that are associated with reoffending.

Understanding sexual offending

Theoretical perspectives into sexual offending have developed in line with the research over the past 30 years. It is generally considered that models that use a number of factors and theory from a number of different perspectives to explain sexual abuse offer more complete accounts of what causes sexual abuse (Ward *et al.* 2006). A comprehensive theory of sexual offending needs to encompass psychological, social, neuro-biological, developmental and situational contributors; and a comprehensive rehabilitative response would ideally also target each of these types of features.

To give an example of a multi-faceted theory of sexual offending, Marshall and Barbaree (1990) argued that a developmental perspective on the aetiology of inappropriate sexual behaviour is necessary to understand fully the processes involved. They stated that 'the task for human males is to acquire inhibitory controls over a biologically endowed propensity for self-interest associated with a tendency to fuse sex and aggression' (Marshall and Barbaree 1990: 257). Thus, they argued that all males have an inherited propensity to engage in sexual behaviour, and a capacity to use sexual aggression, but that not all do so. Developmental and environmental factors are likely to be major determinants in developing inhibitory controls. The early childhood experiences of boys who become sexually aggressive inadequately prepare them for desires that emerge at puberty. They learn to use aggression as a problem-solving technique by modelling the behaviour of their parents, and in particular the childhood environments of abusers limits the possibility of developing strong and positive attachments, resulting in feelings of alienation and emotional loneliness. This can result, in adolescence, in a sense of anger towards females, to whom the individual finds it difficult to relate. The task for adolescents of discriminating between sex and aggression is seen as being a difficult one in any event. Sexual fantasies may put them in a position of power and indifference to the rights of others. Such individuals may be unable to develop intimacy and feel empathy. A dysfunctional view of masculinity emerges. Where there are societal messages that promote interpersonal violence, social acceptance of male domination, and negative attitudes towards women, these dysfunctional schemas can flourish (Marshall and Barbaree 1990). The subsequent presence of situational factors, such as stress, intoxication or sexual stimuli, either overwhelm an individual's coping mechanisms and result in heightened risk of committing a sexual offence, or encourage him to actively seek out deviant sexual activity to meet his needs for intimacy. The reinforcing effects of deviant sexual activity and the development of cognitive distortions thus serve to maintain the abuse.

More recently, Ward and Siegert's (2002) 'pathways' model attempted to integrate the best features of existing theory and in doing so explain child sexual abuse according to a series of vulnerabilities that are present to a greater or lesser extent. The vulnerabilities are in turn caused by 'faulty mechanisms' or faults in 'what makes things work or function' (Ward and Siegert 2002: 332). Mechanisms include impaired cognitive or behavioural skills and mental states such as maladaptive beliefs and desires. The model postulates that abusive men tend to have different developmental pathways into their abusive behaviour. Five pathways are suggested, and although one particular pathway might be the primary one, elements of the others may apply in all cases. Ward and Siegert's (2002) pathways are as follows:

1 Intimacy and social skills deficits, where dysfunctional intimacy and social skills mechanisms inhibit the development of close relationships, resulting in emotional loneliness and isolation.

2 Deviant sexual scripts, meaning mental representations acquired throughout the offender's lifetime reflecting past experience, and organising thoughts related to sexuality. In this particular case, it is thought that scripts that confuse interpersonal closeness and sexuality are of particular importance.

3 Emotional dysregulation, where an individual's ability to control emotional states to meet goals is inhibited. Offenders either become overwhelmed and sexually uninhibited, or use sexual behaviour as a soothing strategy.

4 Antisocial cognitions, where the inappropriate sexual behaviour is part of a general pattern of antisocial behaviour, and where the sexual offending is reflective of a general antisocial outlook on life combined with poor impulse control.

25

5 Multiple dysfunctional mechanisms; offenders with a particular sexual script dysfunction combined with difficulties in all the other pathways. This group of offenders are referred to as 'pure paedophiles'.

Theoretical perspectives such as these, and Marshall and Barbaree's (1990) work, support the notion that children who grow up in supportive, structured environments seem less likely to develop the traits that in later life might lead to sexually abusive behaviour.

Implications: primary prevention

If this sort of explanation is accurate (and it is generally accepted by professionals in this area to be so), then there are implications for public policy, and in particular about when and how we should intervene. In particular, this theoretical perspective suggests a much earlier intervention in the lives of children who might be vulnerable to development of the deficits known to be common to sex offenders. To achieve intervention at this point, a change of focus might be required, from the criminal justice to a social welfare approach. The implications of multi-faceted theories of sexual abuse suggest that a high priority be given to primary prevention; that is, intervention in the lives of children and young people before they develop the vulnerabilities to be sexually abusive. In particular, we argue that approaches that seek to improve parenting abilities might have a protective effect for future generations. Such approaches might also have the additional benefit of improvements in the lives of vulnerable children. It is true that the English government has invested in recent years in improved opportunities for children. While such initiatives as Sure Start are not directed specifically at potential abusers, it will be important in future years, as those generations mature, to determine what impact such programmes have had on sexual and violent offending rates.

Secondary prevention

Theoretical perspectives also point the way to more effective interventions with convicted sex offenders: the secondary prevention approach. Here, the modern approach is to identify those factors that are associated with reconviction, and to provide interventions that can target any and all such factors, but that are flexible enough to be tailored to the particular criminogenic needs of each individual.

Sex offender programmes have developed through a number of phases over the last 30 years, from more basic social skills-training approaches through considerably structured, relapse-prevention programmes, to today's more flexible and individualised cognitive-behavioural interventions.

Recent meta-analyses of treatment programmes for sexual offenders have indicated mixed effectiveness. Some programmes have reported significant reductions in reoffending following treatment, whereas others appear to have had little or no impact. Most recently, Hanson *et al.* (2008) confirmed the application of the general principles of effective practice (known as the 'What Works' principles) in reducing reoffending with sex offenders through a meta-analysis that compared programmes that met none, one, two or all three of the recommended 'risk, need and responsivity' principles (whereby treatment should be proportionate to risk, focused on criminogenic need, and delivered in a manner to which offenders are responsive). Programmes designed in line with all three of these principles produced significant reductions in reoffending, while programmes that met none or just one principle produced no impact on reconviction rates (for more information on the effectiveness of sex offender treatment programmes, see Chapter 5 of this volume).

An effective programme, therefore, would target medium- and higher-risk offenders and would target established dynamic risk factors such as sexual preoccupation, offence supportive attitudes, poor adult attachments, lifestyle impulsivity, poor problem solving, and generalised hostility (see Mann *et al.* (2009) for a current list of evidenced risk factors for sexual offending). Such an effective programme would also be based on cognitive-behavioural principles, would be delivered by skilled and supervised therapists who engage with offenders in a warm and motivational style, and would take place in a context where the wider environment's culture and values are consistent with the principles that the programme is trying to teach to offenders (Mann 2009). While it is possible to articulate such an ideal programme, in practice the implementation of such a programme into a criminal justice system is fraught with difficulty and therefore easier said than done.

Meta-analyses (e.g. Hall 1995) also indicate that cognitive-behavioural treatment can usefully be augmented by pharmacological treatments for offenders with particular features such as sexual pre-occupation or compulsive deviant sexual fantasies. Various medical treatments have been used over the years, many of them aimed at moderation of the hormone testosterone. Such treatments usually involve either surgical castration (removal of the testicles) or the use of anti-androgen drugs (popularly but unhelpfully known as chemical castration), which reduce the synthesis of testosterone, block its access to receptors in its target cells, or increase its breakdown and removal from the body (Grubin 2008). More recently, use has also been made of selective serotonin reuptake inhibitors, the main effect of which is to 'reduce the intensity and frequency of sexual fantasies, and to lessen the force of sexual urges' (41).

Because of the promising research indications, coupled with the difficulty in addressing these risk factors via psychological treatment, increasing use of such medical treatments, mainly as an adjunct to psychological treatments, is being made in the UK, particularly in English and Welsh prisons and probation areas. As Grubin (2008) indicates, such treatments recognise that sexual offending is not just a reflection of underlying emotional problems, but that it is also about sex itself. Because such remedies address out-of-control sexuality, but not underlying emotional causes of sexual offending, it appears they will remain unnecessary for many offenders, and only one part of a wider treatment regime for the small proportion of offenders who require or will benefit from them (for more information on surgical and chemical castration, see Chapter 6 of this volume).

Social approaches

We noted earlier that sexual offending has multiple causes, and therefore multiple responses are required. Sex offender treatment can target the unique psychological features of sexual offenders, and this can be usefully augmented in some cases with medication, as described above. But sexual offending is also a social problem. Few offenders are equally risky in all situations, and those offenders who enjoy social and emotional support from friends, family and professional confidantes have a significantly better prognosis for successful resettlement. This resettlement ideal is a particular challenge to achieve in a society that reviles and rejects sexual offenders as the lowest of the low, and where vigilante action is felt to be a threat. Many sexual offenders (particularly those who have previous convictions) find themselves rejected by friends and family, who no longer wish to be associated with their crimes or who fear the repercussions were their ties to a sex offender found out.

Even offenders who can demonstrate clear benefits from psychological and/or medical treatments will struggle to maintain their efforts to change if they lack support and friendship. Those offenders who have learned to express themselves more healthily and constructively within their relationships will find their new skills quickly rusting if there are no relationships to develop. This is illustrated by the success of the Circles of Support and Accountability (COSA) projects in Canada (Wilson *et al.* 2008). COSA are a means of mobilising volunteers in the community to support and, where necessary, hold certain sex offenders accountable for their actions. The circle operates in the form of a group of trained volunteers meeting regularly with the sex offenders in order to provide a social network, but also to monitor and report on their activities. Wilson *et al.* (2007) report that high-risk sex offenders provided with COSA are significantly less likely to reoffend than those without, although the results should be treated with some caution due to the relatively low number of offenders in the sample. Furthermore the effectiveness of COSA in the UK has yet to be demonstrated conclusively. Nevertheless the importance of COSA seems to be related to the importance of social networks in promoting desistance, but equally such restorative projects may have additional benefits in the positive engagement of communities in managing risky people among them (for more information on restorative justice practices with sex offenders, see Chapter 7 of this volume).

Current practice in England and Wales

Current penal practice in England and Wales has developed roughly in line with the theoretical and research developments outlined above (Murphy and McGrath 2008). An early recognition of the effectiveness of well-designed sex offender treatment programmes, based on cognitive-behavioural methods and meeting the principles of risk, need and responsivity as set out above, resulted in the establishment of a panel of experts to accredit such programmes for use in prisons and probation settings. The panel has so far accredited a range of programmes meeting the needs of various offenders. More recently, specialist programmes addressing the particular emerging needs created by Internet-related crime have been developed. Importantly, sex offender treatment has taken a systems approach, involving not just treatment providers but also offender managers in the delivery of programmes, with complex quality-assurance processes being developed.

The delivery of these programmes is now mandatory for probation areas, and they are also delivered at a number of prisons across the country. Offenders in the community can be mandated to attend for sex offender treatment by conditions in a Community Rehabilitation Order or as part of licence release from prison. In prisons, offenders attend voluntarily, although a strategy is in place to maximise the number of offenders in prisons who consent to treatment.

Efforts to increase the uptake of medical treatments within prison and community treatment settings are in place, as described above, although an offender cannot be required to undertake such treatments; therefore, participation is voluntary. The combination of psychological and medical treatments can ensure that both the emotional and sexual aspects of sexual offending can be addressed.

In addition to such treatment programmes, the overall strategy for the management and treatment of sex offenders includes the consistent use across agencies of RM2000, described above, as an initial risk-assessment tool, the use of Structured Assessment of Risk and Need to assess offenders' progress through treatment, and a pilot of Stable and Acute 2007 (Hanson *et al.* 2007), which is a dynamic risk-assessment tool developed in Canada to improve the assessment and monitoring of sex offenders.

Challenges

For many criminologists the idea that late modern society has become preoccupied with risk, in all forms, has become common wisdom. Some writers (e.g. Lacombe 2008) have drawn attention to the emergence of a risk society, defined by increasing concerns for greater security, and the avoidance of risk. This is linked to the increased wealth and decreased social cohesion that lead to feelings of insecurity and thus a preoccupation with management of risks, including criminal ones (Bottoms 1995; Matravers 2003). McAlinden (2007) argues that governments are abandoning rehabilitative approaches in favour of retributive ones to give the impression that something is being done about sexual crime. The result of this within a criminal justice context is seen as the emergence of a 'culture of control' (Garland 2001), concerned with the management and incapacitation of unruly groups, as opposed to the rehabilitation of individuals. This brings into context the use of actuarial risk-assessment tools such as RM2000 described above, and its use in defining who, among a group of offenders, should receive the most intensive or restrictive interventions. In this way it is argued that notions of just deserts (von Hirsch 1986), a philosophy under which offenders are sentenced according to the seriousness of their crime, are replaced by incapacitation and deterrent sentencing. Indeed, Lacombe (2008) suggested that sex offender treatment itself is designed to reinforce this sense of being different, an outsider, permanently at risk of reoffending, and that within sex offender treatment 'they teach offenders to recognize, acknowledge and internalize what Becker (1963) refers to as a Master Status – a set of characteristics that over-determines identity and overshadows all other aspects of an offender's character' (72). Lacombe's work refers to a US sex offender treatment programme based on management of sexual fantasy – we have examined the UK context above and would argue that here more attention is paid to the development of positive attributes than in the work described by Lacombe. Nevertheless, the allegation that modern sex offender treatment programmes are more concerned with construction of the offender as a significant other, always ready to reoffend and defined by deviant sexuality, is a serious one, not least because there is a growing body of evidence to suggest the importance of social links and bonds in reducing the likelihood of reoffending.

Braithwaite (1989) emphasised the importance of shame as a means of social control of offenders. He distinguishes between reintegrative and disintegrative shaming, the latter occurring when, after committing a crime the offender is prevented from reintegrating with society and treated as a deviant outsider. It is argued that this approach is likely to result in further crimes being committed rather than rehabilitation of the offender, as a result of the offender's being stigmatised and isolated from society. Although Braithwaite's work was not directed specifically at sex offenders, public opinion of sex offenders over the past 20 years could be viewed as an extreme form of disintegrative shaming (McAlinden 2007). Sex offenders have become subjects of moral outrage (Thomas 2005; McAlinden 2007), with media descriptions hardening in recent years. Descriptions of sex offenders as 'monsters', 'paedos', 'beasts', and other derogatory terms have become commonplace, and a scenario in which the role of newspapers in particular appears to have changed from one of reporting the news to one of creating and processing news for entertainment, aimed at a particular market, has been reported (Franklin 1997, cited in Thomas 2005) (for more information on the responsibilities of the media in such reporting, see Chapter 13 of this volume). This is exemplified by the 'name and shame' campaigns held in recent years by certain newspapers, with the aim of notifying the public of the names of sex offenders. Although much of the information disclosed in such campaigns is often already in the public domain as a consequence of court hearings, the information is presented in a way that seems to inflame public opinion to the point where rioting has taken place in some areas of the country where sex offenders were suspected of residing. Bottoms (1995) described the effect this may have upon politicians in provoking punitive, often short-term, policies designed to reduce reoffending by general deterrence or, through the adoption of 'populist punitive' policies (40), to placate public opinion (or at least the opinions of a certain proportion of the electorate). Matravers (2003) argued that the term 'public protection' is used to justify continuing sanctions against unconvicted or released prisoners who have done their time, and notions of just deserts for sex offenders in particular are ignored in the assumption that only longer and more punitive sanctions will reduce the risk from these offenders.

Whether changes in policy and legislation with regard to the treatment and management of sex offenders have been as the result of, for example, public concern, or an inevitable consequence of the growing realisation of the impact of sexual abuse on victims is debatable. What is less debatable is the volume of restrictive techniques and legislation that have emerged in recent years, in an attempt to control and manage sex offenders (Cobley 2003), and perhaps to assuage public opinion with regard to protecting them from sexual offending. This has taken place despite some writers pointing to the scant evidence of the effectiveness of punitive or deterrent responses (e.g. Matravers 2003). The system of management and treatment of sex offenders that we have described, therefore, might be seen in the light of the emergence of the risk society itself.

Conclusion

Over the past 20 years the means of treatment and management of sex offenders has developed dramatically in the UK, in line with the growing recognition of the problem of sexual abuse itself. Interventions are provided by a number of agencies, police, prisons, and probation; some are based on developing internal controls, aimed at changing offenders' thoughts and opinions with regard to their offending, but most are aimed at increasing external controls, physical barriers to reoffending. Systems to assess and identify those offenders who need the most intensive interventions of either kind have been developed. While some writers have related this to an increasing concern about personal risk within society, and criticised the change from a focus upon justice, punishment and rehabilitation to one that seems concerned with managing unruly groups; equally the empirical evidence demonstrating the long-term effects on victims of sexual abuse illustrates the importance of dealing effectively with these people.

The whole project has been complicated by hardening of public and media attitudes towards sex offenders, and the particular manifestation of shaming that has emerged, which has been disintegrative rather than reintegrative. This has made successful rehabilitation and proper management of risky people more difficult.

Finally, although the treatment of known sex offenders is important, there are two reasons to suggest that more general policies that improve the quality of childhood in society in general might improve our ability to reduce the amount of sexual offending in the longer term. These reasons are, firstly, theoretical perspectives that indicate the development of vulnerabilities for sexual offending in childhood backgrounds of offenders, and, secondly, the growing evidence that many, if not most, sex crimes go undetected and unpunished. The criminal justice system can, at best, only address the proportion of sexual crime that has been detected.

References

Andrews, D. A and Bonta, J. (2003) *The Psychology of Criminal Conduct* (3rd edn). Cincinnati, OH: Anderson.

Barnett, G. D., Wakeling, H. C. and Howard, P. D. (2009) 'An Examination of the Predictive Validity of the Risk Matrix 2000 in England and Wales'. Paper under review.

Bottoms, A. E. (1995) 'The Philosophy and Politics of Punishment and Sentencing', in C. Clarkson and R. Morgan (eds), *The Politics of Sentencing Reform*. Oxford: Clarendon Press.

Braithwaite, J. (1989) *Crime, Shame and Reintegration*. Cambridge: Cambridge University Press.

Cobley, C. (2003) 'The Legislative Framework', in A. Matravers (ed.), *Sex Offenders in the Community. Managing and reducing the risks*. Cullompton: Willan.

Cunliffe, J. and Shepherd, A. (2007) *Reoffending of Adults: Results from the 2004 Cohort*. Home Office Statistical Bulletin 06/07, London: Home Office.

Garland, D. (2001) *The Culture of Control. Crime and Social Order in Contemporary Society*. Oxford: Oxford University Press.

Grubin, D. (1998) *Sex Offending Against Children: Understanding the Risk*. Police Research Series Paper 99, London: Home Office.

Grubin, D. (2008) 'The Use of Medication in the Treatment of Sex Offenders', *Prison Service Journal*, 178: 37–43.

Hall, G. C. N. (1995) 'Sexual Offender Recidivism Revisited: A Meta-Analysis of Recent Treatment Studies', *Journal of Consulting and Clinical Psychology*, 63: 802–9.

Hanson, R. K., Bourgon, G., Helmus, L. and Hodgson, S. (2009) *A Meta-Analysis of the Effectiveness of Treatment for Sexual Offenders: Risk, Need and Responsivity*. Report 2009–01, Public Safety Canada.

Hanson, R. K., Harris, A. J. R., Scott, T.-L. and Helmus, L. (2007) *Assessing the Risk of Sexual Offenders on Community Supervision: The Dynamic Supervision Project*. Solicitor General of Canada (Minister of Public Safety and Emergency Preparedness).

Harris, A. J. R. and Hanson, R. K. (2004) Sex *Offender Recidivism: A Simple Question*. Solicitor General of Canada (Minister of Public Safety and Emergency Preparedness).

Hood, R., Shute, S., Feilzer, M. and Wilcox, A. (2002) *Reconviction Rates of Serious Sex Offenders and Assessments of Their Risk*. London: Home Office.

Johnson, P. (2001) 'In Their Own Voices: Report of a Study on the Later Effects of Child Sexual Abuse', *Journal of Sexual Aggression*, 7(2): 41–56.

Lacombe, D. (2008) 'Consumed With Sex: The Treatment of Sex Offenders in Risk Society', *British Journal of Criminology*, 48: 55–74.

Maguire, M., Kemshall, H., Noaks, L. and Wincup, E. (2001) *Risk Management of Sexual and Violent Offenders: The Work of Public Protection Panels*. London: Home Office.

Mann, R. E. (2009) 'Getting the Context Right for Sexual Offender Treatment', in D. Prescott (ed.), *Building Motivation to Change in Sexual Offenders*. Vermont, USA: Safer Society Press.

Mann, R. E., Hanson, R. K. and Thornton, D. (2009) 'Assessing Risk for Sexual Recidivism: Some Proposals on the Nature of Meaningful Risk Factors'.

Marshall, W. L. and Barbaree, H. E. (1990) 'An Integrated Theory of the Etiology of Sexual Offending', in W. L. Marshall, D. R. Laws and H. E. Barbaree (eds), *Handbook of Sexual Assault: Issues, Theories and Treatment of the Offender*. New York: Plenum Press.

Matravers, A. (2003) 'Setting Some Boundaries – Rethinking Responses to Sex Offenders', in A. Matravers (ed.), *Sex Offenders in the Community. Managing and Reducing the Risks*. Cullompton: Willan.

McAlinden, A-M. (2007) *The Shaming of Sex Offenders. Risk, Retribution and Reintegration*. Oxford: Hart Publishing.

Murphy, W. D. and McGrath, R. (2008) 'Best Practices in Sex Offender Treatment', *Prison Service Journal*, 178: 3–8.

Thomas, T. (2005) *Sex Crime: Sex Offending and Society*. Cullompton: Willan.

Thornton, D., Mann, R., Webster, S. *et al.* (2003) 'Distinguishing and Combining Risks for Sexual and Violent Recidivism', *Annals of the New York Academy of Sciences*, 989: 225–235.

von Hirsch, A. (1986) *Past or Future Crimes. Deservedness and Dangerousness in the Sentencing of Criminals.* Manchester: Manchester University Press.

Ward, T., Gannon, T. and Vess, J. (2008) 'Human Rights, Ethical Principles and Standards in Forensic Psychology', *International Journal of Offender Therapy and Comparative Criminology*, 53: 126–144.

Ward, T., Polaschek, D. L. L. and Beech, A. R. (2006) *Theories of Sexual Offending.* Chichester: Wiley.

Ward, T. and Siegert, R. J. (2002) 'Toward a Comprehensive Theory of Child Sexual Abuse: A Theory Knitting Perspective', *Psychology, Crime and Law*, 8: 319–351.

Wilson, R. J., McWhinnie, A. J., Picheca, J. E., Prinzo, M. and Cortoni, F. (2007) 'Circles of Support and Accountability: Engaging Community Volunteers in the Management of High-Risk Sexual Offenders', *Howard Journal*, 46: 1–15.

Wilson, R. J., McWhinnie, A. J. and Wilson, C. (2008) 'Circles of Support and Accountability: An International Partnership in Reducing Sexual Offender Recidivism', *Prison Service Journal*, 178: 26–36.

Part II

Risk management

Chapter 3

Effective multi-agency public protection: learning from the research

Jason Wood and Hazel Kemshall

Introduction

Multi-Agency Public Protection Arrangements (MAPPA) are a key operational structure charged with the community management of sexual and violent offenders. Through local partnerships underpinned by national statutory guidance and legislation, the arrangements bring together three responsible authorities (police, probation and prisons) and a range of 'duty to cooperate' agencies who are charged with assessing risk and providing responsive risk management plans in a context of closer interagency cooperation and shared responsibility.

Drawing on the authors' research, this chapter briefly reviews the development of MAPPA before examining how 'effectiveness' is measured in these arrangements. It considers staff and offender views on effectiveness and demonstrates how lessons from research can be used to strengthen the supervision and management of offenders.

History and context

How to predict, manage and prevent risk has become the central preoccupation of criminal justice practitioners in supervising sex offenders post-custody. The Criminal Justice Act (CJA) 1991 was the first to reframe the role of probation to 'protect the public from serious harm' (Home Office 1990: 2) with public protection becoming the key driver for probation work (Kemshall 2003). The CJA 1991 was to be superseded and expanded by a series of legislative and policy developments throughout the 1990s that would continuously reshape the role of probation in the correctional service. This period saw the service characterised by 'risk aversion, enforced repositioning and blame avoidance' (Kemshall 2003: 85). In police, probation and across other criminal justice agencies, new technical approaches were developed in the pursuit of accurately identifying potential risk of harm. These tools were supplemented by greater inter-agency cooperation and risk management planning.

The wider 'risk context' and the circumstances which led to the development of MAPPA have been discussed elsewhere (e.g. Kemshall and Wood 2007a, 2007b, 2009), but for the purposes of revision, some key contextual debates are reviewed here.

High-profile cases and the punitive turn

Sexual and violent offenders powerfully exercise the imagination of the public, media and policymakers (Kitzinger 2004; Kemshall and Wood 2009): they are the monstrous offenders who have framed much of contemporary penal policy responses to risk (Kemshall 2008). For example, Kitzinger (2004) has commented extensively on how a fixation on the small numbers of offenders actually subject to community supervision has distorted our understanding of the problem of child sexual abuse, and notes how the media framing of such abuse as located almost exclusively in the alien 'Other', 'stranger-danger', has influenced the framing of policy and legislation. Most policy and procedures are geared towards detecting and controlling this outsider, resulting in overwhelming shock and blame when children are harmed by those charged with their care (for example, the case of Victoria Climbié (Laming 2003)).

As a consequence of growing awareness of sexual offending, including increased media attention and the discovery of the predatory paedophile, key cultural shifts began to occur in the public discourse around dangerousness (Kemshall and Wood 2009). Sensitivity to the seemingly rare and dangerous risks was heightened, with studies revealing the extent of child sexual abuse (e.g. Cawson et al. 2000), and the inadequacy of criminal justice responses across the spectrum (Prior et al. 1997). These studies revealed not only the true prevalence, but also the varying types of offence and their degrees of severity (Grubin 1998). The media focus was selective, however: its emphasis on dangerous strangers superseded discussion around, for example, the high proportion of sexual offences that occur within the family. Public safety and security from the unknown dangers mirrored a wider, growing insecurity associated with the now well- documented 'rise of risk' (Kemshall 2003; Nash 2005). The result: a dominant policy focus on the exclusion and distancing of offenders characterised as monsters and 'Others' (Kemshall and Wood 2007b).

National debate centred on key cases (such as the murders of Sarah Payne, Holly Wells and Jessica Chapman) has resulted in political challenges to preventing further incidences of grave crime, and 'Political parties were parading their tough credentials, anxious to appease the press. Little was done to represent the real nature of the risk to an increasingly aware and concerned public' (Nash 2005: 18). The impact of the risk agenda on penal policy can be measured by the volume of legislation and the extensive systems and processes designed for its management (Kemshall 2003; Nash 2006). The impact on key criminal justice agencies has also been significant, with a sea change in the role and responsibility of the Probation Service and a tighter focus on risky offenders for the police (see Kemshall 2003 for a full review). The resulting public protection industry is now extensive, and has led to an 'escalating vocabulary of punitive motives' (Welch et al. 1997: 486) in which ever harsher penal policies against the dangerous are advocated, a situation Sanders and Lyon (1995) have described as 'repetitive retribution'. This retribution has largely crystallised in the sex offender and most notably the paedophile (Kitzinger 2004; Thomas 2005), but has been accompanied by seepage to other offenders and offence types.

Parallel to this was the rise of a new penology of risk and actuarial justice (Feeley and Simon 1992, 1994). As a result of the demise in confidence in liberal crime management strategies and a concern with how to manage the most dangerous and habitual offenders, risk management increasingly took precedence over rehabilitation (Garland 2001; Kemshall and Wood 2007b). This was evidenced by greater measures to increase conviction rates, the introduction of new sentences, and the imposition of new post-custody licence conditions and restrictions. Risk-assessment strategies were developed, as new technical and actuarial procedures were increasingly used in the classification and prediction of offender risk.

The development of multi-agency public protection arrangements

Formal partnerships for protection emerged early within the public protection agenda, most notably in West Yorkshire, with police and probation exchanging information in the early 1990s on high-risk offenders (see Maguire et al. 2001; Kemshall and Maguire 2001;

Wood and Kemshall 2008). Such partnerships gained momentum and legislative force in the Criminal Justice and Court Services Act (CJCSA) 2000; CJA 2003; and guidance (Home Office 2004; Ministry of Justice 2007); and quickly became embedded within the main agencies and processes of criminal justice (Kemshall 2003). These partnerships were concerned largely (although not exclusively) with the statutory supervision of high-risk offenders in the community and with the oversight of high-risk offenders upon release from prison. The partnerships have crystallised into the formal MAPPA.

The CJCSA 2000 placed a responsibility on police and probation (and later prisons through the CJA 2003) to:

> Establish arrangements for the purpose of assessing and managing risks in [the local area] by:
> (a) Relevant sexual and violent offenders, and
>
> (b) Other persons, who, by reason of offences committed by them (wherever committed), are considered by the responsible authority to be persons who may cause serious harm to the public. (CJCSA 2000: s. 62(2))

The level of cooperation between agencies and the resources dedicated to risk management are determined by three levels of management. These levels are designed to match resources and be responsive to the risk assessment:

- **Level 1 – ordinary risk management** where the agency responsible for the offender can manage risk without the significant involvement of other agencies. This level of management is only appropriate for offenders presenting a low or medium risk.

- **Level 2 – local inter-agency risk management** where there is active involvement of more than one agency in risk management plans, either because of a higher level of risk or because of the complexity of managing the offender. It is common for level 3 cases to be referred down to level 2 when risk of harm deflates.

- **Level 3 – Multi-Agency Public Protection Panel (MAPPP)** is for those defined as the 'critical few'. The MAPPP is responsible for risk management, drawing together key partners who will take joint responsibility for the community management of the offender. An offender who should be referred to this level of management is defined as someone who:

(a) Is assessed under OASys [the Offender Assessment System] as being a high or very high-risk of causing serious harm; **AND**

(b) Presents risks that can only be managed by a plan which requires close cooperation at a senior level due to the complexity of the case and/or because of the unusual resource commitments it requires; **OR**

(c) Although not assessed as a high or very high risk, the case is exceptional because the likelihood of media scrutiny and/or public interest in the management of the case is very high and there is a need to ensure that public confidence in the criminal justice system is sustained. (Home Office 2004: para 116).

MAPPA is firmly rooted in the community protection approach to risk management (Connelly and Williamson 2000). Here, public protection agencies manage offenders through restriction, conditions, sanctions, corrective programmes and enforcement with the identification of the public as a potential wider victim group (Kemshall and Wood 2007b).

Controlling and restrictive measures are those conditions attached to supervision orders or licences that restrict where offenders can go and live, what they can or cannot do, and whom they must not approach or contact. For example, a sex offender may have a restriction against using certain leisure facilities (for example, swimming pools) or approaching local schools, and may have a condition to reside in a certain place (for example, a probation hostel). Offenders can also be made the subject of a curfew to restrict their activities at certain times of the day or night when they are known to be more risky. These conditions restrict the opportunity to commit offences and to groom victims. Restrictive conditions are specific to individual offenders, and it is important that they are well matched to the assessed risk factors, and are proportionate, justified and workable in practice.

MAPPA have been subject to three significant research evaluations (Maguire *et al.* 2001; Kemshall *et al.* 2005; Wood and Kemshall 2007). The most recent review conducted in 2006–7 included perceptions from practitioners and offenders on the effectiveness and operation of the arrangements and formed part of the Home Secretary's Child Sex Offender Review (CSOR) that reported in 2007.

Issues in partnership

Partnerships are intended to avoid functional silos by overcoming departmental and specialist barriers and by providing joined-up services (in this case, risk management). They are often argued to be better placed to meet policy objectives by using multiple players and different levels, and to strengthen the link between central government aspirations, targets and guidance and local arrangements. Partnerships also provide a forum for multi-disciplinary expertise and enable the sharing of distinct expert opinions and perspectives (see Newman 2001; Prins 2002; Kemshall and Wood 2007a; Wood and Kemshall 2008).

In the issue of child protection and risk management of dangerousness, they are seen to be given additional impetus on account of previous inter-agency failure to assess and respond adequately to warning signs. Debate about high-profile cases where children have died and abuse was not either adequately detected or responded to is often accompanied by an assessment of the roles of different agencies and the extent to which they communicated effectively with one another. In the context of managing high-risk offenders, partnerships are seen to be best placed in responding to the different aspects of an offender's risk assessment. Police and probation services may have a duty to monitor and enforce conditions, provide corrective programmes and supervision. For agencies to undertake these responsibilities effectively, inter-agency communication, as a minimum, is seen as necessary. Other agencies have significant roles to play in addressing an offender's risk. For example:

- *Social services* may monitor the extent to which offenders have access to children and, in response, will institute child protection procedures where access could lead to further offences.

- *Health services* provide mental health treatment and engagement, and offenders may be subject to intervention by forensic mental health services.

- *Housing agencies* through the local authority and private agencies are responsible for providing social housing to offenders.

- *Employment agencies* provide opportunities for offenders to re-engage in training and employment.

The linkage between traditional criminal justice and other social agencies is theoretically strengthened when greater communication and cooperation are encouraged. This interaction moves beyond mere communication between partners. In the context of MAPPA, police, probation and prisons must work together as responsible authorities, and other agencies have a duty to cooperate with arrangements (Kemshall and Wood 2007a).

The first MAPPA evaluation found significant hurdles to the effective functioning of partnership, most notably value clashes, ideological disputes, inadequate resourcing and protectiveness over agency services, lack of coordination, and lack of a multi-disciplinary approach (Kemshall and Maguire 2001; Maguire et al. 2001). The subsequent evaluation (Kemshall et al. 2005) found significant improvements, but a number of key issues remained. While agency-based value disputes are now relatively less common, boundaries between the MAPPA agencies have become increasingly permeable, resulting in what Nash has famously called a 'polibation officer' (Nash 1999a, 1999b), with the roles and responsibilities of police and probation merged. It is crucial that permeable boundaries do not become fuzzy boundaries, particularly in respect of statutory duties such as enforcement of orders or enforcement of the sex offender register. Role and boundary confusion has been significant in previous risk management failures and inquiries (Sheppard 1996). There is also evidence that MAPPA remains under-resourced, and that the public protection commitment of the relevant agencies has not been sufficiently costed (Kemshall et al. 2005), with subsequent problems in delivering costly interventions such as long-term community surveillance or intensive treatment programmes. In addition, the multi-disciplinary expertise of MAPPA is at present undermined by the lack of cooperation by health services (particularly forensic mental health and psychological services). Where they are making a local contribution, both the risk assessments and risk management plans are improved, and access to relevant services is enhanced (Kemshall et al. 2005).

Difficulties in measuring effectiveness

The issues of investigating effectiveness are likened to the central question of what constitutes a positive outcome in MAPPA (Wood and

Kemshall 2008). Effectiveness can be measured in terms of whether agencies cooperate well together, whether risk assessments are more thorough than they would be in the absence of such cooperation, and whether risk management plans are delivered by all agencies charged with the actions specified. All of these issues are compounded by the nature of the structure of MAPPA, where accountability to the public, between and to stakeholders, and to victims and offenders can be characterised as complex (Wood and Kemshall 2008).

A Home Office report *MAPPA – The First Five Years* noted that the number of serious further offences committed by offenders managed at levels 2 and 3 in 2005/6 was only 0.44 per cent. The biggest impact was at level 3, 'and such a low serious reoffending rate for this particular group of offenders is to be welcomed and supports the view that MAPPA is making a real contribution to the management of dangerousness in the community' (Home Office 2007: 6–7). Enforcement and breach of parole licences and court orders had also risen for levels 2 and 3, in effect, taking action to prevent further offending based upon problematic behaviours or breach of conditions. Action to enforce the Sex Offender Register requirements also increased by 30 per cent (through cautions and further convictions) and affected some 1,295 offenders, '4.3 per cent of the total registered in the community' (7). The years 2005/6 also saw the use of 973 Sexual Offences Prevention Orders (SOPOs) under the Sexual Offences Act 2003. This evidence of impact mitigates the critique of commentators, such as Lieb (2003), who contend that MAPPA is little more than joined-up worrying.

Such worries are confounded by continuing political and public anxiety over the management arrangements. Media interest remains high, often with a focus on shortcomings in supervision at the expense of a more balanced report on the effectiveness of MAPPA. For example, Wood and Kemshall's (2007) evaluation of MAPPA investigated good practice and areas for development and highlighted a range of effective supervision practices in managing high-risk offenders. In response to its publication, media interest focused on comments that if caseloads rise, there may be negative consequences for the effectiveness of supervision. This comment gained prominence in the national press, which concluded that offenders were not being managed enough because of inadequate staffing (with the *Daily Star* reporting it as 'paedos go free'). As another example, the locally produced and published annual reports, designed to inform the public about the work of MAPPA, include details of the number of sex offenders subject to community management. Media reporting each year tends to focus on any increases in the numbers without the corresponding detail or explanation for inevitable rises.

However, the Chief Inspector of Probation in England and Wales has noted the significant impact of low resources and diminished capacity in the adequate supervision of offenders. He referred to the 'Long Squeeze' – a situation over a period of time where resources have not kept pace with rising workload, and increasing public and political expectations of what can be delivered (Her Majesty's Inspectorate of Probation (HMIP) 2007a: 5–6). The Chief Inspector draws the conclusion that if the situation is not addressed, the capacity to supervise adult offenders satisfactorily will be compromised. Practitioners have also reflected this concern (Wood and Kemshall 2007). While a simple causal relationship cannot necessarily be drawn between quantity and quality in the workload (HMIP 2007a), the Effective Supervision Inspections have found that less than 60 per cent of cases had a satisfactory risk of harm assessment carried out (similar to the findings of Kemshall *et al.* 2005 on MAPPA cases), although interventions were satisfactory in around 80 per cent of cases (HMIP 2007b). The joint Police and Probation Inspectorate report on the community management of sex offenders conducted in 2005 found:

- lack of clarity and consistency about the level of MAPPA management for individual sex offender cases
- lack of completion of OASys risk of harm sections
- lack of clear recording in case files
- lack of home visiting and monitoring of sex offenders
- lack of appropriate resourcing for police visits to sex offenders
- risk management plans not always implemented
- poor minute taking and actions not clear
- lack of reviews and no follow-up on failed actions
- lack of appropriate and dedicated resources for MAPPA (summarised from Her Majesty's Inspectorate of Constabulary (HMIC) and HMIP 2005).

The inquiry also noted that 'in the 100 cases we inspected interventions and their level of intensity were not proportionate to the assessed risk of harm in 35 per cent of cases which indicates either more or less input was required in those cases to manage risk of harm' (HMIC and HMIP 2005: 27).

The overuse of restrictive conditions has also been problematic. The HMIP thematic report on sex offenders noted that sex offenders

Table 3.1 Summary of the HMIC and HMIP 2005 findings

% above the line (excellent/sufficient)	SOTI[1]	ESI[2]
(For high/very high risk of harm cases only)		
Has a good-quality risk management plan been produced under MAPPA or other interagency arrangement?	50%	58%
Is this risk management plan being executed appropriately, with effective liaison between the agencies, particularly police and probation, including on accommodation issues?	42%	66%
Has the risk management plan been appropriately reviewed?	50%	66%
(For child protection cases only)		
Has there been probation and police involvement in child protection arrangements – e.g. core group or case conference and liaison between agencies to reduce the risk to the child(ren)?	59%	80%

(HMIC and HMIP 2005: 39, Table 5)

[1]Sex Offender Treatment Inspection.
[2]Effective Supervision Inspection.

subject to restrictive measures may struggle with social isolation and experience difficulties with community reintegration (HMIC and HMIP 2005; Levenson and Cotter 2005). In addition, sex offenders, and particularly high-risk, sexually violent offenders, lack social support and are social isolates. This can affect normal social learning and seems to have a decisive impact on normal and deviant behaviour (Bandura 1977, cited in Gutierrez-Lobos *et al.* 2001). The overuse of exclusion zones has been seen as problematic, preventing employment/education and destroying access to supportive or family networks (Levenson and Cotter 2005; Worth 2005).

Levenson and Cotter (2005) identify 14 states in the USA that have exclusion zones prohibiting sex offenders from living within close proximity to a school, park, day-care centre or school bus stop (168). They note that the zones range from 500 to 2,000 feet, and in California to a quarter of a mile, from a school and prohibit sex offenders from residing within 35 miles of a victim or witness. Interestingly, they cite studies in which the evidence for proximity to children resulting in recidivism is mixed (e.g. Walker *et al.* 2001; Minnesota Department of Corrections 2003; Colorado Department of Public Safety 2004). They contend that the overuse of exclusion zones may result in homelessness and transience, thus making risk management harder. It also produces illogical responses to risk, potentially displacing risk onto more vulnerable people, summed up by one offender thus:

> I couldn't live in an adult mobile home park because a church was 880 ft away and had a children's class that met once a week. I was forced to move to a motel where right next door to my room was a family with three children – but it qualified under the rule. (Levenson and Cotter 2005: 175)

Evaluations of effectiveness

This has proved a difficult area for MAPPA, not least because positive outcomes have not always been clear-cut. For example, a parole recall in response to escalating risk can be viewed both as a negative indicator – supervision has failed, the offender has not succeeded in the community, a costly custodial place will now be required – and as a positive indicator, in that supervision and monitoring have resulted in swift protective action and enforcement; therefore, MAPPA has succeeded in protecting the public. The report *MAPPA – The First Five Years* used reconviction as an indicator of effectiveness, although this was largely limited to 'serious further offences'.

Enforcement was also considered: 'The data relating to breach of licence and court orders is positive as this reflects an increase in action taken in level 2 and 3 cases prior to them having opportunity to commit serious further harm; i.e. to recall to prison' (Home Office 2007: 7). Similarly, action to enforce sex offender requirements through caution and conviction increased to 30 per cent, totalling 4.3 per cent of those in the community. While this report did not explicitly explore additional key performance indicators, it did recognise that broader measures of effectiveness should be taken into account. In particular, the report noted the learning and recommendations of the two serious further offence reviews carried out by the Probation Inspectorate in 2006 (HMIP 2006a, 2006b).

Audits: process and outcome

Audit can take two main forms in respect of MAPPA: process audits that focus on systems, processes, and practice; and outcome audits focusing on reconviction, enforcement and recall. Process audits have been more common, with two evaluations of MAPPA systems and processes (Maguire *et al.* 2001; Kemshall *et al.* 2005), and one audit of supervision practice (Wood and Kemshall 2007). Maguire *et al.* (2001) found inconsistency in operation and standards, and a number of recommendations were implemented with guidance (Home Office 2003, 2004) and by legislation (most notably, CJCSA 2001, sections 67–68). The second evaluation had a slightly extended remit with a focus on effective community management strategies as well as partnership arrangements. While this report found many improvements since the original evaluation report (Home Office 2003), a number of key issues still required further attention. In brief, these were the need for greater effectiveness and appropriateness in the allocation of offenders to the appropriate level of risk management; the full completion of risk assessment tools in all cases; clearer mechanisms for recording risk assessments and risk management decisions, particularly in the case of panel minutes; the need for a case review system that is matched to the risk management plans; and appropriate, dedicated resources for the coordination and administration of MAPPA (Kemshall *et al.* 2005). This report also recommended that MAPPA regularly complete audits of their work, particularly case-based audits (Box 3.1).

Audits by panel personnel of approximately 10 per cent of cases each year would assist reviews of practice standards, encourage consistency, and help to identify system failures and resource gaps early (Kemshall *et al.* 2005). Corrective action could then be taken as a matter of course, integrated within the quality assurance function of MAPPA Strategic Management Boards. The HMIP inspection, for example, found that planned, unannounced visits to the homes of sex offenders actually took place 10 per cent less than originally planned (HMIC and HMIP 2005: 41). This is important quality assurance information and can reveal issues in resource shortfall, lack of integrity in risk management, and conflicting priorities (in this case in policing priorities).

Wood and Kemshall (2007) in an evaluation carried out as part of the CSOR focused on the contribution of MAPPA to the management of high-risk offenders, effective supervision practice, staff views of MAPPA effectiveness, and the views of offenders subject to MAPPA management. The study found that staff were positive about the contribution of MAPPA with the following themes seen as particularly important:

Box 3.1 Criteria for case-based audits

- Check whether the amount of contact with the offender corresponds to the risk of harm they currently pose and that the case file demonstrates the appropriate targeting of resources at the highest risk offenders.

- Assess whether the documentation within the case file clearly demonstrates the systematic, well-informed and timely review of the offender's status and, if subject to probation supervision, their supervision plan objectives.

- Ensure that case files are comprehensively, accurately and well maintained in order that information is consistently and readily accessible.

- Ensure that all National Standards are adhered to under probation supervision.

- Ensure that where a Public Protection Meeting has been held, any action required by the action plan has been evidenced as being carried out within the timescale indicated in the plan.

- Establish whether the appropriate risk assessment tool has been appropriately completed and this information used at the Public Protection Meeting.

- Establish whether review dates are documented in the case file and are appropriately and timely completed.

- Ensure case files are well structured and accessible.

- Establish that a contingency plan is evident and is periodically reviewed.

- Ensure essential resources are available.

(Kemshall *et al*. 2005: 18)

- Effective communication amongst the police, probation and prisons.
- The systematic exchange of information.
- Access to housing and accommodation.
- Access to specialist supervised accommodation (though this was felt to be uneven).
- Link to social services.

- Victim liaison for victim issues.
- MAPPA approved discretionary disclosure.
- Rapid response to escalating risk.
- Option to facilitate supervision of high risk offenders beyond end of licence.
- MAPPA can facilitate access to additional resources (Wood and Kemshall 2007: 8).

The report notes that effectiveness is difficult to measure in MAPPA and relied on police and probation staff views of the perceived added value to identify areas of good practice. Key factors were identified as:

- Timely and focused pre-release work. Facilitated in one area through joint visits by police and probation to prisoners pre-release, and by regular attendance of prison personnel at MAPPP Level 3 meetings. Specific risk management plans were reported to be developed pre-release with appropriate conditions and restrictions and areas operated swift recall policies.

- Panel attendance of victim liaison workers. This enabled presentation of victim issues and a focus on victim protection strategies (for example rapid response phone contact, alarms, etc.).

- Early identification of need and referral to relevant treatment/group work programme, supported by relevant one-to-one work. Communication between programme tutors and the MAPPA co-ordinator had assisted in presenting more informed progress reports at MAPPA meetings in one area. In another area, information was passed on from programme tutors within 24 hours. In both areas, there was a suggestion that treatment providers could attend MAPPA meetings more often.

- Offence-focused individual work, for example working with offenders to develop internal controls and recognise and avoid triggers to offending.

- Attention in one-to-one-supervision to relapse prevention, especially following completion of treatment. This varied across the three areas, appearing to be excellent in one area but less often implemented in another.

- Probation officers working with offenders to jointly manage risk with the goal of engaging offenders in their own regulation. This participatory approach was felt to be effective in ensuring offenders could better self-risk manage post-supervision.

- The use and enforcement of appropriate external controls (curfews, exclusion zones, etc.).

- Use of home visits to check and be 'lifestyle vigilant' – in one area visits were jointly made by police and probation while other areas conducted police visits.

- Police surveillance.

- Swift and appropriate information exchange (for example between police and probation especially when offenders were breaching licence conditions).

- The specialist multi-agency teams of police and probation in two areas showed very well developed specialist expertise and prompt information-sharing practices. Similarly, the specialist police team in another area was well developed, with excellent links with the MAPPA co-ordinator (Wood and Kemshall 2007: 9).

In in-depth interviews with offenders subject to MAPPA, Wood and Kemshall (2007) found that offenders valued and benefited from attention to their personal and social problems, and to their personal goals, needs and desires – an approach promoted by the 'Good Lives Model' (see Ward and Stewart 2003; Ward and Maruna 2007). The balance between external and internal controls was the key to their effective risk management. Various external controls were employed, including legal requirements, parole conditions, curfews, exclusion zones, residence requirements, and the use of unannounced home visiting. While some offenders saw external controls as intrusive, where they could perceive a link between such controls and the management of their behaviour they were more likely to accept and comply with them. 'I understand they have a responsibility to the public to ensure that I do not cross any boundaries' (Wood and Kemshall 2007: 7). In one MAPPA area, this approach was supported by the use of contracts with offenders, and while not legally binding, these provided an important starting point for supervision and engaged offenders in planning their own risk management (Wood and Kemshall 2007: 18–19).

MAPPA offenders were more likely to engage and comply with supervision if the role of MAPPA and their supervision requirements had been properly explained to them (Wood and Kemshall 2007), and many saw MAPPA as having a legitimate role in helping them to avoid future offending and to reintegrate into society. Offenders were able to articulate the techniques helpful in changing behaviours and these included:

- self-risk management including the use of contracts and self-reporting to police or probation if an offender believed they were about to offend

- clear articulation of victim issues, including the recognition of the impact of sexual offending upon children

- the use of distraction techniques to avoid inappropriate sexual thoughts when seeing children. (Wood and Kemshall 2007: 14)

This indicates that offender perceptions are important to evaluating service delivery, targeting appropriately, and ensuring motivation and compliance (Dominey et al. (2005).

In a study of 61 high-risk prisoners, Attrill and Liell (2007) found that prisoners understood the purpose of risk assessment, and recognised that staff were concerned with severity, harm and the imminence of any offending on release. Prisoners were also aware of the key criminogenic risk factors associated with their offending, and recognised that workers would legitimately focus on these. However, a number also pointed out the paradox of risk assessment for most prisoners; in effect, how can prisoners prove their reduced risk without being released, and without demonstrating reduced risk they cannot achieve parole. In addition, prisoners were concerned about the accuracy of written information about them and that decisions could be made on out-of-date information. Other important factors cited by prisoners were the knowledge, skill and competence of the risk assessor; the time taken to 'get to know them'; the level of their inclusion in the assessment; whether they were given sufficient credit for change; and whether negative factors were balanced with positive ones (Attrill and Liell 2007: 195-199). The authors conclude:

The views and comments made by the offenders we met were not unreasonable, unrealistic or naïve. What they often wanted was probably much the same as we do, as professionals involved in risk assessment and decision-making. They wanted accuracy, fairness and a chance to be involved in decisions about their future. In this, and many other things, we have common ground. (Attrill and Liell 2007: 201)

In general terms, staff working in MAPPA considered effectiveness to be a reduction in reconviction, although it was also described as 'holding difficult and high-risk offenders' in the community for longer, reducing victim risk, and avoiding serious further offences (Wood and Kemshall 2007: 15). All areas were publishing reconviction data as part of Annual Reports, and these are aggregated nationally.

Evaluating partnerships

While inter-agency work has often been promoted as a solution to the practice problems of working with people with complex behaviours and complex lives, joining up services from a number of different agencies has often proved more problematic (Kemshall 2001). Translating good intentions into robust actions for the community management of high-risk offenders has often proved more challenging. The Derwent Initiative has helpfully addressed this difficult issue and has progressed standards for inter-agency work (see Hughes 2001). Importantly, Hughes states that:

The art of inter-agency working consists in the bringing together of various agencies, specialities and disciplines as equal partners aligned to a common purpose in order to produce additional value at the point of delivery to the client group, while at the same time acknowledging, maintaining and respecting the integrity of the individual agencies, specialities and disciplines involved. (Hughes 2001: 1)

However, the standards also note the inherently contradictory nature of attempting 'cooperation as equals' with 'maintaining individual integrity' (2). The tension is clear in MAPPA – individual agencies should not allow their aims and objectives to predominate, but the aims and objectives of individual agencies within the MAPPA should be respected. This can be significantly difficult to uphold where there is a distinction between the responsible authorities and duty to cooperate agencies, and where statutory case supervision is vested in a single agency (for example, probation). This tension is partly addressed by making aims and objectives for the inter-agency partnership itself (i.e. for MAPPA) that supersede those of the individual agencies, such as public protection – aims that require the contribution of all to achieve. However, this does not necessarily eliminate disputes about how they should be achieved, nor does it eliminate conflict between these aims and those of individual agencies in other arenas. For example, the police may wish to achieve public protection but may always have a view that this is done through enforcement rather than rehabilitation, a potential source of conflict with probation colleagues. The key issue here is how these tensions are resolved to ensure greater effectiveness of MAPPA management of high-risk offenders, including increased compliance, increased offender disclosures of risky behaviours, and increased behaviour change (see Kemshall 2008 for a full discussion). In this type of scenario, the key test should be risk management that is based on robust research evidence about the most effective means of reducing risky behaviours in the community, and not necessarily the pursuit of risk management strategies that most comply with the value base or routine work patterns of the individual agencies concerned. Mechanisms to counter this trend can be the use of independent chairs, and rotating case management responsibility, or sharing it in joint case supervision (Hughes 2001; Kemshall 2008).

It is also important that MAPPA can demonstrate value added – what is it that MAPPA can achieve that individual agencies working alone cannot? This requires a clear statement of the intended aims and objectives of MAPPA, how they have been achieved, and how they used the services, skills and knowledge of more than one agency in their successful delivery. To some extent, MAPPA annual reports do this, but usually only around individual case story anecdotes. What is required is a broader analysis of the types of plans routinely provided, which agencies are involved and how, and the critical services/interventions in such plans that can be shown to have reduced the risk.

Conclusion

This chapter has reviewed the development of MAPPA as a system of greater cooperation between agencies concerned with the risk assessment and management of sexual offenders. Firmly rooted in the community protection model, these arrangements are characterised by inter-agency information sharing, risk assessment and risk management planning. As a result of more prescriptive guidance, these arrangements have become more formalised, and there is evidence that agencies cooperate in increasingly effective ways.

However, measuring effectiveness in MAPPA remains problematic. What constitutes a positive outcome in MAPPA is contested, and measures of effectiveness operate within the context of high public anxiety about the offender group subject to these arrangements. Media and resource pressures may intensify these issues.

Ultimately, findings from research can inform the work of public protection, especially in terms of demonstrating how supervision staff and offenders define effectiveness and through capturing key elements of good practice. This chapter has shown the importance of audit as a mechanism for quality assurance, not least in ensuring a more systematic way of reviewing risk management outcomes and communicating these to the public. The success of MAPPA will be judged by different stakeholders in different ways: providing a strong evidential narrative is one way of challenging common public misconceptions and media interpretations.

References

Attrill, G. and Liell, G. (2007) 'Offenders' Views on Risk Assessment', in N. Padfield, (ed.), *Who to Release? Parole, Fairness and Criminal Justice.* Cullompton: Willan.

Cawson, P., Wattam, S. and Kelly, G. (2000) *Child Maltreatment in the United Kingdom: A Study of the Prevalence of Child Abuse and Neglect.* London: NSPCC.

Colorado Department of Public Safety (2004) *Report on Safety Issues Raised by Living Arrangements for and Location of Sex Offenders in the Community.* Denver, CO: Sex Offender Management Board.

Connelly, C. and Williamson, S. (2000) *A Review of the Research Literature on Serious Violent and Sexual Offenders.* Edinburgh: Scottish Executive Central Research Unit.

Dominey, D., Knight, V. and Kemshall, H. (2005) 'The Perception of the Participant on Accredited Programmes in the Probation Service', *VISTA,* 10(2): 72–80.

Feeley, M. and Simon, J. (1992) 'The New Penology: Notes on the Emerging Strategy for Corrections', *Criminology,* 30(4): 449–75.

Feeley, M. and Simon, J. (1994) 'Actuarial Justice: The Emerging New Criminal Law', in D. Nelken (ed.), *The futures of criminology.* London: Sage.

Garland, D. (2001) *The Culture of Crime Control: Crime and Social Order in Contemporary Society.* Oxford: Oxford University Press.

Grubin, D. (1998) *Sex Offending Against Children: Understanding the Risk.* London: Home Office.

Gutierrez-Lobos, K., Eher, R., Grunhut, C., *et al.* (2001) 'Violent Sex Offenders Lack Male Social Support', *International Journal of Offender Therapy and Comparative Criminology*, 45(1): 70–82.

Her Majesty's Inspectorates of Constabulary and Probation (HMIC and HMIP) (2005) *Managing Sex Offenders in the Community: A Joint Inspection on Sex Offenders*. London: Home Office.

Her Majesty's Inspectorate of Probation (HMIP) (2006a) *An Independent Review of a Serious Further Offence: Damien Hanson and Elliot White*. London: Home Office.

Her Majesty's Inspectorate of Probation (HMIP) (2006b) *An Independent Review of a Serious Further Offence Case: Anthony Rice*. London: HMIP.

HM Inspectorate of Probation (2007a) *Independent Inspection of Probation and Youth Work. Annual Report 2006-7*. London: HMIP.

HM Inspectorate of Probation (2007b) *Effective Supervision Inspection of the National Probation Service for England and Wales*. London: HMIP.

Home Office (1990) *Crime, Justice and Protecting the Public: The Government's Proposals for Legislation*, Cm 965. London: HMSO.

Home Office (2003) *MAPPA Guidance (Version 1)*. London: Home Office.

Home Office (2004) *MAPPA Guidance (Version 2)*. London: Home Office.

Home Office (2007) *MAPPA – The First Five Years: A National Overview of the Multi-Agency Public Protection Arrangements*. London: Home Office.

Hughes, J. (2001) *Quality Standards in Inter-Agency Work*. Newcastle: The Derwent Initiative.

Kemshall, H. (2001) 'Foreword', *Quality Standards in Inter-agency Work*. Newcastle: Derwent Initiative.

Kemshall, H. (2003) *Understanding Risk in Criminal Justice*. Buckingham: Open University Press.

Kemshall, H. (2008) *Understanding the Community Management of High Risk Offenders*. Maidenhead: Open University Press/McGraw-Hill.

Kemshall, H., Mackenzie, G., Wood, J., Bailey, R. and Yates, J. (2005) *Strengthening Multi-Agency Public Protection Arrangements*. London: Home Office.

Kemshall, H. and Maguire, M. (2001) 'Public Protection, Partnership and Risk Penality: The Multi-Agency Risk Management of Sexual and Violent Offenders', *Punishment and Society*, 3(2): 237-264.

Kemshall, H. and Wood, J. (2007a) 'High-Risk Offenders and Public Protection', in L. Gelsthorpe, and R. Morgan (eds), *Handbook of Probation*. Cullompton: Willan.

Kemshall, H. and Wood, J. (2007b) 'Beyond Public Protection: An Examination of Community Protection and Public Health Approaches to High Risk Offenders', *Criminology and Criminal Justice*, 7(3): 203-222.

Kemshall, H. and Wood, J. (2009) 'Risk and Public Protection: Responding to Involuntary and Taboo Risk', in D. Denney (ed.), *Living in Dangerous Times: Fear, Insecurity, Risk and Social Policy*. Oxford: Wiley Blackwell.

Kitzinger, J. (2004) *Framing Abuse: Media Influence and Public Understanding of Sexual Violence Against Children*. London: Pluto Press.

Laming, Lord (2003) *The Victoria Climbié Inquiry.* London: Crown Copyright. Available at: www.victoria-climbie-inquiry.org.uk/finreport/finreport.htm (accessed on 16 March 2007).

Levenson, J.S. and Cotter, L.P. (2005) 'The Impact of the Sex Offender Residence Restrictions: 1,000 Feet from Danger or One Step from the Absurd?', *International Journal of Offender Therapy and Comparative Criminology*, 49(2): 168-178.

Lieb, R. (2003) 'Joined-Up Worrying: The Multi-Agency Public Protection Panels', in A. Matravers (ed.), *Sex Offenders in the Community: Managing and Reducing Risk.* Cullompton: Willan.

Maguire, M., Kemshall, H., Noaks, L. and Wincup, E. (2001) *Risk Management of Sexual and Violent Offenders: The Work of Public Protection Panels.* Police Research Series Paper 139, London: Home Office.

Ministry of Justice (2007) *MAPPA Guidance 2007* (Version 2.0). Produced by the National MAPPA Team, National Offender Management Service Public Protection Unit. London: Ministry of Justice.

Minnesota Department of Corrections (2003) *Level Three Sex Offenders. Residential Placement Issues.* St Paul, MN: Minnesota Department of Corrections.

Nash, M. (1999a) *Police, Probation and Protecting the Public.* London: Blackwell Press.

Nash, M. (1999b) 'Enter the Polibation Officer', *International Journal of Police, Science and Management*, 1(4): 360-368.

Nash, M. (2005) 'The Probation Service, Public Protection and Dangerous Offenders', in J. Winstone and F. Pakes (eds), *Community Justice: Issues for Probation and Criminal Justice.* Cullompton: Willan.

Nash, M. (2006) *Public Protection and the Criminal Justice Process.* Oxford: Oxford University Press.

Newman, J. (2001) *Modernising Governance.* London: Sage.

Prins, H. (2002) *Will They Do It Again? Risk Assessment and Management in Criminal Justice and Psychiatry.* London: Routledge.

Prior, V., Glaser, D. and Lynch, M. A. (1997) 'Responding to Child Sexual Abuse: The Criminal Justice System', *Child Abuse Review*, 6: 128–140.

Sanders, C. R. and Lyon, E. (1995) 'Repetitive Retribution: Media Images and the Cultural Construction of Criminal Justice', in J. Ferrell and C. Sanders (eds), *Cultural Criminology.* Boston, MA: Northeastern University Press.

Sheppard, D. (1996) *Learning the Lessons: Mental Health Inquiry Reports Published in England and Wales between 1969–1996 and Their Recommendations for Improving Practice* (2nd edn). London: Zito Trust.

Thomas, T. (2005) *Sex Crime: Sex Offending and Society.* Cullompton: Willan.

Walker, J., Golden, J. and VanHouten, A. (2001) 'The Geographic Link Between Sex Offenders and Potential Victims: A Routine Activities Approach', *Justice, Research and Policy*, 3(2): 15–33.

Ward, T. and Maruna, S. (2007) *Rehabilitation.* Key Ideas in Criminology Series. London: Routledge.

Ward, T. and Stewart, C. (2003) 'Criminogenic Needs and Human Needs: A Theoretical Model', *Psychology, Crime and Law*, 31(3): 282–305.

Welch, M., Fenwick, M. and Roberts, M. (1997) 'Primary Definitions of Crime and Moral Panics: A Content Analysis of Experts' Quotes in Feature Newspaper Articles on Crime', *Journal of Research on Crime and Delinquency*, 34: 474–94.

Wood, J. and Kemshall, H. (with Maguire, M., Hudson, K. and Mackenzie, G.) (2007) *The Operation and Experience of Multi-Agency Public Protection Arrangements (MAPPA)*. London: Home Office, Research and Statistics Department, online report 12/07. Available at: www.homeoffice.gov.uk/rds/pubintro1.html (26 October 2009).

Wood, J. and Kemshall, H. (2008) 'Risk Management, Accountability and Partnerships in Criminal Justice: The Case of Multi-Agency Public Protection Arrangements (MAPPA)', in B. Stout, J. Yates and B. Williams (eds), *Applied Criminology*. London: Sage.

Worth, R. (2005) 'Questions About Legality and Effectiveness', *New York Times*, October 3, p.1.

Chapter 4

The sex offender register, community notification and some reflections on privacy

Terry Thomas

Introduction

A central component of the UK's policies for managing sex offenders in the community is that of the sex offender register. The register was introduced in 1997 and requires sex offenders to keep the police notified of their current whereabouts and circumstances, and to notify them every time those details change.

The purpose of the register is to keep police records up to date and more accurate. In this sense the police are the appointed custodians of the register, which has never actually been a register as such but an annotation of the national collection of criminal records stored on the Police National Computer (PNC) to show that certain people are statutorily required to notify on the basis of their offence being a designated sexual offence.[1]

The thinking behind notification and the keeping of police records up to date was that it would assist in the wider aim of greater public protection. The register was not intended to be a punishment. The punishment was the sentence of the court that the offender was given, be it a custodial sentence or a community sentence. The Home Office has been clear that the register is designed to help 'protect the community from sex offenders not an additional penalty for the offender' (Home Office/Scottish Executive 2001: 11).

Sanctions are applied to those sex offenders who fail to comply with the notification requirements, which last for a given period of time dependent on the seriousness of the original offence and the punishment imposed. Registration is for life if a sentence of 30 months or more has been given. Juveniles have their time periods halved.

The purpose of this chapter is to examine the register and its implementation over the last 12 years and to note how it has slowly changed in nature as it has been gradually strengthened and tightened. The chapter will also look at the idea of making the register public in a way comparable to the US policies of community notification or Megan's Law and what this would mean to our understanding of privacy in the UK.

Other legitimate questions that might be asked about the register would include questions about its effectiveness and whether or not the register actually makes a difference. Does it work? Can it be evaluated?

The origins of the UK sex offender register

Going back to the mid-1990s, we have to ask why – at this particular time – did we think – or at least the Home Office think – the UK needed a sex offender register. What were the forces around and the influences on policymakers at that time?

In the USA, sex offender registers had a long history in some states[2] and all states had been mandated to introduce one by the 1994 federal law, the Jacob Wetterling Crimes against Children and Sexually Violent Offenders Registration Act. In the UK we know that some local authorities in the 1980s were keeping their own registers of sexual offenders and that the Home Office was not very happy with this development (Home Office et al. 1991). We know that social workers were in favour of the idea on the basis that it made as much sense as – if not more sense than – keeping child protection registers on abused children (Thomas 2004). We know that some police were quite keen on the idea of a register to keep their records up to date and to track the mobile offender (Hughes et al. 1996) and that it was the Police Superintendents Association (PSA) that first publicly called for a register (Hansard HC Debates, 27 January 1997: columns 23–24).

The Home Office Consultation Document on the register was clear that its primary purpose would be 'to ensure that the information on convicted sex offenders contained within the police national computer was fully up to date' (Home Office 1996: para. 43). The consultation document also proposed three subsidiary aims for the register:

- To help (the police) identify suspects once a crime had been committed;
- *Possibly* help them to prevent such crimes; (and)
- It *might* act as a deterrent to potential re-offenders. (Home Office 1996: para. 43; emphasis added)

The language used in the consultation document to outline these subsidiary aims is tentative. A register might 'possibly' help with prevention and it 'might' act as a deterrent – a degree of uncertainty is present from the outset. These aims are not clearly expressed and the plural policy objectives are vague. Even the identifying of suspects *after* a new crime would mean the register had not contributed to public protection or helped in any way to prevent that crime.

The parliamentary debate on the Sex Offender Bill during 1996–7 was fairly muted (see especially Hansard HC Debates, 4–6 February 1997, Standing Committee D: columns 1–104). A general election was in the offing, and no one wanted to look soft on crime – especially when it came to child molesters and paedophiles (often seen as synonymous with sex offenders). The government was able to report that 87 per cent of respondents to the 1996 consultation document were in favour of introducing a register (Hansard HC Debates, 25 October 1996: WA 965), and the then Labour opposition were clear 'that it is not our intention to delay the Committee' (Hansard HC Debates, 4 February 1997, Standing Committee D: column 4). Some voices criticised the details of registration (e.g. Liberty 1996), but only one journalist declared that there was no reason for it and that it was 'simply a piece of electioneering' (Parris 1997).

The Sex Offenders Act 1997

The Sex Offenders Act 1997 that introduced the register was one of the last acts of the Conservative administration that had started back in 1979, and it was inherited by Labour for implementation in September 1997. Alun Michael for the new Labour Home Office was as hesitant and tentative in his language as the White Paper had been. He wanted the register to work 'fairly and effectively' (Home Office 1997a), but when he announced implementation, he said, 'There is no magic wand – so we will be open to new ideas and initiatives – if changes are necessary I will look at how it can be developed and improved' (Home Office 1997b). The Act outlined the basic requirements to notify, the time periods for doing so, and the sanctions for non-compliance.

The register started slowly and steadily without great fanfare. By 2000, it reportedly held some 8,608 names, and the compliance rate among those required to notify was put at 94 per cent (Plotnikoff and Woolfson 2000); the compliance rate rose to 97 per cent a year later (Home Office/Scottish Executive 2001). The 1997 Act was repealed and replaced by the Sexual Offences Act 2003.

The Sexual Offences Act 2003

The 2003 Act represented a complete overhaul and consolidation of the UK sexual offending laws, which had become fragmented and outdated. The Act essentially kept the requirements of the 1997 law intact with some changes to the reporting times and the number of offences now designated as leading to registration. The Act also introduced new powers to put on the register offenders who had offended abroad (Notification Orders) and new civil laws combining the old Sex Offender Orders and Restraining Orders (Sexual Offences Prevention Orders), new anti-grooming laws (Risk of Sexual Harm Orders), and powers to prevent sexual offenders from travelling abroad (Foreign Travel Orders).

The time periods for registration remained the same and are as outlined in Table 4.1.

Table 4.1 Registration periods for commission of designated sexual offences

---

A person sentenced to imprisonment for life or for more than 30 months – **indefinite registration**

A person admitted to a hospital subject to a restriction order – **indefinite registration**

A person sentenced to imprisonment for a period of 6–30 months – **10 years**

A person sentenced to imprisonment for a period of less than 6 months – **7 years**

A person admitted to hospital without a restriction order – **7 years**

A person cautioned or given a final warning by the police – **2 years**

See Sexual Offences Act 2003, sections 81–82 for full details.

Toughening and strengthening the Sex Offender Register

Apart from the two underpinning Acts – the Sex Offender Act 1997 and the Sexual Offences Act 2003 – the sex offender register has been regularly revised and changed by other laws and administrative interventions. These changes have often been accompanied by the political rhetoric of the register being 'strengthened', 'toughened' and 'tightened'. The words are put in quotation marks because this is the language of successive Home Secretaries when they announced changes to the register (see Table 4.2).

Table 4.2 Statements by Home Office Ministers on strengthening the register

---

I'm not sure how our obligations under the European Court of Human Rights would be affected by a provision that said, 'We shall impose **draconian** conditions on those whom we know about but not on those who have been convicted abroad of a serious sexual offence'. That is not a sensible way to proceed legislatively.

> *David Maclean (Minister of State for the Home Office, Hansard HC Debates,*
> *27 January 1997: column 30)*

I have decided that **tougher** penalties are needed to stop sex offenders from flouting the registration requirements.

> *David Maclean (in Home Office 1997 'Sex Offenders to Face Tougher Penalties*
> *– Maclean' (press release) 27 January – see also Hansard HC Debates,*
> *27 January 1997: columns 30–31)*

[The Sex Offender Bill Clause 1 on Notification Requirements] is **draconian** ... because it is undoubtedly a major obligation, and concerns a sensitive matter. In that sense it is **draconian**, but it is not an extension of the punishment per se – the Government have not said that.

> *Timothy Kirkhope (Under Secretary for the Home Department, Hansard HC*
> *Debates, Standing Committee D, 4 February 1997: column 8)*

The [Sex Offender] Bill sets **tough** periods of registration which will put **a great obligation** on people.

> *Timothy Kirkhope (Hansard HC Debates, Standing Committee D,*
> *4 February 1997: column 24)*

Table 4.2 continues overleaf

Table 4.2 continued

This review (of the register) will help us identify any **areas of weakness**, however small, and to make sure that everything that can be done, is done.

Charles Clarke (in Home Office 2000b)

A series of measures to **strengthen** the operation and effectiveness of the sex offenders register were published for public consultation today by Home Office Minister Beverley Hughes.

Home Office (2001)

We are determined to take every opportunity of building on and **strengthening** the steps already taken to protect the public from these offenders.

David Blunkett (Home Secretary in Home Office/Scottish Executive 2001: 1)

New measures to **strengthen** the sex offenders register and make offenders subject to its strict requirements were announced today by the Home Secretary David Blunkett.

*Home Office (2002a New moves to **tighten** sex offenders 'register' (press release), 2 October)*

This paper puts forward proposals **to further strengthen** the law on sex offenders.

David Blunkett (Home Secretary in the Foreword to Home Office 2002b)

Home Secretary Jacqui Smith said, 'We have some of the **strictest controls on sex offenders in the world** to protect our children'.

(quoted in Johnson 2008)

[Jacqui Smith] emphasised that the UK's rigorous system for managing child sex offenders is already among **the toughest in the world**. 'The changes I'm announcing today will **strengthen** that even further. I want to see everyone who poses a threat to our children dealt with as firmly as possible.'

Home Office (2008 Tightening Rules for Sex Offenders (press release) 20 August)

Emphasis added in bold throughout.

When the register was reviewed in 2001, the terms of reference of the review were quite specifically 'to strengthen [its] operation and effectiveness' (Home Office/Scottish Executive 2001: 3). David Blunkett saw the register as 'a valuable tool' that 'could be strengthened' (*ibid.*: 1), and, by 2008, Home Secretary Jacqui Smith could boast that 'our system for managing child sex offenders is already amongst the toughest in the world' (Home Office 2008; see also Home Office 2002a, 2007a).

Even in the original parliamentary debate in 1997, the Home Office minister described the obligations being put on sex offenders as no less than 'draconian' (Hansard HC Debates, 4 February 1997, Standing Committee D: column 8). The Bill itself had contained two new stronger elements that were never in the 1996 consultation document:

(1) Police Cautions for example, were never mentioned as being criteria for inclusion on the register but they appeared unannounced in the Bill and were put into the law. Cautions are arguably for people thought unlikely to reoffend and therefore not needing to be prosecuted. Registration is premised on precisely the opposite idea that sex offenders *will* reoffend.

(2) The sanctions for non-compliance were also strengthened during the parliamentary debate before we had any experience of the register in practice; this was done at the suggestion of child care organisations and the police. (Home Office 1997c and Hansard HC Debates, 27 January 1997: columns 30–31)

In summer 2000, one high-profile event in particular was the trigger for the start of more strengthening and tightening of the register and a process that has continued until today. The abduction and murder of 8-year-old Sarah Payne became the focus of a newspaper campaign demanding open access to the register and policies of community notification comparable with Megan's Law in the USA. The vigilantism, riots and recriminations of the campaign by *The News of the World* have been well documented (e.g. Thomas 2001; Silverman and Wilson 2002: Chapter 7). The Home Office still held fast against a policy of community notification, but within two months of the campaign's start (23 July 2000) the first changes to the register were announced (Home Office 2000a).

Over the next eight years, further incremental changes have been made to the register and duties imposed upon those required to register; these changes are listed in Table 4.3.

Table 4.3 'Strengthening' and 'tightening' the Sex Offender Register 1997–2009

---

(1) **2001** Criminal Justice and Court Services Act 2000 introduced **five new** conditions that registrants are obliged to comply with:

- Initial reporting must be within 3 days.
- The initial reporting must be in person.
- Reporting must be to prescribed police stations.
- Police are given new powers to photograph/fingerprint on initial registration.
- There is a new duty to notify police if going abroad for more than 8 days.

Non-compliance is made an arrestable offence and sanctions for non-compliance are increased (6 months' custody goes up to 5 years maximum); the new Multi-Agency Public Protection Panels come into being and Restraining Orders are introduced as an option.

(2) **2001** Home Detention Curfew (i.e. early prison release with an electronic tag) is denied to sex offenders.

(3) **2001** – laypeople are to join Multi-Agency Public Protection Panels – announced within days of the conviction of Roy Whiting for the murder of Sarah Payne – they will have an advisory role only and not be privy to information on individual cases.

(4) **2003** – Sexual Offences Act – a further **five new conditions** placed on the registrants:

- All changes must be notified within 3 days.
- Annual verification exercises introduced – personal visits required – no emails or letters.
- Must notify any change of address of longer than 7 days.
- New offences added (created by the Act);
- Notification Orders may be placed on people who have offended abroad when they either visit or come home; these orders put them on the register.

As well as **higher penalties for non-compliance for young offenders**

(5) **2003** Criminal Justice Act, section 327, requires all those on the register to be 'risk assessed' annually by the Multi-Agency Public Protection Panels.

Table 4.3 continues opposite

Table 4.3 continued

---

(6) **2006** in June John Reid demands all those on the register living in probation hostels be moved out of that hostel if near a school.

(7) **2006** Violent Crime Reduction Act (passed in November) allows the police to apply to a magistrate for **powers to force entry to the home of a registered sex offender** to carry out a risk assessment – introduced May 2007.

(8) **2006** in December it was announced* that **another six offences were being added** to the designated offences leading to registration:

- outraging public decency;
- theft;
- burglary with intent to steal;
- child abduction;
- harassment; and
- sending prohibited articles by post.

The Sexual Offences Act 2003 (Amendments of Schedules 3 and 5), Order 2007, no. 296, eventually added these offences to Schedule 5 of the Sexual Offences Act and added three other offences to Schedule 3 that would lead to registration. These offences were:

- causing or inciting child prostitution or pornography;
- controlling a child prostitute or a child involved in pornography; and
- arranging or facilitating child prostitution or pornography.

(9) **2007** a Home Office review** recommends the **collection of five more pieces of information** from those on the register:

- DNA sample be taken;
- e-mail addresses taken;
- passport numbers;
- bank account numbers;
- notify the police of any children under 18 living in the same household; and
- notify the police of any foreign travel – of whatever length;

and two **more obligations** be placed on them:

- to report regularly to a police station if homeless;
- to inform the police of any risk factors that might lead to reoffending.

Table 4.3 continues overleaf

Table 4.3 continued

Plus – possible new drug treatments, satellite tracking using GPS, and polygraphs ('lie detectors') (see below) and more disclosures on request to those with a need to know (see below).

(10) **2007** Offender Management Act, sections 28–30, allows the use of polygraphs on sex offenders.

(11) **2008** new disclosure powers in Criminal Justice and Immigration Act 2008, section 140, amending the Sexual Offences Act 2003 with a new section 327A, contains a new duty to disclose information to the public on request if they have a legitimate concern; a presumption to disclose if children are known to be in a household, whether or not there is a request.

---

*Vernon Coaker for the Home Office explained that 'the offences may not seem inherently sexual, but could have had a sexual motive. These changes are necessary to strengthen the monitoring and management of sex offenders' Home Office (2006).

**Home Office (2007b: 18).

Legal challenges

The sex offender register has shifted on the back of these pressures and has arguably become slowly more onerous for those required to register. The Home Office has clearly been aware of this gradual ratcheting up of the register and at one time speculated about the continuing compliance of the Sex Offender Act 1997 with human rights regulation:

> Challenges to the SOA on human rights grounds have been successfully resisted because the registration requirement has been seen as an administrative consequence of a sentence passed by the court, rather than being a separate sentence in its own right. Were the registration requirement to become more onerous, there could come a point at which the Act could no longer be seen as an administrative requirement. (Home Office/ Scottish Executive 2001: 13)

This statement was made in 2001 and there have been further changes since that date. The Home Office did not say as much but the concern must have been that the requirements would eventually be in breach of Article 8 of the European Convention on Human Rights – the right to privacy (for more on Article 8, see Chapter 14 of this volume).

Subsequent test cases at the European Court of Human Rights have indeed shown that the register does engage Article 8 but in general terms it does not breach it (*Adamson* v. *UK* (1999) 28 EHRR CD 209). A case in Northern Ireland came to a similar finding (*Re Kevin Gallagher* [2003] NIQB 26). In December 2008, the High Court in London ruled that those on the sex offender register for life should at least have the right to appeal against that indefinite requirement to a judicial body having some oversight of the register and the circumstances of those on it; the Home Office was reportedly considering an appeal (*F and Angus Aubrey Thompson* v. *Secretary of State for Justice* [2008] EWHC 3170; see also Green 2008; Whitehead 2008).

Community notification and privacy

One of the abiding questions for policymakers is whether or not the public should have access to the sex offender register; the argument has been made that if the authorities, in the form of the police and probation service, know where these offenders live, then, surely, the public should also know. The public should know whether such an offender lives in their street in order to better protect themselves and their children.

In the USA, such community notification policies exist in all 50 states, as required by the federal Megan's Law of 1996; some states had already put their own laws in place before that date.[3] Megan's Law was named after 7-year-old Megan Kanka, who was attacked and killed by a man living in the same street as her family in New Jersey. The authorities knew the man lived there, but no one on the street did.

Arguments have been made in the UK that we should have community notification policies. The question was raised during the parliamentary debate and ruled out (Hansard HC Debates, 4 February 1997, Standing Committee D: column 43ff), and, as we have noted above, it was raised during the 2000 *News of the World* campaign following the abduction and murder of Sarah Payne; once again it was ruled out as a policy option.[4]

When police in North Wales released details of the sexual offending criminal records of two people to their immediate neighbours in the interests of child protection, the two people concerned applied for a judicial review of the police decision to make that disclosure. The courts ruled in favour of the police actions, saying that it was part of their duty to prevent crime. The courts added that it should not be done on a blanket basis but only for those offenders presenting a significant risk (*R v. Chief Constable of North Wales Police ex p. AB* (1997) *Times*, 14 July 1997). It was this need for an assessment of risk that led eventually to the Multi-Agency Public Protection Arrangements (MAPPA), prompted by the Criminal Justice and Courts Services Act 2000, sections 67–68 and to the policy of 'discretionary disclosure' (Cann 2007) (for more on MAPPA, see Chapter 3 of this volume).

Home Secretary John Reid was said to be close to considering a community notification policy in 2006, and he dispatched his junior minister, Gerry Sutcliffe, to the USA to look at it in practice. Again the government backed down, and instead we had the watered-down idea of the 'presumption to disclose' being added to the existing policies of 'discretionary disclosure' and the idea that some people who cared for children could ask the police for advice on certain people who had contact with their children (Criminal Justice and Immigration Act 2008, section 140).

Discussion

It could be argued that the sex offender register is an example of criminal justice policy made at a political level in response to perceived populist demands and with no real evidence to support it. It is policy made in a research vacuum, with ill-defined and hesitant aims, which is then left 'hanging in the air' to be adjusted and amended by politicians listening to the practitioners and specialist lobby groups as well as the public reactions to the latest high-profile crime against a child.

On one level, the requirement to notify is clearly a success. A reported 97 per cent of offenders comply with their requirements, and we should surmise that police records are, therefore, much more up to date. What is less certain is the contribution the register makes to public protection and safer communities.

In 1997, some background research for the Home Office entailed looking at the experience of registers in the USA. *Keeping Track? Observations on Sex Offender Registers in the US* outlined lessons to be learnt from the USA at the point of implementing the register.

One of the findings was that no research had ever been carried out on the effectiveness of registers even though the first registers in the USA had been created as long ago as the 1940s:

In reviewing the available published literature on evaluation of registration as an investigative and preventive tool, one is struck by the dearth of good research studies. With few exceptions, no substantial effort has been devoted to examining base-rates for offending and the scientific literature on long term re-conviction data, nor even to looking at the career path of offenders and the efficacy of registering all (as opposed to some) sexual offenders. (Hebenton and Thomas 1997: 34)

Subsequent UK evaluations also noted that:

(Police) Forces had no agreed way of quantifying the contribution of sex offender monitoring to improving community safety. In some forces, senior officers had asked for measures to be developed to support cost-benefit analysis ('Best Value'). No single measure of effectiveness emerged from this study as suitable for performance measurement. (Plotnikoff and Woolfson 2000: 50)

The problem for research is a difficult one – how do you demonstrate a negative and show that nothing happened (i.e. further offences) because of your interventions? How do you demonstrate links between registers and recidivism when there are so many other factors to consider? It leaves the register more as an act of faith than an evidence-based policy. Ministers have talked of success in terms of high compliance rates but whether that is the same as a greater public protection and desistance from offending is more of an unknown.[5]

Policy based on high-profile cases can be equally flawed. Using the Sarah Payne case again, we could say that the furore over community notification and a Sarah's Law overlooked and marginalised the fact that the register in itself had been no help at all. The perpetrator of the offence – Roy Whiting – was on the register when he reoffended to abduct and murder, and the fact of being required to notify had had no effect at all on his propensity to reoffend. The furore – if it noted this at all – did so only to argue for community notification as the answer.

We might also note the marginalisation of what research evidence does exist on the more microscale of policy implementation. The reduction of the initial reporting time to 3 days in 2001 ignored the evidence that the police were sometimes unprepared for a person coming in to register within the 14 days they originally had.

'Many designated officers mentioned that they first heard about a registration requirement from the offender himself ... [and] ... failed to receive timely notice from the official sources in the majority of register cases' (Plotnikoff and Woolfson 2000: 21). When the reporting time for all reporting (i.e. not just initial) was reduced to 3 days in 2003 this ignored the consultation document that had suggested it be 8 days because 3 days 'is too short to enable effective action to be taken and would make unreasonable demands on police resources' (Home Office/Scottish Executive 2001: 23).

When the Home Office invited views on the registration of young people (under 18), it again ignored the responses made. A series of more welfare-orientated proposals had been made for young sex offenders (Home Office/Scottish Executive 2001: Chapter 6) which had received a generally warm welcome from the childcare lobby.[6] The Home Office then simply rejected its own proposals and even increased the sanction on young people for non-compliance despite their having a compliance rate of 97 per cent (Thomas 2003, 2009).

The government has been far more comfortable in responding to media influences than to research and evaluation evidence where it existed. The reduction of reporting times from 14 to 3 days (see above) had been demanded by newspapers, and the Home Office has been very conscious of a need to appear tough, and 'Acting out the punitive urges ... [to] assuage popular outrage, reassure the public, and restore the credibility of the system, all of which are political rather than penological concerns' (Garland 2001: 173). The Association of Chief Police Officers (ACPO) spokesman on sexual offending has himself accused the government of following media agendas at the expense of more considered sources (BBC 2006). We might also surmise that the quiet rejection of a welfare approach to young people on the sex offender register (see above) reflected a populist need to be seen to be tough on young offenders rather than show any understanding.

The more specialist lobbyists have also been successful in influencing policy. The NSPCC came out against community notification but in favour of tightening up the requirements to notify foreign travel arrangements (Gillan 1999); such notification was duly tightened up by the Foreign Travel Order, and further new restrictions have been proposed (Home Office 2008).

The government also appears to be more comfortable in listening to the practitioners and making the adjustments that they call for. The activities of some practitioners in this field have strayed to the limits of the law and guidance. The response has been not to criticise or sanction these practitioners but to legitimise their activities with changes in the guidance and law. The police photographing, fingerprinting, and taking DNA swabs of those on the register, for example, was reported in 2000 (Plotnikoff and Woolfson 2000) and later legitimated by the Criminal Justice and Courts Services Act 2000, section 140.

When the police were found to have had difficulty in accessing the homes of sex offenders, in order to complete risk assessments (HMIP/HMIC 2005), the response was again to simply bring in new laws. The Violent Crime Reduction Act 2006, section 58 allows the police to apply for court warrants to force entry to the homes of sex offenders if necessary in order to carry out risk assessments.

In a similar fashion, the police's 'discretionary disclosure' of sex offender registration to certain parties was supposed to be with the authorisation of senior officers. Research found that this was not always happening and that junior officers were taking it upon themselves to make this decision – often spontaneously (Cann 2007). The new law now requires these disclosures to be 'as soon as practicable' (Criminal Justice and Immigration Act 2008, section 140), and this seems to cover spontaneous disclosure and retrospective authorisations.

Policy created in response to public demand, media recommendations and practitioners' wishes, and without reference to research or evidence, is not confined to policies on sex offenders. We have seen the same policy formulation processes in place elsewhere. As Tonry has put it, 'crime and punishment is one of those subjects about which little is said or done [by the Labour government] without what looks like enormous concern for short-term public and media reactions' (Tonry 2004: 38). It is policy based on a 'belief that [the government's] own continuation in office justifies the unnecessary human suffering and waste of public resources that its policies produce' (Tonry 2004: ix). Or we may note Garland's contention that governments today are 'highly attuned to public concerns, particularly to the sentiments that offenders are being insufficiently punished or dangerous individuals inadequately controlled' (Garland 2001: 172). A very expensive-to-maintain bureaucracy has been built up with little or no evidence to demonstrate its worth. Politicians have pushed it in directions that suit their own purposes, and practitioners and campaigners have been able to push it in the directions that they want. The pushing in question has often been based on a high-profile crime against a child and who is going to argue against that?

Notes

1 For ease of expression, this chapter refers to 'the register' throughout.
2 The Californian register started in 1947.
3 The first state community notification law was in 1990 in Washington state.
4 A study for the NSPCC confirmed a further lack of research in the area of community notification and that 'Megan's Law is not an evidence-based policy, but rather a reaction to a series of high-profile crimes against children. Since its implementation, there has been little detailed monitoring and evaluation to ascertain its effectiveness' (Fitch 2006: para 8.1).
5 The same absence of research is still being noted in the USA. Logan has reported that, 'remarkably, given the ostensible public safety premise of [sex offender] registration and notification, it largely remains an untested article of faith that the laws tangibly contribute to community safety' (Logan 2003: 337–351). Logan could find only two US studies trying to assess recidivism by tracking those on the register and control groups over four years, and 'neither study found a statistically significant difference in recidivism' (*ibid.*).
6 A summary of the responses was made available by the Home Office at www.sexualoffencesbill.homeoffice.gov.uk (accessed 5 December 2001).

References

BBC (2006) 'Media "Dictates Paedophile Plans"'. Available at: http://news.bbc.co.uk/1/hi/uk_politics/5096542.stm (accessed 16 March 2009).

Cann, J. (2007) *Assessing the Extent of Discretionary Disclosure Under the Multi-Agency Public Protection Arrangements (MAPPA)*, Home Office online report 13/07. Available at: www.homeoffice.gov.uk/rds/pdfs07/rdsolr1307.pdf (accessed 6 February 2009).

Fitch, K. (2006) *Megan's Law: Does it Protect Children?* (2nd edn). London: NSPCC.

Garland, D. (2001) *The Culture of Control: Crime and Social Order in Contemporary Society*. Oxford: Oxford University Press.

Gillan, A. (1999) 'Paedophile Law Change Sought', *The Guardian*, 23 July.

Green, C. (2008) 'Convicted Sex Attackers Can Challenge Inclusion on Offenders' Register', *The Independent*, 20 December, p. 4.

Hebenton, B. and Thomas, T. (1997) *Keeping Track? Observations on Sex Offender Registers in the US*. Crime Detection and Prevention Series Paper 83, Police Research Group. London: Home Office.

HMIP/HMIC (HM Inspectorate of Probation/HM Inspectorate of Constabulary) (2005) *Managing Sex Offenders in the Community: A Joint Inspection*. London: HMIP.

Home Office (1996) *Sentencing and Supervision of Sex Offenders: A Consultation Paper*. Cm 3304. London: Home Office.

Home Office (1997a) 'Guidelines for Operating Sex Offenders Register Published' (press release), 11 August. London: Home Office.

Home Office (1997b) 'Sex Offenders Register Comes into Effect' (press release) 31 August. London: Home Office.

Home Office (1997c) 'Sex Offenders to Face Tougher Penalties – Maclean' (press release), 27 January. London: Home Office.

Home Office (2000a) 'Government Proposals Better to Protect Children from Sex and Violent Offences' (press release), 15 September. London: Home Office.

Home Office (2000b) 'Sex Offenders Register to be Reviewed' (press release), 26 June. London: Home Office.

Home Office (2001) 'Strengthening the Sex Offenders Act: Public Consultation Published Today' (press release), 30 July. London: Home Office.

Home Office (2002a) 'New Moves to Tighten Sex Offender Register' (press release), 2 October. London: Home Office.

Home Office (2002b) *Protecting the Public: Strengthening Protection Against Sex Offenders and Reforming the Law on Sexual Offences*. Cm 5668. London: TSO.

Home Office (2006) 'Sex Offender Register to be Expanded to Include More Offences' (press release), 18 December. London: Home Office.

Home Office (2007a) 'The Home Office has Unveiled a Range of Tough New Measures to Enhance the Protection of Children from Sex Offenders' (press release), 13 June. London: Home Office.

Home Office (2007b) *Review of the Protection of Children from Sex Offenders*. London: Home Office.

Home Office (2008) 'Tightening Rules for Sex Offenders' (press release), 20 August. London: Home Office.

Home Office, Department of Health, Department of Education and Science and Welsh Office (1991) *Working Together: A Guide to Arrangements for Inter-agency Cooperation for the Protection of Children from Abuse*. London: HMSO.

Home Office/Scottish Executive (2001) 'Consultation Paper on the Review of Part 1 of the Sex Offenders Act 1997'. London: Home Office.

Hughes, B., Parker, H. and Gallagher, B. (1996) *Policing Child Sexual Abuse: The View from Police Practitioners* (Police Research Group). London: Home Office.

Johnson, B. (2008) 'Paedophiles Face Curbs on Internet Use', *The Guardian*, 4 April [online]. www.guardian.co.uk/uk/2008/apr/04/ukcrime.childprotection (accessed 10 April 2009).

Liberty (1996) 'Response to the Home Office Consultation Paper on Sentencing and Supervision of Sex Offenders'. London: Liberty.

Logan, W. (2003) 'Sex Offender Registration and Community Notification: emerging legal and research issues', in R. Prentky, E. Janus and M. Seto (eds) *Sexually Coercive Behavior: Understanding and Management. Annals of the New York Academy of Sciences*, 989: 337–351.

Parris, M. (1997) 'All-Party Witch Hunt', *The Times*, 24 January.

Plotnikoff, J. and Woolfson, R. (2000) *Where Are They Now?: An Evaluation of Sex Offender Registration in England and Wales*. Police Research Series Paper 126. London: Home Office.

Silverman, J. and Wilson, D. (2002) *Innocence Betrayed: Paedophilia, the Media and Society*. Cambridge: Polity.

Thomas, T. (2001) 'Sex Offenders, the Home Office and the Sunday Papers', *Journal of Social Welfare and Family Law*, 23(1): 103–108.

Thomas, T. (2003) 'The Sex Offender Register: The Registration of Young People', *Childright*, 194: 10–11.

Thomas, T. (2004) 'Sex Offender Registers and Monitoring', in H. Kemshall and G. McIvor (eds), *Managing Sex Offender Risk*. London: Jessica Kingsley.

Thomas, T. (2009) 'Children and Young People on the UK Sex Offender Register', *The International Journal of Children's Rights*, 17(3): 491–500.

Tonry, M. (2004) *Punishment and Politics: Evidence and Emulation in the Making of English Crime Control Policy*. Cullompton: Willan.

Whitehead, T. (2008) 'Life on Sex Offender List Breaches Rapist's Rights, Say Judges', *Daily Telegraph*, 20 December, p. 4.

Part III

Treatment and risk reduction

Chapter 5

An introduction to sex offender treatment programmes and their risk reduction efficacy

Sarah Brown

Introduction

The use of sex offender treatment programmes has developed and expanded enormously in recent decades such that they are now used routinely in many countries and in some they have become an integral part of the countries' criminal justice systems' responses to sex offenders. For example, in England and Wales all offenders who are sentenced for a sexual offence and who have time to complete a treatment programme are assessed for their suitability for this form of intervention and to determine which programme(s) they should complete.

In order to meet the principles outlined by the Carlton University Group (see Andrews 1989; Andrews *et al.* 1990a; Andrews and Bonta 2003) of risk (offenders should receive intervention according to their level of risk), need (offenders should receive interventions that address their criminogenic needs), and responsivity (offenders should receive treatment that meets their specific characteristics, such as intellectual functioning) that have been repeatedly shown to be associated with effective interventions (Andrews *et al.* 1990b; Lipsey 1989, 1995) and to allow for large-scale, cost-effective delivery to as large a group of appropriate offenders as possible, England and Wales have a suite of programmes. These have the same underlying principles that fit together so that a package of programmes that is most appropriate for each offender can be delivered. Delivered in both community and custodial settings, a system of accreditation ensures that all programmes (a) are suitable for use, for example, by having a sound underlying theoretical base and model of change that is evidence-based; and (b) are delivered as intended; that is, have programme integrity – for example, by reviewing programme delivery and treatment providers' practice. The suite of programmes is designed so that some offenders, such as those with short sentences and/or lowest risk and/or need, complete a single programme, while others, such as those with long sentences or highest risk and/or need, complete two or more programmes. Some programmes are completed on a rolling format, where offenders join at the start of any module: a format which provides for offenders who have short sentences and limited periods of time in which to complete the intervention. The majority of programmes, however, have specific start and end points, with all offenders starting the programme at the same time. In addition, specific programmes are available for offenders with learning difficulties and for offenders whose sexual offences involved the Internet.

This is just one approach to the implementation of sex offender treatment: there is great variability from country to country and in some countries, such as the USA, from state to state and county to county, although many states now have a system of accreditation for treatment providers. While much of the large-scale provision (for example, in the UK and Canada) has been centred on criminal justice, in some parts of the world sex offender treatment is located within more therapeutic, public health and/or mental health settings. Despite this variation, the most common, though by no means only, treatment approach used for adult male offenders is the cognitive-behavioural approach, which has been shown by the so-called 'What Works' evidence base to be an effective approach for offender intervention (for a review, see Vennard *et al.* 1997). Interventions with juvenile/adolescent sex offenders, which are still being developed and are gradually being used more extensively, use a greater variety of approaches (e.g. Reitzel and Carbonell 2006 and Chapter 9 of this volume). To date multi-systemic treatment has shown good outcome data, though the evidence base for these programmes is still small (Reitzel and Carbonell 2006).

Before looking at the development of sex offender treatment and outlining the principles/content of cognitive-behavioural programmes, it is important to note that although the word 'treatment' is commonly used to refer to this form of offender intervention, it is not the most appropriate term if it conjures up ideas about medical treatment. Cognitive-behavioural programmes require offenders to engage in them actively, learn skills, and assimilate ideas/messages, etc., that they are then expected to employ in order to live non-offending lives in the community. Although medical treatment usually requires some kind of engagement/participation (for example, to take the required amounts of medication at the correct times), it is more passive in nature; for example, it can be administered with great effect to a person who is unconscious. The same could never be said for cognitive-behavioural treatment, which requires the client to be alert, to be motivated to some extent to learn and absorb the messages, skills and ideas of the programme, and to actively implement these thoughts, skills and behaviours in their lives, and in many instances into all aspects of their lives for very long periods of time.

Some forms of treatment for sex offenders are medical, though they are used less commonly. For example, some jurisdictions still use surgical castration; however, ethical and human rights issues tend to mean that this method is used only on a small number of offenders/ men, largely those who volunteer to have the procedure (for more information on surgical castration, see Chapter 6 of this volume). Hormonal treatments are used in some programmes or with some offenders (for a review of evaluation studies and treatment issues, see Chapter 6 of this volume). As discussed by Lösel and Schmucker (2005), hormone treatments are not normally used in isolation, and problems such as negative side effects and potential increased risk following termination mean that the use of this treatment is not likely to be widespread, though it may be particularly useful for some groups of offenders (for example, high-risk offenders, or when sexual arousal plays a significant causal role in offending). Because of these issues, the rest of this chapter will focus on describing cognitive-behavioural programmes, which is the most commonly used approach, in countries such as Canada, the USA, the UK, New Zealand and Australia.

Cognitive-behavioural programmes

The origins of cognitive-behavioural programmes (for a more detailed review of the development of these programmes, see Laws and Marshall 2003; Brown 2005) can be found in the 1970s delivery of traditional behavioural programmes, such as aversion therapy, which were designed to reduce deviant sexual arousal and in some instances, as with orgasmic or masturbatory reconditioning, to increase appropriate sexual arousal (for a more detailed discussion of the range of techniques applied to sex offenders, see Marshall *et al.* 1999; Wood *et al.* 2000; Law and Marshall 2003). The effectiveness of these programmes was limited (Quinsey and Earls 1990; Laws and Marshall 2003), perhaps due to the simplistic idea that sexual arousal is the sole and single motivator for inappropriate sexual behaviours.

At a time when psychology more generally saw a shift from favouring behavioural to cognitive theories and explanations, and the complexity of the causes and motivations for sexual behaviour was increasingly recognised, sex offender treatment programmes also developed and expanded their content. For example, some therapists (Marshall and Williams 1975) reasoned that appropriate sexual relationships would not be formed if offenders were not able to develop relationships with adults, and this was likely to be a problem given that many of their clients had poor social skills; accordingly, they added social skills and sex education elements to their behavioural programme. Throughout the 1970s, the range of factors incorporated into behavioural treatments was expanded upon. By the late 1970s, Abel *et al.* (1978) had added components on assertiveness, sexual dysfunction and gender role behaviour, and by 1980 had also incorporated empathy enhancement (Murphy *et al.* 1980), forming what could arguably be described as one of the first cognitive-behavioural treatment programmes for sex offenders.

Over time, the cognitive element of these programmes expanded such that, although still called cognitive-behavioural programmes, current programmes have a small behavioural element, which is largely centred on behavioural theories and explanations of behaviour; for example, that behaviours have causes and consequences and those that are perceived positively are likely to be repeated. Few current cognitive-behavioural programmes use the more traditional behavioural therapies, such as aversion therapy, although these approaches have seen a small revival in recent years, being employed on an individual basis with some offenders whose motivations for sexual offending and/or risk factors are amenable to these approaches. However, these techniques are more likely to be used as an add-on to cognitive-behavioural, group-based programmes on an individual basis, rather than being used and delivered more routinely. Most programmes do employ techniques that are derived from behavioural principles, such as modelling and role-play.

The shift from behavioural to cognitive-behavioural approaches in sex offender treatment developed in two ways. The first occurred rapidly in North America, with treatment practitioners adding more cognitive components to what had originally been behavioural programmes. Eventually, most programmes explored and attempted to change attitudes towards sexual behaviour and sexually deviant behaviour; attitudes towards women and children and sexual entitlement; cognitive distortions (or thoughts and attitudes encouraging sexually deviant behaviour); offence cycles or offence chains, including thoughts and behaviours leading to sexually deviant behaviour; empathy; self-esteem; and social skills. The other way in which cognitive-behavioural programmes were developed can be illustrated by the introduction of sex offender programmes to the prison service of England and Wales, where, once a decision had been taken at a political level to introduce sex offender treatment programmes, a focus on evidence-based practice led to a review of the 'What Works' literature, which determined that cognitive-behavioural programmes were the most effective programmes (generally and with sex offenders). Thus, the new initiative was introduced, with programmes being modelled on the most promising programmes from North America, incorporating the more general findings and principles from the 'What Works' literature.

In the 1980s, as cognitive-behavioural programmes continued to develop, relapse prevention became an important component of treatment programmes; indeed, some programmes were designed to be centred on these principles (e.g. Marques *et al.* 2005). Although some treatment providers had attempted to develop relapse-prevention-type strategies, it was not until Pithers *et al.* (1983) extended the relapse-prevention model, originally developed in the area of addiction by Marlatt (1982; see also Marlatt and Gordon 1985) that relapse prevention became a key element, if not a central part, of most cognitive-behavioural programmes. The main aim of relapse prevention is to encourage and support the maintenance of treatment-induced abstinence; for example by encouraging offenders to think about how they will respond, and develop skills to respond to lapses/relapses in behaviour (such as having a cigarette or alcoholic drink in the original additions model, or thinking about a sexual offence when adapted for sex offender treatment programmes).

Although popular for a number of years, and argued by Marshall (1996) to be '[w]ithout doubt, the most important development in the 1980s' (180), the enthusiasm for relapse prevention has waned in recent years (for a more detailed discussion see Brown 2005; Mann and Marshall 2009), not helped by the poor outcome of a randomised, control evaluation of a programme centred on relapse prevention (Marques *et al.* 2005; see also Mann and Marshall 2009) and the fact that in their meta-analysis, Gallagher *et al.* (1999) showed no difference in the outcome of cognitive-behavioural with and without relapse-prevention elements. Relapse prevention also encourages a focus on what cannot be done and what should be avoided – that is, avoidance goals; yet, as Mann (1998, cited in Marshall and Serran 2000) observed, research indicates that avoidance goals are more difficult to attain than approach goals. This approach also conflicts with positive models of offender engagement that have become popular in recent years.

Following the incorporation of relapse-prevention techniques, the core elements and principles of cognitive-behavioural treatment for sex offenders had been established and the most significant development in the 1990s and early 2000s was the rapid increase in the use of these programmes. This period also saw the approach being used (with adaptations as necessary) with a broader group of offenders, such as juvenile/adolescent offenders, female offenders and offenders with learning difficulties.

The principles of behavioural theories/approaches show that positive reinforcement for desired behaviour is a much more effective method of adapting behaviour than either negative reinforcement or punishment. It is interesting that, given this, criminal justice systems and frequently offender interventions have been traditionally focused on punishment and negative reinforcement. Recently, coinciding with an increased interest in psychology more generally with positive psychology, work in this area has focused on offender engagement and working with offenders' potential to live good, healthy, non-offending lives in the community. The Good Lives Model (Ward 2002; Ward and Stewart 2003) has been particularly influential. This explains that we all, offenders included, want to live good lives; that is, we want excellence in work, play and agency, knowledge, community, happiness and spirituality, to name a few of the 'goods' identified in this model. It is believed that offenders will be more likely to desist from offending in the future if they are able to achieve these 'goods' and are encouraged to achieve them without offending. Accordingly, it is argued that interventions that focus on offenders' potentials and what they can do will be more encouraging/motivating and more likely to have a positive impact on offenders than programmes that focus solely on offenders' potential to cause harm and on what cannot and should not be done. These principles are currently being integrated into many cognitive-behavioural programmes and into work more generally with offenders, though it is too early to see what impact this will have on treatment efficacy.

Most current cognitive-behavioural programmes, then, have a large cognitive component, in that offenders are encouraged to consider how their thoughts (including their attitudes to women, children, sex, etc.; thoughts about behaviours and their consequences; ideas about the impact of offending behaviours on others or empathy; problem-solving abilities/tendencies; ideas about themselves, and their self-efficacy and self-esteem; attachment styles and relationship patterns, etc.) encourage, justify and/or support their offending behaviour and how these thoughts can be changed so that offending is avoided in the future. Thus, the cognitive-behavioural approach assumes that offenders have control over their behaviour and are able to change their behaviour and avoid offending in the future. Many programmes still also have a relapse-prevention component, or at least encourage offenders to think about how they will live offending free lives in the community and to practise relevant and appropriate skills to aid with this endeavour. This approach means that programmes often have similar elements, although programmes differ in a variety of ways (for example, content, length, number and timing of treatment sessions, etc.).

There is not scope in this chapter to describe programmes in detail (for a more detailed review, see Brown 2005, or programme details/ descriptions that can be found elsewhere in the literature) and so some of the common elements of cognitive-behavioural programmes will be briefly outlined. All cognitive-behavioural programmes review offenders' attitudes and thoughts that may support and/or encourage offending. Most programmes ask offenders to discuss their offending, its causes and its consequences, and thoughts/attitudes that are offence supportive are challenged by training providers and treatment group members. Despite a shift in views about the link between empathy and sexual offending (that is, that most offenders do not have general empathy deficits but do not show appropriate levels of empathy specifically to their own victims (e.g. Fernandez *et al.* 1999), which may be related to thoughts and justifications about the behaviour and what offenders' perceptions are about what the victims apparently wanted) and some concern about the inclusion of empathy work (for more detailed discussions, see Brown 2005; Mann and Marshall 2009), many programmes contain an element that discusses the impact of sexual offending on victims and others who are affected by these offences. Another element involves offenders reviewing their offence chains/offending cycles to identify how behaviour can be changed in the future to eliminate offending, and this may be combined with planning future offence-free lives and practising skills and behaviours that are relevant to each offender. Many programmes also include social and life skills, problem-solving, assertiveness, anger management, attachment and appropriate relationship formation/maintenance, and sex education elements, as many offenders have deficits in these areas. Some work, such as improving self-efficacy and self-esteem, will be less easy to identify in programme content, despite the fact that it will be a core element of work throughout the programme. Some programmes include more idiosyncratic elements such as drama and work with offenders' partners.

Efficacy of cognitive-behavioural programmes

As discussed, cognitive-behavioural treatment programmes have been delivered in some countries since the 1980s, with early forms of the programmes developed in the 1970s. There are many published evaluations of sex offender treatment programmes, and so it would not seem overly ambitious to expect that we would be able to confidently deduce whether these programmes have a positive effect on the offenders who complete them; that is, that they would be less likely to reoffend than offenders who did not receive such intervention. Unfortunately, there is still a great deal of debate regarding the efficacy of sex offender treatment programmes, which is centred on methodological issues. Although it seems relatively easy to assess whether treatment programmes are effective or not (i.e. compare the outcomes of a group of treated offenders with a group of offenders who receive no treatment), there are a number of methodological, practical and ethical difficulties that make it difficult to establish conclusive findings regarding programme efficacy.

Randomised, control trials are widely regarded as the most methodologically robust method of testing programme effectiveness. In theory, randomisation to treatment or non-treatment groups ensures that there are no differences between these groups, such that differences after treatment can be confidently ascribed to the intervention, provided that the treatment and no-treatment groups are treated identically in all respects apart from the application of the relevant intervention. This design is even stronger if recipients, treatment providers and researchers are all blind to the condition of each research participant/client; however, this requires a placebo intervention (one that looks the same as the real intervention such that those receiving the placebo and treatment are not sure what they are receiving), which is either not possible or extremely difficult to formulate with interventions of this sort.

The use of randomised, control trials with sex offender treatment programmes is controversial and keenly debated when evaluations of such programmes are considered (see, for example, the paper by Marshall and Marshall (2007), who conclude that randomised studies are not necessary to determine sex offender treatment efficacy, compared with the paper by Seto *et al.* (2008), who take issue with this point of view and the arguments used by Marshall and Marshall (2007)). Some have argued (Marshall 1993; Marshall and Pithers 1994; Marshall and Marshall 2007) that it is not ethical to withhold sex offender treatment from offenders, making random allocation impossible, because of the consequences for the potential victim(s) of the untreated offenders (note that this view tends to assume that sex offender treatment has positive consequences; that is, something potentially positive is being withheld). Others, such as Quinsey *et al.* (1993), have argued that we have an ethical duty to ascertain whether these programmes are effective and that the only way to do this such that we have firm conclusions is to use random allocation. Under this perspective, it is highlighted that potential victims can be harmed if offenders deemed to be safe following treatment are in fact not safe because the treatment had no impact (note here that the tendency is to assume that programmes are not effective, or that this has yet to be determined).

Aside from these ethical standpoints, there are actually a number of methodological and practical problems that mean that randomised studies are extremely difficult to conduct. For example, unless the sample size is large, random allocation cannot ensure groups are equivalent, and a large pool of offenders assessed as being suitable and in need of treatment needs to be identified prior to random allocation, so that group equivalence can be ensured. In addition, actual practice means that this type of study is extremely difficult or unlikely; for example, in the UK, either offenders are court ordered to complete sex offender treatment, or addressing their offending behaviour through the completion of these programmes is a sort of prerequisite for movement to less strict prison regimes or release into the community. Consequently, it is not possible to randomly allocate offenders under these conditions to no-treatment control groups, or their willingness to be part of the study if it was tried would be unlikely. In effect, this means that very few randomised, control trials have been conducted on sex offender treatment programmes. For example, Lösel and Schmucker (2005) found six (although a seventh study used this design, it was compromised), and Robertson *et al.* (submitted) identified only four studies.

To assess the relative merits of different methodological designs, Sherman *et al.* (1997) developed a coding system, the Maryland Scale of Scientific Rigor, that has become widely used. According to this scale, five, the highest rating, is assigned to studies that employ an uncompromised randomised design. The next best, four, is awarded for designs that apply procedures, such as participant matching or statistical control, to ensure equivalence between the treatment and no-treatment groups. While in theory this is possible in studies that evaluate sex offender treatment programmes, in reality it is difficult (a) to find enough untreated offenders who are not different at pretreatment from treated sex offenders – for example, because they refused treatment, were assessed not to need it, or dropped out of treatment – and (b) if untreated offenders are available, to find that they can be matched with treated offenders on enough variables (such as risk level, number of previous convictions, age, type of offending history, etc.) to enable equivalence to be guaranteed. The result is that there are very few studies that employ these designs, or, when they do, that they are unable to employ the designs in a way such that equivalence is guaranteed. Lösel and Schmucker (2005) identified six studies using this design.

Level three of the Maryland Scale of Scientific Rigor can be applied to studies where offenders are incidentally assigned to treatment and no-treatment groups such that equivalence can be assumed, as where equivalence on relevant variables is demonstrated. The problem of limited numbers of untreated offenders being available for study, which has become increasingly difficult as the use of sex offender programmes has been routinely expanded, also applies to studies trying to use this design. Groups of offenders who are available and have been commonly used in treatment evaluations, such as treatment refusers and drop-outs, do not allow for the assumption of equivalence. Some studies (nearly a quarter (19) of the studies included in Lösel and Schmucker's (2005) study) have been able to adopt this design – for example, by comparing treated offenders with similar offenders who were released before the introduction of sex offender treatment.

A commonly used method (60 per cent, or 48, of the studies identified by Lösel and Schmucker (2005), and 43 per cent, or 23, of the studies identified by Robertson *et al.* (submitted)) is to compare treated offenders with a comparison group, such as treatment drop-outs, treatment refusers, or those assessed as not needing treatment, where equivalence cannot be assumed between the treated and comparison groups. This type of study is given a two on the Maryland Scale and causes controversy, as any post-treatment differences between the groups could be due to their pretreatment differences rather than the result of the impact of treatment. Studies that do not employ a control or comparison group are coded one on the Maryland Scale and are widely agreed to be extremely poor in methodological design, so much so that they are frequently excluded from review or meta-analytic studies (see below).

There are many other difficulties that can only be summarised here (for more detailed discussions of these issues, see Brown 2005; Harkins and Beech 2007). For example, measures of recidivism (such as official conviction rates, arrest rates, and trawls of records/files for evidence of reoffending) vary in their reliability, and the different measures used affect comparability between studies. Sex offenders have persistent, long-term risk of reoffending (Cann *et al.* 2004), meaning that long follow-up periods are needed. The result of this can be that by the time the evaluation outcome is known, the treatment has been modified, discontinued, or become outdated in comparison with the evidence. Most deliveries of programmes are small in scale (for example, 8–10 offenders in each treatment group/delivery) and many offenders drop out of treatment. This makes quantitative analysis of each programme delivery problematic. This is exacerbated by the fact that recidivism rates are relatively low, meaning that large samples are needed to reliably identify statistical differences between treated and control/comparison groups. These issues have resulted in many deliveries of a programme being combined and evaluated as a single programme. While this allows for more reliable statistical analysis, it means that differences between each delivery of the programme, which could be crucial to treatment effectiveness, are overlooked.

In reality, criminal justice requirements/orders mean that unless mandated at a high level or designed into the development and implementation of a programme, evaluators often have little flexibility in the designs they can use, and this means that they often have to use designs and data that are not ideal. Therefore, conclusions about programme efficacy are still being keenly debated, such that there is still a lack of clarity about the efficacy of sex offender treatment programmes: an issue that this chapter will now address. Given the methodological issues outlined above and the amount of evaluation research, it is not possible in this chapter to give a thorough review of all the evaluation research that has tried to examine whether the completion of sex offender treatment programmes reduces the risk of further offending (for a more detailed review, see Brown 2005). However, to provide a summary of the research in this area, the meta-analyses that have been conducted to date will be discussed below.

A meta-analysis pools together treatment effects from a number of studies and so provides a method of assessing the consistency of results across studies, which should allow us to draw some overall conclusions about the efficacy of sex offender treatment programmes. By combining the samples of a number of studies, the power of the statistical analysis is increased, so that even small effects which might not be identified in a single study can be identified. Thus, this method is considered by some to be state-of-the-art in reviewing quantitative evaluation research; however, as we will see in the discussion below, the reliability of any meta-analysis depends on the studies that are included within it. While this may, at first glance, seem relatively straightforward (for example, by including all that have been published), there are a number of issues that make the selection of studies crucial and far from straightforward (for example, including unpublished studies, as there is a tendency for studies that find statistically significant and positive results to be published and/or submitted for publication; for excluding studies with overlapping samples so that the same treatment programme is not over-represented in the analysis; and for including only studies that are seen to be methodologically sound in the analysis, which, as we have seen above, can be extremely difficult to determine, or there may not be a sufficient number of methodologically sound studies to include). Consequently, different researchers include different studies in their analyses.

This means that the meta-analyses, which are supposed to be helpful in that they provide a summary of the research, actually produce conflicting results depending on the studies that have been selected and incorporated into the review. Nevertheless, as discussed above, it is so difficult to conduct the sort of research that would produce *conclusive* results that the outcome of meta-analyses is the best method we have (without reviewing each study) to summarise the research in this area and to attempt to assess whether sex offender treatment has a positive effect on the future offending behaviour of those who complete it.

In 1989, Furby *et al.* attempted a meta-analysis, but the poor quality of the research that had been published at that time meant that they were unable to do this and instead they published a review of the research studies. They concluded that there was no evidence of effectiveness, though it is important to note that many of the programmes included in the review had been discontinued because their approach was deemed obsolete. In addition, Marshall and Pithers (1994) showed that at least one-third of the samples reviewed by Furby *et al.* (1989) overlapped, creating, in this instance, a bias against positive results. So while the no-evidence conclusion may have been justified at the time and Furby *et al.* (1989) claimed to have made only tentative conclusions regarding treatment effectiveness, this review tells us little about the efficacy of current programmes. Despite this, the study has been cited as evidence that treatment is ineffective.

In 1995, Hall conducted a meta-analysis of 12 studies (published after Furby *et al.*'s 1989 review) that he argued had employed relatively rigorous and robust methodology (that is, they compared, using samples of 10 or more, treated offenders with comparison groups, using arrest records for sexual recidivism as outcome data): these 12 studies were selected from 92 studies, with 80 being discarded, as they did not meet his specified methodological requirements. Three of the 12 studies employed randomisation to control and treatment groups, but only four studies evaluated cognitive-behavioural programmes (although Hall categorised five studies as cognitive-behavioural, one was a multi-systemic programme for adolescents that had a particularly large treatment effect). The mean follow-up period was 6.9 years, and the analysis revealed that treated sex offenders had fewer rearrests (9 per cent) compared with untreated controls (12 per cent), with an average effect size of 0.12.

Grossman *et al.* (1999) argued that Hall's conclusion that treatment had a positive impact on recidivism constituted a 'robust finding' (359), but others have criticised this study. As well as reporting problems with the categorisation of treatment as cognitive-behavioural (see above), Becker and Murphy (1998) criticised the small number of studies included, and it is important to remember that the study only included four programmes that used a cognitive-behavioural approach (though these all had a positive treatment effect with effect sizes of 0.14, 0.45, 0.47 and 0.56). In order to rectify this problem, however, Hall would have had to include studies with less robust methodologies, and this would have generated different problems that would no doubt have incurred criticism.

Becker and Murphy (1998) pointed out that some comparison groups received some treatment, while other comparison groups received no treatment, a fact that was not taken into account in the analysis. Furthermore, Hanson *et al.* (2004) argued that a major limitation of the study was that many of the comparison groups were made up of non-completers (drop-outs), a fact that Hall did acknowledge in his report. When Rice and Harris (1997) reanalysed the data from Hall's study, they concluded that the treatment effects were confined to studies using non-completers, and an analysis excluding drop-out studies failed to find a treatment effect.

In 1999, Alexander reported the findings of an analysis of the results of 79 evaluation studies published from 1943 to 1996. Alexander recognised that the majority of studies included in her analysis did not have the methodological rigour of those assessed by Hall (1995), although she, too, excluded studies with fewer than 10 participants. She hoped, however, that the larger data set would reveal patterns that were not so readily discernible in Hall's data set. Alexander omitted studies with overlapping data sets, unclear or no outcome data, biomedical treatment and surgical castration. In addition, data for drop-outs, because of a lack of consistency in data and analyses, were omitted, an omission that Alexander acknowledges could have skewed the results.

Alexander found that less than 11 per cent of the treated sex offenders reoffended, and when offenders were subdivided by type of offence, the efficacy for some groups of offenders became more apparent. Treated offenders had lower recidivism rates than untreated offenders in all categories (rapists, child molesters, exhibitionists, and type not specified), except for type not specified. Rates for treated child molesters averaged 13.9 per cent while those for untreated child molesters averaged 25.8 per cent. Similarly, treated incest offenders had lower recidivism rates (4.0 per cent) than untreated incest offenders (12.5 per cent). There was little difference, however, in comparisons for treated and untreated rapists (20.1 per cent and 23.7 per cent respectively). While Alexander's study seems to suggest that treatment was effective, Hanson et al. (2002) pointed out that there were some anomalies in Alexander's results and suggested that there was too much variance in the methods employed across the range of studies analysed to enable firm conclusions to be drawn. Lösel and Schmucker (2005) highlighted that the majority of the studies contained no control or comparison group, which is very weak in terms of methodological rigour. Including studies from as early as 1943 and evaluations of such a wide range of treatment programmes also means that it is difficult to draw conclusions from this analysis about the efficacy of current treatment methods.

Published in the same year as Alexander's study, Gallagher et al. (1999) included 22 studies, with 25 treatment comparisons in their meta-analysis. They argued that Hall's study was compromised because it included only published studies, and so they broadened and updated Hall's study by including published and unpublished literature that had a measure of sexual reoffence as an outcome measure and a no-treatment comparison group, was reported in the English language after 1975, and delivered treatment after 1970. Gallagher *et al.* criticised Hall for including studies published after 1989, as they said this was an arbitrary date in terms of treatment development, although it was chosen by Hall to include all studies published after Furby *et al.*'s (1989) review. However, like Alexander, Gallagher *et al.* can also be criticised for choosing to have such an early cut-off date, as treatment delivered in the 1970s (and before) differed enormously from that delivered in the 1990s, with the latter programmes being more similar to current treatment methods than the earlier programmes. In addition, the type of programmes included in Gallagher *et al.*'s study varied enormously, including two they categorized as behavioural, two as augmented behavioural, 10 as cognitive-behavioural/relapse prevention, three as cognitive-behavioural, one as surgical castration, four as chemical castration, and three as other psychosocial treatments. Three studies investigated programmes for juvenile offenders, and Becker and Murphy's (1998) criticism of Hall's classification of the multi-systemic programme can also be applied to Gallagher *et al.*'s study.

Of the studies analysed by Gallagher *et al.*, 20 demonstrated a better outcome for treated offenders, four a better outcome in untreated comparisons, and one study revealed no difference between treated and untreated groups. The average effect size was 0.43, which the authors argued could be considered statistically significant and a medium effect size. The behavioural, cognitive-behavioural (both relapse prevention and other), and augmented, chemical-medical programmes showed substantial reductions in post-treatment sexual recidivism. Gallagher *et al.* concluded that cognitive-behavioural programmes were effective, with programmes including relapse prevention being as effective as programmes without it. However, Hanson *et al.* (2004) pointed out that many of the studies reviewed contained threats to validity: many used drop-out comparison groups, and some contained preliminary reports which were contradicted by later studies. In addition, some offenders were double or triple counted, as they formed the treatment sample in more than one study.

In 2002, Hanson *et al.* attempted to bring some order to the methodological concerns and criticisms levelled at previously conducted meta-analyses. They included all credible studies of psychological treatment of sex offenders identified by May 2000 in which treated sex offenders were compared with sex offenders who received no treatment or a form of treatment judged to be inadequate or inappropriate. Forty-three studies with combined sample sizes of 5,078 treated sex offenders and 4,376 untreated sex offenders were reviewed. When more than one study evaluated the same sample of treated offenders, the study with the largest sample size or longest follow-up period was included in the analysis. If a different method was used in more than one study using the same sample, then only the study that was determined to have the best methodology was included. Two studies were omitted due to unresolved anomalies in the data. Twenty-three published studies and 20 unpublished studies were included in the analysis. Most studies were North American (21 US, 16 Canadian) in origin, with five from the UK and one from New Zealand. The median publication year was 1996, with 10 (23 per cent) evaluations published in 1999 or later. The authors argued that the studies were mostly recent, although the earliest publication year was 1977, and treatment was delivered between 1965 and 1999 (80 per cent of the offenders received treatment after 1980). Most studies examined adult male sex offenders, but four investigated adolescent sex offenders, and one studied female offenders. More than half of the programmes evaluated (23 out of 43) were based exclusively in institutions, with 17 based in the community and three in both settings.

Averaged across all the studies, with a mean follow-up period of 46 months, the sexual recidivism rate of 12.3 per cent for treated offenders was lower than the sexual recidivism of 16.8 per cent for untreated offenders. This pattern was similar for general recidivism, with a rate of 27.9 per cent for treated offenders and 39.2 per cent for untreated comparisons. The better outcome displayed by treated offenders was statistically significant, but there was a great deal of variability across studies. The treatment effect was stronger in unpublished studies, a finding which perhaps counters arguments of a publication bias towards positive outcomes. Offenders who dropped out of treatment had higher rates of sexual recidivism, an effect that was consistent across the 18 studies that included drop-out data. However, surprisingly, offenders who refused treatment did not have higher recidivism rates than those who had attended at least some treatment. Offenders referred to treatment based on need had higher recidivism rates than offenders not considered to need treatment. These results suggest that the findings of studies which include comparison groups of drop-outs or offenders assessed as not needing treatment are unreliable, as many have argued. On average, the 20 studies with the best methodological designs revealed an overall treatment effect, although there was a great deal of variability in the effects revealed by these studies. The recidivism rates averaged across the 15 studies evaluating current treatments that were deemed to be the most robust in terms of methodology were 9.9 per cent for treated groups and 17.4 per cent for untreated comparison groups. Institutional and community-based programmes seemed to be equally effective, as were programmes targeting adults or juvenile offenders. Hanson *et al.* concluded that the study undisputedly showed that recidivism rates were lower in treated sex offenders. However, what can be disputed, they argued, is the reason for this: either treatment is effective or other differences between the treated and untreated offenders account for the differences in recidivism. Hanson *et al.* (2002) believe that current treatments are effective at reducing recidivism, but argued that 'firm conclusions await more and better research' (186).

In 2005, Lösel and Schmucker attempted a 'comprehensive, independent, and international review' (Lösel and Schmucker 2005: 119) of treatment effectiveness, following their conclusions from a 2003 review that research analyses 'vary in effect size, type of treatment included, prevailing design quality, categorization of programs, treatment settings and meta-analytic techniques' (119). They also noted that most analyses were restricted to studies reported in English. In their meta-analysis, they included all studies reported in English, German, French, Dutch or Swedish up to 2003 that could be located (attempts were made to identify relevant unpublished studies), that used recidivism (though a broad definition of recidivism was used) as an outcome measure, included a comparison group not receiving the same treatment (could be a no-treatment control group but studies only reporting a drop-out control group were excluded, or some other comparison group that may have received some other form of treatment), and had sample sizes of at least 10.

This produced 80 comparisons from 69 studies, which were discussed in 66 reports. Most of the studies came from North America, one-third contained unpublished data, nearly three-quarters were published after 1990 and nearly one-third since 2000, and half the programmes were assessed as being cognitive-behavioural in approach (and two multi-systemic programmes were included in this category, they argued, due to basic similarities with the cognitive-behavioural programmes). Seven comparisons related to juvenile sexual offenders. Most of the studies (60 per cent) used comparison groups that could not be assumed to be equivalent; for example, in nearly one-quarter of the comparisons the comparison groups consisted of treatment refusers (see discussion above). However, when group differences were tested and reported, the treatment group was more often at higher risk than the comparison group, though no information on group differences was available for 29 comparisons (including all the randomised, control trials). Only six comparisons, which used randomisation, could be given the highest methodological rating.

The mean rate of sexual recidivism was 11.1 per cent for treated offenders, compared with 17.5 per cent of offenders in comparison groups. Lösel and Schmucker (2005) argued that low base rates mean that this represents a reduction in sexual recidivism of nearly 37 per cent, with similar rates also identified for violent and general recidivism. After controlling for methodological and other study characteristics, only programmes with a cognitive-behavioural orientation showed an independent treatment effect, and this is encouraging as it is based on a 'solid number of 35 independent comparisons' (136). Although treatment programmes had an impact on violent and general recidivism as well as sexual recidivism, only programmes designed specifically for sex offenders had an impact. More modern programmes or findings published most recently were not necessarily the most successful. Lösel and Schmucker (2005) concluded: 'Bearing the methodological problems in mind, one should draw very cautious conclusions from our meta-analysis. The most important message is an overall positive and significant effect of sex offender treatment' (135).

To update the two previously discussed reviews, Robertson *et al.* (submitted) included studies published and located up to March 2008 using similar inclusion criteria as the previous studies (recidivism as outcome measure, comparison group of untreated or differently treated offenders, sample sizes of at least 10). In addition, they included only studies reported in English and those that contained recidivism criteria and follow-up periods that allowed for equal comparisons between the treated and control/comparison groups. Fifty-four studies were identified (53 of which reported sexual recidivism and 40 general recidivism), which dated from 1976 to 2005 (34 were published and 20 unpublished). As with other reviews, the majority of the studies were North America (24 US and 18 Canadian), with nine UK studies and one each from New Zealand, The Netherlands and Australia. Four studies evaluated interventions for adolescents, while the remainder focused on adult male sex offenders. The majority of the studies (40) used a cognitive-behavioural approach.

A significant treatment effect for sexual recidivism was demonstrated with a recidivism rate of 9.4 per cent for treated offenders compared with 15.6 per cent for untreated offenders (figures that are reasonably comparable with the two analyses previously discussed). The 31 studies with the strongest designs also demonstrated a treatment effect for sexual recidivism. It is important to note, however, that when all of the strongest 31 studies are considered, a significant variability between studies was demonstrated. Significant treatment effects on general recidivism were also found for all the studies and the 22 most methodologically robust studies, but again there was significant variability between studies in both these analyses. Programmes using a cognitive-behavioural (40) or systemic (2) approach were the only approaches to demonstrate a significant treatment effect on sexual recidivism (supporting the findings of most of the previously discussed reviews). Robertson *et al.* concluded that the results lent support for the efficacy of sex offender treatment programmes but that it was also important to take study design into account during evaluation.

All of the previously discussed reviews have combined adult and juvenile male (and in some cases the extremely limited number of adult female offender studies) sex offenders. Reitzel and Carbonell (2006) conducted a review that focused on juvenile (ages 7–20) sex offenders. Studies had to have a measure of sexual recidivism and a control or comparison group, and nine were identified (four published and five unpublished) and included in the analysis. Published papers dated from 1990 to 2001 with unpublished data from as late as 2003. The low numbers of studies and the usual methodological issues (a concern for a variety of reasons with many of the studies included in this analysis) mean that the conclusions of this analysis must be tentative; however, a significant treatment effect on sexual recidivism was found, with unweighted average recidivism rates of 7.4 per cent for treated and 18.9 per cent for untreated juvenile sex offenders and a weighted average effect size of 0.43 reported.

Conclusion

Despite the methodological problems and slight differences in the findings of these meta-analyses, each has found that treated sex offenders have lower sexual (and often violent and general) recidivism rates than untreated or comparison group sex offenders. These studies show increased support for the efficacy of treatment, although there is great variability across evaluations studies, which perhaps reflects a large variation in the impact of different programmes. The methodological issues, as Hanson *et al.* (2002) highlighted, may also mean that the differences in recidivism rates are a consequence of differences in the control/comparison groups rather than the treatment programmes themselves. It is rather frustrating that it is still difficult to draw firm conclusions about the efficacy of these programmes given the efforts of many researchers to address this issue, the amount of time spent trying to answer the question, and the fact that it is unlikely that firm conclusions can be easily drawn in the future given the wide range of methodological issues that make evaluating the programmes problematic. The key issue still centres on the conclusiveness of the evidence base, with those seeking more conclusive results firstly bemoaning the small number of randomised studies that so many argue are the reference standard of evaluation design and then, secondly, stressing that those that have been conducted have shown no positive treatment effect. However, as Robertson *et al.* (submitted) point out in a recent attempt to provide clear guidance on research designs, the Association for the Treatment of Sexual Abusers' Collaborative Data Committee (CODC) published guidelines on this topic (CODC Guidelines 2007), arguing that it is highly unlikely that a definitive study would provide a clear conclusion to the debate on programme effectiveness. The guidelines suggested that a more definitive conclusion could be drawn from the accumulation of research studies that employed diverse methodologies. According to these principles, the reviews discussed above would seem to suggest that sex offender treatment, and particularly programmes that employ a cognitive-behavioural approach, are effective in reducing risk, at least in adult male sex offenders. If one takes the view that the variable results indicate that programmes have variable impacts on offenders (rather than being solely the artefact of methodological issues), a further problem is that it is difficult to reliably determine (particularly in a time frame that is useful to treatment providers) which programmes are effective, or the most effective and with which type of offenders they have efficacy, or even what exactly it is about the programmes that produces any reduction in risk. Perhaps a switch in focus to trying to assess what it is about programmes that does or does not have an impact on offenders would enable development in our understanding of treatment efficacy, as, currently, we seem to be at an impasse, with those in favour of the approach supported by the CODC arguing that treatment is effective, while many others await more firm and conclusive evidence, which is extremely elusive and unlikely to be produced in the near future (if ever) such that this debate surrounding efficacy can be resolved to everyone's satisfaction.

References

Abel, G. G., Blanchard, E. B. and Becker, J. V. (1978) 'An Integrated Treatment Program for Rapists', in R. Rada (ed.), *Clinical Aspects of the Rapist*. New York: Grune and Stratton.

Alexander, M. A. (1999) 'Sexual Offender Treatment Efficacy Revisited', *Sexual Abuse: A Journal of Research and Treatment*, 11(2): 101–16.

Andrews, D. A. (1989) 'Recidivism is Predictable and Can Be Influenced: Using Risk Assessments to Reduce Recidivism', *Forum of Correction Research*, 1(2): 11–18 [online]. Available at: http://www.csc-scc.gc.ca/text/pblct/forum/e012/12j_e.pdf (accessed 14 April 2009).

Andrews, D. A. and Bonta, J. (2003) *The Psychology of Criminal Conduct* (3rd edn). Cincinnati, OH: Andersen.

Andrews, D. A., Bonta, J. and Hoge, R. D. (1990a) 'Classification for Effective Rehabilitation', *Criminal Justice and Behavior*, 17(1): 19–52.

Andrews, D. A., Zinger, I., Hoge, R. D., Bonta, J., Gendreau, P. and Cullen, F. T. (1990b) 'Does Correctional Treatment Work? A Clinically Relevant and Psychologically Informed Meta-analysis', *Criminology*, 28: 369–404.

Becker, J. V. and Murphy, W. D. (1998) 'What We Know and Do Not Know About Assessing and Treating Sex Offenders', *Psychology, Public Policy and Law*, 4 (1/2): 116–37.

Brown, S. J. (2005) *Treating Sex Offenders: An Introduction to Sex Offender Treatment Programmes*. Cullompton: Willan.

Cann, J., Falshaw, L. and Friendship, C. (2004) 'Sexual Offenders Discharged from Prison in England and Wales: A 21-Year Reconviction Study', *Legal and Criminological Psychology*, 9(1): 1–10.

Collaborative Outcome Data Committee (2007) *Sexual Offender Treatment Outcome Research: CODC Guidelines for Evaluation*. Public Safety Canada Department of Corrections [online]. Available at: http://www.publicsafety.gc.ca/res/cor/rep/codc-en.asp (accessed 14 April 2009).

Fernandez, Y. M., Marshall, W. L., Lightbody, S. and O'Sullivan, C. (1999) 'The Child Molester Empathy Measure: Description and Examination of Its Reliability and Validity', *Sexual Abuse: A Journal of Research and Treatment*, 11(1): 17–37.

Furby, L., Weinrott, M. R. and Blackshaw, L. (1989) 'Sex Offender Recidivism: A Review', *Psychological Bulletin*, 105(1): 3–30.

Gallagher, C. A., Wilson, D. B., Hirschfield, P., Coggeshall, M. B. and MacKenzie, D. L. (1999) 'A Quantitative Review of the Effects of Sex Offender Treatment on Sexual Reoffending', *Corrections Management Quarterly*, 3(4): 19–29.

Grossman, L. S., Martis, B. and Fichtner, C. (1999) 'Are Sex Offenders Treatable? A Research Overview', *Psychiatric Services*, 50(3): 349–361.

Hall, G. C. N. (1995) 'Sexual Offender Recidivism Revisited: A Meta-Analysis of Recent Treatment Studies', *Journal of Consulting and Clinical Psychology*, 63(5): 802–809.

Hanson, R. K., Broom, I. and Stephenson, M. (2004) 'Evaluating Community Sex Offender Treatment Programs: A 12-Year Follow-Up of 724 Offenders', *Canadian Journal of Behavioural Science*, 36(2): 87–96.

Hanson, R. K., Gordon, A., Harris, A. J. R., *et al.* (2002) 'First Report of the Collaborative Outcome Data Project on the Effectiveness of Psychological Treatment for Sex Offenders', *Sexual Abuse: A Journal of Research and Treatment*, 14(2): 169–94.

Harkins, L. and Beech, A. R. (2007) 'Measurement of the Effectiveness of Sex Offender Treatment', *Aggression and Violent Behavior*, 12(1): 36–44.

Laws, D. R. and Marshall, W. L. (2003) 'A Brief History of Behavioral and Cognitive Behavioral Approaches to Sexual Offenders: Part 1. Early Developments', *Sexual Abuse: A Journal of Research and Treatment*, 15(2): 75–92.

Lipsey, M. W. (1989) 'The Efficacy of Intervention for Juvenile Delinquency: Results from 400 Studies'. *41st Annual Meeting of the American Society of Criminology*, Reno, NV.

Lipsey, M. W. (1995) 'What Do We Learn from 400 Research Studies on the Effectiveness of Treatment with Juvenile Delinquents?', in J. McGuire (ed.), *What Works: Reducing Reoffending*. Wiley Series in Offender Rehabilitation. Chichester: Wiley.

Lösel, F. and Schmucker, M. (2005) 'The Effectiveness of Treatment for Sexual Offenders: a Comprehensive Meta-Analysis', *Journal of Experimental Criminology*, 1: 117–46.

Mann, R. E. and Marshall, W. L. (2009) 'Advances in the Treatment of Adult Incarcerated Sex Offenders', in A. R. Beech, L. A. Craig and K. D. Browne (eds), *Assessment and Treatment of Sex Offenders*. Chichester: Wiley-Blackwell.

Marlatt, G. A. (1982) 'Relapse Prevention: A Self-Control Program for the Treatment of Addictive Behaviors', in R. Stuart (ed.), *Adherence, Compliance and Generalization in Behavioral Medicine*. New York: Brunner/Mazel.

Marlatt, G. A. and Gordon, J. R. (1985) *Relapse Prevention: Maintenance Strategies in the Treatment of Addictive Behaviours*. New York: Guilford.

Marques, J. K., Weideranders, M., Day, D. M., Nelson, C. and van Ommeran, A. (2005) 'Effects of a Relapse Prevention Program on Sexual Recidivism: Final Results from California's Sex Offender Treatment and Evaluation Project', *Sexual Abuse: A Journal of Research and Treatment*, 17: 79-107.

Marshall, W. L. (1996) 'Assessment, Treatment, and Theorizing About Sex Offenders: Developments During the Past Twenty Years and Future Directions', *Criminal Justice and Behavior*, 23(1): 162–199.

Marshall, W. L. (1993) 'The Treatment of Sex Offenders: What Does the Outcome Data Tell Us? A Reply to Quinsey, Harris, Rice, and Lalumière', *Journal of Interpersonal Violence*, 8(4): 524–530.

Marshall, W. L. and Marshall, L. E. (2007) 'The Utility of the Random Controlled Trial for Evaluating Sexual Offender Treatment: The Gold Standard or an Inappropriate Strategy?', *Sexual Abuse: A Journal of Research and Treatment*, 19: 175–191.

Marshall, W. L. and Marshall, L. E. (2009) 'Modifying Sexual Preferences', in A. R. Beech, L. A. Craig and K. D. Browne (eds), *Assessment and Treatment of Sex Offenders*. Chichester: Wiley-Blackwell.

Marshall, W. L. and Pithers, W. D. (1994) 'A Reconsideration of Treatment Outcome with Sex Offenders', *Criminal Justice and Behavior*, 21(1): 10–27.

Marshall, W. L. and Serran, G. A. (2000) 'Improving the Effectiveness of Sexual Offender Treatment', *Trauma, Violence and Abuse*, 1(3): 203–222.

Marshall, W. L. and Williams, S. (1975) 'A Behavioral Approach to the Modification of Rape', *Quarterly Bulletin of the British Association for Behavioural Psychotherapy*, 4: 78.

Marshall, W. L., Anderson, D. and Fernandez, Y. M. (1999) *Cognitive Behavioural Treatment Programmes*. Chichester: Wiley.

Murphy, W. D., Abel, G. G. and Becker, J. V. (1980) 'Future Research Issues', in D. J. Cox and R. J. Daitzman (eds), *Exhibitionism: Description, Assessment and Treatment*. New York: Garland STPM Press.

Pithers, W. D., Marques, J. K., Gibat, C. C. and Marlatt, G. A. (1983) 'Relapse Prevention with Sexual Aggressives: A Self-Control Model of Treatment and Maintenance of Change', in J. G. Greer and I. R. Stuart (eds), *The Sexual Aggressor: Current Perspectives on Treatment*. New York: Van Nostrand Reinhold.

Quinsey, V. L. and Earls, C. M. (1990) 'The Modification of Sexual Preferences', in W. L. Marshall, D. R. Laws and H. E. Barbaree (eds), *Handbook of Sexual Assault: Issues, Theories, and Treatment of the Offender*. New York: Plenum.

Quinsey, V. L., Harris, G. T., Rice, M. E. and Lalumière, M. L. (1993) 'Assessing the Treatment Efficacy in Outcome Studies of Sex Offenders', *Journal of Interpersonal Violence*, 8(4): 512–523.

Reitzel, L. R. and Carbonell, J. L. (2006) 'The Effectiveness of Sexual Offender Treatment for Juveniles as Measured by Recidivism: A Meta-Analysis', *Sexual Abuse: A Journal of Research and Treatment*, 18(4): 401–421.

Rice, M. E. and Harris, G. T. (1997) 'The Treatment of Adult Offenders', in D. M. Stoff, J. Breiling and J. D. Master (eds), *Handbook of Antisocial Behaviour*. Toronto: Wiley.

Robertson, C., Beech, A. R. and Freemantle, N. (submitted) 'A Meta-Analysis of Treatment Outcome Studies: Comparisons of Treatment Designs and Treatment Delivery'.

Seto, M. C., Marques, J. K., Harris, G. T., *et al.* (2008) 'Good Science and Progress in Sex Offender Treatment Are Intertwined: A Response to

Marshall and Marshall (2007)', *Sexual Abuse: A Journal of Research and Treatment*, 20(2): 247–255.

Sherman, L., Gottfredson, D., MacKensie, D., Eck, J., Reuter, P. and Bushway, S. (1997) *Preventing Crime: What Works, What Doesn't, What's Promising. Report to the U.S. Congress.* Washington, DC: Department of Justice.

Vennard, J., Sugg, D. and Hedderman, C. (1997) *Changing Offenders' Attitudes and Behaviour: What Works?* Home Office Research Study No. 171. London: HMSO.

Ward, T. (2002) 'Good Lives and the Rehabilitation of Offenders: Promises and Problems', *Aggression and Violent Behavior*, 7(5): 513–528.

Ward, T. and Stewart, C. A. (2003) 'The Treatment of Sex Offenders: Risk Management and Good Lives', *Professional Psychology: Research and Practice*, 34(4): 353–360.

Wood, R. M., Grossman, L. S. and Fichtner, C. G. (2000) 'Psychological Assessment, Treatment, and Outcome with Sex Offenders', *Behavioral Sciences and the Law*, 18: 23–41.

Chapter 6

The use of pharmacotherapy with high-risk sex offenders[1]

Karen Harrison

Introduction

The treatment of sex offenders and specifically that of high-risk sex offenders is a question of importance throughout the world. Arguably, the three main methods of treatment are psychotherapy, surgical intervention and pharmacotherapy, although practices involving restorative justice techniques are also gaining support (psychotherapy has already been looked at in some detail in Chapter 5 of this volume, and restorative justice practices are addressed in Chapter 7 of this volume). This chapter will therefore briefly look at the use of surgical interventions in the forms of neurosurgery and surgical castration, although it will mainly concentrate on the use of pharmacotherapy in the treatment of high-risk sex offenders.

Neurosurgery

The use of neurosurgery upon sex offenders, also known as stereotaxic hypothalamotomy, involves the removal of parts of the hypothalamus in the brain. The operation causes a disruption in the production of male hormonal agents, including testosterone, causing a reduction in sexual arousal and consequently in deviant sexual behaviour (Grossman *et al.* 1999). It was first used on sex offenders in Germany in 1962, where a paedophile had two-thirds of the ventromedial nucleus in his hypothalamus removed (Rieber and Sigusch 1979), eliminating erotic fantasies and deviant urges (Icenogle 1994). Although this practice is used in some parts of Europe, and with some success, the complex interactions between the brain and sexual behaviour are not sufficiently understood for it to be considered safe. It is thus seen as an imprecise procedure that can cause unpredictable behavioural results (Lockhart *et al.* 1989), often contributing to the offender's committing suicide or violent crime.

Surgical castration

Surgical castration or bilateral orchiectomy is the removal of a man's testes. The operation eliminates the primary supply of testosterone, as approximately 95 per cent of testosterone is produced in the testes (Prentky 1997). This has the effect of reducing sexual desire and urges. Surgical castration as a means of treating sex offenders has been used by several European countries, with Switzerland, in 1892, being the first to use it (Carpenter 1998). In The Netherlands, between 1930 and 1969, 400 sex offenders were surgically castrated (Frenken *et al.* 1999); in Denmark, between 1929 and 1959, the figure stood at 738 (Ortmann 1980); while in Germany, between 1955 and 1977, the number was 800 (Prentky 1997). Surgical castration has also been used in the USA, Norway, Sweden, Finland, Estonia, Iceland, Latvia and the Czech Republic.

Evaluation studies on the whole have been positive, and Ohm (1960, cited by Wille and Beier 1989) evaluated 224 castrated sex offenders in Germany, noting that only eight (3.5 per cent) had reoffended. Likewise, in Switzerland, Cornu's study (1973, cited by Wille and Beier 1989) of 121 offenders found the recidivism rate to be 4.1 per cent. Even more encouraging is the study by Sturup (1968, cited by Wille and Beier 1989) in Denmark which found a 0 per cent recidivism rate. More recently, Wille and Beier (1989) compared 99 castrated offenders with 35 non-castrated offenders. Using a follow-up time of 11 years, the research discovered that of the castrated group, only 3 per cent had been involved in another sexual crime, while 46 per cent of the non-castrated group had reoffended. Most of the castrated offenders were also found to have experienced a reduction in sexual desire, sexual ability, erotic fantasies and erectile function.

Despite such positive results, surgical castration, while still legal in many European countries and US states, is now only practised on a very small scale. Many regard the practice as 'barbaric' (*Weems* v *United States*, 217 US 349, 377 (1910)) and in contravention of Article 3 of the European Convention on Human Rights (ECHR), and/or Amendment 8 of the US Constitution (*State* v *Brown*, 326 S.E.2d 410 (S.C. 1985)). Arguably, on matters of family life, it also contravenes Articles 8 and 12 of the ECHR. It is also worth noting that the operation can produce the negative side effects of hot flushes, softening of the skin, lethargy, decrease in muscle mass (Russell 1997) and osteoporosis (Aschwanden and Ermer 2008a). While the operation is irreversible, the effects of the surgery can be modified by testosterone injections, which can be acquired illegally on the black market. Constant monitoring, of even surgically castrated sex offenders, is thus required.

Pharmacotherapy

In contrast to such invasive surgical interventions, pharmacotherapy involves the use of medication to treat offenders, to achieve the *effect* of surgical castration but through less invasive and irreversible means. It is this method of treatment upon which this chapter focuses, with an explanation of the medications used, how they work, their efficacy, and current use in England and Wales. It will also consider some of the ethical and legal issues such as whether the treatment should be voluntary or mandatory; whether it should even be classified as treatment or should instead be seen as punishment and cost.

Usually, and wrongly, referred to under its more emotive title of 'chemical castration' (as the role of these drugs is to reduce abnormally excessive sex drives rather than to render the offender impotent (Miller 1998)), pharmacotherapy involves the use of anti-libidinals, such as medroxyprogesterone acetate (MPA), cyproterone acetate (CPA), luteinising hormone–releasing hormone (LHRH) inhibitors, and long-acting gonadotrophin-releasing hormones (GnRH) agonists, and psychotropic medications such as selective serotonin reuptake inhibitors (SSRIs). While there are several beneficial effects of using such drugs, their main aim is to reduce the sexual desire of the offender, defined by Leiblum and Rosen (1988) as a 'subjective feeling state that may be triggered by both internal and external cues, which may or may not result in overt sexual behaviour' (5).

Anti-libidinal medication

While it may be thought that pharmacotherapy is a new phenomenon in the treatment of sex offenders, this is not the case. The use of drugs to treat sex offenders can be traced as far back as the 1940s, to the use of oestrogen, a predominantly female hormone. In 1940, Dunn (1940) reported how imprisoned male sex offenders were given daily doses of stilboestrol. No toxic side effects were reported and at the end of the 96-day trial, there was a complete absence of libido. The main problem, however, was that from 75 days onwards, patients began to complain of gynaecomastia (enlargement of the breasts). This negative and arguably degrading effect was also reported by Foote (1944) and Hutton and Reiss (1942). While early reports were thus positive, most trials were nevertheless ended due to the negative side effects of the drugs including gynaecomastia, thrombosis, nausea, severe headache and impairment of vision (Bowden 1991).

Largely due to such side effects, the use of oestrogen was succeeded in the 1960s by anti-libidinals, namely MPA in the USA and CPA in Europe, Canada, and England and Wales. More recently, LHRH inhibitors and GnRH agonists have also been used. Anti-libidinals, also classified as anti-androgens or androgen antagonists, are grouped as such because their primary effect is to either stop androgens from being produced or prevent them from working altogether. Testosterone, a predominantly male hormone, is part of the androgen hormone group and is synthesised largely in the testes (Stone et al. 2000). The behavioural effects of testosterone are mediated through androgen receptors, which are distributed throughout the brain; thus, anti-libidinals work by reducing levels of testosterone (Briken et al. 2003). This is important when treating sex offenders, as testosterone influences activational effects in the body such as sexual arousal and responsiveness (Grubin 2008), with sexual activity increasing levels of testosterone, and causing a positive feedback cycle (Briken et al. 2003). Thus, it is thought that a reduction in testosterone consequently leads to a reduction in a man's libido and desire to engage in sexual activity.

Testosterone-reducing agents will therefore reduce an offender's sexual drive, decrease erotic and deviant fantasies (Hicks 1993), and lessen potency, sperm production, sexual frustration, and the frequency and pleasure of masturbation (Craissati 2004). Anti-libidinals also work to reduce an offender's frustration and anger levels, making him more relaxed and thus able to concentrate on other forms of treatment such as psychotherapy (Weiss 1999). Thus, it is argued that, to achieve the most effective results, pharmacotherapy should always be used alongside and in conjunction with psychotherapy and other treatment methods (Craissati 2004; Harrison 2007).

Medroxyprogesterone acetate (MPA)

MPA is the main hormonal agent used on sex offenders in the USA for the purpose of reducing sexual desire. Known more commonly under its trade name of Depo-Provera, it can reduce blood levels of testosterone from approximately 575 nanograms (ng) per 100 ml of blood to 125 ng/100 ml. Depo-Provera also affects the brain by causing a tranquillising effect. This is why the drug is often said to calm offenders and provide relief from urges that were previously 'insistent, commanding and not subject to voluntary control' (Melella *et al.* 1989: 225). It is usually administered by intramuscular (IM) injection and comes in two concentrations of 100 and 400 mg/ml (Money 1987). The second concentration is much thicker in volume and so can be quite painful when injected into the patient. Both concentrations are injected into the buttock, whereby the drug binds to the muscle and is gradually released into the body (Fitzgerald 1990). There is no evidence that a patient will develop a tolerance to the drug, so once the correct dosage is found, it does not need altering even if used for an extended period of time.

MPA has been used for the treatment of sexually deviant behaviour since the late 1950s (Saleh *et al.* 2004), and has been popular in the USA from the 1960s onwards following studies of its use at Johns Hopkins University (Money 1970, 1972). The first study looking at MPA and its effect of reducing sex drive was carried out by Heller *et al.* (1958). The main effects of the drug were noted after 3–4 weeks, including a reduction in testicular size, a reduction in spermatozoa production, a complete loss of libido, and difficulty in producing seminal fluid through masturbation. Libido increased 2 weeks after medication ceased and returned to normal 6 weeks later (Bradford 1983). Berlin and Meinecke (1981) additionally argue that MPA is particularly good for the treatment of unconventional sexual cravings; but does not show as positive outcomes when used with offenders who abuse alcohol/drugs, are sexually impulsive, have a history of sociopathy or violence, or have difficulty in complying with the taking of medication.

A larger study involving the use of MPA with 40 men between the ages of 16 and 78 was carried out by Meyer *et al.* (1992). Of those involved, 23 were paedophiles, 10 exhibitionists and seven rapists. IM injections of 400 mg/week were given to the men for durations ranging from 6 months to 12 years. Results were compared with 21 men who had refused MPA treatment and were receiving only psychotherapy. Follow-up rates ranged from 2 to 12 years. Of the 40 men who began MPA treatment, 18 per cent reoffended while still receiving medication and 35 per cent reoffended after the course of treatment had finished, rates which, while high, were still lower than the 58 per cent reoffending rate of those receiving psychotherapy alone. Of those who did reoffend, either on or following MPA treatment, offences were usually non-touching and less serious than their previous offences. Rapists and exhibitionists were also more likely to reoffend than paedophiles. Plasma testosterone in those receiving MPA treatment fell to within the normal female range. The researchers concluded that while treatment with MPA was not successful in all, it was useful for those who had been carefully selected, were motivated to change, and were well informed about all potential side effects.

Maletzky and Field (2003) and Maletzky et al. (2006) have also carried out extensive research into the Oregon Depo-Provera programme. Of the 18 offenders receiving Depo-Provera in 2002, none had since been charged with a sexual offence, although it was accepted that the follow-up period at this stage was extremely short (Maletzky and Field 2003). To rectify this, a further investigation into the first 4 years of the programme was undertaken. Of the 275 inmates who had been evaluated for their suitability for MPA, 134 were deemed to be appropriate for treatment and 141 unsuitable. Of those 134, 79 (59 per cent) went on to receive treatment (Maletzky et al. 2006). Results from the study found that those who were receiving MPA treatment were significantly less likely to reoffend sexually than those receiving no treatment, and in the follow-up period, none of the 79 men had returned to prison. In addition, those on treatment were more likely to keep to their parole conditions and be considered to be doing well by their parole officers, with any reoffending being non-sexual in nature. The authors conclude that while the study still requires further follow-up it does provide evidence that MPA can be a 'valuable addition to a treatment program for selected offenders' (312).

Unlike surgical interventions, castration through medication is reversible. Although MPA is estimated to stay in a patient's bloodstream for 6–8 weeks, it is thought that the effects of it reduce within days of treatment withdrawal (Carpenter 1998), with the ability to achieve erections and ejaculate restored within 7–10 days (Fitzgerald 1990). Wincze et al. (1986) reported the return of unwanted sexual urges within one month of treatment removal, with one patient feeling so out of control at this time that MPA was reinstated.

While MPA can work for some offenders, the main criticism about its use concerns its negative side effects. One of the first to report on this was Gagne (1981). He noted how the drug caused weight gain (in 58 per cent of the patients), hot and cold flushes (29 per cent); headaches (20 per cent), nausea (14 per cent), and phlebitis (inflammation of a vein) (2 per cent). MPA treatment can also cause lethargy, nightmares, leg cramps, gallstones, depression including suicidal thoughts, insomnia, difficulty in breathing (Harrison 2007), and fluid retention, so medical practitioners need to monitor patients who suffer from epilepsy, migraine headache, asthma, and/or cardiac/renal dysfunction. More serious effects include thrombophlebitis (blood clots in superficial veins), pulmonary embolism (blockages in the pulmonary arteries) (Bradford 1983), hyperglycaemia, hypertension, shrinkage of the prostate vessels, diabetes and gynaecomastia (Craissati 2004). Depo-Provera has also been noted to cause cancer in female beagle dogs and uterine cancer in monkeys (Fitzgerald 1990); Mellella *et al.* (1989) describe it as a 'chemical straitjacket' (230).

Cyproterone acetate (CPA)
CPA, a synthetic steroid analogue, works in a similar way to MPA, in that it inhibits testosterone production, by competing with testosterone at organ receptor sites (Bowden 1991). It is more commonly known under its brand name, Androcur, which was granted a product licence for use in England and Wales in January 1974. CPA is usually given orally at doses ranging from 50 to 200 mg/day but is also available as an IM injection at dosages ranging from 300 to 600 mg, which are given every 1 or 2 weeks (Bradford 1983).

The first reported use of CPA with sex offenders was in Germany in 1966 (Laschet and Laschet 1971, cited in Bradford and Pawlak 1993). Results with 110 patients, of whom approximately 50 per cent were sexual offenders, produced reductions in sexual drive, erections, and the ability to orgasm. Such effects were achieved with 100 mg/day with 80 per cent of the cases, and through 200 mg/day for the remaining 20 per cent. Cooper *et al.* (1972) also reported use of 100 mg/day for 12 weeks with one man. Plasma testosterone was reduced by 50 per cent, morning erections disappeared, and the patient was unable to masturbate to orgasm. Based on these results, a larger investigation was undertaken (Cooper 1981) involving nine men, who received 4-week phases of no treatment, 50 mg/day of CPA/placebo, no treatment, 50 mg/day placebo/CPA, and finally no treatment, resulting in a 20-week test period. The results showed a 'significant action for cyproterone acetate ... in reducing sexual interest and concomitant physiological arousal' (461), with a parallel 30 per cent reduction in plasma testosterone levels.

A double-blind study of CPA has also been carried out by Bradford and Pawlak (1993). The research involved 19 repeat sexual offenders who alternated between 3 months of CPA treatment and 3 months of placebo, for a period of 13 months. Four 3-month treatment periods were used, with an initial 1-month baseline of no treatment. All patients received their treatment in identical tablets with CPA dosage ranging from 50 to 200 mg/day. Patients noted that while on CPA they felt calmer and less sexually preoccupied, noticing more significant reductions in sexual arousal and activity when compared to the placebo and baseline stages. During the study, two withdrew: within 3–6 months, one had reoffended and the other admitted that his deviant fantasies had returned, although he had not acted upon them.

Additional studies on the use of CPA with sex offenders suggest that an offender's libido is usually decreased within 2 weeks of treatment beginning (Ott and Hoffet 1968, cited by Bradford and Pawlak 1993; Mothes *et al.* 1971, cited by Bradford and Pawlak 1993), and that it can have a tranquillising effect, making patients less irritable, more relaxed, and thus amenable to treatment. Both psychological and physiological effects are reversed within 4 weeks of withdrawal (Cooper 1981), although its positive effects in controlling deviant behaviour may last much longer (Craissati 2004).

Like MPA, CPA can also produce negative side effects, including fatigue, hypersomnia (sleepiness), lethargy, depression, decrease in body hair, increase in scalp hair, and weight gain (Bradford and Pawlak 1993). Other effects include liver damage, bone mineral loss, nausea, indigestion, skin rashes, galactorrhoea (abnormal production of breast milk), shortness of breath, and decreased production of oil from sebaceous glands in the skin (NetDoctor 2008). Of interest, however, is the claim that CPA does not cause gynaecomastia; this would make it, for many, an obvious choice over MPA (Davis 1974).

Luteinising-hormone-releasing hormone (LHRH) inhibitors and gonadotrophin-releasing hormones (GnRH) agonists

LHRH and GnRH are hormones synthesised by a network of cells in the basal forebrain within the hypothalamus and are secreted directly into the circulation (Briken *et al.* 2003). The secretion initiates the release of follicle-stimulating hormone (FSH) and luteinising hormone (LH) in the pituitary gland, which stimulates the production of testosterone in the testes. LHRH inhibitors and GnRH agonists[2] are thus synthetic hormones that diminish the release of FSH and LH, consequently inhibiting the production of testosterone in the body

(Saleh *et al.* 2004), resulting in levels equivalent to surgical castration. However, for the first 2–4 weeks of medication, there is actually an increase in sex hormone production, known as the 'flare-up effect' (Briken 2002). Therefore, for the first period of the treatment, it is also necessary to prescribe MPA/CPA or SSRIs to counteract this reaction. On the whole, these anti-libidinals are thought to be better than MPA/CPA, as they cause less serious side effects, and in some cases where the offender showed no response to MPA or CPA, some effect was felt from the use of either a LHRH inhibitor or a GnRH agonist.

One of the reasons they are thought to work with sex offenders who display hypersexual behaviour is based on the work of Gaffney and Berlin (1984) and Bain *et al.* (1988). Both studies found that paedophiles, when injected with LHRH inhibitors, responded with a marked increase of LH when compared with non-paedophiles. They consequently formed the hypothesis that paedophilia is caused by a disorder in hormone regulation (Briken 2002), and thus argued that LHRH inhibitors could control such deviant behaviour.

One LHRH inhibitor, leuprolide acetate (Lupron), has been used to treat paedophilia since the early 1990s. Saleh *et al.* (2004) evaluated the effectiveness of leuprolide acetate, looking at six patients, all of whom had at least one paraphilia and had been involved in previous unsuccessful treatment efforts. When the subjects were given 7.5 mg/ month, all of them reported a reduction in their sexually deviant symptoms, although, for one, this was only achieved with additional weekly injections of MPA. There was a marked reduction in the frequency of masturbation to deviant sexual thoughts and imagery and also in the frequency of inappropriate behaviour, although most reported a reduction in their behaviour and thoughts rather than complete eradication. While the optimal duration on LHRH inhibitors is unknown, it is thought that for some offenders, it could be for as little as 9–12 months, which would allow time to stabilise thoughts and behaviour and engage with psychotherapy. For others, however, it is conceded that duration could be forever. Other positive studies on leuprolide acetate have been undertaken by Krueger and Kaplan (2001); Czerny *et al.* (2002); Schober *et al.* (2005), and Saleh (2005).

Briken *et al.* (2001) also looked at LHRH inhibitors testing the effect of Trenantone on 11 men with severe paraphilia over a period of 12 months. Sexually aggressive behaviour was eradicated and patients reported a reduction in penile erection, ejaculation, masturbation, and sexually deviant impulses and fantasies, with no sexual reoffending during the treatment period. Testosterone levels were significantly reduced after 3 months, with six men who had previously used CPA or SSRIs feeling that Trenantone was better at reducing their deviant fantasies. Despite such positive findings, the negative side effects of LHRH inhibitors include weight gain, depression, pain at the injection site (Briken *et al.* 2001), mild to moderate bone demineralisation, nausea, depression, and mild gynaecomastia (Krueger and Kaplan 2001). Aschwanden and Ermer (2008a) also record instances of allergic reactions to the drug (leuprorelin), which cause redness and swelling at the injection site, but, which more importantly, can affect the effectiveness of the medication. These authors also warn that long-term use may result in cognitive problems. Grasswick and Bradford (2002, cited by Briken *et al.* 2003) additionally report concerns of osteoporosis, which can be lessened by adding etidronate (a bisphosphonate used to strengthen bones) and vitamin D to the treatment package.

The effectiveness of triptorelin (Trelstar), a GnRH agonist, has been analysed by Rousseau *et al.* (1990). Serum testosterone levels were reduced to castration levels within 4 weeks, eradicating all exhibitionist behaviour. Erectile capacity was maintained, as were coital activities and masturbation ability. Triptorelin was also studied by Rösler and Witztum (1998), where 30 paraphiliac outpatients were treated with 3.75 mg/month, for periods ranging from 8 to 42 months. Nine had been unsuccessfully treated with CPA and seven with SSRIs. During the course of the treatment, no sexual offences were committed, testosterone levels decreased significantly, deviant sexual fantasies and urges disappeared completely, and masturbation frequency was reduced. Three patients withdrew due to negative side effects, although the study does not comment on what these were. All three were alternatively given 200 mg/day of CPA, although while on CPA two reoffended and were sent to prison. Twenty-one noted progressive erectile failure, with other negative side effects being hot flashes, hypogonadism (lack of gonad function), muscle tenderness, pain at the injection site, and asthenia (physical weakness). Eleven also reported a significant decrease in bone mineral density, although the same authors in a 2000 study (Rösler and Witztum 2000) noted that this could be controlled by including 25–50 mg/month of testosterone enanthate (Delatestryl) in the treatment programme. While this allows patients to achieve erections, the suppression of paraphiliac fantasies is still maintained. Delatestryl might therefore be a sensible addition when using GnRH agonists, not just to ensure that bone mineral density is not affected, but also to give patients or offenders some sexual functioning, which should decrease attrition rates, especially if medication is voluntary. Management of bone demineralisation was also achieved by Dickey (2002) by using 10 mg/day of Fosamax (a drug often used in the treatment of osteoporosis), 1 g/day of calcium and vitamin D supplements.

The use of triptorelin, (Decapeptyl) was also assessed by Thibaut et al. (1996). Six patients, aged between 17 and 43 years, received 3.75 mg/month IM injections, and 200 mg/day of CPA was also administered for the first 4 weeks to prevent the initial flare-up effect. While all patients involved were still able to achieve erection and were able to masturbate, none were able to ejaculate. Non-sexual aggressiveness remained, although testosterone levels dropped to castration levels and, in five, deviant sexual behaviour was eradicated and sexual fantasies and activities were significantly reduced. Side effects were not significant, although one patient complained of hot flushes and asthenia and one of episodic, painful erections. A slight decrease in femoral bone density was also reported. Two patients withdrew, one after 12 months and the other after 3 years. Both reoffended within 8–10 weeks. The researchers felt that long-term effectiveness following treatment withdrawal had a better chance of success if there was a phasing-out programme rather than an abrupt withdrawal; to be achieved by adding increasing amounts of testosterone to the medication. In one case where this was practised, testosterone levels and fantasies returned to pretreatment levels; but deviant behaviour did not, even after 33 months from withdrawal.

Briken et al. (2003) note that when taking LHRH inhibitors and GnRH agonists, each prospective patient should be tested at the beginning of the programme, and every 6 months, for FSH, LH and testosterone levels; kidney function; complete blood count; and cardiovascular status and monitored by electrocardiograms. Baseline bone density should also be monitored and repeated on an annual basis. While such testing is imperative, it would obviously add to the cost of the programme.

A comparison of anti-libidinal medication
Cooper et al. (1992) looked at the use of CPA and MPA in seven paedophiles, who received a mixture of placebos, MPA and CPA in alternating phases. All drugs were given in tablet form, and the staff involved were also blind as to what the drugs actually were. Results showed that both medications worked equally well, with greater effects occurring at the 200 mg/day level when compared with either the placebo or the 100 mg/day dosage. Five patients stated that they preferred MPA and two, CPA.

When comparing LHRH inhibitors with CPA, Allolio *et al.* (1985, cited by Briken *et al.* 2003) found that when treated with CPA, testosterone levels in a group of patients were within the normal range, although once the medication had been switched to leuprolide acetate, serum testosterone dropped, with subsequent reductions in the paedophilic symptoms noted. However, a larger review (Czerny *et al.* 2002), involving 2,070 patients in 67 German forensic psychiatric hospitals, found little difference between CPA and LHRH inhibitors and argued that CPA was better at reducing sexual activity while LHRH inhibitors were more effective at reducing deviant fantasies. Thibaut *et al.* (1996), however, argue that treatment with GnRH agonists has three advantages over that with CPA: triptorelin is more potent, has fewer negative side effects, and, because it is available through IM injection, can be given in monthly dosages, thus increasing compliance. Polak and Nijman (2005) similarly argue that goserelin, a LHRH inhibitor, is more powerful in reducing testosterone levels than CPA and, again, has fewer negative side effects. Gottesmann *et al.* (1997, cited by Briken *et al.* 2003) also found similar results when comparing LHRH agonists with MPA. Four men, three of whom had experienced unsuccessful treatment with MPA, were given 3.75 mg/month of leuprolide acetate for a period of 10 months. All noticed a decrease in erections, ejaculations, paraphiliac fantasies and behaviour. Testosterone levels were recorded as being lower than with MPA. Rösler and Witzum (2000) argue that 'Long-acting GnRH analogues are currently the most effective and promising medications ... with the fewest side effects compared to other anti-androgens' (49).

Psychotropic medication

While several areas of the brain affect sexual behaviour and arousal, the two most closely associated are the hypothalamus and the limbic system. A number of hormones and neurotransmitters are active in this region of the brain, although those most closely linked to sexual performance are dopamine and serotonin (Grubin 2008). Dopamine is commonly associated with the pleasure system of the brain, playing a major role in both mood and emotion. Testosterone promotes the desire for sex and the chemical that sends this signal is dopamine. While dopamine can thus be said to increase sexual functioning, serotonin, conversely, inhibits it. Serotonin is naturally produced in the pineal gland and is thought to control appetite, sleep, memory and learning, temperature regulation, mood, sexual behaviour, cardiovascular function, muscle contraction, endocrine regulation, and depression (Acampora 2003). Low levels of serotonin are thought to contribute to depression, obsessive compulsive disorder (OCD), and other anxiety disorders; hence medication designed to treat such conditions works by increasing levels of serotonin in the body.

Selective serotonin reuptake inhibitors (SSRIs)
One such category of drugs, SSRIs, inhibits the reuptake of serotonin, and this has the effect of increasing serotonin concentration levels in the synaptic cleft (Adi *et al.* 2002). Enhancing central serotonin inhibits or reduces sexual functioning, sexual desire, and associated sexual performance behaviours (Kafka 1997). SSRIs are commonly used in the treatment of depression, bulimia nervosa and OCD (Adi *et al.* 2002) and were not initially designed to be used with sex offenders. However, in the early 1990s, it was thought that they could be effective due to the similarities between the characteristics of OCD and sexually deviant behaviour. Researchers such as Pearson (1990), and Kafka and Coleman (1991) believed that similar drugs could work for each category of patient, although work carried out by Kruesi *et al.* (1992) disputes that such a link exists. SSRIs are the most commonly prescribed medication in sex offender treatment programmes in North America (Kafka 2006).

The most common drugs are fluoxetine (Prozac), paroxetine (Seroxat), citalopram (Cipramil), sertraline (Lustral) and fluvoxamine (Faverin) (Adi *et al.* 2004). The main purpose of the drugs is to lessen the frequency and intensity of sexual fantasies, subsequently leading to a reduction in sexual urges and resulting deviant behaviour (Grubin 2008). Other positive effects include reductions in anxiety, depression and irritability and a diminishing of low self-esteem (Kafka 2001). Duration of SSRI treatment for sex offenders is, however, unknown, arguably making their use 'highly uncertain' (Adi *et al.* 2002: 10). Dosage levels are the same as usual antidepressants levels, with effects starting to occur by the 4-week stage (Kafka 2001).

To assess how effective SSRIs are in treating sex offenders, Adi *et al.* (2002) conducted a review concentrating on nine US studies, involving 225 subjects. In psychometric tests to analyse and record change, most showed a level of improvement while on either fluoxetine or sertraline, and in six of the nine studies these improvements were statistically significant. Only one study showed insignificant improvements, with only three out of 13 patients experiencing positive change. Reported side effects included delayed ejaculation, insomnia, blurred vision, sexual dysfunction, increased depression, gastrointestinal distress, and, in one case, worsening of sexual symptoms. Bradford *et al.* (1995, cited by Greenberg *et al.* 1996) looked at the use of sertraline in the treatment of 21 paedophiles. Results showed a decrease in paedophilic fantasies, urges and arousal; but, interestingly, conventional relations with adults were maintained. When some psychotherapy programmes work to encourage sex offenders, particularly child sex offenders, to have age-appropriate relationships, medication which allows this must be seen in a better light than that which does not.

Greenberg *et al.* (1996) conducted a study comparing fluoxetine, fluvoxamine and sertraline with 94 patients at the Royal Ottawa Hospital. Patients were given one of the three medications and assessed retrospectively at the 4-, 8- and 12-week stages. Results from the study showed that there were significant reductions in paraphilia fantasies but no difference in effectiveness across the drugs. Negative side effects included insomnia in eight men, delayed ejaculation (in eight); headache (in seven), nausea (in three), and blurred vision (in two). The same authors (Greenberg and Bradford 1997) also looked at a group of 95 paraphilics treated with SSRIs, comparing them with 104 patients receiving psychosocial interventions. Results showed that following a 12-week period, those patients who were part of the SSRI group had significantly more reduction in fantasies and urges than the control group. Other results comparing SSRIs have been varied. When comparing fluvoxamine, desipramine and a placebo which resembled fluvoxamine, Zohar *et al.* (1994) found that in one case of exhibitionism, the impulse to expose himself was reduced only when taking fluvoxamine, with no treatment effect noticed with desipramine or the placebo. Dosage levels of fluvoxamine began at 300 mg/day, with deviant impulses disappearing within 2 weeks, although doses were later reduced to 200 mg/day to eradicate dizziness and anorexia with no change of effectiveness noticed. The patient's desire for his wife remained unchanged.

While the possible side effects are considered to be less severe than those associated with MPA/CPA, they can still include gastrointestinal problems, increased appetite and weight gain, rashes, anxiety, headache, sweating, convulsions and hallucinations. SSRIs should therefore not be used if the patient is hypersensitive to the drug or enters into a manic phase, is receiving electroconvulsive therapy, or has a history of epilepsy, cardiac disease, diabetes, renal and hepatic impairment, or bleeding disorders (Adi *et al.* 2002). While positive results have been reported, Adi *et al.* (2002) note that many studies are vulnerable to bias, comparative control groups are rarely used, and there are few or no follow-up periods. Similarly, Beech and Mitchell (2005) argue that while there are several examples of SSRI use, many are single-case studies; meaning that more research including large-scale, double-blind, randomised, controlled trials is required, an opinion also shared by Maletzky and Field (2003). A double-blind, controlled trial of SSRIs in imprisoned sex offenders was commissioned to take place in England and Wales, by the National Programme on Forensic Mental Health; but to date this has not been achieved (Grubin 2007).

The hierarchy of medication

In view of the different types of drugs available and within each type the variety of medications which can be used, it is a potential minefield for practitioners to know which type of drug and, within that category, which actual medication is the best for their individual patient. Briken *et al.* (2003: 896) suggest that while all patients plagued with deviant thoughts and behaviour should be treated with a combination of psychotherapy and pharmacotherapy, a hierarchical order of medication does exist. This can be seen in Figure 6.1. This is

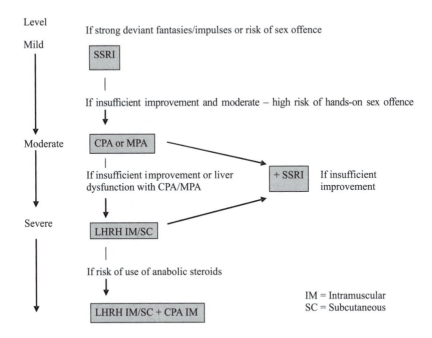

Figure 6.1 Hierarchy of medication for controlling sexually deviant behaviour

confirmed by Kafka (2006), who argues that SSRIs should be used as the first-line drug, while Rösler and Witztum (2000) state that LHRH inhibitors are the most potent of all anti-libidinals.

Use in England and Wales

Previous use

Data on the use of pharmacotherapy with sex offenders are limited, so it is unclear what practices and which drugs have previously been used in England and Wales. It is apparent, however, that benperidol, an antipsychotic drug often used to treat schizophrenia, was available in prisons between 1971 and 1973 for the treatment of deviant behaviour, despite the fact that its product licence was not granted until July 1973 (Sim 1990). In 1971, Field conducted a study on its use at Wormwood Scrubs. Of the 28 men involved, all noticed a reduction in sexual desire, although for two, this was not accompanied by additional decreases in erotic fantasies (*The Times*, 10 September 1973: 3). CPA was also available between 1970 and 1974, with trials ending due to the effects of gynaecomastia (Sim 1990). Figures for November 1975–November 1978 suggest that 138 sex offenders in British prisons were involved in one or more types of drug treatment for deviant sexual behaviour (Sim 1990), with a 1987 survey reporting 18 imprisoned men involved in such treatment (Bowden 1991).

Current use

While it would appear that some sex offenders are being prescribed CPA by psychiatrists and other health professionals, there are no data in England and Wales to show exactly how many offenders are involved in such practices (Grubin 2008). Since June 2007 (Home Office 2007), the role of referral for sex offender medication has been given to the Ministry of Justice through the National Offender Management Service (NOMS). Medication is offered on a voluntary basis, in conjunction with other treatment programmes and is available only to convicted offenders through referrals by prison or probation personnel (NOMS 2007). Offenders are deemed to be appropriate for referral where either 'specific mental health issues are identified that relate directly to assessment or treatment (for instance, where mental illness is thought to contribute to the risk of reoffending)', or where there is evidence of hyper-arousal, intrusive sexual fantasies or urges, sexual urges that are difficult to control, and/or sexual sadism (NOMS 2007: 3). Depending on the needs of the offender SSRIs, CPA or LNRH inhibitors will be used.

Treatment has been available in England and Wales since 1 December 2007, with a contract being issued to Northumberland Tyne and Wear NHS Trust to run the pilot scheme for an initial period of 3 years. In addition to the provision of treatment, the Sexual Behaviour Unit in Newcastle also provides a national advisory service for NOMS and arranges for psychiatric assessments to establish whether a mental health problem has contributed to sexual offending (NOMS 2007). Detailed information on how the offender will be assessed as medically suitable and then how his health will be monitored is not yet readily available, but it is assumed that provisions will be put in place including tests to assess and then periodic monitoring of the physical, emotional and/or mental state of every offender involved. Such tests and assessments are imperative to ensure that, first, the offender is medically suitable and, second, continues to be so throughout the period of treatment; otherwise, the government may open itself up to human rights claims and, if negative side effects become too great to tolerate, offenders will simply withdraw consent and leave the programme.

Legal and ethical issues[3]

Voluntary or mandatory

Arguably, one of the most contentious issues concerning the use of pharmacotherapy is whether it should be provided on a voluntary or mandatory basis. Many US states, such as California, Florida and Montana, use MPA on a mandatory basis, often tying it to prison or parole release (Connelly and Williamson 2000). While this can be viewed positively in that if such treatment does work, then it is better to have offenders treated with it than not, there are still problems with maintaining compliance, especially when the treatment is in pill form and administered by the offender. There are also ethical considerations to take into account, as prison is effectively being exchanged for medication, and this can cause serious side effects. In England and Wales, however, as discussed above, the treatment is currently offered on a voluntary basis.

If the treatment is taken voluntarily, there are still some concerns over the issue of consent, including whether that consent is valid and whether the offender truly understands what he is consenting to, including all of the possible side effects. Meyer and Cole (1997) argue that before voluntary treatment is allowed, the offender should be examined by at least two mental health professionals to ensure that he is not being motivated by self-hate and a desire for self-punishment, to check that there are no mental disorders, and to check that the offender understands all of the risks involved. A neutral party should then be appointed to ensure that the offender's consent is valid and freely given, and, finally, if relevant, that the offender's spouse be told of the risks and consequences of the drugs. It has also been argued that since the long-term effects of the drugs are unknown, no offender can truly give informed consent (Harrison and Rainey 2009; for more information on this, see Chapter 14 of this volume).

When deciding whether such treatment should be voluntary or mandatory, perhaps one thing to bear in mind is compliance evidence with voluntary versus involuntary groups of offenders. Work of this nature has been carried out by Maletzky (1980), whose study compared 100 self-referred and court-referred paedophiles and exhibitionists. Self-referred offenders were described as those who: 'entered therapy of [their] own accord without coercion from a legal source', while court-referred offenders were those who had 'entered therapy under coercion from a legal source' (308). Treatment compliance rates were measured through a combination of self-reported behaviours, penile plethysmography and observers' reports. On the whole, no difference was found between the two groups. While there was marginally better compliance from self-referred offenders, this was not significantly different, and while court-referred subjects had better attendance, again, this was not significantly different. Work of a similar nature was also carried out by Alexander (1993, cited by Munafo 1994), who compared offenders involved in mandatory and voluntary treatments. Of the 2,296 offenders receiving voluntary treatment, 12.4 per cent reoffended, while of the 1,470 receiving mandatory treatment, only 10.4 per cent reoffended. While she suggests that legislating treatment would make it more effective and beneficial to the offender and thus society at large, this view is not shared by the author, as the results were not radically different. If there is no significant difference in effectiveness between voluntary and mandatory participants, then it may be that the only difference lies in the motivation of the offender – how much does he really want to engage with the treatment and subsequently change? There appears to be little research on this; but if, as with cognitive-behavioural programmes, most success comes from those offenders who are motivated, for whatever reason, to change, the best results may come from those who have voluntarily agreed to participate. As argued by Brody and Green (1994), offenders who participate in treatment against their will are often less likely to respond positively.

Treatment or punishment

Throughout this chapter, pharmacotherapy has largely been referred to as a method of treatment, but this section looks at whether the use of medication with sex offenders should be used as part of a treatment package or as a method of punishment (for more details, see Harrison and Rainey 2009). Money (1979) argues that if people misuse others with no concern for their victims, they should be imprisoned and punished. However, if they are at the mercy of intense cravings, while they must assume responsibility for their actions, medical treatment, if available, should be given to help with their difficulties. Whether we view pharmacotherapy as treatment or punishment may be inextricably linked with whether it is voluntary or mandatory, with voluntary participation arguably seen as treatment and mandatory participation as punishment.

Although referring to surgical castration, Baker (1984) argues that the critical point is whether the offender, in addition to being prevented from offending, is also prevented from legally permissible sexual activity. The question is therefore whether the treatment exceeds the cure. As surgical castration prevents both forms of activity, he claims that it can only be classified as punishment and never treatment. As the research literature has indicated, however, this is not the case with pharmacotherapy. Many offenders taking medication to reduce testosterone levels can still achieve erections and engage in age-appropriate sexual relationships. If this is true for every offender involved, then it might be fitting to regard the use of pharmacotherapy as treatment, especially if that use is also voluntary.

Another issue, due to the prevalence and intensity of the negative side effects, is whether participation can be described as treatment, even if participation is voluntary, with exposure to the risks of gynaecomastia and liver damage easily classified as punishment. Despite this view, it may be better to label the use of anti-libidinals as treatment, as it is easier to justify pain when it is classified as treatment rather than as punishment, as even if pain is involved in the cure, it is not intended as pain. Rather, it is intended to help the patient and is consequently more ethically acceptable (Christie 1982). Such a classification, however, may not suit those who actually want the offender to suffer, and subsequently does not fit in with populist punitiveness and longer than commensurate sentencing, a view shared by Icenogle (1994): 'The emotional reaction engendered by criminal sexual behaviour makes it unlikely that society will accept treatment as a sentencing option unless it is clearly viewed as punishment' (280). On the other hand, it is also noted that while the public demand punitiveness when the offender is a stranger, they are often more sympathetic and accepting of treatment when the offender is a family member. Bearing in mind that the vast majority of offenders are known to their victims, this need for punishment may not be as accurate as it is often assumed.

Meyer and Cole (1997) argue that while pharmacotherapy might contribute positively to treating a sex offender, biological interventions may give offenders a 'medical problem' excuse (13) for their behaviour rather than their having to be responsible for their own actions. They argue that it is the brain which is the offending organ and not the penis. However, they do acknowledge that the endocrine system, which the testes are a part of, does affect the quality and intensity of sexual arousal, and thus biology probably does have a part to play in deviant sexual behaviour. Bradford and Pawlak (1993) similarly argue that sex is one of the basic biological drives (like sleep, hunger and thirst) and thus is controlled by the biological regulatory system and, arguably, cannot be regulated by willpower alone. If treatment can be offered and if suitable medication exists, then this should be the first priority when deciding on availability. If this is the case, then surely it would be more appropriate to class such therapy as a component of a treatment package rather than part of a punishment agenda.

However, it must be remembered that while drugs will diminish the strength of deviant sexual interest and desires, in all likelihood they will not cure or change the direction of them (Bowden 1991). This is also argued by Gys and Gooren (1996), who state that while hormonal treatments can reduce deviant desires and arousals, they cannot alter their form. Fitzgerald (1990), moreover, points out that MPA cannot change an offender's sexual orientation, and, as Money *et al.* (1976) note, it is just a threshold or barrier to sexual arousal and not a cure. If this viewpoint is accepted, can pharmacotherapy be classed as a treatment method, especially if it is accepted that a cure can never be achieved? If so, then perhaps the use of pharmacotherapy is neither punishment nor treatment but instead should be classified as a risk-management strategy and should be brought into play after punishment has been served, and alongside and in conjunction with other treatment techniques.

Cost

Involved costs largely depend on which drug or combination of drugs is used and how often such drugs are required. In England and Wales, leuprolide acetate is estimated to cost in the region of £2,000–3,000 per year (Murphy 2007), while in Germany leuprorelin costs US$900 per month (Aschwanden and Ermer 2008b). Adi *et al.* (2002) found that including SSRIs in a treatment package was annually more expensive than the alternative option of CPA, with annual costs for SSRIs amounting to £100-800 depending on the medication used and the dose. Likewise, LHRH inhibitors are more expensive than MPA (Saleh 2005). The true cost of using pharmacotherapy, however, is much more than just the basic cost of the drugs, additional costs including initial referral and assessment, drug delivery, and the monitoring of offenders involved.

The final question is, who will pay for it? One argument is that it should be the offender, who could perhaps contribute through prescription charges. Thus, an offender could pay £7.20 per prescription, £28.25 every 3 months, or £104 per year if prepayment certificates were bought in advance (Department of Health 2009). While this would not cover all of the expenses involved, it may go some way in contributing to the cost. One concern, however, is that if an offender has to pay for his own drugs, there is a risk that such treatment would not be commenced or completed because of the costs involved, although if finances were an issue, and money was collected through the prescription scheme, then presumably such an offender would be exempt from the prescription charges in any event.

At the moment the research trials in England and Wales are being funded by the Ministry of Justice, but should this be the case? If pharmacotherapy is a matter of punishment, then this may be correct, but if a matter of treatment, should it not be the Department of Health that foots the bill? While drug treatment and the necessary treatment programmes which need to accompany it are not cheap, when costed out, they will be less expensive than the costs of an offender reoffending, both in terms of costs involved in police investigation, trial and sentence, and in the provision of medical and psychological services needed to aid a victim's recovery and the intangible costs of fear to the public at large (Prentky and Burgess 1990).

Conclusion

This chapter has briefly looked at the use of surgical interventions to treat high-risk sex offenders but has largely concentrated on the use of medication. Pharmacotherapy is the use of drugs to lower testosterone and in consequence lower and in some cases eradicate libido, fantasies and deviant behaviour. It is widely accepted that it should be used in conjunction with psychotherapy and arguably also in conjunction with newer restorative justice practices. It would appear that SSRIs are the first line of defence; rising to anti-libidinals, with a combination of LHRH inhibitors/GnRH agonists and CPA as the most potent combination. While there is a multitude of positive research studies, Grubin (2007) concludes that evidence for the use of medication with sex offenders is supportive rather than robust, so while there may be good reasons to include pharmacotherapy in a treatment package, more research and trials are still needed.

In addition to effectiveness studies, it is also important to note the plethora of potential negative side effects, all of the drugs displaying some risk of these. One interesting question, however, is whether the drug companies know that their drugs are being used for such purposes. If they do not, maybe there is a way to manufacture drugs which exhibit the positive effects required but eliminate those which are not. Other matters to take into consideration include whether medication should be given on a voluntary or mandatory basis, with most academics believing that it should be given only to those offenders who are medically suitable and who have freely and validly consented.

Pharmacotherapy is currently availably in England and Wales for convicted sex offenders through a referral system with NOMS. While this is a positive step forward in treatment methods, it is argued that treatment should be made available to all. While an absolute right to treatment does not exist in England and Wales (for more detail, see Harrison and Rainey 2009), surely it would be better to provide it to those who need it so that offending can be prevented rather than only using it to reduce recidivism. When the primary goal of NOMS is public protection,

> if legislation and punishment alone cannot fully solve the problem, medicine and science need to be called into action. And if society can be made safer by such means, why not use them? (Berlin 1994: 2)

Notes

1 I would like to thank Professor Adrian Edwards, School of Medicine, Cardiff University and Iain McDonald, Bristol Law School, UWE – Bristol, for their comments on earlier drafts. Any errors are of course my own.
2 The terms 'LHRH agonists/inhibitors' and 'GnRH agonists' are often used interchangeably in the literature to mean the same thing, although, strictly speaking, they do refer to different types of drugs used. For the sake of clarity, the chapter will use the separate terms 'LHRH inhibitors' and 'GnRH agonists' to show this differentiation.
3 For more detail on legal and ethical issues, see Harrison (2008).

References

Acampora (2003) *The Structure, Properties, Function, and Synthesis of Serotonin and Serotonin's Similarity to LSD* [online]. Available at: http://www.totse. com/en/technology/science_technology/seroton.html (accessed 16 March 2009).

Adi, Y., Ashcroft, D., Browne, K., Beech, A., Fry-Smith, A. and Hyde, C. (2002) *Clinical Effectiveness and Cost-consequence of Selective Serotonin Reuptake Inhibitors in the Treatment of Sex Offenders*. London: Home Office.

Aschwanden, R. and Ermer, A. (2008a) 'Leuprorelin Allergy as a Side Effect of Chemical Castration and, as a Consequence, the Discussion About Surgical Castration'. *IATSO Conference*, Capetown, August 2008.

Aschwanden, R. and Ermer, A. (2008b) 'The Impressive Effectiveness of Chemical Castration with Leuprorelin on a Homosexual Sadistic and Schizoid Sexual Murderer with Elimination of the Previously Dominating Sadistic Thoughts and Drive'. *IATSO Conference*, Capetown, August 2008.

Bain, J., Langevin, R., Hucker, S., Dickey, R., Wright, P. and Schonberg, C. (1988) 'Sex Hormones in Paedophiles, 1: Baseline Values of Six Hormones, 2: The Gonadotropin Releasing Hormone Test', *Sexual Abuse: A Journal of Research and Treatment*, 1(3): 443–54.

Baker, W. L. (1984) 'Castration of the Male Sex Offender: A Legally Impermissible Alternative', *Loyola Law Review*, 30: 377-399.

Beech, A. R. and Mitchell, I. J. (2005) 'A Neurobiological Perspective on Attachment Problems in Sexual Offenders and the Role of Selective Serotonin Reuptake Inhibitors in the Treatment of Such Problems', *Clinical Psychology Review*, 25: 153-182.

Berlin, F. S. (1994) 'The Case for Castration, Part 2', *Washington Monthly*, 26(5): 28.

Berlin, F. S. and Meinecke, C. (1981) 'Treatment of Sex Offenders with Anti-androgenic Medication: Conceptualization, Review of Treatment Modalities and Preliminary Findings', *American Journal of Psychiatry*, 138(5): 601–607.

Bowden, P. (1991) 'Treatment: Use, Abuse and Consent', *Criminal Behaviour and Mental Health*, 1: 130–141.

Bradford, J. W. (1983) 'The Hormonal Treatment of Sexual Offenders', *Bulletin of the American Academy of Psychiatry and the Law*, 11: 159–169.

Bradford, J. M. W. and Pawlak, A. (1993) 'Double-Blind Placebo Crossover Study of Cyproterone Acetate in the Treatment of the Paraphilias', *Archives of Sexual Behavior*, 22(5): 383–402.

Briken, P. (2002) 'Pharmacotherapy with Luteinizing Hormone-releasing Hormone Agonists', *Archives of General Psychiatry*, 59: 469–470.

Briken, P., Hill, A. and Berner, W. (2003) 'Pharmacotherapy of Paraphilias with Long-acting Agonists of Luteinizing Hormone-releasing Hormone: A Systematic Review', *Journal of Clinical Psychiatry*, 64(8): 890–897.

Briken, P., Nika, E. and Berner, W. (2001) 'Treatment of Paraphilia with Luteinising Hormone-releasing Agonists', *Journal of Sex and Marital Therapy*, 27: 45–55.

Brody, A. L. and Green, R. (1994) 'Washington States' Unscientific Approach to the Problem of Repeat Sex Offenders', *Bulletin of the American Academy of Psychiatry and the Law*, 20: 343–356.

Carpenter, A. (1998) 'Belgium, Germany, England, Denmark and the United States: The Implementation of Registration and Castration Laws as Protection Against Habitual Sex Offenders', *Dickinson Journal of International Law*, 16(2): 435–457.

Christie, N. (1982) *Limits to Pain*. Oxford: Robertson.

Connelly, C. and Williamson, S. (2000) *A Review of the Research Literature on Serious Violent and Sexual Offenders*. Edinburgh: Scottish Executive Central Research Unit.

Cooper, A. J. (1981) 'A Placebo-controlled Trial of the Anti-Androgen Cyproterone Acetate in Deviant Hypersexuality', *Comprehensive Psychiatry*, 22(5): 458–465.

Cooper, A. J., Ismail, A. A. A., Phanjoo, A. L. and Love, D. L. (1972) 'Antiandrogen (Cyproterone Acetate) Therapy in Deviant Hypersexuality', *British Journal of Psychiatry*, 120: 59-63.

Cooper, A. J., Sandhu, S., Losztyn, S. and Cernovsky, Z. (1992) 'A Double-Blind Placebo Controlled Trial of Medroxyprogesterone Acetate and Cyproterone Acetate with Seven Pedophiles', *Canadian Journal of Psychiatry*, 3: 687–693.

Craissati, J. (2004) *Managing High Risk Sex Offenders in the Community. A Psychological Approach*. New York: Routledge.

Czerny, J. P., Briken, P. and Berner, W. (2002) 'Antihormonal Treatment of Paraphilic Patients in German Forensic Psychiatric Clinics', *European Psychiatry*, 17: 104-106.

Davis, T. S. (1974) 'Cyproterone Acetate for Male Hypersexuality', *Journal of International Medical Research*, 2: 159–163.

Department of Health (2009) *NHS Costs and Exemptions* [online]. Available at: http://www.dh.gov.uk/en/Healthcare/Medicinespharmacyandindustry/Prescriptions/NHScosts/index.htm (accessed 16 February 2009).

Dickey, R. (2002) 'Case Report: The Management of Bone Demineralization Associated with Long-Term Treatment of Multiple Paraphilias with Long-Acting LNRH Agonists', *Journal of Sex and Marital Therapy*, 28: 207–210.

Dunn, C. W. (1940) 'Stilboestrol Induced Gynaecomastia in the Male', *Journal of the American Medical Association*, 115: 2263–2264.

Fitzgerald, E. (1990) 'Chemical Castration: MPA Treatment of the Sexual Offender', *American Journal of Criminal Law*, 18(1): 1–60.

Foote, R. M. (1944) 'Hormonal Treatment of Sex Offenders', *Journal of Nervous and Mental Disorders*, 99: 928–929.

Frenken, J., Gijs, L. and Van Beek, D. (1999) 'Sexual Offender Research and Treatment in the Netherlands', *Journal of Interpersonal Violence*, 14(4): 347–371.

Gaffney, G. and Berlin, F. (1984) 'Is There a Hypothalamic-Pituitary-Gonadal Dysfunction in Paedophilia? A Pilot Study', *British Journal of Psychiatry*, 145: 657–660.

Gagne, P. (1981) 'Treatment of Sex Offenders with Medroxyprogesterone Acetate', *American Journal of Psychiatry*, 138: 644–646.

Greenberg, D. M. and Bradford, J. M. (1997) 'Treatment of the Paraphilic Disorders: A Review of the Role of the Selective Serotonin Reuptake Inhibitors', *Sexual Abuse: A Journal of Research and Treatment*, 9(4): 349–360.

Greenberg, D. M., Bradford, J. M., Curry, S. and O'Rourke, A. (1996) 'A Comparison of Treatment of Paraphilias with Three Serotonin Reuptake Inhibitors: A Retrospective Study', *Bulletin of the American Academy of Psychiatry Law*, 24(4): 525–532.

Grossman, L. S., Martis, B. and Fichtner, C. G. (1999) 'Are Sex Offenders Treatable? A Research Overview', *Psychiatric Services*, 50(3): 349–361.

Grubin, D. (2007) *Second Expert Paper: Sex Offender Research, NHS National Programme on Forensic Mental Health Research and Development*. Liverpool: Forensic Mental Health.

Grubin, D. (2008) 'The Use of Medication in the Treatment of Sex Offenders', *Prison Service Journal*, 178: 37–43.

Gys, L. and Gooren, L. (1996) 'Hormonal and Psychopharmacological Interventions in the Treatment of Paraphilias: An Update', *Journal of Sex Research*, 33(4): 273–290.

Harrison, K. (2007) 'The High Risk Sex Offender Strategy in England and Wales: Is Chemical Castration an Option?', *Howard Journal*, 46(1): 16–31.

Harrison, K. (2008) 'Legal and Ethical Issues When Using Antiandrogenic Pharmacotherapy with Sex Offenders', *Sexual Offender Treatment*, 3(2) [online]. Available at http://www.sexual-offender-treatment.org/2-2008_01.html (accessed 29 July 2008).

Harrison, K. and Rainey, B. (2009) 'Suppressing Human Rights? A Rights-Based Approach to the Use of Pharmacotherapy with Sex Offenders', *Legal Studies*, 29(1): 47–74.

Heller, C. G., Laidlaw, W. M., Harvey, H. T. and Nelson, W. O. (1958) 'Effects of Progestational Compounds on the Reproductive Processes of the Human Male', *Annals of the New York Academy of Sciences*, 71: 649–665.

Hicks, P. (1993) 'Castration of Sexual Offenders: Legal and Ethical Issues', *Journal of Legal Medicine*, 14: 641–667.

Home Office (2007) *Review for the Protection of Children from Sex Offenders*. London: Home Office.

Hutton, E. L. and Reiss, M. (1942) 'The Hormone Treatment of Acromegaly', *Journal of Mental Science*, 88: 550–553.

Icenogle, D. L. (1994) 'Sentencing Male Sex Offenders to the Use of Biological Treatments. A Constitutional Analysis', *Journal of Legal Medicine*, 15: 279–304.

Kafka, M. P. (1997) 'A Monoamine Hypothesis for the Pathophysiology of Paraphilic Disorders', *Archives of Sexual Behavior*, 26(4): 343–358.

Kafka, M. P. (2001) 'The Role of Medications in the Treatment of Paraphilia-related Disorders', *Sexual and Relationship Therapy*, 16(2): 105-112.

Kafka, M. P. (2006) 'Pharmacological Treatments for Sexual Offenders: How Can We Reduce Sexual Motivation and Impulsivity Associated with Sexual Offending?', *IATSO conference*, Hamburg, 2006.

Kafka, M. P. and Coleman, E. (1991) 'Serotonin and Paraphilias: The Convergence of Mood, Impulse and Compulsive Disorders', *Journal of Clinical Psychopharmacology*, 11: 223-224.

Krueger, R. B. and Kaplan, M. S. (2001) 'Depot-Leuprolide Acetate for Treatment of Paraphilias: A Report of Twelve Cases', *Archives of Sexual Behaviour*, 30(4): 409–422.

Kruesi, M. J. P., Fine, S., Valladares, L., Phillips, R. A. Jr. and Rapoport, J. L. (1992) 'Paraphilias: A Double-Blind Crossover Comparison of Clomipramine Versus Desipramine', *Archives of Sexual Behavior*, 21(6): 587–593.

Leiblum, S. R. and Rosen, R. C. (1988) 'Changing Perspectives on Sexual Desire', in S. R. Leiblum and R. C. Rosen (eds), *Sexual Desire Disorders*. New York: Guilford Press.

Lockhart, L. L., Saunders, B. E. and Cleveland, P. (1989) 'Adult Male Sexual Offenders: An Overview of Treatment Techniques' in J. S. Wodarski and D. L. Whitaker (eds), *Treatment of Sex Offenders in Social Work and Mental Health Settings*. Philadelphia: Haworth Press.

Maletzky, B. M. (1980) 'Self-Referred Versus Court-referred Sexually Deviant Patients: Success with Assisted Covert Sensitization', *Behavior Therapy*, 11: 306–314.

Maletzky, B. M. and Field, G. (2003) 'The Biological Treatment of Dangerous Sexual Offenders: A Review and Preliminary Report of the Oregon Pilot Depo-Provera Program', *Aggression and Violent Behavior*, 8: 391–412.

Maletzky, B. M., Tolan, A. and McFarland, B. (2006) 'The Oregon Depo-Provera Program: A Five-Year Follow-Up', *Sex Abuse*, 18: 303–316.

Melella, J. T., Travin, S. and Cullen, K. (1989) 'Legal and Ethical Issues in the Use of Anti-Androgens in Treating Sex Offenders', *Bulletin of the American Academy of Psychiatry and the Law*, 17(3): 223–31.

Meyer, W. J. and Cole, C. M. (1997) 'Physical and Chemical Castration of Sex Offenders: A Review', *Journal of Offender Rehabilitation*, 25(3/4): 1–18.

Meyer, W. J., Cole, C. and Emory, E. (1992) 'Depo-Provera Treatment for Sex Offending Behavior: An Evaluation of Outcome', *Bulletin of the American Academy of Psychiatry and the Law*, 20(3): 249–259.

Miller, R. D. (1998) 'Forced Administration of Sex-Drive Reducing Medications to Sex Offenders: Treatment or Punishment?', *Psychology, Public Policy and Law*, 4(1/2): 175–199.

Money, J. M. (1970) 'Use of Androgen-Depleting Hormone in the Treatment of Sex Offenders', *Journal of Sex Research*, 6: 167–172.

Money, J. M. (1972) 'The Therapeutic Use of Androgen-Depleting Hormone', *International Psychiatry Clinics*, 8: 165–174.

Money, J. M. (1979) 'Ideas and Ethics of Psychosexual Determinism', *British Journal of Sexual Medicine*, May: 27–32.

Money, J. M. (1987) 'Treatment Guidelines: Anti-androgen and Counselling of Paraphilic Sex Offenders', *Journal of Sex and Marital Therapy*, 13(3): 219–223.

Money, J., Wiedeking, C., Walker, P. A. and Gain, D. (1976) 'Combined Antiandrogenic and Counselling Program for Treatment of 46, XY and 47, XYY Sex Offenders', in E. J. Sachar (ed.), *Hormones, Behavior and Psychopathology*. New York: Raven.

Munafo, R. (1994) *Sex Offender Treatment Project: Literature Review*. University of Alaska Anchorage: Justice Center.

Murphy, C. (2007) 'Can Drugs Help Sex Offenders?', *BBC News* [online]. Available at: http://news.bbc.co.uk/1/hi/uk/6748789.stm (accessed 18 July 2008).

NetDoctor (2008) *Androcur* [online]. Available at: http://www.netdoctor. co.uk/medicines/100000131.html (accessed 29 July 2008).

NOMS (2007) *Medical Treatment for Sex Offenders*. Probation Circular 35/2007. London: NOMS.

Ortmann, J. (1980) 'The Treatment of Sexual Offenders: Castration and Antihormone Therapy', *International Journal of Law and Psychiatry*, 3: 443–51.

Pearson, H. J. (1990) 'Paraphilias, Impulse Control, and Serotonin', *Journal of Clinical Psychopharmacology*, 10: 233.

Polak, M. A. and Nijman, H. (2005) 'Pharmacological Treatment of Sexually Aggressive Forensic Psychiatric Patients', *Psychology, Crime and Law*, 11(4): 457–465.

Prentky, R. A. (1997) 'Arousal Reduction in Sexual Offenders. A Review of Antiandrogen Interventions', *Sexual Abuse: A Journal of Research and Treatment*, 9(4): 335–347.

Prentky, R. and Burgess, A. W. (1990) 'Rehabilitation of Child Molesters: A Cost-Benefit Analysis', *American Journal of Orthopsychiatry*, 60(1): 108–117.

Rieber, I. and Sigusch, V. (1979) 'Psychosurgery on Sex Offenders and Sexual "Deviants" in West Germany', *Archives of Sexual Behavior*, 8(6): 523–527.

Rösler, A. and Witztum, E. (1998) 'Treatment of Men with Paraphilia with a Long-Acting Analogue of Gonadotropin-releasing Hormone', *New England Journal of Medicine*, 338: 416–422.

Rösler, A. and Witztum, E. (2000) 'Pharmacotherapy of the Paraphilias in the Next Millennium', *Behavioral Sciences and the Law*, 18: 43–56.

Rousseau, L., Couture, M., Dupont, A., Labrie, F. and Couture, N. (1990) 'Effect of Combined Androgen Blockade with an LHRH Agonist and Flutamide in One Severe Case of Male Exhibitionism', *Canadian Journal of Psychiatry*, 35(4): 338–341.

Russell, S. (1997) 'Castration of Repeat Sexual Offenders: An International Comparative Analysis', *Houston Journal of International Law*, 19: 425–459.

Saleh, F. (2005) 'A Hypersexual Paraphilic Patient Treated with Leuprolide Acetate: A Single Case Report', *Journal of Sex and Marital Therapy*, 31: 433–444.

Saleh, F. M., Niel, T. and Fishman, M. J. (2004) 'Treatment of Paraphilia in Young Adults with Leuprolide Acetate: A Preliminary Case Report Series', *Journal of Forensic Science*, 49(6): 1343–1348.

Schober, J. M., Kuhn, P. J., Kovacs, P., Earle, J., Byrne, P. and Fries, R. (2005) 'Leuprolide Acetate Suppresses Pedophilic Urges and Arousability', *Archives of Sexual Behavior*, 34: 691–705.

Sim, J. (1990) *Medical Power in Prisons: The Prison Medical Service in England 1774–1989*. Buckingham: Open University Press.

Stone, T. H., Winslade, W. J. and Klugman, C. M. (2000) 'Sex Offenders, Sentencing Laws and Pharmaceutical Treatment: A Prescription for Failure', *Behavioral Sciences and the Law*, 18: 83–110.

Thibaut, F. Cordier, B. and Kuhn, J.-M. (1996) 'Gonadotropin Hormone Releasing Hormone Agonist in Cases of Severe Paraphilia: A Lifetime Treatment?', *Psychoneuroendocrinology*, 21(4): 411–119.

Weiss, P. (1999) 'Assessment and Treatment of Sex Offenders in the Czech Republic and in Eastern Europe', *Journal of Interpersonal Violence*, 14(4): 411–421.

Wille, R. and Beier, K. (1989) 'Castration in Germany', *Annals of Sex Research*, 2: 103–133.

Wincze, J. P., Bansal, S. and Malamud, M. (1986) 'Effects of Medroxyprogesterone Acetate on Subjective Arousal, Arousal to Erotic Stimulation, and Nocturnal Penile Tumescence in Male Sex Offenders', *Archives of Sexual Behaviour*, 15(4): 293–305.

Zohar, J., Kaplan, Z. and Benjamin, J. (1994) 'Compulsive Exhibitionism Successfully Treated with Fluvoxamine: A Controlled Case Study', *Journal of Clinical Psychiatry*, 55(3): 86–88.

Chapter 7

Restorative justice and the reintegration of high-risk sex offenders

Anne-Marie McAlinden

This chapter considers the use of restorative justice as a means of reducing the risk posed by high-risk sex offenders.[1] A number of restorative schemes have been developed in recent years largely as a rejoinder to the failings of traditional popular and state-led responses to managing sex offenders in the community. Official measures such as sex offender notification and popular responses by the media and the public in the form of 'Name and Shame' campaigns have resulted in the marginalisation of sex offenders and a possible increased risk of reoffending. Circles of Support and Accountability (COSA), which originated in Canada but are beginning to be developed in other jurisdictions including England and Wales, have been used successfully with high-risk sex offenders who are re-entering the community on release from prison. Based broadly on restorative principles, these programmes entail the development of informal networks of support and treatment involving the offender, the wider community, and state or voluntary agencies.

This chapter argues that restorative programmes may operate as a practical means of addressing the core problems concerning the reintegration of high-risk sex offenders, namely meeting the offender's rehabilitative needs and allaying public anxieties concerning the presence of sex offenders in the community. The growing empirical evidence demonstrates that restorative justice has been effective not only in reducing sex offender recidivism but also in providing a means of positive engagement with the local community around sex offender reintegration. It will be argued that criminal justice policy and practice need to recognise the potential of restorative programmes in this context and adopt these on a more extensive basis. Arguably, two of the most contentious issues in contemporary restorative justice debates are whether restorative justice should be applied to serious forms of offending, and the nature of its relationship with formal criminal justice (Dignan *et al.* 2007). These two issues lie at the heart of discourses on devising alternative responses to the reintegration of high-risk sex offenders and will be discussed further below.

The case for restorative justice: the failure of retributive responses

The advancement of restorative justice as a response to sexual crime has arisen, in large part, from the failings of retributive public shaming approaches (McAlinden 2005, 2007). The last decade has been marked by heightened public and official concerns over the dangers posed by released sex offenders. However, punitive legislative and judicial responses to sexual crime, together with vengeful media and public attitudes, have impeded offender reintegration and ultimately undermined effective risk management.

State-led responses to sexual crime

As noted elsewhere in this volume, recent legislative and policy attempts at offender reintegration, particularly within the UK, have been heavily premised on risk assessment and management. The related notions of risk, regulation and governance have featured prominently in socio-political discourses on security and justice (Ericson and Haggerty 1997; Shearing 2000; Loader and Walker 2007). These in turn have been translated into a range of criminal justice policies which are focused on pre-emptive regulatory approaches to crime (O'Malley 2004; Ericson 2007; Zedner 2009), most notably in relation to regulating the behaviour of sex offenders on release from custody (Hebenton and Thomas 1996; Kemshall and Maguire 2001; Matravers 2003).

In the UK, in the mid-1990s, a range of policy proposals aimed at controlling sex offenders in the community more effectively (Home Office 1996a, 1996b) eventually became embodied in a range of legislation. The most notable perhaps of these recent measures is sex offender registration and community notification, which is discussed in Chapter 4 of this volume. Following the enactment of Megan's Law in the USA, Part II of the Sexual Offences Act 2003[2] requires certain classes of sex offender to register their details with the police. Registration of the offender's personal details and notification of this information to the community in particular may result in a social stigma being attached to the offender (Edwards and Hensley 2001; McAlinden 2005). Such concerns have been particularly prevalent in the USA where there is a much wider degree of notification permitted to the local community (Bedarf 1995; Earl-Hubbard 1996; van Dujn 1999).

In many US states, mandatory self-notification variously requires sex offenders to wear a scarlet letter 'S' on the front of their clothing to denote their status as a convicted sexual offender, to hand out flyers or notices to their neighbours which contain their photograph and details of their offending history, or go door to door personally informing local residents that they are a convicted sexual offender (Bedarf 1995; Petrunik 2002). In addition, law enforcement officials may also distribute information about offenders via wanted posters and online databases and email alerts of all known local sex offenders (van Dujn 1999). The UK has thus far resisted public calls for a similarly constituted Sarah's Law that would permit a much wider degree of public disclosure (Rutherford 2000; Thomas 2003). The pilot scheme, however, to allow single parents in particular to have access to the offending history of those who have regular contact with their children indicates that legislation in this area is a real possibility[3] (for more information on this, see Chapter 13 of this volume).

In addition, a minority of judges in the USA have also used shame penalties as part of probation conditions, particularly for sex offenders (Brilliant 1989; Massaro 1991; Karp 1998). The courts have required, *inter alia*, convicted sex offenders to post signs on their car and on the door of their home in large lettering that read: 'Dangerous Sex Offender – No Children Allowed',[4] or to place ads in the local newspaper publicising their offences (Massaro 1991). Clearly, the aim of such sanctions is public protection by warning society of the potential danger these offenders pose. However, the threat of social stigma and exclusion also attaches to those who are subject to such penalties.

Popular responses to sexual crime

Official concerns over the risk posed by released sex offenders in the community have also been reflected in popular discourses. As part of what has been termed a vicious policy cycle (Brownlee 1998; McAlinden 2007), punitive political rhetoric fuels public concerns about sexual offenders and at the same time provides a rationale and increased demand for regulatory measures meant to alleviate these fears.

One of the best illustrations of punitive public attitudes towards sex offenders and their attendant consequences is perhaps the aftermath of *The News of the World*'s 'Name and Shame' media crusade in the wake of the murder of Sarah Payne in July 2000. The campaign aimed to publicly identify suspected and known paedophiles by printing their photographs, names and addresses, along with details of their offending history. At the height of the campaign, public hysteria and vigilante activity was rife in Portsmouth, where local residents protested at the presence of paedophiles in their community. Protesters demonstrated outside the homes of suspected paedophiles issuing threats, with attendant criminal damage to properties and vehicles. Famously, the work premises of a local paediatrician were also vandalised due to the mistaken association with the word 'paedophile'. As a result, several families fled the area, one convicted paedophile disappeared, and two suspected paedophiles committed suicide (Ashenden 2002; Williams and Thompson 2004a, 2004b).

This example illustrates the fact that punitive popular responses to released sex offenders by the media and the public may, at worst, lead to violence or vigilante action by vengeful members of the community on suspected paedophiles. Stigmatisation of the offender, however, in the form of both state-led and popular responses to sexual offending, may have a number of other detrimental consequences for sex offender reintegration.

The effects of public shaming approaches

The disintegrative effects of public shaming approaches that undermine effective rehabilitative efforts with sex offenders can best be explained by reference to Braithwaite's (1989) dichotomy of disintegrative and reintegrative shaming. According to this theory, the ways in which not only the state, but also society, the community and the family sanction deviance affect the extent to which their members engage in criminal behaviour. Braithwaite makes the distinction between two types of society and related shaming practices. He argues that communitarian societies (where there is a high degree of interdependence and strong cultural commitments to group interests) are better able than others (where there is a lower level of interdependence and greater concern for individualism) to informally sanction deviance and reintegrate deviants by shaming the offence, rather than permanently stigmatising the offender through formal penal measures (Braithwaite 1989).

Reintegrative shaming reinforces an offender's membership in civil society (Braithwaite 1989). It involves the overt disapproval of the delinquent act (shaming), rather than the person, by socially significant members and, at the same time, the inclusion of the offender within an interdependent relationship (reintegration) (Zhang 1995). In contrast, with disintegrative shaming, little or no effort is made to forgive offenders and therefore reinforce their membership in the law-abiding community. Stigmatisation shuns offenders and treats them as outcasts and may as a result provoke a rebellious and criminal reaction from them (Karp 1998).

The concept of disintegrative shaming has for the most part informed contemporary state-led and popular responses to the reintegration of high-risk sex offenders. Official measures, such as registration and notification, and novel probation conditions, in common with popular name and shame campaigns, may serve to label and stigmatise the offender and isolate him from the rest of the community in a number of ways (Winick 1998). Firstly, it may impede his successful reintegration, his ability to obtain employment or accommodation, and therefore his ultimate rehabilitation (Bedarf 1995; Soothill and Francis 1998). Secondly, heightening the offender's sense of isolation may increase the chance of subsequent delinquent behaviour as a coping mechanism (Braithwaite and Mugford 1994; Edwards and Hensley 2001). Thirdly, from the deviancy amplification spiral[5] of the labelling perspective (Wilkins 1964), offenders who are isolated from normal law-abiding society may be forced to associate with similar offenders, from whom they learn more sophisticated techniques. Fourthly, if an offender becomes ostracised in the area where he lives, he will simply go underground thereby increasing or displacing the risk of reoffending (Soothill and Francis 1998).

Consistent with Braithwaite's thesis, disintegrative public shaming practices in the form of punitive criminal justice or social responses will not deter offenders, protect victims, or reduce recidivism levels, except perhaps in the short term. Without structured community programmes to support offender readjustment, help victims to protect themselves, and engage communities in a constructive way, stigmatisation may well result in more incidents of sexual offences in the long term (Finstad 1990; Braithwaite and Daly 1994; Hudson 1998).

Restorative justice: the contemporary policy context

As noted at the outset, the growth of restorative programmes can in one sense be attributed to the failings of modern criminal justice and the attendant need to develop a more effective response. Restorative justice, however, generally assumes that the offender has already accepted responsibility for an offence. It is therefore, not a fact-finding process aimed at determining guilt, but is concerned rather with developing an appropriate response to acknowledged behaviour. Moreover, restorative schemes may operate either in conjunction with formal justice or as a diversionary process. As will be explained further below, it is the former model which is envisaged here as a response to sexual offending.

In comparison with retributive justice, restorative justice views crime not as a violation of a legal norm that necessitates punishment but as harm to people and relationships and, as the term suggests, seeks to redress or undo that harm (Zehr 1990; van Ness and Strong 1997). In this respect, restorative or reintegrative approaches are usually based on the following core values and principles: empowerment of and respect for all the parties affected by the offence; collective, non-coercive participation and decision making; and a neutral process that aims to deal with the aftermath of the offence (Marshall 1999). Additionally, the restorative paradigm has a number of related aims: engaging with offenders to help them appreciate the consequences of their actions, encouraging appropriate forms of reparation by offenders to their victim or the wider community, seeking reconciliation between the victim and offender where this is desirable, and preventing future offending and reintegrating the offender (Zehr 1990; Braithwaite 1999).

'Restorative justice' is in one sense an umbrella term used to cover a growing body of practices and processes that seek to respond to crime in a more productive way than through the use of conventional criminal justice (Galaway and Hudson 1996). The main variants, however, are mediation (Marshall 1991; Davis 1992; Umbreit 1994) and conferencing (Retzinger and Scheff 1996; Morris and Maxwell 2000). The traditional domain of restorative justice has generally been low-level crime and first-time or young offenders. In the UK, for example, it has been used to transform criminal justice policies in key areas such as youth justice.[6] The restorative conferencing programmes in England and Australia deal only with adult and juvenile offenders charged with moderately serious crimes. Similarly, New Zealand applies restorative practices to adult offenders who have committed relatively serious offences (Morris and Maxwell 2003) and to all juvenile crimes except murder and manslaughter (Morris and Maxwell 2000).

More recently, however, a number of initiatives have emerged that have adopted restorative interventions for adult offenders and for very serious social problems. In this vein, it has been used in the Truth and Reconciliation Commissions of South Africa (Villa Vincenzo 1999) and Rwanda (Drumbl 2000) in relation to genocide, mass torture and rape and with respect to paramilitary violence in Northern Ireland (McEvoy and Mika 2001). In the USA, victim–offender mediation has been used with homicide and serious sexual assault and also between a murderer on death row and the family of his victim (Umbreit *et al.* 1999). Similarly, intimate abuse circles have also been considered by American judges, albeit with some controversy, as a response to domestic violence (Mills 2003). These circles, closely based on restorative principles and derived in large part from the Truth and Reconciliation Commissions of South Africa, are similar in some respects to their Canadian counterpart, COSA, which will be discussed below. They provide a medium for addressing the abusive process and, depending on the extent of the violence and the wishes of the participants, may involve both parties and a care community, comprising family, friends or the clergy, who come together to promote offender accountability and rehabilitation. On balance, it is perhaps the application of the restorative paradigm to sexual offending that remains the most controversial.

Restorative justice and sexual offending

With sexual offences, a few isolated initiatives have developed that are based on reintegrative or restorative principles. In South Australia, for example, young people charged with sexual offences who admit their behaviour are diverted from court processes and participate instead in a family conference (Daly 2006). The family decision-making model in Australia and North Carolina has also used a conference-style process with children and families affected by child sexual abuse and domestic violence, although usually the offender is excluded (Pennell 2006). In Arizona, the RESTORE programme has used restorative justice as a response to date and acquaintance rape by first-time adult offenders and those charged with misdemeanour sexual offences (Koss *et al.* 2003). Two of the best-known international programmes, however, are 'Stop It Now!', and COSA.

Stop It Now!

The Stop It Now! programme originated in Vermont, but now also operates across the USA as well as in the UK, the Republic of Ireland and Australia. It is in essence a prevention programme aiming to stop child sexual abuse by encouraging abusers and potential abusers to recognise their behaviour as abusive, and by educating the public about child sexual abuse so that people are more open about abuse and can take the necessary steps to protect children. These aims of protection and prevention are delivered through a number of local projects, including media campaigns, public information leaflets, training for professionals, and public meetings. In addition, a free confidential national helpline has also been set up, offering advice and support to people who suspect that someone they know presents a risk to a child and as an avenue to treatment resources for those abusers seeking help to desist.

The programme is based on the following core values: protecting children, by raising awareness and understanding of the nature and scale of sexual abuse and the ways in which abusers operate; balancing understanding with accountability, by recognising that sex offenders are not the monsters of popular imagination, while at the same time holding them responsible for the consequences of their behaviour; developing a public health approach, by acknowledging that the scale of the problem requires a social response to prevention; and working together, by building partnerships between key statutory and voluntary agencies in the areas of child protection, criminal justice, and health and in developing links with the local community in specific areas.

Many of the core elements of the programme, in particular media and information campaigns and organised community forums, have strong restorative or reintegrative potential. These schemes constitute a very positive social response to child sexual abuse and the problem of managing the risk posed by sex offenders in the community. They promote understanding of child sexual abuse and abusers and encourage responsible action on the part of the community. At the same time, however, they also offer a means of holding offenders accountable and providing them with support in their effort to desist. The ethos of the programme is well encapsulated in the following:

> With the majority of these people, even if they go to prison, they will be released into the community.... To ensure community safety, we need to be able to support them.... A sex abuser

who is isolated and driven underground is much more likely to reoffend than one who has support in place in the community. (Gatos 1999).

Circles of Support and Accountability

One of the most established programmes is perhaps COSA. Circle programmes originated in Canada more than a decade ago as a response to the reintegration of several high-profile and high-risk sex offenders (Cesaroni 2001; Petrunik 2002; Wilson *et al*. 2002).[7] More recently, circles have been extended to other jurisdictions such as Northern Ireland and England and Wales on a pilot basis. Here they have been used to support the work of the police, the probation service and other agencies in the multi-agency approach to sex offender risk management. Important differences, therefore, exist between these two main models. While the Canadian model is said to be organic, the model which exists in England and Wales is rather more systemic (Quaker Peace and Social Witness 2005).

At a broad level, these post-release schemes involve the development of support and treatment networks for sex offenders where the community works in partnership with the offender and professional agencies (McAlinden 2005, 2007). The schemes are based on the twin philosophies of safety and support. They operate as a means of addressing public concerns and also the offender's needs concerning reintegration. Each circle is individually tailored around the offender as the core member. The offender and other members of the circle enter into a covenant that specifies each member's area of assistance. The trained volunteers provide high levels of support and guidance for the offender, and can mediate between the police, media and the wider community to minimise risk and assist with reintegration. This includes addressing all aspects of the offender's life necessary for successful reintegration, including finding suitable accommodation and employment, and not just their abusive behaviour. The offender agrees, in turn, to relate to the circle, pursue treatment, and act responsibly in the community. The offender has contact with someone from the circle each day in the high-risk phase following release. The circle remains in place as long as the risk to the community and the offender are above average.

Programmes are tailored in particular to elements of reintegrative shaming as outlined above (Braithwaite 1989). Circles are accompanied by one of the principal hallmarks of reintegrative shame cultures – the aim is to control wrongdoers within a communitarian society and informally sanction deviance by reintegration into cohesive networks, rather than by formal restraint (Braithwaite 1989). Reintegrative shaming mechanisms bring relevant community members together in an organised forum that evokes shame in the offender and promotes reintegration. As Petrunik (2002) puts it, 'Rather than being driven from neighborhood to neighborhood like some tormented Frankenstein and perhaps reoffending in despair that he can never be any different, the sex offender is given a chance to redeem himself under the caring but ever so watchful eyes of a concerned community' (506). Circles aim to allay the fears of the local community and, at the same time, reduce the likelihood of further offending by holding offenders accountable to their commitment not to reoffend. In this vein, evaluations of their effectiveness have shown positive results.

The effectiveness of restorative justice with sexual offending

Advocates of restorative justice generally contend that it is more likely than retributive justice to reduce sexual recidivism rates because of its central concern for the safety of victims. The majority of evaluation studies have been carried out on the two main models of mediation and conferencing (Miers *et al.* 2001; Kurki 2003). At a general level, these studies have demonstrated that restorative justice can have a reductive effect in certain cases and can change the behaviour of some offenders.

At the same time, however, restorative justice has wider outcome measures than traditional regulatory responses. Aside from rates of reoffending, there are other important measures of outcome. These include, *inter alia*, overall contribution to community safety, victim, offender and community involvement, offender reintegration,[8] improvement in the relationship between offenders and their families and the local community, and reparation to victims and the wider community (Maxwell and Morris 1999, 2002). Some of these aspects have also been captured in recent evaluations of programmes involving sexual offending.

An archival study of nearly 400 court and conference cases of youth sexual assault in South Australia over a 6½-year period demonstrates that the conference may be less victimising than the court process and may produce more effective outcomes (Daly 2006). Overall, the rate of reoffending was much higher for those young offenders dealt with by the court (66 per cent) than by the conference process (48 per cent). Several studies have examined the effectiveness of the Stop It Now!

programme (Tabachnik and Chasan-Taber 1999; Klein and Tabachnik 2002). In Vermont, 50 persons reported for treatment between 1995 and 1997. This figure comprised 11 adults who self-reported and 39 adolescents who entered treatment as a result of a parent or guardian (Tabachnik *et al*. 2001). An earlier study also found that the incidence of reoffending dropped from 38 per cent to 6 per cent.[9]

The growing empirical data emerging from the evaluation of circle programmes in particular demonstrate that they can be effective in enhancing community safety and offender desistance on two important levels: reducing recidivism rates (Wilson *et al*. 2002, 2007c) and engaging communities in the reintegrative process (Quaker Peace and Social Witness 2005; Wilson *et al*. 2007a, 2007b). One evaluation of circles in Ontario found that recidivism was reduced by more than 50 per cent where each incident of reoffending was less invasive and severe than the original offence for which the offender had been imprisoned (Wilson *et al*. 2002). In a more recent study by Wilson and colleagues, offenders who participated in the project had significantly lower levels of any type of reoffending – there was a 70 per cent reduction in sexual recidivism, a 57 per cent reduction in all types of violent recidivism, and a 35 per cent reduction overall (Wilson *et al*. 2007c). Early evaluations of these projects in England and Wales have also shown that circles have been effective in reducing expected rates of recidivism and assisting in offender rehabilitation. Moreover, despite early misgivings, communities were willing to play a constructive role in this process (Quaker Peace and Social Witness 2005).

In addition to actual reconviction rates, which may not always provide an accurate picture of actual criminality (Friendship and Thornton 2001; Friendship *et al*. 2002), the literature also refers to pro-offending behaviour, which might precede eventual recidivism (Falshaw *et al*. 2003). Research also suggests that these soft data, routinely held by circles, are crucially important in evaluating the effectiveness of interventions (Bates *et al*. 2004; Quaker Peace and Social Witness 2005). In the pilot projects in England and Wales, only 8 out of 20 core members were identified as displaying early recidivist behaviour, including activities known to be part of the *modus operandi* of previous offences. Of these offenders, only three men were recalled to prison for breaching the terms of their release, none of whom had committed further sexual offences. One core member, however, was reconvicted of breaching a sexual offences prevention order (Quaker Peace and Social Witness 2005).[10] In each case, the recall was facilitated by information passed to the authorities by circle members. Without the intervention of the circle at such an early stage, progression to reoffence may well have occurred (Quaker Peace and Social Witness, 2005).

Taken together, these findings are highly indicative of the account-ability aspect of the work of circles and demonstrate effectively the critical role that they may have in managing high-risk sex offenders in the community. Moreover, they also highlight the fact that the circle model potentially offers professional agencies a clear means of actively and positively engaging with the local community on controversial sex offender issues (Quaker Peace and Social Witness 2005).

Addressing the critics

Conceptions and processes of restorative justice have been subjected to rigorous debate. On one level, opponents of restorative justice as a whole have pointed out the latent dangers of a communitarian approach to justice, chiefly the need to secure legitimacy (Paternoster *et al.* 1997), accountability (Roche 2003), and adequate safeguards (Ashworth 2002; Wright 2002). On another level, opinions also differ on the types of offences for which restorative processes are suitable. While some scholars accept the viability of restorative justice in dealing with low-level offending, they are usually more reluctant to extend this paradigm to serious and persistent forms of offending (Johnstone 2003).

More recently, there has been increased feminist engagement with new forms of justice (Daly and Stubbs 2006) and a growing recognition that restorative justice initiatives may have a role in dealing with intimate violence and abuse (Mills 2003; Cameron 2006; Coker 2006) in carefully selected or managed contexts. For the most part, however, as Daly (2006) puts it, 'sexual offences have been excluded from the RJ agenda' (334). Many writers have highlighted the particular unsuitability of restorative programmes in the domain of sexual or domestic violence (Koss 2000; Presser and Gaarder 2000; Busch 2002; Stubbs 2007). The majority of critiques have been formulated in the context of restorative systems involving adult victims and those who commit non-sexual offences. However, for critics, the application of the restorative approach to sexual offending and to child sexual abuse in particular, adds extra dimensions to the problem (Cossins 2008).

In this respect, a number of traditional critiques are advanced by opponents of restorative justice as applied to sexual crime. For these critics, sexual offending is considered an inappropriate or too delicate an area within which to use a restorative response. Without a wish to oversimplify their arguments, it is proposed within the space constraints to summarise these core arguments and how they can be overcome. In the main, it has been suggested by the detractors that restorative justice trivialises what is a very serious crime, particularly where children and the vulnerable are concerned; it fails to hold the offender accountable and allows the offender to reject responsibility for the offence; it reinforces the imbalance of power ingrained in abusive relationships and leads to possible revictimisation; and it promotes vigilantism (McAlinden 2007; Cossins 2008).

Proponents, on the other hand, have addressed these critiques concerning so-called hard cases in both theoretical and empirical contexts (Hudson 1998, 2002; Daly 2002, 2008; Morris and Gelsthorpe 2000; Morris 2002; McAlinden 2005). They counter that even though formal criminal law remains an important moral symbol of state sanctioning and social condemnation, restorative processes that involve the offender's immediate family and the community can meet the expressive need for censure in sexual offences cases; that while the criminal justice system does little to hold offenders accountable and address established patterns of offending, restorative justice seeks genuine engagement with offenders to help them acknowledge the effects of their wrongdoing, as it focuses on the empowerment of victims in a supportive environment in which the victim can make clear to the offender the effects of the abuse on them; that by offering constructive rather than purely penal solutions, it may be employed at an earlier stage in the victim's experience of abuse; and, finally, that distortions of power, including abuse of community control, are addressed when programmes adhere closely to restorative principles.

In addition, critics of reintegrative theory also argue that there are a number of more practical difficulties, meaning that such schemes will not easily be implemented in contemporary Western society (McAlinden 2007). These include the lack of empirical research to date, the lack of social and norm cohesion in contemporary society, the difficulties in promoting social inclusion, and the contestable nature of the terms 'community' and 'partnership'. Advocates, however, contend that restorative justice, as argued above, has outcome measures that are much broader than reoffending rates (Maxwell and Morris 1999, 2002); that popular responses to sex offending demonstrate that, if anything, there is clear consensus concerning the wrongness of sexual relationships between adults and children in particular (Hacking 1999); that the provision of accurate information about the nature and extent of sexual crime and appropriate responses to it, should dispel the commonly held misconceptions, shift public opinion, and help to promote social inclusion (Grubin 1998); and, finally, that the involvement of professional agencies in community-based schemes will help to keep the community in check while also ensuring state and organisational accountability (Crawford 1999). In effect, contrary to the major arguments put forward by the critics, it is argued here and elsewhere (McAlinden 2005, 2007) that some sex offenders may be suitable for a restorative approach in carefully managed contexts. The question then becomes, how would this be workable in practice?

Extending the use of restorative justice to manage risk

As noted at the outset, for advocates, restorative justice is ultimately envisaged as a more proactive and effective response to the problems of gendered and sexualised violence (Hudson 2002) than that currently provided by the traditional criminal law. Contrary to the concerns of critics, it has been argued that it provides a viable means of addressing the offender's rehabilitative needs while at the same time safeguarding the concerns and interests of victims and communities in terms of effective public protection. Extending the use of restorative justice with sexual offenders beyond the largely piecemeal approach that exists at present in turn raises a number of issues. These include the nature of the relationship with formal state justice and the necessary prerequisites, if any, of adopting such schemes.

The relationship of restorative justice with retributive justice

Some scholars continue to emphasise the difference of the restorative vision as a fundamental shift in criminal law (Zehr 1990, 1995; Bazemore 1996; Barnett 2003). Others, however, call for recognition of alternative forms of justice and highlight the compatibility of restoration and retribution. According to this view, the two concepts may be integrated as part of the same system of justice where they would complement each other rather than operate as dichotomous systems (Zedner 1994; Daly 2000; Duff 2002, Hudson 2002).[11]

As noted above, in practice, restorative justice may operate either within or outside the traditional justice system (Zehr 1990).

An example of the latter is the use of community restorative justice schemes with paramilitary groups in Northern Ireland (McEvoy and Mika 2001). An example of the former is the use of restorative justice as the mainstay of the youth justice system in England and Wales, where criminal justice remains as the formal backdrop to be used as a last resort with more persistent offenders (Crawford and Newburn 2003). In relation to sexual offences, however, it is contended that programmes should be extended as part of the current mainstream criminal justice response. All but the most minor of sexual offences could be processed through the criminal justice system initially. Restorative community programmes would then be available on release from custody on the basis of a referral by a statutory criminal justice agency. Schemes could be integrated into and accredited by the formal criminal justice system as part of multi-agency approaches to risk where the local community works in partnership with professional agencies (Crawford 1999). Such an approach would also go some way towards addressing the central concerns of critics as discussed above.

It is submitted, however, that there are a number of conditions which must first be put in place (McAlinden 2007). In particular, consensual and voluntary participation by both victims and offenders must be established as a cornerstone of the process. To force victims to participate could lead to further victimisation, while forcing offenders to do so may undermine the effectiveness of programmes (McAlinden 2005). There is also a very real need for a rigorous public education and awareness programme, driven by government, designed to provide accurate information about the nature and extent of sexual offending, including in particular that the greatest danger to children lies with those closest to them rather than predatory strangers (Grubin 1998). Such a programme would hopefully provide fertile ground for the fuller inception of reintegrative shaming practices by reducing the social exclusion and stigmatisation of offenders that can often undermine effective reintegration.

Addressing levels of risk

Moving from a purely punitive response to sex offending to one where retribution and restoration are combined will facilitate the management of both the known and unknown risks posed by sexual offenders. In short, in combination with the formal criminal justice system, restorative justice is itself presented as a regulatory approach to sexual crime (McAlinden 2007).

In this respect, research by Soothill and colleagues (Soothill *et al.* 2005) has identified three main categories of offender: known and high-risk, known but low-risk, and unknown risk. Restorative justice offers a practical means of managing the risk posed by each of these categories of offender. For example, known and high-risk offenders could continue to be prosecuted in the normal way and then reintegrated into the community via COSA on release. For known and low-risk or low to middle-risk offenders, circles could be used as an effective alternative to prosecution. As now happens with young offenders in England and Wales, the legal framework and more punitive sanctions, however, can be retained for use with habitual offenders (Crawford and Newburn 2003). This approach is similar, in some respects, to Braithwaite's enforcement pyramid which envisages restorative justice as part of an overall regulatory framework that includes deterrence and incapacitation, but, explicitly, not retribution (Braithwaite 1999, 2002). Moreover, by encouraging more offenders and victims to come forward, principally by reducing public vilification of offenders and the threat of punitive sanctions, it may also offer a critical means of probing and managing the unknown risk where offenders may be strongly suspected of sexual crime but have not actually been adjudicated upon.

Conclusion

Extending the restorative paradigm more fully to the domain of sexual offences raises a number of difficult theoretical questions, including what is appropriate terrain for restorative justice and the legitimate role of the state in such processes (Dignan *et al.* 2007). At the same time, it also raises more practical challenges concerning how this would fit within contemporary Western society, which has been dominated largely by the public shaming and vilification of sex offenders, particularly those against children. Restorative justice, in this respect, is presented as both a realistic and a workable response to the failings of formal criminal justice and as a way of extending the theoretical thinking on the use of restorative justice in hard cases. A growing body of evidence has demonstrated its effectiveness in terms of addressing the pivotal issues concerning the reintegration of high-risk sex offenders. These include rehabilitating offenders, improving public protection, and providing reassurances for victims and communities while at the same time engaging the community in the dynamic process of sex offender reintegration.

Notes

1   Arguments in this chapter are more fully developed in other recent works by the author (see McAlinden 2005, 2007).
2   This Act replaces Part I of the Sex Offenders Act 1997.
3   See, for example, 'Parents Get New Sex Crime Checks', *BBC News On-line*, 17 February 2008, Available at: http://news.bbc.co.uk/1/hi/uk/7249043. stm (accessed 20 February 2008).
4   *State v Bateman* 95 Or. Ct. App. 456, 771 P.2d 314 (1989).
5   This circuitous process begins when society becomes less tolerant of certain behaviour. This leads to more acts being defined and more action against criminals, who are more severely punished. In turn, this generates more crime by deviant groups. The net result is further social intolerance and alienation of deviants by conforming society, and the process begins all over again.
6   Under the Crime and Disorder Act 1998, the Youth Justice and Criminal Evidence Act 1999, and amending legislation, a range of restorative options is used with first-time young offenders.
7   In Canada, 'Sentencing Circles' (SC) are commonly used as well as 'Circles of Support and Accountability' (COSA). Although the terms are often used interchangeably they are distinct processes. SC can be utilised at the outset of the sanctioning process for a range of offences, while COSA focus specifically on the reintegration of high-risk sex offenders (Wilson *et al.* 2002).
8   Recent research in this respect has argued that restorative justice can be effective in promoting engagement with the idea as well as the process of desistance (Robinson and Shapland 2008).
9   See http://www.stopitnow.com/about.htm (accessed 22 October 2003).
10 Sexual Offences Prevention Orders, enacted under Part 2 of the Sexual Offences Act 2003, can be used to prohibit the offender from engaging in specified conduct in order to protect the public from serious harm. This particular offender secretly purchased a car, part of his previous *modus operandi*, and two girls aged 6 and 14 were found in his flat.
11 For others, however, restoration is potentially corroded by a partnership with retribution (Boyes-Watson 1999).

References

Ashenden, S. (2002) 'Policing Perversion: The Contemporary Governance of Paedophilia', *Cultural Values*, 6(1-2): 197–122.

Ashworth, A. (2002) 'Responsibilities, Rights and Restorative Justice', *British Journal of Criminology*, 42(3): 578–595.

Barnett, R. E. (2003) 'Restitution: A New Paradigm of Criminal Justice', in G. Johnstone (ed.) *A Restorative Justice Reader: Texts, Sources, Context.* Cullompton: Willan Publishing.

Bates, A., Falshaw, L., Corbett, C., Patel, V. and Friendship, C. (2004) 'A Follow-Up Study of Sex Offenders Treated by Thames Valley Sex Offender Group Work Programme 1995-99', *Journal of Sexual Aggression*, 10: 29–38.

Bazemore, G. (1996) 'Three Paradigms for Juvenile Justice', in B. Galaway and J. Hudson (eds), *Restorative Justice: International Perspectives*. Monsey, NY: Criminal Justice Press.

Bedarf, A. (1995) 'Examining Sex Offender Community Notification Laws', *California Law Review*, 83(3): 885-939.

Boyes-Watson, C. (1999) 'In the Belly of the Beast? Exploring the Dilemmas of State-Sponsored Restorative Justice', *Contemporary Justice Review*, 2(3): 261–281.

Braithwaite, J. (1989) *Crime, Shame and Reintegration*. Sydney: Cambridge University Press.

Braithwaite, J. (1999) 'Restorative Justice: Assessing Optimistic and Pessimistic Accounts', in M. Tonry (ed.), *Crime and Justice: A Review of Research*. Chicago: University of Chicago Press.

Braithwaite, J. (2002) *Restorative Justice and Responsive Regulation*. Oxford: Oxford University Press.

Braithwaite, J. and Daly, K. (1994) 'Masculinities, Violence and Communitarian Control', in T. Newburn and E. Stanko (eds), *Just Boys Doing Business? Men, Masculinity and Crime*. London: Routledge.

Braithwaite, J. and Mugford, S. (1994) 'Conditions of Successful Reintegration Ceremonies', *British Journal of Criminology*, 34(2): 139–171.

Brilliant, J. A. (1989) 'The Modern Day Scarlet Letter: A Critical Analysis of Modern Probation Conditions', *Duke Law Journal*, 5: 1357–1385.

Brownlee, I. (1998) 'New Labour – New Penology? Punitive Rhetoric and the Limits of Managerialism in Criminal Justice Policy', *Journal of Law and Society*, 25(3): 313–335.

Busch, R. (2002) 'Domestic Violence and Restorative Justice Initiatives: Who Pays If We Get It Wrong?', in H. Strang and J. Braithwaite (eds), *Restorative Justice and Family Violence*. Melbourne: Cambridge University Press.

Cameron, A. (2006) 'Stopping the Violence: Canadian Feminist Debates on Restorative Justice and Intimate Violence', *Theoretical Criminology*, 10(1): 49–66.

Cesaroni, C. (2001) 'Releasing Sex Offenders into the Community Through "Circles of Support" – A Means of Reintegrating the "Worst of the Worst"', *Journal of Offender Rehabilitation*, 34(2): 85–98.

Coker, D. (2006) 'Restorative Justice, Navajo Peacemaking and Domestic Violence', *Theoretical Criminology*, 10(1): 67–85.

Cossins, A. (2008) 'Restorative Justice and Child Sex Offences: The Theory and the Practice', *British Journal of Criminology*, 48(3): 359–378.

Crawford, A. (1999) *The Local Governance of Crime: Appeals to Community and Partnerships*. Oxford: Oxford University Press.

Crawford, A. and Newburn, T. (2003) *Youth Offending and Restorative Justice: Implementing Reform in Youth Justice*. Cullompton: Willan.

Daly, K. (2000) 'Revisiting the Relationship Between Retributive and Restorative Justice', in J. Braithwaite and H. Strang (eds), *Restorative Justice: Philosophy to Practice*. Aldershot: Ashgate.

Daly, K. (2002) 'Sexual Assault and Restorative Justice', in H. Strang and J. Braithwaite (eds), *Restorative Justice and Family Violence*. Melbourne: Cambridge University Press.

Daly, K. (2006) 'Restorative Justice and Sexual Assault: An Archival Study of Court and Conference Cases', *British Journal of Criminology*, 46(2): 334–356.

Daly, K. (2008) 'Setting the Record Straight and a Call for Radical Change: A Reply to Annie Cossins', *British Journal of Criminology*, 48(4): 557–566.

Daly, K. and Stubbs, J. (2006) 'Feminist Engagement with Restorative Justice', *Theoretical Criminology*, 10(1): 9–28.

Davis, G. (1992) *Making Amends: Mediation and Reparation in Criminal Justice*. London and New York: Routledge.

Dignan, J., Atkinson, A., Atkinson, H. *et al.* (2007) 'Staging Restorative Justice Encounters Against a Criminal Justice Backdrop: A Dramaturgical Analysis', *Criminology and Criminal Justice*, 7(1): 5–32.

Drumbl, M. (2000) 'Sclerosis: Retributive Justice and the Rwandan Genocide', *Punishment and Society*, 2(3): 287–307.

Duff, A. (2002) 'Restorative Punishment and Punitive Restoration', in L. Walgrave (ed.), *Restorative Justice and the Law*. Cullompton: Willan.

Earl-Hubbard, M. (1996) 'The Child Sex Offender Registration Laws: The Punishment, Liberty, Deprivation and Unintended Results Associated with the Scarlet Letter Laws of the 1990s', *Northwestern University Law Review*, 90(2): 788–862.

Edwards, W. and Hensley, C. (2001) 'Contextualising Sex Offender Management Legislation and Policy: Evaluating The Problem of Latent Consequences in Community Notification Laws', *International Journal of Offender Therapy and Comparative Criminology*, 45(1): 83–101.

Ericson, R. V. (2007) *Crime in an Insecure World*. Cambridge: Polity Press.

Ericson, R. V. and Haggerty, K. D. (1997) *Policing the Risk Society*. Oxford: Clarendon Press.

Falshaw, L., Friendship, C. and Bates, A. (2003) *Sexual Offenders – Measuring Reconviction, Reoffending and Recidivism*. Home Office Research Findings No. 183. London: Home Office.

Finstad, L. (1990) 'Sexual Offenders Out of Prison: Principles for a Realistic Utopia', *International Journal of Sociology*, 18(2): 157–177.

Friendship, C., Beech, A. R. and Browne, K. D. (2002) 'Reconviction as an Outcome Measure in Research: A Methodological Note', *British Journal of Criminology*, 42(2): 442–444.

Friendship, C. and Thornton, D. (2001) 'Sexual Reconviction for Sexual Offenders Discharged from Prison in England and Wales: Implications for Evaluating Treatment', *British Society of Criminology*, 41(2): 285–292.

Galaway, B. and Hudson, B. (eds) (1996) *Restorative Justice: International Perspectives.* Monsey, NY: Criminal Justice Press.

Gatos, P. (1999) 'Dealing with Child Sexual Abuse When a Loved One Is the Abuser', *Valley News*, 30 July.

Grubin, D. H. (1998) *Sex Offending Against Children: Understanding the Risk.* Police Research Series Paper No. 99. London: Home Office.

Hacking, I. (1999) *The Social Construction of What?* Cambridge, MA: Harvard University Press.

Hebenton, B. and Thomas, T. (1996) 'Sexual Offenders in the Community: Reflections on Problems of Law, Community and Risk Management in the USA and England and Wales', *International Journal of the Sociology of Law*, 24(4): 427–443.

Home Office (1996a) *Protecting the Public: The Government's Strategy on Crime in England and Wales.* Cm 3190. London: HMSO.

Home Office (1996b) *Sentencing and Supervision of Sex Offenders: A Consultation Document.* Cm 3304. London: HMSO.

Hudson, B. (1998) 'Restorative Justice: The Challenge of Sexual and Racial Violence', *Journal of Law and Society*, 25(2): 237–256.

Hudson, B. (2002) 'Restorative Justice and Gendered Violence: Diversion or Effective Justice?', *British Journal of Criminology*, 42(3): 616–634.

Johnstone, G. (2003) (ed.) *A Restorative Justice Reader: Texts, Sources, Context.* Cullompton: Willan.

Karp, D. R. (1998) 'The Judicial and the Judicious Use of Shame Penalties', *Crime and Delinquency*, 44(2): 277–294.

Kemshall, H. and Maguire, M. (2001) 'Public Protection, Partnership and Risk Penality: The Multi-Agency Risk Management of Sexual and Violent Offenders', *Punishment and Society*, 3(2): 237–264.

Klein, A. and Tabachnick, J. (2002) 'Framing a New Approach: Finding Ways to Effectively Prevent Sexual Abuse by Youth', *The Prevention Researcher*, 9(4): 8–10.

Koss, M. P. (2000) 'Blame, Shame, and Community: Justice Responses to Violence Against Women', *American Psychologist*, 55(11): 1332–1343.

Koss, M. P., Bachar, K. J. and Hopkins, C. Q. (2003) 'Restorative Justice for Sexual Violence: Repairing Victims, Building Community, and Holding Offenders Accountable', *Annals of the New York Academy of Sciences*, 989: 384–377.

Kurki, L. (2003) 'Evaluating Restorative Justice Practices', in A. von Hirsch, A. Roberts and A. Bottoms (eds), *Restorative and Criminal Justice: An Exploratory Analysis.* Oxford: Hart Publishing.

Loader, I. and Walker, N. (2007) *Civilizing Security.* Cambridge: Cambridge University Press.

Marshall, T. (1991) *Victim–Offender Mediation.* Home Office Research Bulletin No. 30. London: HMSO.

Marshall, T. (1999) *Restorative Justice: An Overview.* A Report by the Home Office Research Development and Statistics Directorate. London: HMSO.

Massaro, T. M. (1991) 'Shame Culture and American Criminal Law', *Michigan Law Review*, 89: 1880–1944.

Matravers, A. (ed.) (2003) *Sex Offenders in the Community: Managing and Reducing the Risks.* Cullompton: Willan.

Maxwell, G. and Morris, A. (1999) *Understanding Re-offending.* Wellington: Institute of Criminology, Victoria University of Wellington.

Maxwell, G. and Morris, A. (2002) 'The Role of Shame, Guilt and Remorse in Restorative Justice Processes for Young People', in E. Weitekamp and H. J. Kerner (eds), *Restorative Justice: Theoretical Foundations.* Cullompton: Willan.

McAlinden, A. (2005) 'The Use of Shame in the Reintegration of Sex Offenders', *British Journal of Criminology*, 45(3): 373–394.

McAlinden, A. (2007) *The Shaming of Sexual Offenders: Risk, Retribution and Reintegration.* Oxford: Hart Publishing.

McEvoy, K. and Mika, H. (2001) 'Policing, Punishment and Praxis: Restorative Justice and Non-Violent Alternatives to Paramilitary Punishments in Northern Ireland', *Policing and Society*, 11(3-4): 259–282.

Miers, D., Maguire, M., Goldie, S. *et al.* (2001) *An Exploratory Evaluation of Restorative Justice Schemes.* Crime Reduction Research Series Paper No. 9. London: Home Office.

Mills, L. G. (2003) *Insult to Injury: Rethinking Our Responses to Intimate Abuse.* Princeton, NJ: Princeton University Press.

Morris, A. (2002) 'Critiquing the Critics: A Brief Response to Critics of Restorative Justice', *British Journal of Criminology*, 42(3): 596–615.

Morris, A. and Gelsthorpe, L. (2000) 'Re-Visioning Men's Violence Against Female Partners', *Howard Journal*, 39(4): 412–428.

Morris, A. and Maxwell, G. (2000) 'The Practice of Family Group Conferences in New Zealand: Assessing the Place, Potential and Pitfalls of Restorative Justice', in A. Crawford and J. Goodey (eds), *Integrating a Victim Perspective in Criminal Justice.* Aldershot: Ashgate.

Morris, A. and Maxwell, G. (2003) 'Restorative Justice for Adult Offenders: The New Zealand Experience', in L. Walgrave (ed.), *Repositioning Restorative Justice.* Cullompton: Willan.

O'Malley, P. (2004) *Risk, Uncertainty and Government.* London: Glasshouse Press.

Paternoster, R., Backman, R., Brame, R. and Sherman, L. (1997) 'Do Fair Procedures Matter? The Effect of Procedural Justice on Spousal Assault', *Law and Society Review*, 31(1): 163–204.

Pennell, J. (2006) 'Stopping Domestic Violence or Protecting Children? Contributions from Restorative Justice', in D. Sullivan and L. Tifft (eds), *Handbook on Restorative Justice: A Global Perspective.* New York: Routledge.

Petrunik, M. G. (2002) 'Managing Unacceptable Risk: Sex Offenders, Community Response, and Social Policy in the United States and Canada', *International Journal of Offender Therapy and Comparative Criminology*, 46(4): 483–511.

Presser, L. and Gaarder, E. (2000) 'Can Restorative Justice Reduce Battering? Some Preliminary Considerations', *Social Justice*, 27(1): 175–195.

Quaker Peace and Social Witness (2005) *Circles of Support and Accountability in the Thames Valley: The First Three Years – April 2002 to March 2005*. London: Quaker Communications.

Retzinger, S. M. and Scheff, T. J. (1996) 'Strategy for Community Conferences: Emotions and Social Bonds', in B. Galaway and J. Hudson (eds), *Restorative Justice: International Perspectives*. Monsey, NY: Criminal Justice Press.

Robinson, G. and Shapland, J. (2008) 'Reducing Recidivism: A Task for Restorative Justice', *British Journal of Criminology*, 48(3): 337–358.

Roche, D. (2003) *Accountability in Restorative Justice*. Clarendon Studies in Criminology, Oxford: Oxford University Press.

Rutherford, A. (2000) 'Holding the Line on Sex Offender Notification', *New Law Journal*, 150: 1359.

Shearing, C. (2000) 'Punishment and the Changing Face of Governance', *Punishment and Society*, 3(2): 203–220.

Soothill, K. and Francis, B. (1998) 'Poisoned Chalice or Just Deserts? (the Sex Offenders Act 1997)', *Journal of Forensic Psychiatry*, 9(2): 281–293.

Soothill, K., Harman, J., Francis, B. and Kirby, S. (2005) 'What Is the Future Repeat Danger from Sexual Offenders Against Children? Implications for Policing', *Police Journal*, 78(1): 37–45.

Stubbs, J. (2007) 'Beyond Apology?: Domestic Violence and Critical Questions for Restorative Justice', *Criminology and Criminal Justice*, 7(2): 169–188.

Tabachnick, J. and Chasan-Taber, L. (1999) 'Evaluation of a Child Sexual Abuse Prevention Program', *Sexual Abuse: A Journal of Research and Treatment*, 11(4): 279–292.

Tabachnick, J., Chasan-Taber, L. and McMahon, P. (2001) 'Evaluation of a Child Sexual Abuse Prevention Program – Vermont, 1995-1999', *Journal of the American Medical Association*, 285(9): 114–115.

Thomas, T. (2003) 'Sex Offender Community Notification: Experiences from America', *Howard Journal*, 42(3): 217–228.

Umbreit, M. (1994) *Victim Meets the Offender: The Impact of Restorative Justice and Mediation*. Monsey, NY: Criminal Justice Press.

Umbreit, M., Bradshaw, W. and Coates, R. B. (1999) 'Victims of Severe Violence Meet the Offender: Restorative Justice Through Dialogue', *International Review of Victimology*, 6(4): 321–343.

van Dujn, A. L. (1999) 'The Scarlet Letter Branding', *Drake Law Review*, 47(3): 635–659.

van Ness, D. and Strong, K. H. (1997/2002) *Restoring Justice*. Cincinnati, OH: Anderson.

Villa Vincenzo, C. (1999) 'A Different Kind of Justice: The South African Truth and Reconciliation Commission', *Contemporary Justice Review*, 1(4): 403–428.

Wilkins, L. (1964) *Social Deviance: Social Policy, Action and Research*. London: Tavistock.

Williams, A. and Thompson, B. (2004a) 'Vigilance or Vigilantes: The Paulsgrove Riots and Policing Paedophiles in the Community: Part 1 – The Long Slow Fuse', *Police Journal*, 77(2): 99–119.

Williams, A. and Thompson, B. (2004b) 'Vigilance or Vigilantes: The Paulsgrove Riots and Policing Paedophiles in the Community: Part 2 – The Lessons of Paulsgrove', *Police Journal*, 77(3): 193–206.

Wilson, R. J., Huculak, B. and McWhinnie, A. (2002) 'Restorative Justice Innovations in Canada', *Behavioural Sciences and the Law*, 20(4): 363–380.

Wilson, R. J., McWhinnie, A., Picheca, J. E., Prinzo, M. and Cortoni, F. (2007a) 'Circles of Support and Accountability: Engaging Community Volunteers in the Management of High-Risk Sexual Offenders', *Howard Journal*, 46(1): 1–15.

Wilson, R. J., Picheca, J. E. and Prinzo, M. (2007b) 'Evaluating the Effectiveness of Professionally-Facilitated Volunteerism in the Community-Based Management of High-Risk Sexual Offenders: Part One – Effects on Participants and Stakeholders', *Howard Journal*, 46(3): 289–302.

Wilson, R. J., Pichea, J. E. and Prinzo, M. (2007c) 'Evaluating the Effectiveness of Professionally-Facilitated Volunteerism in the Community-Based Management of High-Risk Sex Offenders: Part Two – A Comparison of Recidivism Rates', *Howard Journal*, 46(4): 327–357.

Winick, B. (1998) 'Sex Offender Law in the 1990s: A Therapeutic Analysis', *Psychology, Public Policy and Law*, 4(1/2): 505–570.

Wright, M. (2002) 'The Court as Last Resort', *British Journal of Criminology*, 42(3): 654–667.

Zedner, L. (1994) 'Reparation and Retribution: Are They Reconcilable?', *Modern Law Review*, 57(2): 228–250.

Zedner, L. (2009) 'Fixing the Future? The Pre-emptive Turn in Criminal Justice', in B. McSherry, A. Norrie and S. Bronitt (eds), *Regulating Deviance: The Redirection of Criminalisation and the Future of Criminal Law*. Onati International Series in Law and Society, Oxford: Hart Publishing.

Zehr, H. (1990) *Changing Lenses: A New Focus for Crime and Justice*. Scottdale, PA: Herald Press.

Zehr, H. (1995) 'Justice Paradigm Shift? Values and Vision in the Reform Process', *Mediation Quarterly*, 12(3): 207–216.

Zhang, S. X. (1995) 'Measuring Shame in an Ethnic Context', *British Journal of Criminology*, 35(2): 248–262.

Part IV

Special offender groups

Chapter 8

Female sexual offenders: a special subgroup

Franca Cortoni

Introduction

While women commit much fewer crimes than men, they are increasingly coming to the attention of the criminal justice system for sexual offences. Consequently, the demand for assessments of risk of recidivism and developments of treatment and strategies to manage and reduce the risk of reoffending among this special subgroup of sexual offenders are increasing. Yet, professionals tasked with the assessment and treatment of these women have very little systematic information on which to base their evaluations. Although research is still in its infancy, there is now a growing empirical body of information about female sexual offenders that goes beyond clinical case studies. This chapter will provide a review of the current knowledge in the area of risk of sexual recidivism, assessment, and treatment needs of women who sexually offend. Specifically, the prevalence of female sexual offending, recidivism rates, risk factors, and assessment and treatment issues will be discussed.

Prevalence

The true prevalence rate of female sexual offending is difficult to ascertain. Historically, some authors have doubted the existence of women who commit sexually motivated offences. For example, Freund *et al.* (1984) stated that 'pedophilia ... does not exist at all in women' (193). Other authors believe that sexual offending by females is more common than believed, but these offenders are unreported or diverted from the criminal justice system (Vandiver and Walker 2002). Debates about the prevalence of sexual offending by women continue today, albeit no longer on the existence of sexual offending by women, but rather on its true extent. This issue is extremely difficult to resolve since different researchers utilise different sources of information and varying samples to attempt to establish the prevalence of sexual offending by women. Information ranges from victimisation surveys to reports on convicted sexual offenders, as well as various official criminal justice statistics.

In a victimisation survey, Finkelhor *et al.* (1990) interviewed over 2,500 US men and women by telephone to establish incidence and prevalence of sexual victimisation. About 16 per cent of the men and 27 per cent of the women reported having been sexually victimised. While the majority stated their abuser was male, 17 per cent of the men but only 1 per cent of women reported having been abused by a female. In a similar line of research, in the UK, the Child Line research (NSPCC 2007) showed that among children who report sexual abuse, 5 per cent of girls and 44 per cent of boys identify the perpetrator of their abuse as female.

Data on victimisation was also obtained from offenders. Allen (1991) surveyed 75 males and 65 females convicted of sexual offences against children. Among these offenders, 36 per cent of the males reported that they had been sexually abused as children. Of those, 45 per cent reported their abuser had been female. Among the female offenders, 72 per cent reported sexual victimisation, and 6 per cent of these reported that their sexual abuser had been female.

Finally, data from official criminal justice statistics indicate a low frequency of sexual offending by women. Data from the US Department of Justice (2006) show that 1.3 per cent of those charged with forcible rape and 8.7 per cent charged with sexual offences in general were female. In the UK, Home Office figures for 2006 show that 2 per cent of adults convicted of a sexual offence were female (Home Office 2007). In Canada, statistics from the Canadian Centre for Justice Statistics (Kong *et al.* 2003) show that in 2002, 3 per cent of adults reported to the police for sexual assault were female.

In efforts to provide more systematic information about female sexual offenders, Cortoni and Hanson (2005) estimated the proportion of sexual offenders who are women from two general sources of information. The first source of information was official police or Court reports that detail the gender of the offender. Information was available for Australia, Canada, New Zealand, the UK, and the US. Based on official records, Cortoni and Hanson (2005) found the proportion of all sexual offenders who were female ranged from 0.6 per cent in New Zealand to 8.3 per cent for non-rape sexual offenders in the USA. When these numbers were averaged across all countries in the study, women constituted approximately 4 per cent of all sexual offenders.

The second source of information was victimisation surveys. When victimisation studies were examined, Cortoni and Hanson (2005) found that the proportion of sexual offenders who were female, as reported by victims, ranged from 3.1 per cent for New Zealand to 7.0 per cent for Australia. Across the various victimisation studies, women constituted an average 4.8 per cent of all sexual offenders.

In summarising the results, Cortoni and Hanson (2005) established that, when compared with male sexual offenders, women commit sexual offences at a ratio of approximately 1 to 20 based on both official reports and victimisation surveys. Interestingly, official reports and results from victimisation surveys were remarkably consistent with each other and showed that women are responsible for 4–5 per cent of all sexual offences. Using data from the USA, the only country for which direct comparisons between official rates and victimisation reports were possible, Cortoni and Hanson (2005) noted differential rates of police arrests according to the gender of the offender in relation to victimisation survey results. Specifically, 34 per cent of the sexual offences committed by men resulted in police arrest, whereas 57 per cent of the sexual offences committed by women resulted in police arrest. These findings suggest that further research is needed to understand the personal and criminal justice responses to victimisation by female offenders versus male sexual offenders.

Overall, research indicates that sexual offending by women is significant enough to warrant its own attention. This is not to say, however, that sexual offending by women is a new and dangerous phenomenon. This is one of the dangers associated with providing attention to an under-recognised issue. Instead, these findings indicate that it is important, particularly for mental health and child protection professionals, not to ignore the possibility that women can and do commit sexual offences.

Recidivism rates of female sexual offenders

Although tremendous advances have been made in understanding the recidivism rates of adult male sexual offenders, similar knowledge is still extremely limited for female sexual offenders. To examine this issue, Cortoni *et al.* (submitted) undertook a review of the recidivism rates of 1,421 female sexual offenders who had been officially detected and sanctioned by the criminal justice system. The review was accomplished by a thorough search of published and unpublished literature. Included in the review were conference presentations, government reports, official recidivism data drawn from websites or through direct communication with government agencies, and reports of unpublished studies obtained directly from researchers. Information was obtained from Australia, Canada, England, The Netherlands, and the USA.

The review showed that the sexual reoffending rates of female sexual offenders are very low. Specifically, Cortoni *et al.* (submitted) found, in a follow-up period of approximately 6 years, a 5 per cent sexual recidivism rate, a 12 per cent violent recidivism rate, and an overall rate of any type of recidivism of 30 per cent. It is noted that these rates were disproportionally influenced by a study by Vandiver (2007) of 491 female sexual offenders registered in the state of Texas. Vandiver found an identical sexual recidivism rate of 11 per cent in both male and female sexual offenders. When that study was removed from the review, sexual recidivism rates dropped to less than 2 per cent, while violent and any recidivism rates dropped to 6.5 per cent and 20.3 per cent respectively (Cortoni *et al.* forthcoming). In comparison, meta-analyses of large samples of male sexual offenders show that the 5-year recidivism rates for male sexual offenders are 13–14 per cent for sexual crimes, 25 per cent for any violent crime (including sexual offending), and 36–37 per cent for any new crime (Hanson and Bussière 1998; Hanson and Morton-Bourgon 2005). Not surprisingly, Cortoni and Hanson (2005) noted that the differences between the recidivism rates for the male and female sexual offenders were statistically significant for all types of recidivism, confirming that female sexual offenders have much lower rates of all types of recidivism than male sexual offenders. In addition, it is important to note that recidivist female sexual offenders, just like their male counterparts, are much more likely to commit new non-sexual crimes rather than sexual offences.

Assessing risk of recidivism

The factors related to sexual recidivism among male sexual offenders are now well established (Hanson and Morton-Bourgon 2005). This knowledge of risk factors among male offenders has led to the development of validated risk assessment instruments that consistently outperform traditional clinical judgement in predictive accuracy (Hanson and Morton-Bourgon 2009). The situation is very different for female sexual offenders. The lower recidivism rates of female sexual offenders have to date precluded the development of risk assessment tools specifically for women. Low recidivism rates mean that it is difficult to assess or predict who will engage in the given behaviour (Quinsey *et al.* 2006). For example, in a follow-up of 115 American female sexual offenders for an average of 5.5 years (ranging from 2 months to 10 years), Peterson *et al.* (2001) found a zero rate of sexual recidivism. All the women in that study had been in or continued to be in treatment for their sexually offending behaviour. Given the lack of recidivism among these women, it was impossible to determine what factors might be related to sexual recidivism among women.

Because tools for male sexual offenders have not been validated for women, using these tools to assess risk of recidivism among female sexual offenders is inappropriate. In addition, simply extrapolating from the male sexual offender literature to assess risk in female sexual offenders is likely to lead to invalid risk appraisal and unintended consequences. For example, in Washington state in the USA, female sexual offenders have been civilly committed as sexual predators, despite the lack of evidence regarding the risk of recidivism posed by these women (Aylward *et al.* 2003). Until sufficient knowledge has accumulated to permit the development of appropriate risk assessment tools for female sexual offenders, the approach to their assessment should be an empirically guided clinical judgement. This is a prediction based on a clinical judgement of the extent and combination of the risk factors present in the case. Risk factors are those characteristics that have an empirically established link with recidivism. Therefore, the factors used in this type of assessment must be those that have been shown through research to be related to recidivism. As we will see, research is now beginning to provide some indications of these factors among female sexual offenders.

Static risk factors

Notwithstanding the low recidivism rates among female sexual offenders, the recidivism research on these women now contains sufficiently large numbers to permit an examination of their risk factors. There are two types of risk factors: static and dynamic. Static factors are unchangeable aspects in the offender's history that are related to recidivism. For example, among *male* sexual offenders, static risk factors for general and violent (non-sexual) recidivism include being at a younger age, being single, having a history of lifestyle instability and rule violations, and prior criminal history (Hanson and Morton-Bourgon 2005; Andrews and Bonta 2007). Static factors specifically related to sexual recidivism include prior sexual offences, and having male, stranger, and/or unrelated victims (Hanson and Thornton 2000).

Research with female sexual offenders suggests that a prior criminal history is also indicative of a higher risk of recidivism among women. In her follow-up of 471 women, Vandiver (2007) found an 11 per cent sexual recidivism rate. Among the recidivists, she found that the number of prior convictions for any type of offence predicted rearrest for new general and violent offences. She could not, however, establish any factor that specifically predicted new sexual offences among the women in her sample.

In their examination of 390 female sexual offenders registered in the state of New York, Freeman and Sandler (2008) found that 1.5 per cent (six women) had been rearrested for a new sexual offence, while an additional 22.8 per cent (89 women) had been rearrested for a new non-sexual crime. In their research, Freeman and Sandler (2008) were able to establish a number of characteristics that differentiated women who committed new crimes from those who did not. Specifically, the number of prior drug offence arrests, the number of prior violent offence arrests, the number of prior incarceration terms, and being younger at arrest for the index sexual offence were related to a rearrest for new general (i.e., non-sexual and non-violent) offences. Contrary to the findings by Vandiver (2007), they did find some static factors that distinguished the six women who had been rearrested for a new sexual offence. Specifically, high risk (as assessed by the New York state risk assessment system), the number of prior arrests for sexual offences and, interestingly, the number of prior child abuse offences (of any type) were all related to sexual recidivism among the women in their sample.

Finally, in their follow-up of 61 female sexual offenders incarcerated in Canada between 1972 and 1998, Williams and Nicholaichuk (2001) found a sexual recidivism rate of 3.3 per cent (two cases out of 61). In their detailed analysis, these authors found one marker that differentiated these two women from the other female sexual offenders in their sample: these two women had previously engaged exclusively in solo offending with no co-offender present during the sexual assaults. This particular finding is noteworthy and may serve as an important risk marker for sexual recidivism among women, but it requires additional validation, as this particular finding was not found in the US recidivism research discussed above. It is noted, however, that the presence of a co-offender did not appear to have been explicitly examined by Vandiver (2007) or Freeman and Sandler (2008), rendering any direct comparison of this factor difficult.

Dynamic risk factors

Dynamic factors are those aspects of the offender that are amenable to change and that are directly related to the offending behaviour (Hanson 2006). Unlike static risk factors, there is still no systematic empirical information on the dynamic risk factors of female sexual offenders. Consequently, the assessment of the risk of women who sexually offend should be based on the elements that are revealed through the examination of the offending patterns of these women. Clinical research suggests that relationship problems, attitudes and cognitions that support the offending behaviour, the use of sex to regulate emotional states, and emotional dysregulation problems are common among female sexual offenders (Grayston and De Luca 1999; Eldridge and Saradjian 2000; Nathan and Ward 2002). Sexual gratification, a desire for intimacy (with either a victim or a co-defendant), or instrumental goals such as revenge or humiliation are also associated with female sexual offending (Gannon *et al.* 2008). Finally, as female sexual offenders, just like their male counterparts, also engage in other criminal behaviour, factors such as the presence and extent of antisocial attitudes, antisocial associates, and substance abuse as a precursor to the offending behaviour should also be considered in the assessment (Ford and Cortoni 2008).

Problematic relationships appear particularly relevant for female sexual offenders, particularly in the context of the offending. An element unique to female sexual offenders is the frequent presence of a co-offender (Grayston and De Luca 1999). Between one-third and two-thirds of female sexual offenders commit their crimes in the company of a co-offender, typically a male, although female co-offenders have been noted (Vandiver 2006). Of the women who have a co-offender, a subgroup is clearly identified as having been coerced into the offending, typically by a male, while another subgroup of offenders co-offend willingly. In addition, some women will actually be the initiators of the offending behaviour. From these findings, the role of the co-offender needs to be carefully assessed to determine the full extent of the woman's willingness to participate in the abuse.

165

Different dynamic factors are likely to emerge if the woman was coerced into the abuse, as opposed to being a willing participant or an initiator. A coerced offender may demonstrate significant deficits in assertiveness and an exaggerated dependence on her co-offender. Until she develops better assertiveness and relationship skills, she may remain at risk of reoffending. Deviant arousal and fantasising, and attitudes that condone sexual abuse, may appear more frequently in initiators or willing participants. In these cases, a continued adherence to distorted beliefs that support sexual abuse may put her at greater risk of reoffending. In the context of the assessment, an in-depth examination of the elements that motivated the offender to co-offend and her current views of the offending behaviour will be enlightening.

Gannon *et al.* (2008) provide further evidence that problematic relationships are inherent in female sexual offenders. In their examination of the offence pathways of female sexual offenders, these authors found that practical and emotional support from family and friends was lacking in all cases, and that they were frequent victims of domestic violence. Similarly, in their study of 139 female sexual offenders, Wijkman and Bijleveld (2008) found that women with more than one documented sexual offence were particularly vulnerable, physically and socially abused women. The accumulated findings on the relationship problems of female sexual offenders indicate that not only the presence and dynamics of the relationship with the co-offender but also the general quality of their social and familial support are important components of the evaluation of female sexual offenders.

Linked to problematic relationships is a victimisation history. In general, among female offenders, past victimisation is related to future recidivism (Blanchette and Brown 2006). Among female sexual offenders, a past history of physical, emotional, or sexual victimisation may be linked to the woman's current offending behaviour. If sexual victimisation is present, it is important, however, not to automatically view it as the cause of her sexual offences. Research has shown that only a proportion of female sexual offenders were themselves sexually victimised (Weigel *et al.* 2003), and it is highly unlikely that victimisation is the main reason why the woman chose to engage in the abuse herself. Paying undue attention to the victimisation history could cloud other issues that are related to the offending behaviour, such as attitudes supportive of sexual abuse. In addition, such a focus may also inadvertently reinforce distorted beliefs about the woman's lack of responsibility for the offending behaviour, and for making the necessary changes to her life (Eldridge and Saradjian 2000). Instead, past sexual victimisation is more likely to be related to the offending behaviour by dysfunctional patterns of relating to others, as well as patterns of coping, that the woman developed as a result of the victimisation.

The woman's sexual development and history are also important areas to assess. In the assessment, the role that sex and sexuality play in the woman's life should be examined to establish their potential motivational roles in the offending behaviour. In addition, a careful examination of the coping patterns of women is required to determine the role sexual activity in general and sexual abuse in particular may play in alleviating negative emotional states or fulfilling dependence or intimacy needs (Grayston and De Luca 1999; Nathan and Ward 2002; Gannon *et al.* 2008). Female sexual offenders, like male sexual offenders, often do not understand their emotional states, mislabel them, or manage them through sexual activity (Eldridge and Sarajdian 2000). The presence and extent of deviant sexual fantasies and arousal are typically best examined within this context. Tied to this area is the meaning of sex in the woman's life: her beliefs about sexual activity, and by extension sexual abuse, may be linked to her beliefs about gender roles, a sense of entitlement, a refusal to acknowledge the harm caused by the abuse, or even antisocial attitudes. Such pro-offending beliefs may contribute to sexual offending.

The link between pro-offending attitudes and criminal behaviour for all types of offenders of both genders is firmly established (Blanchette and Brown 2006; Andrews and Bonta 2007). Among male sexual offenders, pro-abuse attitudes are a major dynamic risk factor (Hanson and Harris 2001). Similarly, female sexual offenders also have distorted beliefs about the sexual abuse and their victims (Saradjian 1996; Grayston and De Luca 1999). Any assessment would therefore need to elucidate the presence of pro-offending attitudes and other distorted beliefs and to determine their likely contribution to the offending behaviour. Core beliefs about relationships, children, and gender roles are likely to be intertwined with these pro-offending attitudes (Eldridge and Saradjian 2000; Mann and Beech 2003).

Treatment

The overarching goal of the treatment of female sexual offenders is to address the factors related to their sexually offending behaviour. Some of the factors related to offending among female sexual offenders are frequently found among women offenders in general. These common factors include antisocial attitudes, emotional dysregulation, victimisation issues, and substance abuse (Blanchette and Brown 2006). In addition, female sexual offenders also share a few factors with male sexual offenders: denial and minimisation of the offending behaviour, distorted cognitions about the sexual offences, attitudes that condone sexual abuse, intimacy deficits, and the use of sex to regulate emotional states or to fulfil dependence or intimacy needs (Grayston and De Luca 1999; Eldridge and Saradjian 2000; Nathan and Ward 2002). Finally, for at least some female offenders, a desire for sexual gratification is directly related to the abuse (Nathan and Ward 2002).

The manifestation and the relative importance of these factors in women may be different from their relevance in men. For example, common to both male and female sexual offenders are denial and minimisation of the offending behaviour. After female sexual offenders acknowledge their sexual offending behaviour, however, they tend to show much less minimisation of their behaviour than males (Matthews 1993). Further, when the sexually deviant behaviour occurred in the company of co-offenders, many of these women tend to wrongly take responsibility for the deviant behaviour of their offending partners (Matthews 1993). Similarly, although both male and female sexual offenders have problematic relationships with significant others (Matthews 1993; Grayston and De Luca 1999; Hanson and Morton-Bourgon 2005), women tend to demonstrate particularly excessive dependence or over-reliance on the men in their lives (Eldridge and Saradjian 2000). Finally, while some female sexual offenders do report deviant sexual interests (Grayston and De Luca 1999; Nathan and Ward 2002), such interests do not appear to be as predominant as those of male sexual offenders (Wiegel *et al.* 2003).

When these issues are taken into consideration, the treatment of female sexual offenders therefore focuses on five broad areas: (1) cognitive processes, (2) emotional processes, (3) intimacy and relationship issues, (4) sexual dynamics, and (5) social functioning. The treatment addresses the interrelationships among these factors and develops a self-management plan to include goals for a healthier, offence-free life. This approach recognises that sexual offending behaviour is not treated in isolation from the rest of the woman's life, ensures that all areas of functioning are targeted, and allows flexibility to tailor the treatment according to each woman's individual treatment needs (Ford and Cortoni 2008).

Eldridge and Saradjian (2000) presented a model of sexual deviance in women in which they posited that for female sexual offenders, unmet needs result in aversive emotional states that are alleviated by the offending behaviour. These behaviours in turn become rewarding in themselves, leading to the development or reinforcement of knowledge, beliefs, and attitudes that facilitate further sexually deviant behaviour. Drawing from the broader literature on women and their clinical experience with female sexual offenders, these authors suggest that effective treatment with these women has to meet a number of goals. In treatment, women have to identify their sexually deviant patterns, including the related thoughts, emotions, and behaviours. In addition, they need to understand the needs met by the offending behaviour and generate non-offending ways to meet those needs. Treatment concurrently should address the factors that gave rise to those otherwise unmet needs, including victimisation histories, distorted abuse-related cognitions, and negative emotional states. Finally, the women need to develop coping strategies to deal directly with the factors that immediately place them at risk of sexually acting out.

In their writings, Eldridge and Saradjian (2000) highlighted that the modification of cognitive distortions directly related to the offending behaviour was a central feature of treatment. Denov and Cortoni (2006) pointed out that, while important, targeting only these distortions was insufficient: treatment should also address the broader maladaptive cognitive patterns that influence the woman's life beyond the sexual deviance. Cognitions influence behaviour in all areas of one's life (Alcock et al. 1988), and faulty cognitive patterns are a central feature in a variety of pathological conditions, including violence (Beck 1999). Consequently, treatment needs to target broader problematic cognitions related to all areas of the woman's life, and not just those specifically related to the offending behaviour.

Within this context, an examination of the woman's entire life, and not just the offending behaviour, is important. Ellerby et al. (2000) presented a model that incorporates sexual offending within the framework of a negative life pattern. This negative life cycle consists of emotions, negative styles of thinking, and unproductive or counterproductive coping strategies that eventually give rise to inappropriate sexual thoughts or fantasies and eventual offending. According to Ellerby et al. (2000), cognitive elements are integral to this negative life pattern. Using the woman's history, core beliefs that facilitate the sexual deviance, as well as habitual patterns of thinking, can be identified and examined in terms of their impact on all spheres in the woman's life (Mann and Beech 2003; Denov and Cortoni 2006).

Additional treatment considerations

In addition to factors specifically related to the sexually offending behaviour, a portion of female sexual offenders demonstrate mental health difficulties; high levels of substance abuse; personality disorders, including antisocial and borderline personality disorders; post-traumatic stress syndrome and depression; severe interpersonal difficulties, particularly in the area of romantic relationships; and general psychosocial deficits (Grayston and De Luca 1999). The treatment of female sexual offenders therefore should additionally address the broader, additional problematic psychological and psychosocial factors that are part of the woman's negative life cycle and that have set the stage for the offending behaviour. In addition, given these difficulties, female sexual offenders will likely benefit from additional help to improve their general community functioning, with a particular focus on their ability to develop and maintain a more stable lifestyle with less dependence on others.

Finally, because women tend to be the primary caregivers of children, special attention should be paid to the likely presence of other types of child maltreatment. As found by Freeman and Sandler (2008), the presence of child maltreatment offences is related to increased recidivism. Consequently, a thorough understanding of the woman's attitudes and behaviours that are likely to lead to significant harm to a child is necessary, particularly if reunion with her children is contemplated (Saradjian 1996). Any reunion effort should occur only when children clearly wish to reunite with their mother and should include the involvement of child protection services and family therapists skilled in dealing with abused children. The continued involvement of agencies is also crucial to monitor progress and to detect warning signs that the woman is deteriorating (Matthews 1993).

Conclusion

This chapter has reviewed the prevalence of sexual offending by females, their recidivism rates, and the factors related to their offending. Generally, female sexual offenders have much lower rates of any types of offending and tend to recidivate at much lower rates than males. While some female sexual offenders share some of the same characteristics as male offenders, some important differences must be taken into account when assessing and treating women offenders. Specifically, the context in which the offences took place in interaction with the woman's life needs to be examined. Women's lives and their societal experiences differ from those of men, and their experiences influence both their criminal behaviour and their rehabilitation. Although female sexual offenders present some prototypical features commonly associated with sexual offending, these features tend to manifest themselves in different ways when compared with males. Given these differences, it is clear that current knowledge of male sexual offenders cannot simply be extended to female offenders, and much research is required to improve our understanding of why women engage in sexually offending behaviour.

References

Alcock, J. E., Carment, D. W. and Sadava, S. W. (1988) *A Textbook of Social Psychology*. Scarborough, Ontario: Prentice-Hall Canada, Inc.

Allen, C. M. (1991) *Women and Men Who Sexually Abuse Children: A Comparative Analysis*. Orwell, VT: Safer Society Press.

Andrews, D. A. and Bonta J. (2007) *The Psychology of Criminal Conduct* (4th edn). Cincinnati, OH: Anderson.

Aylward, A., Christopher, M., Newell, R. M. and Gordon, A. (2002) 'What About Women Who Commit Sex Offences?', *21st Annual Research and Treatment Conference, Association for the Treatment of Sexual Abusers*, Montréal, QC, Canada, October 2002.

Beck, A. T. (1999) *Prisoners of Hate: The Cognitive Basis of Anger, Hostility, and Violence*. New York: HarperCollins.

Blanchette, K. and Brown, S. L. (2006) *The Assessment and Treatment of Women Offenders*. Chichester: Wiley.

Cortoni, F. and Hanson, R. K. (2005) *A Review of the Recidivism Rates of Adult Female Sexual Offenders*. Research Report R-169. Ottawa, ON: Correctional Service Canada.

Cortoni, F., Hanson, R. K, and Coache, M. E. (submitted) 'The Recidivism Rates of Female Sexual Offenders are Low: A Meta-Analysis'.

Denov, M. S. and Cortoni, F. (2006) 'Adult Female Sexual Offenders', in C. Hilarski and J. Wodarski (eds), *Comprehensive Mental Health Practices with Sex Offenders and Their Families*. New York: Haworth Press.

Eldridge, H. and Saradjian, J. (2000) 'Replacing the Function of Abusive Behaviors for the Offender: Remaking Relapse Prevention in Working with Women Who Sexually Abuse Children', in D. R. Laws, S. M. Hudson and

T. Ward (eds), *Remaking Relapse Prevention with Sex Offenders: A Sourcebook.* Thousand Oaks, CA: Sage.

Ellerby, L., Bedard, J. and Chartrand, S. (2000) 'Holism, Wellness, and Spirituality', in D. R. Laws, S. M. Hudson and T. Ward (eds), *Remaking Relapse Prevention with Sex Offenders: A Sourcebook.* Thousand Oaks, CA: Sage.

Finkelhor, D., Hotaling, G., Lewis, I. A. and Smith, C. (1990) 'Sexual Abuse in a National Survey of Adult Men and Women: Prevalence Characteristics, and Risk Factors', *Child Abuse and Neglect,* 14: 19–28.

Ford, H. and Cortoni, F. (2008) 'Sexual Deviance in Females: Assessment and Treatment', in D. R. Laws and W. O'Donohue (eds), *Sexual Deviance* (2nd edn). New York: Guilford Press.

Freeman and Sandler (2008) 'Female and Male Sex Offenders: A Comparison of Recidivism Patterns and Risk Factors', *Journal of Interpersonal Violence,* 23: 1394–1413.

Freund, K., Heasman, G., Racansky, I. G. and Glancy, G. (1984) 'Pedophilia and Heterosexuality vs. Homosexuality', *Journal of Sex and Marital Therapy,* 10: 193–200.

Gannon, T. A., Rose, M. and Ward, T. (2008) 'A Descriptive Model of the Offense Process for Female Sexual Offenders', *Sexual Abuse: A Journal of Research and Treatment,* 20: 352–374.

Grayston, A. D. and De Luca, R. V. (1999) 'Female Perpetrators of Child Sexual Abuse: A Review of the Clinical and Empirical Literature', *Aggression and Violent Behavior,* 4: 93–106.

Hanson, R. K. (2006) 'Stability and Changes: Dynamic Risk Factors for Sexual Offenders', in W. L. Marshall, Y. M. Fernandez, L. E. Marshall and G. A. Serran (eds), *Sexual Offender Treatment: Controversial Issues.* Chichester: Wiley.

Hanson, R. K. and Bussière, M. T. (1998) 'Predicting Relapse: A Meta-Analysis of Sexual Offender Recidivism Studies', *Journal of Consulting and Clinical Psychology,* 66: 348–362.

Hanson, R. K. and Harris, J. R. (2001) 'A Structured Approach to Evaluating Change Among Sexual Offenders', *Sexual Abuse: A Journal of Research and Treatment,* 13: 105–122.

Hanson, R. K. and Morton-Bourgon, K. E. (2005) 'The Characteristics of Persistent Sexual Offenders: A Meta-Analysis of Recidivism Studies', *Journal of Consulting and Clinical Psychology,* 73: 1154–1163.

Hanson, R. K. and Morton-Bourgon, K. E. (2009) 'The Accuracy of Recidivism Risk Assessments for Sexual Offenders: A Meta-Analysis of 118 Prediction Studies', *Psychological Assessment,* 21: 1–21.

Hanson, R. K. and Thornton, D. (2000) 'Improving Risk Assessments for Sex Offenders: A Comparison of Three Actuarial Scales', *Law and Human Behavior,* 24: 119–136.

Home Office (2007) *Criminal Statistics England and Wales 2006–2007.* London: HMSO.

Kong, R., Johnson, H., Beattie, S. and Cardillo, A. (2003) *Sexual Offences in Canada* (No. 85-002-XPE), 23, 6. Ottawa, ON, Canada: Canadian Centre for Justice Statistics.

Mann, R. E. and Beech, A. R. (2003) 'Cognitive Distortions, Schemas, and Implicit Theories', in T. Ward, D. R. Laws and S. M. Hudson (eds), *Sexual Deviance: Issues and Controversies*. Thousand Oaks, CA: Sage.

Matthews, J. K. (1993) 'Working with Female Sexual Abusers', in M. Elliot (ed.), *Female Sexual Abuse of Children*. New York: Guilford Press.

Nathan, P. and Ward, T. (2002) 'Female Sex Offenders: Clinical and Demographic Features', *Journal of Sexual Aggression*, 8: 5–21.

NSPCC (2007) *Calls to ChildLine About Sexual Abuse. ChildLine Case Notes* [online]. Available at: http://www.nspcc.org.uk/Inform/publications/ Serials/ChildLineCasenotes/CLcasenotessexualabuse_wdf48189.pdf (accessed 22 March 2009).

Peterson, K. D., Colebank, K. D. and Motta, L. L. (2001) 'Female Sexual Offender Recidivism', *20th Annual Research and Treatment Conference of the Association for the Treatment of Sexual Abusers*, San Antonio, Texas, November 2001.

Quinsey, V. L., Harris, G. T., Rice, M. E. and Cormier, C. L. (2006) *Violent Offenders: Appraising and Managing Risk* (2nd edn). Washington, DC: American Psychological Association.

Saradjian, J. (1996) *Women Who Sexually Abuse Children: From Research to Clinical Practice.* Chichester: Wiley.

US Department of Justice (2006) *Crime in the United States 2006.* Washington, DC: Federal Bureau of Investigation.

Vandiver, D. M. (2006) 'Female Sex Offenders: A Comparison of Solo Offenders and Co-offenders', *Violence and Victims*, 21: 339–354.

Vandiver, D. (2007) *An Examination of Re-arrest Rates of 942 Male and 471 Female Registered Sex Offenders.* Academy of the Criminal Justice Sciences, Feature Panel on Sex Offenders: Seattle, WA.

Vandiver, D. M. and Walker, J. T. (2002) 'Female Sex Offenders: An Overview and Analysis of 40 Cases', *Criminal Justice Review*, 27: 284–300.

Wiegel, M., Abel, G. G. and Jordan, A. (2003) 'The Self-Reported Behaviors of Adult Female Child Abusers', *22nd Annual Research and Treatment Conference, Association for the Treatment of Sexual Abusers*, St. Louis, Missouri, October 2003.

Wijkman, M. and Bijleveld, C. (2008) 'Female Sex Offenders: Recidivism and Criminal Careers', *8th Annual Conference of the European Society of Criminology*, Edinburgh, Scotland, September 2008.

Williams, S. M. and Nicholaichuk, T. (2001) 'Assessing Static Risk Factors in Adult Female Sex Offenders Under Federal Jurisdiction', *20th Research and Treatment Conference, Association for the Treatment of Sexual Abusers*, San Antonio, Texas, November 2001.

Chapter 9

Enhancing community collaboration to stop sexual harm by youth[1]

Joann Schladale

> *Never doubt that a small group of thoughtful committed citizens can change the world; indeed, it's the only thing that ever does.*
>
> Margaret Mead

Introduction

Addressing sexual harm by youth creates a significant challenge for communities intent on providing safety and protection from sexual abuse for all citizens. Media sensationalism about sexual harm often creates a false sense of fear, and concerned adults may be at a loss about what to believe when it comes to this topic. At the opposite end of the spectrum, gender attitudes to male sexual behaviour can inhibit prevention and adequate intervention. While children's services are everywhere, few child-serving agencies provide an empirically driven response to the problem (Grimshaw 2008; Steinberg 2008). Many communities struggle to address the challenges effectively. The purpose of this chapter is to provide a foundation for a comprehensive, community-based response to sexual harm by youth.

Defining the challenge

Sexual harm by youth encompasses a broad range of behaviour. While juvenile sexual offenders are defined as 'adolescents from age thirteen–seventeen who commit illegal sexual behavior as defined by the sex crimes statutes of the jurisdiction in which the offense occurred' (Chaffin *et al.* 2003: 1), most youth who sexually abuse are never involved in juvenile justice. Children with sexual behaviour problems are defined as children under the age of 13 who 'initiate behaviours involving sexual body parts ... that are developmentally inappropriate or potentially harmful to themselves or others' (Association for the Treatment of Sexual Abusers (ATSA) 2006, Section 1: 3). For the purpose of this chapter, sexual harm by youth will refer to children of all ages who engage in sexual behaviour that causes harm to others.

Research indicates that 'most adolescent sex offenders pose a manageable level of risk to the community' (Chaffin *et al.* 2003: 2). The Task Force Report on Children with Sexual Behavior Problems states that 'after receiving appropriate short-term, outpatient treatment, children with sexual behavior problems have been found to be at no greater long-term risk for future sex offenses than other clinic children (2 per cent–3 per cent)' (ATSA 2006: 2). Such important information provides a foundation to best address the needs of these youth, their families, their victims, and the community at large, where research indicates they are best served in the most cost-effective manner (Borduin *et al.* 1990; ATSA 2000; Borduin and Schaeffer 2001; Thornton *et al.* 2002; Chaffin *et al.* 2003; Hunter *et al.* 2004; Schladale *et al.* 2007).

Prevalence

There is no way to quantify sexual harm by youth. Even if everyone shared a common definition of problematic sexual behaviour, diverse professionals see children for such a broad array of services, in such a large number of settings, that it would be impossible to accurately survey the problem. Such a challenge in no way impedes an effective response to the issue.

The most recent available data indicate that juvenile sexual offences resulting in disposal have risen in the UK from 1,664 in 2002–3, to 1,988 in 2005–6 (Grimshaw 2008). These statistics, however, seldom reflect the full extent of the problem (Cawson *et al.* 2000). While available data do not adequately convey the breadth, or depth, of the challenge, they do provide information necessary for enhancing community response. When geographic breakdown of the numbers is available, it can inform analysis of community strengths, and vulnerabilities for adequately addressing needs.

Diversity

Young people who sexually abuse are a very diverse group who defy categorisation and efforts to create valid and reliable typologies (Hunter *et al.* 2003). Most youth brought to the attention of authorities for causing sexual harm are males between the ages of 13 and 15 (Chaffin 2009). It is important to note that a very small percentage of youth adjudicated for sexual crimes are female (Grimshaw 2008). A significant number of young people who sexually abuse suffer co-occurring problems, such as co-morbid psychiatric diagnoses and developmental disabilities (Hickey *et al.* 2006). Most have experienced family disruption and significant trauma, exhibit poor social skills, and lack core competencies that impede criminal activity (Righthand and Welch 2001; Torbet and Thomas 2005; Schladale 2006, 2007a). Many share traits in common with those who exhibit non-sexual delinquent behaviour (Seto and Lalumiere 2006). Professionals intent on obtaining more specific details can do so by obtaining information from the Youth Justice Board at www.yjb.gov.uk and ATSA at www.atsa.com.

Risk factors

Trajectories leading to sexual harm are multi-determined (Becker 1998), and recidivism rates indicate that youth who have caused sexual harm are at significantly greater risk of committing non-sexual criminal offences than of reoffending sexually (Becker 1990; Borduin *et al.* 1990; Kahn and Chambers 1991; Schram *et al.* 1991; Langstrom and Grann 2000; Chaffin *et al.* 2003; Hunter *et al.* 2004). It is therefore critical that community responses focus on empirical evidence for all youth violence prevention and delinquency intervention. It is also important to be aware of specific risk factors for the small number of youth who do go on to commit other sexual offences.

Information about static, stable, and dynamic risk factors (Prentky and Righthand 2003; Epperson *et al.* 2006) has come from diligent and persistent efforts to empirically identify factors critical for prevention. Chaffin *et al.* (2003) identify the following six factors that indicate risk of recidivism for sexual harm by youth: history of multiple sexual offences, especially if any occur after adequate treatment; history of repeated non-sexual offences; clear and persistent sexual interest in children; failure to comply with sex-offence-specific treatment; self-evident indications of risk, such as disturbances of arousal and dysregulation, and verbal threats of intent to reoffend; and parental or guardian resistance to adequate supervision and treatment compliance.

According to current evidence, Worling and Langstrom (2006) identify the following risk factors:

- *Empirically supported risk factors*: deviant sexual interest, prior criminal sanctions for sexual offending, sexual offending against more than one victim, sexual offending against a stranger victim, social isolation, and uncompleted offence-specific treatment.

- *Promising risk factors*: problematic parent–adolescent relationship and attitudes supportive of sexual offending.

- *Possible risk factors*: high-stress family environment; impulsivity; antisocial interpersonal orientation; interpersonal aggression; negative peer associations; sexual preoccupation; sexual offending against a male victim; sexual offending against a child; threats, violence, or weapons in sexual offence; and environment supporting reoffending.

- *Unlikely risk factors*: adolescent's own history of sexual victimisation, history of nonsexual offending, sexual offending involving penetration, denial of sexual offending and low victim empathy.

Detailed knowledge of prevalence, diversity, and empirically based risk factors relating to juvenile sexual offending can enhance a comprehensive response by providing a factual basis from which to build a foundation for collaboration.

Collaboration

The word 'collaboration' gets a lot of press. It is a term often used and not always practised. The *Encarta World English Dictionary*'s (2009) first definition of 'collaboration' is 'the act of working with someone to create or produce something'. The same source includes 'traitorous cooperation with an enemy' as another definition. Efforts to coordinate service provision for young people who sexually abuse are at risk of resembling traitorous cooperation with an enemy when opposing values and beliefs about this work collide in an environment that does not support respect for diverse thought and transparent exploration of opposing views.

According to the US Department of Justice's Center for Sex Offender Management (2000), collaboration involves the exchange of information, altering of activities, sharing resources, and enhancement of the capacity of another for the mutual benefit of all in order to achieve a common purpose. Genuine collaboration involves dedication and persistence in the exploration and implementation of empirically based service provision for addressing sexual harm by youth. It is not for the faint of heart!

The following example illustrates typical difficulties in collaboration. In one family with seven children, where all seven were sexually abused, and six sexually abused each other, multiple service providers have been collaborating for over 3 years, across a broad geographic area, in an effort to prevent recidivism. Numerous private and public agencies have been involved at different times, and three of the children have been placed in multiple residential facilities due to extremely high-risk behaviour. On one occasion, staff at a residential programme lied, and falsified documents about a youth's behaviour, in order to influence another programmer's decision to accept the youth for services. Another time, an angry programme manager hung up on the service coordinator after yelling about his dissatisfaction with decision making in a team meeting. Such experiences create a range of challenges and threaten community safety.

Dedicated multi-disciplinary communication and collaboration are essential to achieve a comprehensive, clearly defined, and structured community-based approach for addressing sexual harm by youth (Grimshaw 2008). The Center for Sex Offender Management reports that:

> in numerous jurisdictions, criminal justice agencies and community organizations have successfully forged partnerships, recognizing the enormous potential for impacting crime and reducing cost when agencies share information, develop common goals, create compatible internal policies to support those goals, and join forces to analyze problems and create responsive solutions. (Center for Sex Offender Management 2000: 1).

It is imperative that juvenile justice systems partner with child protective services, mental health services for children, and local schools (Steinberg 2008). Children's services reform in the UK influenced the creation of youth offending teams developed to explain legal implications for youth and families, and collaborate with the Crown Prosecution Service to inform decision-making. Additionally, Local Safeguarding Children Boards were formed to ensure the interests of all children, including those who cause sexual harm. Such reorganisation has resulted in greater understanding, clarity, and interagency cooperation. The Youth Justice Board's source document, *Young People Who Sexually Abuse* (Grimshaw 2008), provides an outstanding resource on the current state of the UK's response to this problem. This chapter addresses specific ways communities can implement recommendations from that document and enhance community safety for all citizens.

Effective collaboration is necessary for compiling evidence of empirically driven interventions that inform best practices and promote successful outcomes. It is critical in coordinating efforts for harm reduction and community safety through resource development and utilisation. Excellent collaboration utilises optimum elements, and channels of communication that streamline access to services. Transparent communication and collaboration reveal harsh realities that must be faced in order to overcome obstacles threatening successful outcomes. Finally, collaboration is necessary for successfully exploring the most cost-effective ways to stop sexual harm by youth.

Barriers to effective collaboration

When a community has not established a collaborative process, potential participants may perceive that complex multi-system coordination is unattainable. Concerns about funding and resource allocation can reduce cooperation, and increase unnecessary competition. Potential participants may be fearful or unmotivated when research indicates a need for change. Responsibilities associated with designated tasks may feel threatening or overwhelming. A lack of defined leadership and focus can prevent successful task completion. Inadequate planning impedes satisfactory implementation. Isolated communities and/or a lack of family involvement are often the major cause of collaboration failure.

Developing a unified response

Standardisation

Effective community collaboration requires a standardised approach involving a shared mission, vision, core values, and philosophy of care that guide all service provision (Center for Sex Offender Management 2000; Schladale *et al.* 2007; Grimshaw 2008). It is critical that all participants contribute to the creation of such fundamental information in order to ensure compliance. When an approach is dictated rather than shared, communities risk division, and/or noncompliance that may impede progress and reduce community safety.

A unified response provides a documented foundation that serves as a map for service provision. Just like a road map, it illustrates how a multitude of avenues can all lead to the same location, or outcome. It addresses both content and processes for effective intervention.

A standardised approach is not a manual that dictates rigid adherence. Interdependent components are interwoven across a continuum from formal to informal documentation and communication. General guidelines are adequate in some situations while specific protocols are required for other activities. Published standards provide an overarching foundation (Bengis *et al.* 1999; Schladale *et al.* 2007), while protocols such as those for family reconciliation and reunification provide general guidelines (Schladale 2006), and designated agenda formats entail specific guidelines for facilitation (Grimshaw 2008).

Documented programme descriptions, service and safety plans are required for all service provision. Service and safety plans are confidentially disseminated among all collaborating partners, and reviewed throughout the full continuum of care. Such information provides clarity about specific interventions, responsibility, and accountability. Without such important information it is difficult to focus, assess strengths and vulnerabilities, and monitor progress in a clearly defined and structured way that streamlines decision making.

While different entities may have unique documents based upon differing situations, core information should be conveyed in all documentation. For instance, all mission statements should include a commitment to community safety such as, 'Our mission is to stop sexual harm by youth'. A vision may be a comprehensive, community-based response to sexual harm by youth that promotes common goals through transparent communication, shared responsibility, mutual authority, and accountability for success. Examples of foundation documents are available at resourcesforresolvingviolence.com, or by contacting the author directly.

When developing a unified response, plan for conflict, and embrace it! It is a normal part of the process. Acknowledging potentially divergent missions, values, and philosophies as soon as possible can reduce conflict throughout the intervention process. When discrepancies are openly acknowledged early in the creation of collaborative efforts, effective communication can honour varied interests, and provide a foundation for diverse thought and action. Protocols can be established if case opposition results in deadlock.

A uniform response requires general agreement about what constitutes best practices for harm reduction, commitment to adhere to such practices, and motivation to implement evidence-based interventions. Standards can help identify sexual harm by youth, promote effective interventions, enhance effective systems of care, and promote a competent response.

Eliminating sexual harm by youth

If you treat an individual as he is, he will stay as he is, but if you treat him as if he were what he ought to be and could be, he will become what he ought to be and could be.

Johann Wolfgang von Goethe

It is important to base a community's response on all relevant research relating to positive youth development, core competencies for court-involved youth, sexual harm by youth, trauma, affect regulation, resilience and protective factors, and youth violence prevention (Schladale *et al.* 2007; Schladale 2008). Two relevant documents highlight the state of the research relating to effective screening, assessment, and intervention. They are, as previously mentioned, the document, *Young People Who Sexually Abuse* (Grimshaw 2008), and *Community-Based Standards for Addressing Sexual Harm by Youth* (Schladale *et al.* 2007).

All collaborating entities should be required to demonstrate the following: how interventions contribute to the reduction of sexual harm, how relevant service providers are involved in a way that enhances successful outcomes, how dispositions focus on the least restrictive placement, and how evaluation and continuous assessment guide a clearly defined process of service and safety planning throughout all transitions across the full continuum of care, and are cost-effective. Competency development and treatment are parallel processes that must both be completed in order to effectively achieve successful long-term change.

Competency development

Competency development is youth's ability to enhance knowledge and skills in order to become 'productive, connected, and law-abiding members of their community' (Torbet and Thomas 2005: 3). Competency development is not treatment. 'Youth do not become competent just because they complete a treatment program' (Torbet and Thomas 2005: 5). Conversely, just because youth demonstrate competency does not necessarily mean they are finished with treatment.

Some youth receiving services are involved with the juvenile justice system. According to the Juvenile Justice and Delinquency Prevention Committee of the Pennsylvania Commission on Crime and Delinquency, the purpose of juvenile justice is:

> to provide for children committing delinquent acts programs of supervision, care and rehabilitation which provide balanced attention to the protection of the community, the imposition of accountability for offenses committed, and the development of competencies to enable children to become responsible and productive members of the community. (Torbet and Thomas 2005: 1)

The role of the juvenile justice system is to 'facilitate efforts that advance youths' competencies so that offenders are less likely to take part in anti-social, delinquent behaviours and are better able to become responsible and productive members of their communities' (Torbet and Thomas 2005: 12). Whether or not youth services are court mandated, developing pro-social competencies is critical for lifelong success.

It is important to recognise that education does not equal change. Research indicates five core competency domains: social skills (interaction, cognition and self-control), moral reasoning, academic skills, workforce development skills, and independent living skills. All youth must be able to integrate knowledge into consistent practice in order to demonstrate measurable progress.

Treatment

Successful treatment to stop sexual harm by youth is not limited to behavioural modification of sexually harmful behaviour. A holistic, individualised approach based upon empirically driven best practices for youth violence prevention is indicated (Schladale *et al.* 2007; Torbet and Thomas 2005; Chaffin 2009). Approaching youth as multifaceted individuals addresses relevant needs that contribute to a youth's overall, long-term success. A youth's support by, and connection to, the community are critical for successful treatment outcomes. Family-sensitive services that embrace strength, competency, and resilience provide the most direct and effective route to therapeutic solutions.

Sources for youth violence prevention indicate a need for multi-modal treatment focusing on parents and family, home-visiting, mentoring and social-cognitive strategies (Office of the Surgeon General 2001; Thornton *et al.* 2002; Center for the Study and Prevention of Violence 2006).

A trauma-sensitive foundation for positive youth development is replacing the historical, pathology-based approach derived from conventional wisdom for incarcerated adult sex offenders (Chaffin and Bonner 1998; Schladale 2008). Current evidence indicates that the most effective treatment is based upon a foundation of non-judgemental attitude, empathy, genuineness, and warmth (Hubble *et al.* 1999; Miller and Rollnick 2002; Hunter and Chaffin 2005). Additionally, studies indicate that successful outcomes in psychotherapy are based upon four factors (Hubble *et al.* 1999). They are therapeutic technique (15 per cent), creation of hope and expectation for change (15 per cent), the therapeutic relationship between service providers and clients (30 per cent), and client characteristics (40 per cent), including strengths, resources, social support, and living environment.

Treatment begins with a thorough evaluation in order to best meet a youth's goals for change (Prescott 2006; Schladale *et al.* 2007; Schladale 2008). Ongoing assessment of individual and environmental protective factors and core competencies creates a foundation for the positive youth development vital to harm reduction. This information guides safety and treatment planning throughout the therapeutic process.

Therapeutic change occurs in the context of relationship. While progress is measured through competency development (Torbet and Thomas 2005), the treatment process is not based on linear progression. Services may be more accurately described as analogous to weaving. Therapeutic issues are introduced into a treatment process and are interwoven in ways that integrate themes and connections to each family member's life experiences. Many threads are similar and repetitive throughout the fabric of treatment. The entire process and content of a healing experience creates a unique pattern that illuminates the changing tapestry of a youth's life story. Therapeutic components, or threads, that create the weaving, provide a pattern design for treatment.

These components of treatment occur in a holistic, ecological framework throughout the full continuum of care. Utilising a family focus that addresses physical, social, psychological, and spiritual elements of therapeutic change enhances potential for long-term successful outcomes. According to *Community-Based Standards For*

Addressing Sexual Harm by Youth (Schladale *et al.* 2007), generally agreed-upon treatment components involve elimination of harm by:

- teaching affect regulation (Groves 2002; Schore 2003; Stien and Kendall 2004; Torbet and Thomas 2005)

- teaching social problem solving, including resolving interpersonal disputes (Henderson 1996; Office of the Surgeon General 2001; Thornton *et al.* 2002; Torbet and Thomas 2005)

- building social skills to enhance greater self-confidence and social competency (Office of the Surgeon General 2001; Thornton *et al.* 2002; Torbet and Thomas 2005)

- promoting social perspective taking to enhance empathy for and sensitivity to the negative impact of sexual harm on victims, families, and communities (Office of the Surgeon General 2001)

- mentoring youth (Ferber *et al.* 2002; Thornton *et al.* 2002; Center for the Study and Prevention of Violence 2006)

- helping youth to understand and intervene in disturbances of arousal that may influence sexually harmful behaviour (Stien and Kendall 2004; van der Kolk 2004)

- promoting positive self-worth and self-confidence (Henderson *et al.* 1996; Ferber *et al.* 2002)

- developing an appreciation for and connection to one's culture (Center for Sex Offender Management 1999; Hunter *et al.* 2000)

- clarifying and modelling values related to respect for self and others (Henderson *et al.* 1996)

- teaching and modelling social psychology of gender as a component of harm reduction (Burn 1996)

- teaching sexual health (Ryan and Lane 1997; Center for Sex Offender Management 1999; Hunter *et al.* 2000; Brown and Schwartz 2006)

- healing trauma (McMackin *et al.* 2002; Schore 2003; Creeden 2004, 2006; Kauffman Best Practices Report 2004; Schladale 2006).

Interventions with youth who have caused sexual harm are continually evolving. Empirically based studies are emerging in the field and guiding practice. It is imperative to acknowledge that advances in research will influence ongoing change in best practices for eliminating sexual harm by youth. Staying abreast of such important research requires responsive and flexible collaboration, as new research renders current best practices outdated.

Effective collaboration

Effective collaboration is a fluid and unique process for each community. Urban, suburban and rural environments present a broad array of diverse challenges, resources, or a lack of resources. Cultural attitudes and human diversity play a significant role in accessing services, and active engagement in such services. Attitudes, values and beliefs influence all collaboration.

Successful collaboration requires continuous evaluation of who should be involved. Each community should have key members who oversee and manage formal structures and processes that provide the community infrastructure for addressing sexual harm by youth. Additionally, multidisciplinary treatment teams have responsibility for actively engaging youth, parents (or guardians), and social support network members in activities for youth violence prevention. This is an inclusive, rather than exclusive, process. The more people involved in eliminating sexual harm, the greater is the potential for successful outcomes.

If communities do not have a Youth Offending Team, or Local Safeguarding Children Board, efforts should be made to develop them. When responsibility has not been designated, a steering committee can be formed to determine who should conduct strengths-and-needs evaluation of the designated community, or facilitate the process themselves. Recommendations from such an evaluation provide the foundation from which specific efforts begin.

Designating the most cost-effective, empirically driven interventions ensures streamlined implementation and monitoring. When all entities with designated services for addressing sexual harm by youth are identified, and agree to participate in a community collaborative, a standardised process for implementation, and monitoring progress, is established. Comprehensive service and safety plans provide a map for so doing.

Finally, a system for tracking outcomes is developed through assessment of competency development (Torbet and Thomas 2005). When all components of the community collaborative are in motion, continual assessment of service provision is provided through consumer feedback.

Above all else, explicit, respectful interdependence is the key to successful collaboration. It is also the most professionally exciting way to perform the often gruelling and gut-wrenching work of eliminating sexual harm by youth. Professionals, youth, and family members working diligently to heal such pain can join together in a committed effort to restore victim justice and community safety. When this happens, the secrecy and isolation associated with violence and sexual abuse are reduced, attachments are formed, and restorative experiences occur.

Recommendations

When collaborating with families to stop sexual harm by youth, it is imperative that we:

- create a context of respect, care, and concern for the development of trust in working relationships

- promote sharing of all resources

- involve families, teachers, coaches, clergy, and anyone else willing to support these youth in their efforts at harm reduction

- embrace distrust, ambivalence, and resistance

- engage and motivate participants to integrate positive change into their lives

- ask permission to talk about sensitive issues

- allow each youth and family to lead the process

- recognise challenges to addressing the pain of sexual abuse

- advocate for and support all participants in utilising untapped strengths and competencies in order to prevent recidivism

- expect disclosure of significant trauma that may include family dissolution, violence, substance abuse, poverty, discrimination, illness, and/or disabilities

- ensure that all participants are emotionally prepared for the impact of addressing sexual harm by youth

- teach all participants affect regulation in order to prevent further harm
- use the trauma outcome process to provide an understanding of the behavioural change necessary for harm reduction
- help participants become pro-social community members
- provide ongoing support as indicated.

Dedicated service providers can use the following empirical actions or policies to enhance collaboration and harm reduction:

- Be genuine.
- Define clear expectations.
- Don't judge.
- Practise empathy.
- Express warmth.
- Exercise patience.
- Provide hope and optimism for a youth's success.
- Give clear instruction and support for truth telling.
- Find out about each youth's interests and dreams.
- Help them explore and pursue those interests and dreams.
- Discuss and explore feelings in an emotionally safe environment.
- Explain differences and varieties of touch.
- Teach youth about benevolent touch for themselves and others.
- Respect privacy by having rules about bathing, dressing and sleeping.
- Develop a positive, non-punitive plan for managing challenging behaviours such as night terrors, bedwetting, soiling, aggression, masturbation, etc.
- Do things kids and families like to do.
- Create a plan to ensure respect for each child's physical and emotional boundaries.

- Share any concerns with treatment team members.

- Promote and have fun!

- Celebrate any success no matter how small, or seemingly insignificant.

- Celebrate yourself, and your colleagues, every day, for a job well done!

A single professional seldom sees youth who have caused sexual harm throughout the full continuum of care. Most often, these youth and families experience a multitude of child-serving agencies, and a diverse array of professionals. The complex nature of sexual harm by youth requires thoughtful consideration of research relating to youth violence prevention. Clearly defined, comprehensive community collaboration provides a structured way to enhance successful outcomes that affect all facets of society.

Note

1 This work is adapted from *Resources For Resolving Violence, Inc.* (resourcesforresolvingviolence.com), and *Community-Based Standards for Addressing Sexual Harm by Youth* (Schladale *et al.* 2007).

References

Association for the Treatment of Sexual Abusers (ATSA) (2000) *The Effective Legal Management of Juvenile Sex Offenders* [online]. Available at: http://www.atsa.com/ppjuvenile.html (accessed on 17 March 2009).

Association for the Treatment of Sexual Abusers (ATSA) (2006) *Report of the Task Force on Children with Sexual Behavior Problems* [online]. Available at: http://www.atsa.com/ppjuvenile.html (accessed on 17 March 2009).

Becker, J. (1990) 'Treating Adolescent Sexual Offenders', *Professional Psychology: Research and Practice*, 21(5): 362–365.

Becker, J. (1998) 'What We Know About the Characteristics and Treatment of Adolescents Who Have Committed Sexual Offenses', *Child Maltreatment: Journal of the American Professional Society on the Abuse of Children*, 3: 317–329.

Bengis, S., Brown, A., Freeman-Longo, R. *et al.* (1999) *Standards of Care for Youth in Sex Offense-Specific Residential Programs*. National Offense-Specific Residential Standards Task Force. Holyoke, MA: NEARI Press.

Borduin, C., Henggeler, S., Blaske, D. and Stein, R. (1990) 'Multisystemic Treatment of Adolescent Sexual Offenders', *International Journal of Offender Therapy and Comparative Criminology*, 34: 105–113.

Borduin, C. and Schaeffer, C. (2001) 'Multisystemic Treatment of Adolescent Sexual Offenders: A Progress Report', *Journal of Psychology and Human Sexuality*, 13(3/4): 25–42.

Brown, S. and Schwartz, C. (2006) 'Promoting Healthy Sexuality in Sexually Abusive Youth', in R. Longo and D. Prescott (eds), *Current Perspectives: Working with Sexually Aggressive Youth and Youth with Sexual Behavior Problems*. Holyoke, MA: NEARI Press.

Burn, S. (1996) *The Social Psychology of Gender*. New York: McGraw-Hill.

Cawson, P., Wattam, C., Brooker, S. and Kelly, G. (2000) *Child Maltreatment in the United Kingdom. A Study of the Prevalence of Child Abuse and Neglect*. London: NSPCC.

Center for Sex Offender Management (1999) *Understanding Juvenile Sexual Offending Behavior: Emerging Approaches and Management Practices* [online]. Available at: http://www.csom.org/ (accessed 17 March 2009).

Center for Sex Offender Management (2000) *The Collaborative Approach to Sex Offender Management* [online]. Available at: http://www.csom.org/ (accessed 17 March 2009).

Center for the Study and Prevention of Violence (2006) *Blueprints for Violence Prevention*. Institute of Behavioral Science, University of Colorado at Boulder [online]. Available at: http://www.colorado.edu/cspv/blueprints/ (accessed 17 March 2009).

Chaffin, M. (2009) 'Public Policy Concerning Children with Sexual Behavior Problems and Teenage Sex Offenders'. *The 23rd Annual San Diego International Conference on Child and Family Maltreatment*, Rady Children's Hospital San Diego, January 2009.

Chaffin, M. and Bonner, B. (1998) 'Don't Shoot, We're Your Children: Have We Gone Too Far in Our Response to Adolescent Sexual Abusers and Children with Sexual Behavior Problems?', *Child Maltreatment*, November: 314–316.

Chaffin, M., Bonner, B. and Pierce, K. (2003) *NCSBY Fact Sheet: What Research Shows About Adolescent Sex Offenders*. Oklahoma City, OK: Center on Child Abuse and Neglect, University of Oklahoma Health Sciences Center.

Creeden, K. (2004) 'Integrating Trauma and Attachment Research in the Treatment of Sexually Abusive Youth', in M. C. Calder (ed.), *Children and Young People Who Sexually Abuse: New Theory, Research, and Practice Developments*. Lyme Regis, Dorset, UK: Russell House Publishing.

Creeden, K. (2006) 'Neurological Impact of Trauma and Implications', in R. Longo and D. Prescott (eds), *Current Perspectives: Working with Sexually Aggressive Youth and Youth with Sexual Behavior Problems*. Holyoke, MA: NEARI Press.

Encarta World English Dictionary [online] (2009) Available at: Macbook Dashboard (accessed 17 March 2009).

Epperson, D., Ralston, C., Fowers, D., Dewitt, J. and Gore, K. (2005) 'Development of the Juvenile Sexual Offense Recidivism Risk Assessment Tool (J-SORRAT)', *Conference of the Minnesota Association for the Treatment of Sexual Abusers*, Minneapolis, MN.

Epperson, D., Ralston, C., Fowers, D., Dewitt, J. and Gore, K. (2006) 'Juvenile Sexual Offense Recidivism Rate Assessment Tool-II (JSORRAT-II)', in D. Prescott (ed.), *Risk Assessment of Youth Who Have Sexually Abused*. Oklahoma City, OK: Wood 'N' Barnes Publishing and Distribution.

Ferber, T. and Pittman, K. with Marshall, T. (2002) *Helping All Youth to Grow Up Fully Prepared and Fully Engaged*. Takoma Park, MD: Forum for Youth Investment.

von Goethe, J. (no date) [online]. Available at: http://www.quotationsbook. com (accessed 17 March 2009).

Grimshaw, R. (2008) *Young People Who Sexually Abuse*. Youth Justice Board [online]. Available at: http://www.yjb.gov.uk/en-gb/ (accessed 17 March 2009).

Groves, B. (2002) *Children Who See Too Much: Lessons from the Child Witness to Violence Project*. Boston, MA: Beacon Press.

Henderson, N., Benard, B. and Sharp-Light, N. (eds) (1996) *Resiliency in Action: Practical Ideas for Overcoming Risks and Building Strength in Youth, Families and Communities* [online]. Available at: http://www.resiliency. com/ (accessed 3 June 2006).

Hickey, N., Vizard, E., McCrory, E. and French, L. (2006) *Links Between Juvenile Sexually Abusive Behavior and Emerging Severe Personality Disorder Traits in Childhood*. DSPD Programme: Dangerous People and Severe Personality Disorder, Department for Health, Home Office and National Offender Management Service. London: HMSO.

Hubble, M., Duncan, B. and Miller, S. (1999) *The Heart and Soul of Change*. Washington, DC: American Psychological Association.

Hunter, J. and Chaffin, M. (2005) *NCSBY Bulletin: Ethical Issues in the Assessment and Treatment of Adolescent Sex Offenders*. Oklahoma City, OK: Center on Child Abuse and Neglect, University of Oklahoma Health Sciences Center.

Hunter, J., Figueredo, A., Malamuth, N. and Becker, J. (2003) 'Juvenile Sex Offenders: Toward the Development of a Typology', *Sexual Abuse: A Journal of Research and Treatment*, 15: 27–48.

Hunter, J., Gilbertson, S., Vedros, D. and Morton, M. (2004) 'Strengthening Community-Based Programming for Juvenile Sexual Offenders: Key Concepts and Paradigm Shifts', *Child Maltreatment*, 9: 2.

Hunter, J., Hazelwood, R. and Slesinger, D. (2000) 'Juvenile-Perpetrated Sex Crimes: Patterns of Offending and Predictors of Violence', *Journal of Family Violence*, 15 (1), 81–93.

Kahn, T. J. and Chambers, H. J. (1991) 'Assessing Reoffense Risk with Juvenile Sexual Offenders', *Child Welfare*, 70(3): 333–345.

Kauffman Foundation Best Practices Project (2004) *Closing the Quality Chasm in Child Abuse Treatment: Identifying and Disseminating Best Practices* [online]. Available at: http://www.capacitybuilding.net/ (accessed 28 January 2007).

Langstrom, N. and Grann, M. (2000) 'Risk for Criminal Recidivism Among Young Sex Offenders', *Journal of Interpersonal Violence*, 15: 855–871.

McMackin, R., Leisen, M., Cusack, J., LaFratta, J. and Litwin, P. (2002) 'The Relationship of Trauma Exposure to Sex Offending Behavior Among Male Juvenile Offenders', *Journal of Child Sexual Abuse*, 11(2): 25–40.

Mead, M. (no date) Available at: http://www.quotationsbook.com (accessed 17 March 2009).

Miller, W. and Rollnick, W. (2002) *Motivational Interviewing*. New York: Guilford Press.

Office of the Surgeon General (2001) *Youth Violence: A Report of the Surgeon General* [online]. Available at: http://www.surgeongeneral.gov/ (accessed 27 January 2007).

Prentky, R. and Righthand, S. (2003) *Juvenile Sex Offender Assessment Protocol II: Manual*. Washington, DC: Office of Juvenile Justice and Delinquency Prevention.

Prescott, D. (2006) *Risk Assessment of Youth Who Have Sexually Abused*. Oklahoma City, OK: Wood 'N' Barnes Publishing.

Righthand, S. and Welch, C. (2001) 'Characteristics of Youth Who Sexually Offend', *Journal of Child Sexual Abuse*, 13: 15–32.

Ryan, G. and Lane, S. (1997) *Juvenile Sexual Offending*. San Francisco, CA: Jossey-Bass.

Schladale, J. (2006) 'Family Matters: The Importance of Engaging Families in Treatment with Youth Who Have Caused Sexual Harm', in R. Longo and D. Prescott (eds), *Current Perspectives: Working with Sexually Aggressive Youth and Youth with Sexual Behavior Problems*. Holyoke, MA: NEARI Press.

Schladale, J. (2007) 'Family Reconciliation and Reunification with Youth Who Have Caused Sexual Harm', in D. Prescott (ed.), *Applying Knowledge to Practice: Challenges in the Treatment and Supervision of Sexual Abusers*. Oklahoma City, OK: Wood 'N' Barnes Publishing.

Schladale, J. (2008) 'Empirically Driven Assessment of Juvenile Offenders', *The Sex Offender*, Vol. 6: *Offender Evaluation and Program Strategies*. Kingston, NJ: Civic Research Institute.

Schladale, J., Langan, T., Barnett, P. *et al.* (2007) *Community Based Standards for Responding to Sexual Harm by Youth* [online]. Available at: http://www.resourcesforresolvingviolence.com (accessed 17 March 2009).

Schore, A. (2003) *Affect Regulation and the Repair of the Self*. New York: W. W. Norton.

Schram, D., Milloy, C. and Rowe, W. (1991) *Juvenile Sex Offenders: A Follow-Up Study of Reoffense Behavior*. Olympia, WA: Washington State Institute for Public Policy.

Seto, M. and Lalumiere, M. (2006) 'Conduct Problems and Juvenile Sexual Offenders: A Comprehensive Meta-Analysis', in H. Barbaree and W. Marshall (eds), *The Juvenile Sexual Offender* (2nd edn). New York: Guilford Press.

Stien, P. and Kendall, J. (2004) *Psychological Trauma and the Developing Brain*. New York: The Haworth Press.

Steinberg, L. (2008) 'Juvenile Justice: Introducing the Issue', *The Future of Children*, 18: 2.

Thornton, T., Craft, C., Dahlberg, L., Lynch, B. and Baer, K. (2002) *Best Practices of Youth Violence Prevention: A Sourcebook for Community Action* (Revised). Atlanta, GA: Centers for Disease Control and Prevention, National Center for Injury Prevention and Control.

Torbet, P. and Thomas, D. (2005) *Advancing Competency Development: A White Paper for Pennsylvania.* Pittsburgh, PA: National Center for Juvenile Justice.

van der Kolk, B. (2004) 'Frontiers of Trauma Research'. *Cape Cod Institute Conference*, Cape Cod, MA: 12–16 July.

Worling, J. and Langstrom, N. (2006) 'Risk of Sexual Recidivism in Adolescents Who Offend Sexually: Correlates and Assessment', in H. Barbaree and W. Marshall (eds), *The Juvenile Sex Offender*. New York: Guilford Press.

Chapter 10

Mentally disordered sexual offenders

Brad Booth

Introduction

The term 'mentally disordered sexual offender' (MDSO) is used to describe individuals who have committed sexual offences and who have co-morbid major mental disorders (not including substance or personality disorders). This important distinction must be considered when formulating a treatment plan to manage an offender's risk in the community. This special category of sexual offender has emerged with the trans-institutionalisation seen over the past four decades. MDSOs require a specialised approach for effective risk management and treatment, both in custody and in the community. This chapter will describe the trans-institutionalisation phenomenon, the prevalence of major mental disorders among sexual offenders, and the special considerations and approaches for MDSOs.

Trans-institutionalisation

Prior to the 1960s, seriously mentally ill individuals were warehoused in asylums. However, two major factors came into play, resulting in an emptying of the asylums, originally termed 'deinstitutionalisation' (Talbott 2004). Firstly, antipsychotic medications became available in the 1950s, providing the first effective treatments for serious mental illness such as schizophrenia and bipolar disorder. Secondly, the civil rights movement of the 1960s extended to the mentally ill. Institutions with abhorrent conditions were targeted and required to provide a therapeutic environment with appropriate numbers of trained staff. This requirement exponentially increased the cost of providing care for the mentally ill. Furthermore, civil commitment legislation became much stricter, often requiring that the mentally ill individual pose an *imminent* risk of *serious* harm to themselves or others before they could be committed to a mental institution. The end result of these factors was a dramatic reduction in the number of chronic care beds for the severely mentally ill. For some, this meant significant increases in liberty and true community reintegration. However, for a large number of people with mental illness, this meant a lack of appropriate community supports, leaving many without stable housing and needed supervision. Many of these individuals migrated into the criminal justice system as part of trans-institutionalisation.

The concept of trans-institutionalisation is not new, with a historical paper from 1939 noting the inverse relationship between beds for the mentally ill and the rates of incarceration in 14 European countries (Penrose 1939). This trend can clearly be seen in Figure 10.1. This phenomenon has been observed internationally (Fakhoury and Priebe

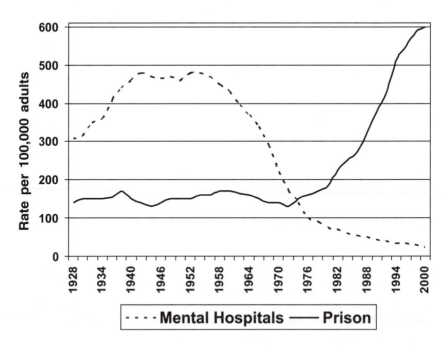

Figure 10.1 Rates of institutionalisation in the USA (per 100,000 adults) (reproduced from Harcourt 2006)

2002), including England and Wales (Gunn 2000), Canada (Sealy and Whitehead 2004), and the USA (Konrad 2002; Harcourt 2006). The end result is high rates of mental illness among inmates, including sexual offenders.

Mental illness among sexual offenders

The precise rate of severe mental illness among sexual offenders is not known. However, several studies have examined this issue. Dunsieth *et al.* (2004) noted in a sample of 113 sexual offenders that 85 per cent had a substance use disorder, 74 per cent had paraphilia, 58 per cent had mood disorder, 38 per cent had impulse-control disorder, 23 per cent had anxiety disorder, 9 per cent had an eating disorder, and 56 per cent had antisocial personality disorder. Alden *et al.* (2007) demonstrated that psychotic disorders co-morbid with personality disorders and substance use disorders are associated with increased risk of sexual offending. In another study of outpatients with paraphilia and paraphilia-related disorders (including a number of sexual offenders), Kafka and Hennen (2002) described high rates of mood disorders (71.6 per cent), anxiety disorders (38.3 per cent), and alcohol/substance abuse (40.8 per cent). In yet another study, Ahlmeyer *et al.* (2003) found high rates of anxiety, dysthymia and depression. Within our Canadian psychiatric hospital for provincially sentenced offenders, the rate of serious mental illness is high among sexual offenders, with 43 per cent being diagnosed with depressive disorder, 13 per cent bipolar disorder, 28 per cent anxiety disorder, 16 per cent psychotic disorder, 10 per cent dementia, 31 per cent mental retardation/developmental delay, 42 per cent alcohol dependence, 38 per cent substance dependence, 20 per cent attention deficit hyperactivity disorder (ADHD), and 47 per cent personality disorder (unpublished data).

The role of these mental disorders in offending is unclear. Some evidence suggests that mental disorders increase recidivism and reincarceration in general offenders (Baillargeon *et al.* 2009) and in MDSOs (Langstrom *et al.* 2004; Fazel *et al.* 2007). However, some evidence suggests that psychotic disorders actually decrease risk in sexual offenders, as noted in one meta-analysis (Bonta *et al.* 1998) and in the Sex Offender Risk Appraisal Guide (Quinsey *et al.* 1998). It is possible that the varying results are a function of whether the underlying mental disorder was detected and appropriately treated; methodological issues in the study design may also be a factor.

Regardless, sexual offenders with mental disorders require a modified treatment approach that includes consideration and treatment of their underlying psychiatric disorder.

Treatment of MDSOs

Unfortunately, MDSOs have been unrecognised in the literature as a unique group requiring specialised treatment. As such, the evidence for treatment is limited to clinical experience, derived from evidence-based approaches available for general sexual offenders and for the mentally ill. In reality, there is no simple approach. Instead, treatment of each MDSO should be tailored to the individual, the mental disorder being one of many factors that may be relevant to treatment. Treatment should be focused on diagnosis initially, and then targets for treatment should be examined and prioritised for different categories of mental disorders.

Our treatment programme includes an inpatient unit which is part of the provincial jail system. The unit is part of a 100-bed psychiatric hospital for provincially sentenced offenders, the first of its kind in Canada. The inpatient interdisciplinary team includes psychiatrists, psychologists, social workers, nurses, substance abuse counsellors, recreation therapists and vocation staff. During the referral process, residents are flagged by corrections staff as potentially having a mental disorder. When the resident arrives in the institution, he undergoes an initial assessment by psychiatry and nursing, including a comprehensive risk assessment and several standardised rating scales. The team prioritises the treatment needs of the offender. The treatment plan usually includes medication treatment. We also use the self-regulation group therapy programme for sexual offenders described by Marshall et al. (2006), including a modified programme for developmentally delayed or other cognitively impaired offenders. Anger management and substance use treatment are also core programmes for many residents. At times, severely ill offenders require initial psychiatric stabilisation prior to engaging in group therapy. Our outpatient services are centralised at our Mental Health Centre in Ottawa, Canada, with a sexual behaviours clinic. The clinic provides evaluations to the courts and evaluation and treatment of sexual offenders and self-referred paraphiles. Similar approaches are utilised in the clinic.

Diagnosing MDSOs

The first step in effective treatment for MDSOs is clarifying the diagnoses and evaluating the potential role of the MDSO's diagnoses in the sexual offence. There are often systemic barriers to doing this. For example, in the correctional setting, MDSOs may have been placed among the general prison population or in protective custody without any screening for mental health issues. They may not be seen by a mental health professional or be sent to a treatment facility. Alternatively, if they do come into a treatment programme for sexual offenders, their psychiatric symptoms may be written off as behavioural issues. In the community, MDSOs may be managed primarily by probation and parole officers, who may not recognise illness nor have been trained to do so. Similarly, community treatment may be provided by individuals with insufficient knowledge about mental illness. Often, there is insufficient availability of psychiatric care for sexual offenders.

Ideally, all sexual offenders would be evaluated by appropriately trained individuals for the presence of mental disorders and have appropriate treatment for these disorders. Similarly, all individuals who treat and manage sexual offenders should have some training in the diagnosis and treatment of mental disorders. Finally, MDSOs may best be treated in specialised programmes that can address both their sexual offence behaviour and co-morbid illnesses.

Prioritisation of treatment needs

Once symptoms of mental illness are identified, they must be balanced against other treatment issues, prioritising these issues and looking at available resources. Symptoms may include psychosis, mood problems, anxiety, substance use, cognitive deficits, attention deficits and others. MDSOs should be evaluated for the severity of these symptoms and how these symptoms might affect sexual offender treatment (discussed below). The therapist should prioritise the treatment needs. For example, at times, the mental disorder may prevent addressing sexual offending issues and may require stabilisation before treating sexual issues. Symptoms may also be difficult to treat (for example, negative symptoms of schizophrenia) and require an alteration of regular treatment. At times, optimal treatment may involve treating both issues (the sexual disorder and other mental disorder) at the same time. Alternatively, treatment may simply involve addressing the sexual issue and leaving treatment of the mental disorder to others.

Examining the role of the mental disorder in offending

Once an MDSO's diagnoses are clarified and the treatment needs prioritised, individuals involved in the risk management of MDSOs should examine the role that the individual's mental disorder played in sexual offending. At times, it may be that the mental disorder caused the behaviour or contributed significantly, providing a clear target for treatment. In other cases, the mental disorder may have been ancillary to the offence, but may become an issue in treatment. In the end, the role of the mental disorder must be acknowledged and considered in treatment and risk management.

Discussion of co-morbid disorders and their potential role in offending should also be introduced into group therapy. Although this approach should always be individualised, there are general issues seen within specific MDSO populations (including psychotic disorders, mood disorders, anxiety disorders, dementing disorders, attention-deficit disorders, substance use disorders and personality disorders) that should be brought up for group discussion. Mental retardation and developmental disorders also require a specialised approach (for more detail on this, see Chapter 11 of this volume).

Specific MDSO populations

Psychotic disorders

MDSOs suffering from chronic psychotic disorders, such as schizophrenia, schizoaffective disorder and delusional disorder, can be some of the most challenging individuals to treat and manage. In our specialised unit for MDSOs, 16 per cent suffer from one of these chronic psychotic illnesses. We also see fewer but still significant numbers of individuals with psychosis in our outpatient clinic and within our system for MDSOs found 'not criminally responsible on account of mental disorder' (NCR). Despite having quite profound illnesses, most MDSOs will not be in the NCR system or equivalent system in other jurisdictions, such as 'not guilty by reason of insanity' (NGRI). For example, in Canada between 1992 and 2005, sexual assault and other sexual offences accounted for only 4.3 per cent of the total offences among NCR individuals (Latimer 2006). Those who do qualify for an NCR/NGRI defence may have their treatment needs regarding sexual offending overlooked, the treatment team focusing primarily on the mental illness. Treatment should address both the sexual offending and the mental disorder.

Once an MDSO with a psychotic disorder is identified, treatment first involves an analysis of how the illness influenced his actions. Did it contribute directly to the behaviour or is it simply an ancillary issue? For example, if a known offender with exhibitionism and schizophrenia had stopped his antipsychotic medications prior to offending, his sexual offending may have resulted from auditory hallucinations urging his behaviour. Issues around medication non-compliance would need to be a part of the treatment plan, and long-acting intramuscular antipsychotic medications may be indicated. In another MDSO with these same illnesses and behaviours, the offending may have been primarily motivated by other issues, such as the presence of paraphilia.

Once the treating team has an understanding of the role the psychotic illness played in the offence, the individual's current symptoms should be evaluated, including delusions, hallucinations, negative symptoms, and cognitive impairment and disorganisation. Does the patient need to have his antipsychotic medications adjusted? For example, an MDSO who is religiously preoccupied may blame the Devil for his actions and thus be unable to focus on how his behaviour led to offending. Such delusions may respond to adjustments in antipsychotic medications. At other times, chronic residual symptoms that do not tend to respond well to medications, such as cognitive deficits or negative symptoms, might interfere and require alteration of the treatment programme. For example, we offer our self-regulation programme sessions in the afternoon to account for sedation from medications as well as negative symptoms such as anergy and avolition. Further, we put those with cognitive deficits and mild developmental delays in a modified self-regulation programme, with a slightly simplified approach and more repetition.

At times, the treatment of psychosis may supersede the sexual issue, and medication intervention may be required to stabilise psychotic symptoms prior to commencing therapy. Despite this, residual psychosis is not an absolute contraindication to group therapy. Florid psychosis with active delusions regarding the offending would usually be an exclusion criterion for self-regulation groups. We have had a number of individuals who were able to effectively address offending behaviour despite residual symptoms of their illnesses. It should be noted that leaders of such groups will need to feel comfortable with psychotic content.

When MDSOs with psychotic disorders enter the community, risk management will likely need to involve community supports that are not usually a part of most sexual offender programmes. For example, individuals may benefit from living in a group home or supervised setting where medication compliance can be ensured. Further, individuals may benefit from the support of community outreach programmes, such as an assertive community treatment team or other outreach programme. Unfortunately, our institution's experience has been that all MDSOs may face discrimination from these outreach organisations. It may prove quite difficult to overcome the stigma associated with sexual offending. Advocacy and education about MDSOs may be helpful.

Probation and parole officers who supervise MDSOs with psychosis would also benefit from training about these illnesses to better manage risk in the community. For example, when an MDSO has difficulty with conditions imposed by the court, an evaluation should be done to look at the role that mental illness might be playing. Illness may best be managed through hospitalisation and adjustment of medications, rather than incarceration. Similarly, non-compliance with court conditions should not automatically be written off as being due to mental illness and, at times, is more appropriately managed through the court. Communication between court officers and the treatment team is important to help address these issues.

Mood disorders

Mood disorders, especially depression and dysthymia, are highly prevalent in sexual offenders (Kafka *et al.* 2002; Dunsieth *et al.* 2004; Baillargeon *et al.* 2009). Many offenders describe symptoms of depression at the time of the offences that may have contributed to their behaviour. Further, sexual offenders are frequently vilified in the criminal justice system. Physical assaults, sexual assaults and scapegoating are not uncommon in prisons (Dumond 2003; Jones and Pratt 2008), particularly for individuals with offences against children. For many sexual offenders, conviction for a sexual offence will bring loss of employment, family, friends, status and financial security. All of these factors likely contribute to increase the offender's risk of developing depression. The end result is that the offender presenting for treatment and community management may have significant symptoms of depression, which must be considered, as they can affect treatment outcome. For example, guilty ruminations can limit gains in therapy if they take a shame basis (Hudson *et al.* 19992; Bumby *et al.* 1999; Proeve and Howells 2002), poor concentration can limit the person's ability to benefit from group therapy and can prevent the assimilation of information between sessions, low energy can prevent the person from completing homework assignments, and hopelessness can interfere with the patients' desire to benefit from treatment if they feel they have nothing to live for. Depressed mood and pessimism can also prove detrimental to the group's milieu and negatively affect other members.

Once again, depression may need to be the target of treatment initially, with consultation to colleagues if required for complex cases. If symptoms are too severe, or if the depressed person has psychotic symptoms, this would be a relative contraindication to beginning group work. If medications are not proving to be effective in treating the depression, electroconvulsive therapy (ECT) may be appropriate in some cases. For example, we have sent a number of clients with severe depression for ECT when treatment with antidepressants was ineffective. In one case, a client being managed in the jail system who was suffering from undetected depression presented to us with near catatonia, renal failure and emaciation. The seriousness of this offender's mental health condition resulted from a general lack of awareness and understanding of mental health issues among correctional staff. Once his illness was appropriately identified and his course of ECT was completed, he was able to engage effectively in the therapeutic process.

Although depression can prevent someone from participating in a group, we have also found that the supportive atmosphere of the group can significantly improve depressive symptoms. At times we will prioritise some individuals to join the group with the goal of addressing guilty ruminations and losses, especially if there are group members with similar losses.

In MDSOs suffering from depression with co-morbid paraphilia or hypersexuality, we will often offer selective serotonin reuptake inhibitors (SSRIs) to treat depression, hypersexuality and paraphilia at the same time (Greenberg and Bradford 1997; Bradford 2001; Adi et al. 2002; Hill et al. 2003) (for more information on the use of SSRIs with sex offenders, see Chapter 6 of this volume).

Bipolar illness is less frequent in this population, but again can contribute to offending or be an issue in treatment. Mania and hypomania are usually stabilised prior to entering group therapy. The potential role of these disorders in disinhibiting the offender and in increasing sexual drive should be part of group therapy discussion.

All individuals with mood disorders may require treatment for these disorders that extends beyond the treatment for sexual offending. Again, resistance from mental health professionals to treat sexual offenders may pose a barrier.

Anxiety disorders

MDSOs suffering from anxiety disorders are also quite prevalent (Raymond *et al.* 1999; Hoyer *et al.* 2001; Kafka and Hennen 2002), social phobia, obsessive compulsive disorder (OCD), post-traumatic stress disorder (PTSD), panic disorder, and generalised anxiety disorder (GAD) being most relevant.

Anxiety, as part of all of these disorders, can interfere with effective group treatment for sexual offenders. Social phobia may prevent the MDSO from participating in group discussions and fully benefiting from therapy. Alternatively, they may entirely decline to attend group therapy. A lack of familiarity with these disorders may cause therapists to misinterpret the lack of participation as resistance to treatment rather than fear of social judgement. Prior to commencing treatment, it may be necessary first to treat the social phobia with medications or cognitive-behavioural therapy. At the same time, many individuals with less severe social phobia experience the acceptance of the therapy group as extremely validating and can really come out of their shells in the context of the group.

Once in therapy, the role of social phobia in offending should be examined during the offence analysis and risk management planning stages. For example, a socially shy man with paedophilia may have found the acceptance from children comforting, causing him to seek out children for social acceptance. Therapy should include strategies for increasing social acceptance and contact within age-appropriate relationships.

Trauma histories and PTSD appear to be prevalent among MDSOs (Marshall and Marshall 2000; McMackin *et al.* 2002), possibly contributing to offending behaviour. Further, PTSD may occur in the offender due to his offences (Gray *et al.* 2003; Crisford *et al.* 2008). Sexual victimisation of sexual offenders in prison can also occur (Dumond 2003; Wolff *et al.* 2007; Jones and Pratt 2008) and cause PTSD. Active symptoms of PTSD can complicate treatment by causing uncontrollable anxiety, dissociation and worsening of sleep, and distracting the offender from group discussions. Groups which focus on detailed descriptions of offences can unmask or worsen PTSD symptoms. However, at times, discussion of trauma issues within the group can assist other group members to see first-hand the effects that their offending may have had on the victim. When discussion of offences exacerbates PTSD symptoms, it may be necessary to work on trauma issues prior to entering sexual offender group therapy. Alternatively, the MDSO with PTSD may need additional individual support around the PTSD beyond that which can be provided in group. If not interfering with treatment, trauma issues may best be left to deal with at a time when the MDSO's life is more stable.

For individuals suffering from other causes of anxiety, including OCD, GAD and depression, the symptoms should be evaluated for their role in the offence and potential role in treatment. All individuals may require separate treatment for the anxiety disorder that complements or extends beyond the duration of sex offender therapy. Once again, issues of stigma may interfere with the individual's ability to obtain such therapy from other mental health providers.

Attention deficit hyperactivity disorder (ADHD)

Adult ADHD is under-recognised and often under-treated (Barkley *et al.* 2008). Again, the exact prevalence among sexual offenders is not known. However, in a consecutive group of outpatients in a sexual behaviours clinic, the retrospective rate of childhood ADHD was 36 per cent (Kafka 2002). Additionally, it was noted that childhood ADHD was associated with paraphilic disorders (Kafka and Prentky 1998). In our inpatient unit, the adult ADHD rate among MDSOs is 20 per cent. Symptoms of ADHD, such as impulsivity and difficulty in evaluating consequences, may contribute to offending behaviour or interfere with group treatment.

In group treatment, residual hyperactive and impulsive symptoms may interfere with the person's ability to interact in the group. He may interrupt frequently, talk too much, or blurt out derogatory comments to other group members. Additionally, he may have a limited ability to remain seated and quiet for the duration of the group. Deficits in attention can limit his ability to benefit from other group members' comments. He may also have difficulty in completing group assignments or organising an effective risk management plan.

Given the potential role of ADHD in offending and in interfering with group therapy as well as the general impairments caused by untreated ADHD, MDSOs with ADHD should be offered pharmacologic treatment. Interestingly, methylphenidate, a psychostimulant used in the treatment of ADHD, was added to augment SSRI treatment in a single study of 26 men with paraphilia or paraphilia-related disorders (Kafka and Hennen 2000). The addition of methylphenidate in this study was associated with further significant decreases in total sexual outlet and average time spent per day in paraphilia or paraphilia-related behaviour. These gains appeared to be independent of the presence of ADHD. This suggests a possible additional benefit to prescribing methylphenidate for ADHD treatment in individuals with paraphilia. Of note, this was a small study which has not been replicated.

Despite the potential benefits of ADHD treatment, sexual offenders have high rates of substance abuse (Kafka and Prentky 1994; Raymond et al. 1999 Langstrom et al. 2004). Thus, there is a potential for diversion or abuse of these medications. As such, stimulants should be prescribed in a slow release form (such as OROS-methylphenidate). Alternatively, non-stimulant treatment for ADHD (such as atomoxetine or bupropion) may be preferred.

Dementing disorders

Dementing disorders, such as Alzheimer's dementia and multi-infarct dementia, are also becoming increasingly prevalent among MDSOs. As noted by Fazel et al. (2002), about half of male prisoners over 59 are incarcerated for sexual offences, making the possibility of dementia in the sexual offender population quite realistic. However, dementia was an infrequent diagnosis in his group. In our facility, dementia affects approximately 10 per cent of the population. We also have had a number of MDSOs with dementia who have been found permanently 'unfit to stand trial' and are managed in the NCR/NGRI system. Regardless of the rates, the MDSO with dementia often has specialised treatment needs and risk management considerations.

As with other MDSOs, the initial step is diagnostic clarification. One must attempt to confirm the cause of the dementia, the prognosis, the deficits present, and the treatment needs of the offender. The diagnostic work-up could include neuropsychological testing, cognitive testing, MRI/CT of the head, and blood testing, such as vitamin B_{12} level and a syphilis screen.

Once the diagnosis is clarified, the role of dementia in the index offences should be established. MDSOs with dementia may come to attention as part of a current offence or from offences committed years before. Although, statistically, frontal lobe disinhibition in the elderly does not appear to be an important factor in sexual offending (Fazel et al. 2002), it nonetheless may have played an important role for an individual offender. Was underlying paraphilia acted on due to reduced inhibition from dementia? Was this a de novo offence that appears to be a personality change (as can occur in frontal lobe dementia)? Also, individuals with dementia are more susceptible to developing delirium – was the offence part of a delirium? At times, nursing homes or the legal system may misinterpret sexual behaviours which occur as part of dementia as intentional and illegal behaviours.

Dementia frequently becomes relevant to treatment and risk management. The MDSO with dementia may have difficulty in remembering the offence, which limits the role of treatments that focus on detailed analysis and discussion of the offence. Memory deficits may also interfere with remembering group discussions beyond the session or between sessions. If patients are able to learn and retain information, then it is likely to be worthwhile to have them in group. However, individuals with moderate and severe dementia would be unlikely to significantly benefit from these approaches.

In some MDSOs with dementia, the risk management may need to focus on other issues. For example, treatment may focus on slowing further cognitive decline through the use of acetylcholinesterase inhibitors or through control of hypertension and hypercholesterolaemia. Reversible causes of dementia, such as nutritional deficits and tertiary syphilis, should be treated. Treatment may also entail pharmacologic interventions aimed directly at sexual offending, such as SSRIs or antiandrogen therapy. However, given high rates of physical illness, consultation from other medical colleagues may be required prior to initiating such therapies.

Ultimately, risk management of the MDSO with dementia may need to focus on appropriate housing and supervision in a structured environment. For individuals with offences against children, there may be a theoretically increased risk in some residences; for example, through having access to children who come to visit grandparents in a nursing home. Usually, this risk can be entirely controlled through education of the staff and appropriate supervision. Unfortunately, again due to stigma, the more common problem is getting nursing homes and other residences for the elderly to accept an MDSO with dementia. Usually, education and close partnerships with these institutions will help.

Conclusion

Sexual offenders suffering from mental disorders are common and require appropriate diagnosis and treatment of their mental disorders in order to optimise treatment outcomes. Often these mental disorders play a role in sexual offending and require special attention in order to provide appropriate treatment and manage risk. Individuals involved in the care and supervision of sexual offenders should be aware of mental illness and its potential impact on treatment.

References

Adi, Y., Ashcroft, D., Browne, K., Beech, A., Fry-Smith, A. and Hyde, C. (2002) 'Clinical Effectiveness and Cost-Consequences of Selective Serotonin Reuptake Inhibitors in the Treatment of Sex Offenders', *Health Technology Assessment*, 6(28): 1–66.

Ahlmeyer, S., Kleinsasser, D., Stoner, J. and Retzlaff, P. (2003) 'Psychopathology of Incarcerated Sex Offenders', *Journal of Personality Disorders*, 17(4): 306–318.

Alden, A., Brennan, P., Hodgins, S. and Mednick, S. (2007) 'Psychotic Disorders and Sex Offending in a Danish Birth Cohort', *Archives of General Psychiatry*, 64(11): 1251–1258.

Baillargeon, J., Binswanger, I. A., Penn, J. V., Williams, B. A. and Murray, O. J. (2009) 'Psychiatric Disorders and Repeat Incarcerations: The Revolving Prison Door', *American Journal of Psychiatry*, 166(1): 103-109.

Barkley, R. A., Brown, T. E., Barkley, R. A. and Brown, T. E. (2008) 'Unrecognized Attention-Deficit/Hyperactivity Disorder in Adults Presenting with Other Psychiatric Disorders', *CNS Spectrums*, 13(11): 977–984.

Bonta, J., Law, M. and Hanson, K. (1998) 'The Prediction of Criminal and Violent Recidivism Among Mentally Disordered Offenders: A Meta-Analysis', *Psychological Bulletin*, 123(2): 123–142.

Bradford, J. M. (2001) 'The Neurobiology, Neuropharmacology, and Pharmacological Treatment of the Paraphilias and Compulsive Sexual Behaviour', *Canadian Journal of Psychiatry*, 46(1): 26–34.

Bumby, K. M., Marshall, W. L. and Langton, C. M. (1999) 'A Theoretical Model of the Influences of Shame and Guilt on Sexual Offending', in B. K. Schwartz (ed.), *The Sex Offender: Theoretical Advances, Treating Special Populations and Legal Developments*. Thousand Oaks, CA: Sage.

Crisford, H., Dare, H. and Evangeli, M. (2008) 'Offence-Related Posttraumatic Stress Disorder (PTSD) Symptomatology and Guilt in Mentally Disordered Violent and Sexual Offenders', *Journal of Forensic Psychiatry and Psychology*, 19(1): 86–107.

Dumond, R. (2003) 'Confronting America's Most Ignored Crime Problem: the Prison Rape Elimination Act of 2003', *Journal of the American Academy of Psychiatry and the Law*, 31(3): 354–360.

Dunsieth, N. W., Jr., Nelson, E. B., Brusman-Lovins, L. A., *et al.* (2004) 'Psychiatric and Legal Features of 113 Men Convicted of Sexual Offenses', *Journal of Clinical Psychiatry*, 65(3): 293–300.

Fakhoury, W. and Priebe, S. (2002) 'The Process of Deinstitutionalization: An International Overview', *Current Opinion in Psychiatry*, 15(2): 187–192.

Fazel, S., Hope, T., O'Donnell, I. and Jacoby, R. (2002) 'Psychiatric, Demographic and Personality Characteristics of Elderly Sex Offenders', *Psychological Medicine*, 32(2): 219–226.

Fazel, S., Sjostedt, G., Langstrom, N. and Grann, M. (2007) 'Severe Mental Illness and Risk of Sexual Offending in Men: A Case-Control Study Based on Swedish National Registers', *Journal of Clinical Psychiatry*, 68(4): 588–596.

Gray, N. S., Carman, N. G., Rogers, P., MacCulloch, M. J., Hayward, P. and Snowden, R. J. (2003) 'Post-traumatic Stress Disorder Caused in Mentally Disordered Offenders by the Committing of a Serious Violent or Sexual Offence', *Journal of Forensic Psychiatry and Psychology*, 14(1): 27.

Greenberg, D. and Bradford, J. M. (1997) 'Treatment of the Paraphilic Disorders: A Review of the Role of the Selective Serotonin Reuptake Inhibitors', *Sexual Abuse: A Journal of Research and Treatment*, 9: 349–361.

Gunn, J. (2000) 'Future Directions for Treatment in Forensic Psychiatry', *British Journal of Psychiatry*, 176(4): 332–338.

Harcourt, B. E. (2006) 'From the Asylum to the Prison: Rethinking the Incarceration Revolution', *Texas Law Review*, 84(7): 1751–1786.

Hill, A., Briken, P., Kraus, C., Strohm, K. and Berner, W. (2003) 'Differential Pharmacological Treatment of Paraphilias and Sex Offenders', *International Journal of Offender Therapy and Comparative Criminology*, 47(4): 407–421.

Hoyer, J., Kunst, H. and Schmidt, A. (2001) 'Social Phobia as a Comorbid Condition in Sex Offenders with Paraphilia or Impulse Control Disorder', *Journal of Nervous and Mental Disease*, 189(7): 463–470.

Hudson, S. M., Ward, T. and Marshall, W. L. (1992) 'The Abstinence Violation Effect in Sex Offenders: A Reformulation', *Behaviour Research and Therapy*, 30(5): 435–441.

Jones, T. R. and Pratt, T. C. (2008) 'The Prevalence of Sexual Violence in Prison: The State of the Knowledge Base and Implications for Evidence-Based Correctional Policy Making', *International Journal of Offender Therapy and Comparative Criminology*, 52(3): 280–295.

Kafka, M. P. and Hennen, J. (2000) 'Psychostimulant Augmentation During Treatment with Selective Serotonin Reuptake Inhibitors in Men with Paraphilias and Paraphilia-Related Disorders: A Case Series', *Journal of Clinical Psychiatry*, 61(9): 664–670.

Kafka, M. P. and Hennen, J. (2002) 'A DSM–IV Axis I Comorbidity Study of Males (*n* = 120) with Paraphilias and Paraphilia-Related Disorders', *Sexual Abuse: A Journal of Research and Treatment*, 14(4): 349–366.

Kafka, M. P. and Prentky, R. A. (1994) 'Preliminary Observations of DSM–III–R Axis I Comorbidity in Men with Paraphilias and Paraphilia-Related Disorders', *Journal of Clinical Psychiatry*, 55(11): 481–487.

Kafka, M. P. and Prentky, R. A. (1998) 'Attention-Deficit/Hyperactivity Disorder in Males with Paraphilias and Paraphilia-Related Disorders: A Comorbidity Study', *Journal of Clinical Psychiatry*, 59(7): 388–396.

Konrad, N. (2002) 'Prisons as New Asylums', *Current Opinion in Psychiatry*, 15(6): 583–587.

Langstrom, N., Sjostedt, G. and Grann, M. (2004) 'Psychiatric Disorders and Recidivism in Sexual Offenders', *Sexual Abuse: A Journal of Research and Treatment*, 16(2): 139–150.

Latimer, J. (2006) *The Review Board Systems in Canada: Overview of Results from the Mentally Disordered Accused Data Collection Study*. Ottawa, Canada: Department of Justice.

Marshall, W. L. and Marshall, L. E. (2000) 'The Origins of Sexual Offending', *Trauma, Violence and Abuse*, 1(3): 250–263.

Marshall, W. L., Marshall, L. E., Serran, G. A. and Fernandez, Y. M. (2006) *Treating Sexual Offenders: An Integrated Approach*. New York: Routledge.

McMackin, R. A., Leisen, M. B., Cusack, J. F., Lafratta, J. and Litwin, P. (2002) 'The Relationship of Trauma Exposure to Sex Offending Behavior Among Male Juvenile Offenders', *Journal of Child Sexual Abuse*, 11(2): 25–40.

Penrose, L. S. (1939) 'Mental Disease and Crime: Outline of a Comparative Study of European Statistics', *British Journal of Medical Psychology*, 18: 1–15.

Proeve, M. and Howells, K. (2002) 'Shame and Guilt in Child Sexual Offenders', *International Journal of Therapy and Offender Comparative Criminology*, 46(6): 657–667.

Quinsey, V. L., Harris, G. T., Rice, M. E. and Cormier, C. A. (1998) *Violent Offenders: Appraising and Managing Risk*. Washington, DC: American Psychological Association.

Raymond, N. C., Coleman, E., Ohlerking, F., Christenson, G. A. and Miner, M. (1999) 'Psychiatric Comorbidity in Pedophilic Sex Offenders', *American Journal of Psychiatry*, 156(5): 786–788.

Sealy, P. and Whitehead, P. C. (2004) 'Forty Years of Deinstitutionalization of Psychiatric Services in Canada: An Empirical Assessment', *Canadian Journal of Psychiatry*, 49(4): 249–257.

Talbott, J. A. (2004) 'Deinstitutionalization: Avoiding the Disasters of the Past', *Psychiatric Services*, 55(10): 1112–1115.

Wolff, N. P. D., Blitz, C. L. P. D. and Shi, J. M. S. (2007) 'Rates of Sexual Victimization in Prison for Inmates With and Without Mental Disorders', *Psychiatric Services*, 58(8): 1087–1094.

Chapter 11

Intellectually disabled sexual offenders: subgroup profiling and recidivism after outpatient treatment

Joan van Horn, Jules Mulder and Ine Kusters

Introduction

What do we know about intellectually disabled (ID) offenders? Research findings are inconclusive as to their characteristics and criminal conduct. It is believed that ID offenders are over-represented in the offending population. Why do we think of ID offenders as high-risk offenders and what do we know about their background and criminal history? Can subgroups of ID offenders be identified or are they basically one group with similar characteristics? These and other related questions are addressed in this chapter. Findings presented here show that ID offenders can be clustered into three subgroups, each displaying distinct patterns of criminal behaviour, family background, and treatment characteristics. Implications for treatment are also discussed.

Prevalence estimates of ID offenders

In The Netherlands, little is known about the prevalence of ID persons in the offending population. A review study by Jones (2007), which exclusively consisted of international studies, showed that prevalence estimates of offenders with intellectual disabilities are very inconsistent. Estimates varied between 2 and 40 per cent. These inconsistent findings can be explained by several factors. The first factor is that levels of intellectual disability were based on different methods or criteria. For instance, in some studies, special school attendance was used as a criterion, whereas in others, intelligence tests were used (Simpson and Hogg 2001; LeGrand *et al.* 2003; Lambrick and Glaser 2004). Nowadays there is more consensus about the use of validated tests like the Wechsler Adult Intelligence Scale (WAIS) to assess the level of cognitive functioning. However, according to the DSM criteria, there are other criteria that have to be met in order to diagnose the presence of an intellectual dysfunction, including impairments in adaptive and social functioning, and the presence of an intellectual disability from childhood. There are numerous measures available to assess the level of adaptive and social functioning, but they are difficult to compare. So far there are no reference standards available. The presence of an intellectual disability from childhood is also difficult to assess. For instance, it is possible that adaptive and social dysfunctions are the result of trauma or physical or mental illness after a period of normal development. The second factor that can be held responsible for the inconsistent prevalence data is that most studies are based on criminal records. These records represent actual arrest and conviction rates and do not give any information on the prevalence or incidence of persons with an intellectual disability in the general offending population. Hence, criminal records cannot be used to draw conclusions about the over- or under-representation of ID people in the offending population.

Recidivism and risk factors

Several studies show that, once known to the police, ID offenders are often rearrested or reconvicted. Recidivism rates range from 30 to 50 per cent among ID offenders (LeGrand *et al.* 2003; Lindsay *et al.* 2004; Cockram 2005). Older studies reported even higher percentages, around 70 per cent (Gibbons and Robertson 1983; Brownlee 1995). Recent studies suggest that ID offenders tend to reoffend at a high rate because they cannot cope with the increased demands associated with community living. Some studies, however, offer alternative explanations; for example, ID behaviour is more often interpreted as aggressive or sexually inappropriate than the same behaviour in a normal population (Sinclair and Murphy 2004). High re-arrest rates among ID people can be explained by unclear definitions of what may be characterised as challenging behaviour instead of offending behaviour. Moreover, rearrest rates themselves are said to be biased. It is also generally believed that ID sex offenders select easily accessible victims, especially children. A study by Thompson

(1997), however, showed that the response to alleged offending by men with an intellectual disability depends crucially on the nature of the victim. Sex offences are reported more often when children are involved than when adults are involved: 73 per cent versus 11 per cent, with offences against ID people or women staff being the least likely to be reported.

It has also been suggested that the police sometimes have some significant biases against people with an intellectual disability: they think alleged ID offenders are less trustworthy and their crimes more serious. As a result, ID offenders are caught in what is called a 'deviancy amplification spiral'. This means that when you come from a poor neighbourhood, look unusual, or behave unusually you have a much greater chance of being caught up in the law enforcement net. These biases against ID people are believed to be unjust because, arguably, ID people cannot be held fully responsible for their criminal actions (Holland *et al.* 2002). ID people do not know that their behaviour is illegal and cannot grasp the detrimental impact of their actions. In the criminal justice system, an offence is defined not only by the actual behaviour or its impact (*actus reus*) but also by the degree of accountability of the offender (*mens rea*). Lambrick (2003) suggests that the majority of ID people who enter the judicial system function at 'borderline' level (average IQ score of 65–75)[1] and live mainly independently in the community. When one assumes that ID people with a borderline IQ level cannot be held fully accountable for their actions, they are deprived of the chance to adapt to more socially accepted behaviour and to reduce relapse of offending through intervention. Although studies into the treatment effectiveness of ID offenders are limited, there is a consensus that treatment is more successful if it is tuned to their way of thinking (concrete versus abstract and impulsive versus reflective) and responsive to their intellectual skills (see the responsivity principle in Bonta 2000; Lindsay 2002).

High recidivism rates are found among ID offenders due to their increased visibility: the way they commit their offences is often less sophisticated, increasing the probability of detection (Craig *et al.* 2006). In summary, from the international studies presented here, there seems to be little empirical support for the view that ID people are over-represented in the actual offending population.

Despite the discussion on whether or not ID people have a criminal predisposition, an intellectual disability is still regarded as a risk factor for criminal behaviour, especially for committing violent, sexual and property offences (Hudson *et al.* 2002; Barron *et al.* 2004). Some factors related to intellectual functioning contribute to an increased risk of criminal behaviour, of which the most important are impulsiveness, inadequate coping skills, unemployment, limitations in social and interpersonal functioning, and unstable living conditions (Green *et al.* 2002; Cockram 2005). However, these factors were also found to enhance criminal conduct within the general population. Thus, it is still unclear whether disabled intellectual functioning exists as a risk factor or not.

Information on ID offenders in terms of group characteristics and recidivism is accordingly very limited. The authors therefore decided to add to this literature through a study carried out in The Netherlands. The objective of this study was to identify subgroups of ID offenders and retrieve more information about their offending behaviour following intensive outpatient treatment.

The De Waag study

The study was conducted at De Waag, centre for outpatient forensic psychiatry. With eight offices located in different parts of the country and more than 4,000 new clients per year, De Waag is the largest outpatient forensic psychiatric treatment centre in The Netherlands. Treating not just sex offenders, De Waag also has treatment programmes for domestic violence, aggression and Internet offences. ID sex offenders are treated by the intensive outpatient group therapy (IOG) programme.

Intensive outpatient group therapy

Generally, sex offenders with an IQ score between 60 and 90 qualify for IOG, although offenders with a too rapidly incurring tension or inadequate coping skills, and clients with higher IQ scores can also be accepted. In the current study, five offenders had an IQ score over 90. Clients who qualify for IOG must meet other criteria as well. According to the therapist's clinical judgement or observation: 1) clients must have some capacity for abstraction; 2) they have to be able to read and write to some extent; 3) they must be able to function in a group; and 4) there has to be some treatment perspective; that is, that in the long run clients can take more responsibility for their offending behaviour (Prevoo 1999). Exclusion criteria are complete denial of the offence, and risk of psychotic decompensation and autistiform impairment, leading to the offender's being unable to function in a group. The aim of treatment is the prevention or reduction of recidivism. To reach this goal, treatment consists of the making of a relapse-prevention plan, increasing social and problem-solving skills, enhancing self-confidence, learning to reflect on and talk about emotions, learning to distinguish thoughts from emotions, and sexual education. The programme is divided into two phases: main treatment and follow-up. At present, the main treatment phase consists of 1½ days a week for one year. After completion, clients attend the follow-up phase, consisting of treatment sessions lasting 45 minutes once a month for one year. At the start of this study, the main treatment phase consisted of three days per week. This was reduced to 1½ days because clients had insufficient time to look for a job or maintain one. To guarantee the continuity of treatment as much as possible, five therapists are responsible for every specific module of the treatment. Preferably, in each treatment module a male therapist and a female therapist are deployed. On indication, pharmaceutical sexual drive inhibitors, such as Androcur, can be prescribed for obsessive or hypersexual offenders. Androcur blocks the androgen receptors, as a result of which the frequency and intensity of sexual desire and agitation decrease, without totally oppressing the sexual desire (van Renesse 1999) (for more information on Androcur, see Chapter 6 of this volume). Sexual drive inhibitors were prescribed for 12 (26.7 per cent) of the 45 IOG clients in the current study.

Sample

The sample consisted of 45 ID male sex offenders who entered treatment between 1999 and 2004. The average age at the start of the treatment was 35 years (SD = 12.22; range 18–62 years). The full-scale IQ score was 80 (SD = 8.25; range 62–95) with a mean verbal scale score of 76 (SD: 7.50) and a mean performance scale score of 90 (SD: 11.42). By the WAIS classification system, 31.1 per cent (n = 14; range 86–95) were classified as below average in intellectual functioning (total IQ score of 85–99), 55.6 per cent (n = 25; range 72–84) as borderline level, and 13.3 per cent (n = 6; range 62–70) as mild mental retardation (total IQ score of 50–70).

Treatment was voluntary for 17.8 per cent of the sample and mandatory for 82.2 per cent. The programme was completed by 68.9 per cent of the total sample, with an attrition rate of 31.1 per cent. The main reason for dropping out was a serious lack of motivation for treatment. In Table 11.1 additional characteristics of the sample are described.

Table 11.1 shows that over 50 per cent of the offenders suffered from one or more early-life traumas. These offenders grew up in *multi-problem* families, illustrated by severe negligence, physical and/or sexual abuse, divorce of parents, and custodial placement.

Table 11.1 Sample characteristics (*n* = 45)

Demographic characteristics	*n*	%	Criminal history and index offence	*n*	%
Age categories			**Police arrests***		
≤ 29 years	16	35.6	Sex offences	73	61.9
29–38 years	13	28.9	Violent offences	15	12.7
≥ 39 years	16	35.6	Vandalism	5	4.2
Marital status			Property offences	24	20.4
With partner	6	13.3	Arson	1	.8
Single	39	86.7	**Convictions***		
Origin			Sex offences	46	68.7
Dutch	43	95.6	Violent offences	8	11.9
Migrant	2	4.4	Vandalism	2	3.0
Current living conditions			Property offences	11	16.4
			Arson	–	–
Independent	10	22.2	**Index offence**		
With family	17	37.8	Hands-off sexual offence	7	15.6
Under supervision	18	40.0	Sexual assault	17	37.8
Education level			Rape	21	46.7
Regular education	12	26.7	**Gender of victim**		
Special education	33	73.3	Female	15	33.3
Employed			Male	30	66.7
Yes, cleaning and public gardens	29	64.4	**Age of victim**		
			≤ 12 years	24	54.5
No	16	35.6	12–16 years	11	25.0
Life trauma before 18			> 16 years	9	20.5
No	20	44.4	**Relationship with victim**		
Yes	25	55.6	Related	13	28.9
Co-morbidity			Not related	18	40.0
No	28	62.2	Stranger	14	31.1
Yes	17	37.8	**Frequency of abuse**		
			Once	20	44.4
			Multiple times	25	55.6

*Twenty-two sex offenders were arrested (118 arrests in total) and convicted (67 convictions in total) multiple times. Percentages shown in the table are based on the total number of arrests and convictions.

Based on the DSMIV–TR criteria, 17 offenders were diagnosed with co-morbid clinical and/or traits of a personality disorder. Alcohol abuse was found among nearly 18 per cent of the sample. A small number of offenders were diagnosed with other clinical disorders such as attention deficit hyperactivity disorder (ADHD) or pervasive developmental disorder. Almost 10 per cent showed traits of antisocial personality disorder (for more information on mentally disordered sex offenders, see Chapter 10 of this volume).

Table 11.1 shows also that 22 offenders had prior arrests or convictions for multiple types of offences. The majority of the offenders (64 per cent) were charged for the first time with a sexual offence. This was mostly child molesting (45 per cent) or exhibitionism (34 per cent). Offenders arrested for child abuse were convicted more often (67 per cent) than those arrested for exhibitionism (40 per cent). Detailed information on the victims was only available for the index sexual offence. The majority of the offenders were arrested for child abuse or exhibitionism. Victims of child abuse were generally aged under 12 and male. Arrest for child abuse more often led to a conviction. The average age at first arrest was 28 years (SD=11.15; range 10–54 years) and 30 years when convicted for the first time (SD=10.29; range 14–54 years).

Criminal history and recidivism

Police records from the Recognition Service System (RSS) and conviction data from the Judicial Documentation System (JDS) were used to map the criminal history and recidivism rates of the 45 ID offenders (criminal records were collected on 6 March 2007). The RSS is a database with nationwide coverage that has been used since 1996 by the police to register reported crimes against identified suspects aged 12 and over. The JDS, managed by the Central Judicial Documentation service, is a database consisting of an overview of the criminal activities of all persons who come into contact with the Dutch justice system.

In this study, all convictions from the JDS were included with separate offences added in one sentence counted separately. From the RSS and JDS, 10 offences were registered prior to the index offence and 10 reoffences were noted starting from the date on which the treatment was concluded. The follow-up period (the time between end of treatment and the date on which the criminal records were collected) ranged from 1 to 77 months, with an average of 39 months (SD: 20.50).

Previous offences (rearrests and convictions) were classified as sexual offences, (threat of) physical violence against persons, vandalism, property crimes and arson. Recidivism rates were calculated for all types of offences (general recidivism), sexual, property, and violent offences.

Instruments

The level of intellectual functioning was assessed by the WAIS (Wechsler 1955; translated into Dutch by Stinissen *et al.* 1969). For reasons of comparison, the WAIS was used even after the release of the WAIS-III (Wechsler 1999).

Since there are no validated risk assessment instruments available in The Netherlands normed on people with intellectual disabilities, the *Sexual Violence Risk-20* (SVR-20) (Boer *et al.* 1997; authorised Dutch translation: Hildebrand *et al.* 2000) was used to assess the level of risk of reoffending. The SVR-20 is a structured method to assess clinically the chance of future offending behaviour among adult offenders. It comprises 20 risk factors divided into three major sections: psychosocial adjustment items (11 items), which deals with issues like employment factors, substance abuse, and relationship problems; sexual offences (seven items), which evaluates risk factors such as high density of sex offences, multiple sex offence types, and escalation in frequency and severity of sex offences; and the third section (two items), which concerns future plans and negative attitudes towards intervention.

All risk factors were scored by a trained diagnostician using file information. Items were coded on a three-point scale: 'risk factor not applicable' (0), 'risk factor to some extent applicable' (1), and 'risk factor applicable' (2). The level of risk of reoffending was categorised as 'low risk', 'moderate risk' or 'high risk'. The SVR-20 item 'psychopathy' was excluded from the risk assessment because previous studies showed that the score did not contribute to the predictive validity of the total SVR-20 score (Douglas *et al.* 1999; De Vogel *et al.* 2004). In the present study, the section 'psychosocial adjustment' consisted of 10 rather than 11 risk factors.

Analysis

To determine the interrater reliability of SVR-20, 10 sex offenders were evaluated by two raters on their recidivism risk. Intraclass correlation coefficients (ICC) were used to assess the interrater reliability for SVR-20 sections. Based on the guidelines of Shrout and Fleiss (1979), the single-measure ICCs were calculated for the two-way random effect model, an absolute agreement being the criterion. The single-measure ICC values are given in order to get a clear understanding of the reliability of the assessment, assuming it had been carried out by a single assessor. Critical values for single measure ICCs were as follows: ICC $\geq$ .75 = excellent; .60 $\leq$ ICC < .75 = good; .40 $\leq$ ICC < .60 = moderate; ICC < .40 = poor (Landis and Koch 1977). The agreement between the raters was (with exception of the section 'future plans', ICC = .21) good to excellent: psychosocial functioning, ICC = .85; sexual offences, ICC = .61; total SVR-20, ICC = .86; and clinically assessed recidivism risk, ICC = .94.

Recidivism rates were calculated by Kaplan–Meier survival analysis. This is a statistical method to calculate the recidivism rates and the time interval for recidivism in a group or subgroup. This calculation takes into account the adjustment for individual differences in the time intervals between ending the treatment and the reference date. Every initial reoffence implies an increase in the recidivism curve; later reoffending is disregarded (for a more extensive explanation on survival analysis, see Wartna 2000). A two-step cluster analysis was performed to identify meaningful clusters (subgroups) of ID sex offenders. Two-step cluster analysis gives the ability to create clusters based on both categorical and continuous variables.

Results

From cluster analysis, three subgroups emerged, each representing about one-third of the total sample. The subgroups can be described as low-risk offenders (n = 10, 24.4 per cent), specialists (n = 16, 39 per cent), and generalists (n = 15, 36.6 per cent)[2]. These subgroups are profiled along three sections: 1) criminal history, recidivism risk and recidivism; 2) demographic characteristics and family background; and 3) treatment and co-morbidity. It is important to note that most of the characteristics included in the analysis were present in all three subgroups, but predominantly in either one of the three groups. In particular, specialists and generalists showed some common features as well.

Criminal history, recidivism risk, and recidivism (rearrests and reconvictions)

Low-risk offender
The low-risk offender was arrested and convicted for the first time at age 35 for committing a sex offence (M = 35 years, SD = 11.96). In

the course of his life, he committed multiple types of relatively minor offences such as vandalism, exhibitionism and property offences. Recidivism rates showed that he was rearrested for minor offences, but was not convicted for any of these offences (Figure 11.1). His recidivism risk for committing sexual offences was estimated as being low to moderate.

Specialist

The specialist was arrested for the first time in his late twenties. He committed multiple types of sex offences, varying from exhibitionism to hands-on sex offences against adults and children. His criminal history showed an escalation of sexual offences in frequency and/

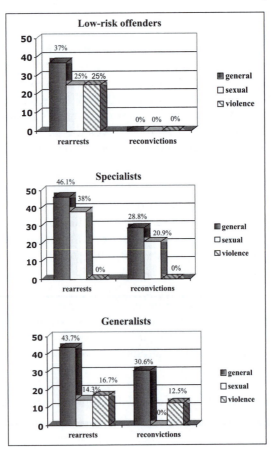

Figure 11.1 Rearrests and reconviction rates (%) among low-risk offenders, specialists, and generalists

or severity. The specialist violated parole conditions on a structural basis. As can be seen from Figure 11.1, this group was rearrested and reconvicted for, in particular, sexual offences.

Generalist

The generalist profile displays quite a different pattern. The typical generalist commits his first offence at a much younger age, in his early twenties. His first offence was a violent offence, and his criminal history comprises mainly violent offences. His violent behaviour continued after treatment, displayed by relatively high rearrest and reconviction rates for violent offences. Interestingly, the generalist tends to minimise and also deny having committed sexual offences.

Demographic characteristics and family background

Low-risk offender

The typical low-risk offender is a single white male, employed in a sheltered workshop or public garden. He lives independently. His IQ score is between 71 and 84, which qualifies for borderline intellectual functioning (BIF). The low-risk offender did not experience early-life trauma.

Specialist

From profiling the specialist, quite a different pattern emerged. He is of Dutch origin and intellectually functions below average (IQ score ranging 85–99) which is the highest level of all three subgroups). The specialist lives with his family and in his childhood suffered from various early-life traumas, such as sexual and/or physical abuse or neglect. ID offenders particularly in this group had serious suicidal thoughts.

Generalist

The generalist is of Dutch origin or an immigrant. With IQ score ranging from 50 to 70 (mild mental retardation), the intellectual functioning of the generalist is the lowest of all subgroups. He lives under supervision. His parents were divorced when he was very young. Compared with the other two subgroups, generalists show serious problems in their working history: they frequently switch jobs, and are regularly unemployed. They share some common features with the specialist as well: in both groups, the intimate relationships of the ID offenders can be described as unstable and problematic.

Treatment and co-morbidity

Low-risk offender

As for the treatment characteristics and co-morbidity, the low-risk offender entered treatment in his late thirties (M = 37.4; SD = 13.52). Treatment was mandatory and he successfully completed the programme. Overall, no co-morbid diagnosis was assessed. However, when co-morbidity was present, the low-risk offender was diagnosed with ADHD. Overall, no medication was prescribed.

Specialist

The specialist also entered treatment on a mandatory status. He was diagnosed with co-morbid clinical disorder, namely alcohol abuse and sexual deviancy. His treatment attitude was extremely negative and finally resulted in treatment dropout. The specialist had a history of violation of parole conditions. Obviously, being a dropout, he violated the current mandatory status of his treatment. Overall, no pharmacological treatment had been offered (73 per cent).

Generalist

As for the generalist profile, no distinct characteristics emerged from cluster analyses other than that they started treatment voluntarily, and were clinically diagnosed with aggressive impulses and co-morbid traits of antisocial personality disorder.

Discussion

From cluster analysis, three subgroups of ID offenders (total sample of 45 ID offenders) emerged with a distinct profile. Each subgroup accounted for about one-third of the total sample: low-risk offenders (24.4 per cent), specialists (39 per cent) and generalists (36.6 per cent). Relatively high general recidivism rates (above 35 per cent) were found in all three groups. However, in focusing on the types of offences, some interesting findings emerge. While low-risk offenders commit minor offences, specialists and generalists seem to focus on committing one particular offence type, respectively, sexual and violent offences. This finding sheds a different light on the general idea that intellectual impairment increases the risk of offending. It seems that the level of cognitive functioning in itself does not increase the risk of reoffending, but rather seems to be linked to committing specific types of offences. Findings suggest that higher IQ scores correlate with offences that require a more sophisticated and organised approach. Specialists, for instance, intellectually function at below average level, which is the highest of all three subgroups. They specialise in committing different types of sexual offences, including child abuse. Clearly, there has to be at least some degree of planning and coordination to perform (non-physical aggressive) sexual acts with children (grooming). In contrast, the generalists, most of whom were diagnosed with mild mental retardation, commit all kinds of offences, with violent offences holding a prominent place. Aggressive impulses and traits of antisocial personality disorder seem to underlie their tendency to carry out criminal behaviour in general, and violent offending in particular. Little organisation is required to commit these kinds of offences. Possibly, impulsiveness can also be seen in their sexual offences.

It has been suggested by Lambrick (2003) that the majority of ID offenders who enter the judicial system function at BIF. In this study, the BIF offender group was the smallest, and they were profiled with the least problematic family background and criminal history. In terms of treatment, they seemed to have the best fit with the IOG: they all successfully completed the programme and had the lowest rearrest and reconviction rates.

Implications for treatment

What are the treatment implications for the specialists and generalists? Both groups showed some misfits with the IOG programme. Regarding the specialist group, the IOG programme seems to lack the structure and intensity to reduce reoffending behaviour. Given their relatively high drop-out rate, specialists would probably benefit more from treatment if they start with motivational sessions. The duration of the treatment should be shorter, but much more intensive; for example, 3–5 days a week for a period of 6 months. The focus of the treatment should be on changing patterns of thinking related to sexual offending and changing sexual deviant patterns of arousal. From this study, it became apparent that 73 per cent of the specialists did not receive additional medical treatment. Given the fact that sexual deviancy was an important risk factor in this group, medical treatment should be offered as well. As for the generalists, clearly, other treatment elements are needed than are currently offered in the IOG programme. IOG particularly lacks some basic elements to increase the ability to control aggressive impulses and restrain antisocial conduct. A therapy in which sexual and aggressive elements are combined is clearly needed. Hence, in line with Bonta's principle of responsivity (Bonta 2000), intervention should be tuned to their low level of intellectual functioning.

Future research

Forensic psychiatric research lacks theoretical notions on criminal behavior. Theory-driven research attempts to gain more insight into (the relapse into) criminal behaviour. A promising theory in this area is the self-regulation model of Ward *et al.* (1998). In short, the theory describes ineffective chains of thoughts, feelings, and behaviour that lead to criminal conduct (pathways). These chains are primarily driven by self-regulation styles to (passively or actively) avoid, maintain or achieve criminal behaviour. Offenders with passive avoidance strategies are characterised by a strong degree of denial and/or the use of ineffective strategies to control deviant sexual preferences (under-regulation). The second form of dysfunctional self-regulation is called misregulation. This refers to the person who engages in some effort to avoid offending, but the effort is misplaced (for example, using alcohol to control deviant fantasies). This is usually associated with negative emotional states. The final form of self-regulation is effective self-regulation, and describes the offender whose goal is to commit a sexual offence. The problem with these offenders is the choice of goals (to sexually offend), rather than dysfunctional self-regulation. These offenders experience positive emotions during the offence process.

These self-regulation styles explain the why and how of criminal behaviour and therefore offer an alternative for effective treatment. While the empirical validation of the model is still under way, the research conducted into this model to date has been promising. The first empirical support was found in a sample of inmates (Hudson *et al.* 1999) and child molesters (Bickly and Beech 2002). The model has not been tested in a group of ID sex offenders yet, but Keeling and Rose (2005) suspect that self-regulation styles among ID offenders will be recognised as 'passive avoidance' or 'automatic approach' style (that is, offences are impulsively committed with minimum planning).

Notes

1 Borderline intellectual functioning (BIF) falls into an area of delayed intellectual, emotional and/or adaptive functioning that balances on the edge of mental retardation but does not actually qualify for that specific diagnosis. While BIF people function at a higher level than those classified as mentally retarded, their cognitive functioning is nevertheless limited. It can create problems for everyday functioning, judgement, and academic or occupational achievement. They are thus at a disadvantage when entering unfamiliar and stressful situations.
2 Four ID offenders were excluded from the analysis due to missing data.

References

Barron, P., Hassiotis, A. and Banes, J. (2004) 'Offenders with Intellectual Disability: A Prospective Comparative Study', *Journal of Intellectual Disability Research*, 48(1): 69–76.

Bickly, J. A. and Beech, A. R. (2002) 'Implications for Treatment of Sexual Offenders of the Ward and Hudson Model of Relapse', *Sexual Abuse: A Journal of Research and Treatment*, 15(2): 121–134.

Boer, D. P., Hart, S. D., Kropp, P. R. and Webster, C. D. (1997) *Manual for Sexual Violence Risk-20*. Simon Fraser University: the Mental Health, Law and Policy Institute.

Bonta, J. (2000) 'Offender Assessment: General Issues and Considerations', *Forum on Corrections Research,* 12: 2.

Brownlee, I. D. (1995) 'Intensive Probation with Young Adult Offenders', *British Journal of Criminology*, 35: 599–612.

Cockram, J. (2005) 'Careers of Offenders with an Intellectual Disability: The Probabilities of Re-arrest', *Journal of Intellectual Disability Research*, 47(70): 525–536.

Craig, L. A., Stringer, I. and Moss, T. (2006) 'Treating Sexual Offenders with Learning Disabilities in the Community', *International Journal of Offender Therapy and Comparative Criminology*, 50(4): 369–390.

Douglas, K. S., Ogloff, J.R., Nicholls, T. L. and Grant, I. (1999) 'Assessing Risk for Violence Among Psychiatric Patients: The HCR-20 Violence Risk Assessment Scheme and the Psychopathy Checklist: Screening Version', *Journal of Consulting and Clinical Psychology*, 67: 917–930.

Gibbens, T. C. and Robertson, G. (1983) 'A Survey of the Criminal Careers of Restriction Order Patients', *British Journal of Psychiatry*, 143: 370–375.

Green, G., Gray, N. S. and Willner, P. (2002) 'Factors Associated with Criminal Convictions for Sexually Inappropriate Behaviour in Men with Learning Disabilities', *Journal of Forensic Psychiatry*, 13(3): 578–607.

Hildebrand, M., de Ruiter, C. and van Beek, D. (2000) *Handleiding van de Nederlandse Sexual Violence Risk-20. Professionele richtlijnen ter beoordeling van risico op seksueel gewelddadig gedrag* ['Dutch SVR-20 Manual. Professional guidelines for assessing the risk of violent sexual behaviour']. Utrecht: Uitgave Forum Educatief, Dr H. Van der Hoevenkliniek Utrecht.

Holland, T., Clare, I. C. H. and Mukhopadhyay, T. (2002) 'Prevalence of "Criminal Offending" by Men and Women with Intellectual Disability and the Characteristics of "Offenders": Implications for Research and Service Development', *Journal of Intellectual Disability Research*, 46(1): 6–20.

Hudson, S. M., Wales, D. S., Bakker, L. and Ward, T. (2002) 'Dynamic Risk Factors: The Kia Maranma Evaluation', *Sexual Abuse: A Journal of Research and Treatment*, 14(2): 103–119.

Hudson, S. M., Ward, T., and McCormack, J. C. (1999) 'Offence Pathways in Sexual Offenders', *Journal of Interpersonal Violence*, 14(8): 779–798.

Jones, J. (2007) 'Persons with Intellectual Disabilities in the Criminal Justice System. Review of Issues', *International Journal of Offender Therapy and Comparative Criminology*, 51(6): 723–733.

Keeling, J. A. and Rose, J. L. (2005) 'Relapse Prevention with Intellectually Disabled Sexual Offenders', *Sexual Abuse: A Journal of Research and Treatment*, 17(4): 407–423.

Lambrick, F. (2003) 'Issues Surrounding the Risk Assessment of Sexual Offenders with an Intellectual Disability', *Psychiatry, Psychology and Law*, 10(2): 353–358.

Lambrick, F. and Glaser, W. (2004) 'Sex Offenders with an Intellectual Disability', *Sexual Abuse: A Journal of Research and Treatment*, 16(4): 381–392.

Landis, J. R. and Koch, G. G. (1977) 'The Measurement of Observer Agreement for Categorical Data', *Biometrics*, 33: 159–174.

LeGrand, B., Lutjenhuis, B. and Solodova, A. (2003) 'Behandeling van zwakbegaafde en licht verstandelijke gehandicapte plegers van seksueel misbruik' ['Treatment of intellectually disabled sex offenders']', *Directieve Therapie*, 24: 82–102.

Lindsay, W. R. (2002) 'Research and Literature on Sex Offenders with Intellectual and Developmental Disabilities', *Journal of Intellectual Disability Research*, 46(1): 74–85.

Lindsay, W. R., Smith, A. H. W., Law, J. *et al.* (2004) 'Sexual and Nonsexual Offenders with Intellectual and Learning Disabilities', *Journal of Interpersonal Violence*, 19(8): 875–890.

Prevoo, N. (1999) 'Ambulante behandeling van de zwakbegaafde seksuele delinquent' ['Outpatient treatment of intellectually disabled offenders'], in C. de Ruiter and M. Hildebrand, (eds), *Behandelingsstrategieën bij forensisch psychiatrische patiënten*. Houten/Diegem: Bohn Stafleu Van Loghum.

van Renesse, J. H. (1999) 'Farmacologische behandeling van forensisch psychiatrische patiënten' ['Pharmacological treatment of forensic psychiatric patients'], in C. de Ruiter and M. Hildebrand, (eds), *Behandelingsstrategieën bij forensisch psychiatrische patiënten*. Houten/Diegem: Bohn Stafleu Van Loghum.

Shrout, P. E. and Fleiss, J. L. (1979) 'Intraclass Correlations: Uses in Assessing Rater Reliability', *Psychological Bulletin*, 86(2): 420–428.

Simpson, M. K. and Hog, J. (2001) 'Patterns of Offending Among People with Intellectual Disability: A Systematic Review. Parts I and II', *Journal of Intellectual Disability*, 45: 340–406.

Sinclair, N. and Murphy, G. (2004) 'Preliminary Outcome of Group Cognitive-Behavioral Treatment for Men with an Intellectual Disability at Risk for Sexual Offending', *4th Annual Conference of the International Association of Forensic Mental Health Services*, Stockholm, Sweden, 6–9 June 2004.

Stinissen, J., Willems, P. J., Coetsier, P. and Hulsman, W. L. L. (1969) *Handleiding bij de Nederlandstalige bewerking van de Wechsler Adult Intelligence Scale (W.A.I.S.)* ['Dutch manual for WAIS']. Lisse: Swets & Zeitlinger.

Thomson, D. (1997) 'Profiling the Sexually Abusive Behaviour of Men with Intellectual Disabilities', *Journal of Applied Research in Intellectual Disabilities*, 10(2): 125–139.

de Vogel, V., de Ruiter, C., Hildebrand, M., Bos, B. and van de Ven, P. (2004) 'Different Ways of Discharge and Risk of Recidivism Measured by the HCR-20: A Retrospective Study in a Dutch Sample of Treated Forensic Psychiatric Patients', *Journal of Forensic Mental Health*, 3: 149–165.

Ward, T., Hudson, S. M. and Keenan, T., (1998) 'A Self-Regulation Model of the Sexual Offense Process', *Sexual Abuse: A Journal of Research and Treatment*, 10(2): 141–157.

Wartna, B. (2000) 'Recidive-onderzoek en survival analyse. Over het meten van de duur van de misdrijfvrije periode' ['Recidivism research and survival analysis. Measuring the duration of the offence-free period'], *Tijdschrift voor Criminologie*, 42: 2–20.

Wechsler, D. (1955) *Wechsler Adult Intelligence Scale*. London: Psychological Corporation.

Wechsler, D. (1999) *Wechsler Adult Intelligence Scale* (3rd edn). London: Psychological Corporation.

Part V

Social and moral responsibilities

Chapter 12

Cyber-sex offences: patterns, prevention and protection

Majid Yar

Introduction

It would not be unduly dramatic to claim that, of all the issues that elicit public and political concern about the Internet and new communication technologies, the problem of child-oriented sexual offending has been paramount. In the early and mid-1990s, when the Internet was undergoing a period of exponential expansion, public and media attention fell upon the circulation and possession of computerised images of child sex abuse and sexualised representations of minors (child pornography). Sensitivity to this issue was heightened, firstly, by a number of high-profile cases in which public figures were arrested and convicted for possession of such images (the pop stars Gary Glitter (Paul Gadd) and Pete Townsend being two such individuals in the UK). Secondly, there were a number of extensive international police investigations of online paedophile rings who shared child pornographic images (such as the Wonderland Club (1998) and those targeted by Operation Ore (2003)). Since 2000, concerns about Internet child pornography have been paralleled by the attention directed to online interactions between sex offenders and children, primarily through the online chat rooms and social networking sites that have become increasingly popular among children and young people. Police investigations and academic studies appear to indicate that children are extremely vulnerable to such predation, be it virtual abuse that occurs in the online environment (the exposure of children to sexually explicit speech) or grooming in which offenders use online interaction to prepare minors for subsequent face-to-face meetings. The emergence of online sex offending as a crime problem has incited a wide range of new legal innovations that have served to further tighten the definition of child sex offences and created new categories of offence oriented to the electronic environment (such as chat room grooming and the prohibition of electronically generated, so-called pseudo-photographs of minors in sexual scenarios). Equally, a whole range of new preventive and protection initiatives have emerged, often making recourse to a wide range of non-state and voluntary actors who are now charged with policing the Internet for child sex offences.

This chapter has three primary aims. Firstly, it will review the emergence of online child sex offending, and attempt to offer some insights into the scope, scale and patterns of such offending. Secondly, it will review the legal innovations that have emerged in response to the (real or imagined) extent of such online offending. Thirdly, it will examine the new apparatus of child protection and crime prevention and detection that is now in place, together with a critical evaluation of its effectiveness and implications in terms of dealing with online sex offences.

Internet child pornography: developments and legal responses

At the outset, we must acknowledge that the definition of what counts as child pornography is a complex matter fraught with ambiguity and subject to both constantly shifting interpretations and significant intra- and cross-cultural disagreement (Quayle and Taylor 2003). In extreme cases, of the kind that tend to be associated with child pornography in the public mind and media discussion, the illegal nature of such images will be unambiguous, as, for example, where images clearly show prepubescent children being subjected to, or engaged in, explicitly sexual acts, of which the image represents a permanent record. However, in many other cases, the classification of an image as child pornography may be considerably less clear-cut. Firstly, for example, it is not always immediately clear that the individual or individuals depicted *are* in fact legal minors, especially when they are clearly post-pubescent; secondly, just *who* counts as a legal minor will vary across legal and cultural contexts; thirdly, there may be considerable dispute as to whether or not any particular image of a child is in fact pornographic or sexual in nature (Quayle and Taylor (2003) note, for example, the controversy over the nude photographs of her own children taken by well-known photographer Sally Mann – responses to these images have varied from *Time* magazine's selection of Mann as 'Photographer of the Year' to her work being vilified as criminal garbage and incestuous). The issue of legal definitions of child pornography will be further discussed later, but for the moment we must bear in mind that an estimation of the extent of child pornography will be inevitably constructed in part on the basis of subjective assessments about the status of such images.

Gauging the precise extent of child pornography online is a difficult task, not only because of the classificatory problems noted above, but also because a significant portion of such material is likely to be hidden from direct public visibility given its illegal nature. Very little child pornography (especially of the most explicit kind) is likely to be openly visible or accessible via the Internet. Rather, it is likely to be secreted behind password-protected sites that can only be accessed by those who have been granted access. An early study, conducted in January 1998, found that 0.07 per cent of 40,000 news groups examined (28 sites) contained child erotica or pornography; in addition, the study found 238 girl-related child pornography or erotica web pages (Akdeniz 2000). A more recent study claims that in the period between 2002 and 2004, the number of child pornography and paedophile websites has doubled to 19,246 (Telofono Arcobaleno 2004). This same study found that over half of these reported websites were hosted in the USA, with Americans also figuring as the most prominent visitors to such web pages, constituting over 32 per cent of global users (Telofono Arcobaleno 2004). The majority of such sites were commercial in character, and it has been estimated that the online trade in child pornography is worth some $3 billion per annum (Internet Filter Review (IFR) 2004). While it is often claimed that the amount of child pornographic images on the Internet has increased rapidly, this conclusion is often extrapolated from the number of such images *reported* by Internet users. It is not therefore entirely clear whether there has in fact been an increase in the availability of such material or whether more of it is simply being reported as bespoke mechanisms for doing so have become more readily available and better publicised (such as the website of the Internet Watch Foundation (IWF)). It is similarly unclear what proportion of such images fall into different categories or levels of pornographic representation. Child pornographic images can be classified along a descriptive scale, from the least to the most explicit ('Indicative – Nudist – Erotica – Posing – Erotic Posing – Explicit Erotic Posing – Explicit Sexual Activity – Assault – Gross Assault –

Sadism/Bestiality' (Quayle and Taylor 2003: 32)). It is to be expected that material of all different kinds appear on the Internet in varying degrees.

Turning from the presence of child pornography online to legal responses, the past few decades have seen concerted legal efforts to address child pornography in general and Internet pornography in particular. In the UK, the Protection of Children Act 1978 makes it a criminal offence 'to take, distribute, exhibit, or possess even one indecent photograph of a child' (End Child Prostitution, Child Pornography and Trafficking of Children for Sexual Purposes (ECPAT) 1997: 9; Akdeniz 2001a: 6). Just what counts as indecent is left unspecified, thereby creating considerable uncertainty as to which images may or may not fall under its remit. Moreover, the Act removed the provision of previous legislation (such as the Obscene Publications Act 1959), which stated that the issues of context or artistic merit could be considered when evaluating a representation; this led to the censorship of a number of highly regarded films on the grounds of indecent representations of children, including Louis Malle's *Pretty Baby* (1978) and the Oscar-winning *Tin Drum* (1979).

Other countries have introduced such laws specifically aimed at tackling child pornography, both on- and off-line, including the USA, The Netherlands, Denmark, Switzerland, Sweden, Norway, Germany, France, Ireland, Austria, Canada, Taiwan, the Philippines, Sri Lanka, South Africa, New Zealand and Australia (ECPAT 1997; Akdeniz 2001b). However, such laws vary considerably across the globe. For example, Japanese law prohibits only commercial production, publication and distribution of child-related pornographic material, but not its possession. Indeed, in Japan, the production and distribution of child pornography were legal until November 1999, and current law still 'preserves the individual's right to possess child pornography and distribute it, recreationally, online' (Graham 2000: 471–472). At the time of writing, legislative proposals are under discussion to prohibit possession, but the issue remains as yet unresolved.

Changes in UK law have not only sought to extend obscenity laws to cover the production and online publication of child pornography, but have also shifted and extended definitions of child pornography. For example, for the purposes of the 1978 Act, a child was defined as a person under the age of 16 years; however, under the later provisions of the Sexual Offences Act 2003, the definition of a child (for the purposes of indecent photography) was extended to cover all those under 18 years of age. Thus, we have seen an upward extension of the legal classification of a child, thereby making illegal sexually explicit images of 16- and 17-year-olds that were previously not covered under the law. A further legal innovation, one that has proved controversial, relates to the prohibition of sexual imagery of children that is electronically generated, including so-called pseudo-photographs. It is widely acknowledged that 'in most cases, child pornography is a permanent record of the sexual abuse of an actual child' (Akdeniz 2001a: 6). However, this is not the case with pseudo-photographs; these comprise one or more images that have been digitally manipulated to produce a pornographic representation involving a minor. These, for example, may take the form of a child's face transposed onto the image of a naked adult performing a sexual act. They may also comprise digital images which have been computer generated from scratch, and thus no image of an actual child has been used in creating the representation. Under UK law, following the Criminal Justice and Public Order Act 1994, all such pseudo-photographs are prohibited alongside real pornographic images of actual children. The legal position remains different in other countries. For example, attempts under the US Child Pornography Prevention Act 1996 to prohibit virtual child pornography were struck down by the Supreme Court on grounds of their unconstitutional restriction on First Amendment (free speech) rights (Mota 2002). The aforementioned initiative to prohibit possession of child pornography in Japan also exempts virtual pornography, especially the extremely popular *anime* (animated) genre (the specific subgenre of *hentai* (meaning abnormality or perversion) typically features highly explicit sexual representations, including those of schoolgirls in scenarios such as rape and sadomasochistic sexual torture). Given that *hentai* now has a worldwide following via the Internet, and is freely available to view and download, the UK's provisions against pseudo-imagery would appear to be largely ineffective.

Online sexual predation: virtual abuse and chat-room grooming

We move our attention now from child pornography to online interactions between sex offenders and children. Since the 1980s, the USA and UK in particular have seen intense anxiety about the problem of child abuse in general, and sexual abuse in particular. Commonplace media discussion of organised ritual abuse, stranger child abduction, and recovered memories of repressed childhood abuse have contributed incrementally to this heightened sense of children's vulnerability. This sensitivity has been further heightened by a number of widely reported cases in which children have been abducted, abused, and then murdered by paedophiles, such as the case of Megan Kanka in the USA and Sarah Payne in the UK. In the late 1990s, the focus upon paedophilia turned increasingly to the online environment. We have already explored the attention devoted to child pornography. The problem of Internet-oriented abuse is often discussed in tandem with the circulation of obscene images of children; indeed, the two issues are frequently treated as different facets of the same problem (for example, Forde and Patterson 1998 and Stanley 2002). It is claimed that many of those investigated for child pornography offences have also participated in the actual sexual abuse of children. For example, British police estimate that some 35 per cent of those targeted by Operation Starburst for possession of child pornography had also physically abused children. Similarly, the FBI claim that something approaching 50 per cent of child pornography collectors have themselves committed sexual offences against children (National Crime Intelligence Service (NCIS) 1999). However, a question remains over the possible causal relationship between these forms of behaviour: does interest in, and consumption of, child pornography encourage or lead to child sexual abuse? Or is it that those already disposed to abusive behaviour inevitably also take pleasure in pornographic representations of similar activities? The UK and US figures cited above imply that those who abuse are in fact a *minority* among child pornography enthusiasts, and that the majority of consumers of such images *do not* engage in any actual physical abuse. This suggests that the relationship between child pornography and child sex abuse is more complicated than is often supposed (Stanley 2002). However, this complexity is seldom explored in public discussion, and the two phenomena are typically treated as synonymous or continuous.

Online child sex abuse can be divided into that which remains virtual (restricted to communicative abuses committed via the Internet) and that which serves as a preparation method for later physical contact and abuse (so-called grooming of potential physical abuse victims). Each will be discussed in turn below.

UK-based research by Rachel O'Connell and her colleagues at the Cyberspace Research Unit (CRU) claims to have uncovered a wide range of 'cybersexploitation' practices taking place in Internet chatrooms. In such cases, adults or older adolescents with a sexual interest in young children use online communication in order to 'identify, deceive, coerce, cajole, form friendships with and also to abuse potential victims' (O'Connell 2003: 2). This may entail, firstly, adults engaging children in sexually explicit conversations. Examples include asking questions of the child such as 'have you ever been kissed?' or 'do you ever touch yourself?' (O'Connell 2003: 7). Secondly, such behaviour may entail the fantasy enactment of sexual scenarios through online conversation with a child. Thirdly, it may entail what is described as cyber-rape, in which coercion and threats are used to force a child into acting out the sexual scenarios proposed by the abuser. It has been suggested by many commentators that adult abusers exploit the Internet to disguise their identity, posing as children or adolescents in order to win the friendship and trust of their victims (Feather 1999; NCIS 1999). Children may thus be blissfully unaware that their Internet friend is in fact an adult whose aim is to deceive them into participation in sexual conversation and interaction. O'Connell *et al.* claim that surveys of children's online interaction show that 53 per cent of chatroom users aged between 8 and 11 reported having had sexual conversations online (O'Connell *et al.* 2004). However, it is unclear what proportion of such conversations involved an adult interlocutor; indeed, given the ease with which disguise is possible, it may be virtually impossible to determine whether a given conversation is an adult–child interaction, or a case of child-to-child or teen-to-teen cyber-flirting. Indeed, only 6 per cent of children aged 9–16 reported that 'online conversations of a sexual nature were unpleasant or offensive' (O'Connell *et al.* 2004: 6). Putting the above points together, it may be suggested that the vast majority of children's online interactions of a sexual nature are nothing more than explorations of a burgeoning curiosity about physical relationships. Such curiosity is unremarkable, especially in the context of a consumer culture that actively encourages children and adolescents to take an interest in sex and sexuality. However, this does not imply that adult–child sexual interactions online are a non-existent problem. In the aforementioned studies conducted by the CRU, researchers registered themselves online under the guise of a child, typically a girl aged between 9 and 12 years. Subsequently, a number of self-professed adults engaged this child in conversations of an explicitly sexual kind. The UK's Sexual Offences Act 2003 makes it a criminal act to incite a child to engage in sexual activity; 'for example, persuading children to take their clothes off, causing the child to touch themselves sexually, sending indecent images of themselves' (O'Connell *et al.* 2004: 6). Thus, those online child–adult interactions in which the child may be encouraged to engage in sexual acts is defined as non-contact abuse and is punishable by up to 14 years' imprisonment.

The second area of online paedophile activity is linked to the commission of off-line contact abuse. Recent years have witnessed a growing concern that paedophiles are using Internet chatroom contacts with children in order to establish a relationship of apparent friendship and trust, which can then be exploited to arrange face-to-face meetings in which sexual abuse can take place. O'Connell (2003) identifies a number of stages to such grooming, starting with friendship formation (getting to know the child), progressing to relationship formation (becoming the child's best friend), and leading to the exclusivity stage (where intimacy, trust and secrecy are established). It is only when such a bond has been formed that the paedophile will move on to suggesting sexual contact. One US-based survey of 10–17-year-old Internet users found that 19 per cent reported having been approached for sex online (Stanley 2002). In response to such findings, the Sexual Offences Act 2003 introduced an offence of Internet grooming 'designed to catch those aged 18 or over who undertake a course of conduct with a child under 16 leading to a meeting where the adult intends to engage in sexual activity with a child' (Home Office 2004: 25). Conviction for this offence can result in a custodial sentence of up to five years. The precise extent of such grooming activity is difficult to assess, as its identification depends upon a judgement about an individual's ultimate intention to abuse. No physical abuse need actually be attempted in order to secure a conviction, merely a perception that an individual *intended* to use a meeting set up via the Internet to engage in the sexual abuse of a minor. As Bennion points out:

> The object is to catch adults who try to make friends with children so as later to have sex with them. But how is that to be proved? If the suspect goes on to carry out a sexual assault that can be charged as an offence in itself, but there is then no need for the preliminary offence of grooming. Where no assault later ensues how can preliminary grooming be established? (Bennion 2003: 63).

While implementation of this law may be beset with evidential dilemmas, what is clear is the conviction among most politicians, child protection organisations, and members of the public that Internet grooming is a real and palpable threat that must be tackled through criminal legislation.

Child sex offences online: from policing to prevention

The heightened levels of public, mass media and political attention directed towards online child sex offences has clearly been reflected in the high priority accorded such problems by the police (especially compared with other variants of Internet-oriented offences, which have been consistently marginalised within policing priorities). Police commitment to addressing online child-oriented offences is reflected not only in the significant resources directed towards investigation, but also in the unprecedented levels of international criminal justice cooperation that have taken shape. In 1995, for example, police from across Europe, the USA, South Africa, and the Far East were involved in Operation Starburst, an investigation of a paedophile ring using the Internet to distribute child pornography; 37 men were arrested worldwide (Akdeniz 2001a). Similarly, in 1998, investigators from the British National Crime Squad, US Customs, and Interpol coordinated an operation against the Wonderland Club, an organised ring of paedophiles spanning at least 33 countries, which had been using the Internet to distribute child pornography for a number of years. Across Europe and Australia 47 suspects were arrested, along with 32 in the USA (Graham 2000). Even more recently, Operation Ore (2003) led to 1,600 arrests in the UK of individuals who had subscribed to a US-based child pornography website (Creighton 2003); the arrests were made possible by cooperation with US law-enforcement authorities, who provided credit card details of UK residents who had subscribed to the service.

A number of countries have also broadened attempts to combat child pornography by involving Internet service providers (ISPs) and other Internet intermediaries. In some nations, this has taken the form of establishing ISPs' legal liability for third-party content placed on sites that they host or provide access to. Thus, for example, ISPs in both Germany and France have faced criminal charges of providing access to child pornography (Akdeniz 2001a). Other countries, such as the UK, have favoured self-regulation and cooperation with ISPs. In such cases, child pornography has been targeted by organisations such as IWF, which have established hotlines through which the public can report suspicious material online; the IWF then passes the information to ISPs so that they can remove the web pages, and to the police so that they can investigate with a view to bringing criminal charges against those responsible for posting the offending material (Akdeniz 2001a; Sutter 2003). In 2007, the IWF received almost 35,000 such reports via its Internet hotline, some 2,700 of which were confirmed as potentially illegal (IWF 2008). Such hotlines now exist across Europe, the USA and elsewhere, and are coordinated by associations such as Internet Hotline Providers in Europe (INHOPE) (Williams 1999). The online adult pornography industry has also involved itself in efforts to eradicate child pornography. The Association of Sites Advocating Child Protection (ASACP), for example, is an alliance of US-based, adult pornographic content providers which undertakes measures such as self-regulation through approved membership and certification of legitimate adult sites, informing member providers about child protection laws, engaging in educational and outreach activities directed toward government and the public, and providing a hotline through which both adult content providers and consumers can report child pornography identified on the Internet (ASACP 2009).

However, while all of the above initiatives (public and private) are undoubtedly valuable, they are by their nature *reactive* in character. In other words, they respond *ex post facto* to offences already committed, and seek to remove offending content from the Internet and seek the identification, arrest, prosecution and conviction of those responsible. While this is both laudable and necessary, and may (or may not) have a valuable deterrent effect, the abuse involved in the production of child pornographic images has nevertheless already taken place. Moreover, relatively few of the child victims abused during the production of such materials are successfully identified during the investigation process, leaving them vulnerable to further and ongoing abuse. Therefore, significant efforts have also been directed in recent years to *preventive* action that can curtail online abuse before it begins or in its early stages, especially in relation to virtual contact abuse and grooming. The emphasis upon interaction in online forums (such as chat rooms, social networking sites, and instant messaging services) reflects the massive take-up of such online communications technologies by children and young people. For example, a 2008 study found that 49 per cent of 8–17-year-olds who have Internet access also have a personal profile on a social networking site such as Bebo, MySpace and Facebook (Ofcom 2008). Concerns are further increased by findings that age restrictions on membership of such sites (typically set at 13 or 14 years of age) are seldom enforced, meaning that much younger children also make use of such sites in significant numbers.

The first type of preventive strategy has been an increased emphasis upon educating children and young people about the potential dangers presented by sexual predators online. For example, the UK government's Child Exploitation and Online Protection Centre (CEOP) provides a programme of education and advice for Internet users as young as five (with content tailored to different age groups), and disseminates Internet safety advice for those who use social networking sites, email, chat services and the like (CEOP 2009). For example, they advise 11–16-year-old users that:

- It's best not to give out your personal details to online mates.
- If you publish a picture or video online – anyone can change it or share it.
- SPAM/junk email and texts: don't believe it, reply to it or use it.
- Some people lie online.
- It's better to keep online mates online. Don't meet up with any strangers without an adult you trust. Better to be uncool than unsafe!
- It's never too late to tell someone if something makes you feel uncomfortable.

Advice and education for younger users make use of cartoons and animations, and offers a downloadable Safety Button application that children can hit if they see something that makes them confused or uncomfortable. In addition to such advice, the CEOP also provides a hotline for young users to report inappropriate content or contacts, as well as an online service that children can use for a private one-to-one chat with a representative from the children's charity NSPCC. The CEOP also provides educational resources aimed at parents and carers, which includes explanations of 'What Is Grooming?', and information about how social networking sites, chat forums, blogs and instant messaging services work. Similarly, parents and carers are offered advice and tips about how best to keep children safe when using such online technologies. Anticipating a competence gap between parents and their children (wherein children may well be more knowledgeable and competent in Internet usage than their elders), parents are encouraged to learn to use the applications that their children access, as well as monitor their children's online activities. The kind of programmes offered by the CEOP are by no means unique – there now exists a vast array of such initiatives, many produced by charitable organisations.

A second level at which preventive initiatives have emerged is that of technological innovation. The first generation of such applications were primarily aimed at regulating children's access (intentional or unintentional) to pictorial materials of a sexually explicit nature, deemed unsuitable for minors. Using such software, parents could set controls so as block access to unsuitable sites and images. There now exist a wide range of commercially available filtering packages, such as Cyber Patrol, X-Stop, Cyber Sitter, Net Nanny, Child Safe, Cyber Sentinel, Content Protect, and WinGuardian. Despite question marks over their efficacy (they may variously under-filter and fail to block access to offending material or over-filter and block access to non-offensive content), they remain popular with parents. A second generation of safety applications has evolved to reflect wider social concerns about online child victimisation. Applications such as KidsWatch offer tools such as a chat room monitor that logs the use of inappropriate words in children's chat sessions (any one of 1,630 suspect words or phrases), and can be configured to send email alerts to parents once such words are detected as being used.

At a third level, the providers of online services such as social networking have invested considerable resources in monitoring and managing the use of their sites, often acting in a pre-emptive manner to exclude those who are identified as potential or actual sex offenders. For example, in April 2008, the social networking company MySpace announced that it had barred 29,000 US registered sex offenders from its sites. MySpace used software that cross-referenced users' details with data publicly available on the details and addresses of registered sex offenders (a consequence of the adoption of the so-called Megan's Law). Given that such data about registered sex offenders are not publicly available in the UK (despite campaigns for the introduction of a similar Sarah's Law), some observers have raised concerns that large numbers of such offenders are using social networking sites undetected, and may present a significant threat to children (Wallop 2008). However, caution is warranted in receiving such figures for a number of reasons. Firstly, while MySpace may have excluded 29,000 registered sex offenders, only a small proportion of these are likely to have committed sex offences against children. Secondly, while it is relatively easy (at least in the USA) to match sex offenders against those who have registered online using their own details, there is nothing to prevent those wishing to avoid detection from registering with an alias. Other social networking sites have taken even more draconian steps in an attempt to curtail the possibility of online offences against children. For example it was reported in 2008 that the social networking site Faceparty had deleted the accounts of all users who were (or had declared themselves to be) over 36 years of age (*The Register* 2008). Proposals were also brought forward in 2008 for the UK government to share the email details of registered sex offenders with social networking sites (*BBC News* 2008a). However, the efficacy of any such provisions is suspect, to put it mildly, since anyone can set up as many email accounts with different providers, using different names, as they wish. A possibly more effective strategy, focused upon designing online interaction software with built-in safeguards against potential abuse, may pave the best way forward. Such a strategy has been adopted by the social networking site Bebo, who in 2006 appointed Rachel O'Connell, an academic expert on online child sex abuse, as its chief safety officer, in an attempt to mediate refined understandings of predatory behaviour into the foundations of website design.

Challenges for policing and protection

While the focused attention upon preventing, detecting and prosecuting child-oriented online sex offences is to be welcomed, there are a number of significant problems and challenges raised by the nature of current provisions.

First, we must note that the global and dispersed network character of the Internet renders it almost impossible to have a centralised system of monitoring or policing. As Jewkes and Yar (2008) note, the sheer proliferation of websites, pages and content on the Internet far outstrip the resources for monitoring available to public authorities, who must struggle to distribute finite manpower to deal with a wide range of crime, welfare and social order problems. Consequently, what we see today is an array of public, quasi-public and private actors involved in addressing online child abuse problems. In effect, the governance gap has been filled by a shifting and multi-lateral assembly of groups, organisations and individuals who seek (both collaboratively and individually) to address problems of online child sex offences. However, this distributed and decentralised mode of monitoring and regulation inevitably raises questions of efficacy and efficiency. Following the old dictum of too many hands, we see that there now exists a plethora of organisations that undertake same or similar regulatory actions over the same terrain, often duplicating efforts. Moreover, the absence of a single authoritative organisation responsible for addressing a specific problem (be it child pornography or child safety in online forums) serves to create uncertainty and confusion in the minds of Internet users in terms of who is responsible, to whom they should report offences, and so on.

A second, and in some ways even more pressing, issue is that of accountability. The history of public policing in Western democracies has typically been a balancing act between upholding the authority of the police as agents of the state in enforcement of its laws, and ensuring their accountability to the public to whom they are ultimately responsible. Thus, there have developed, over time, mechanisms to ensure that the police are subject to public scrutiny and to whom they must provide justification for their decisions (be they decisions to act, or not to act, in response to particular crime problems and situations). For example, in the UK, each police force is accountable to an elected police authority, comprising local councillors, magistrates and members of the general public. Through such mechanisms, the public interest can be upheld and the public voice on policing decisions heard. However, no such mechanisms exist where private policing is concerned (Loader 1997, 2000; Loader and Walker 2004, 2006). Any individual or group can potentially set themselves up with a brief to police the Internet, according to their own interests, priorities or moral convictions (thus, for example, members of particular ethnic and religious minorities police the Internet for what they deem instances of hate speech; women's rights activists do likewise with pornography; those interested in child protection tackle child sexual abuse images). Inevitably, conflicts can and do arise about whether the actions of such groups are actually in the wider public interest (as opposed to any given group's sectional interest), and when controversial decisions are taken, there is no direct mechanism through which they can be held accountable. Thus, the proliferation of such initiatives brings with it a democratic deficit and a potential legitimacy gap, insofar as private actors are considerably harder to oversee and regulate.

The above problem is clearly illustrated by a recent controversy relating to online child pornography. The IWF is a private organisation (set up in 1996 by the UK Internet industry) that monitors the Internet for child pornography (or as they prefer to say, child sex abuse images). Through a series of conventionalised agreements, it liaises with the UK government and the police, and advises ISPs about illegal material that needs to be removed from the Web. In late 2008, there emerged a dispute in the UK following the IWF's judgement that a page on the Internet encyclopaedia *Wikipedia* potentially contravened child pornography laws, and its subsequent actions to have access to this page blocked for those using UK-based ISPs. The page in question dealt with the veteran German rock band, the Scorpions, and featured the cover of an album, *Virgin Killer*, with a photograph of a naked, prepubescent girl (*BBC News* 2008b). Critics of the IWF's action objected on a number of grounds: firstly, because by denying users access to the offending page, the IWF were effectively blocking access to its non-illegal text content as well as its potentially (yet unproven) illegal imagery; secondly, the block on this one page had knock-on effects for UK users of *Wikipedia*, and for some time they were unable to edit any of the encyclopaedia's pages (*Wikipedia* 2008); thirdly, it has been argued that the album in question has been freely available across Europe for more than 30 years since its initial release (in 1976), and during that time no legal challenge has been presented on the grounds that it contravenes obscenity or child pornography laws. Consequently, the IWF acted as police, judge and jury in bypassing due legal process and deciding unilaterally to censor Internet content. Some 24 hours later, the IWF retracted its ban, stating that, 'in light of the length of time the image has existed and its wide availability, the decision has been taken to remove this webpage from our [black] list' (*BBC News* 2008c – UK-based readers can now view the offending image and judge for themselves, at http://en.wikipedia.org/wiki/Virgin_Killer). Critics may be less than reassured by these developments, as the IWF's *volte-face* may be seen as something only forced upon them by public outcry and negative media coverage (Richmond 2008). Moreover, it raises wider issues around the private regulation of the Internet insofar as such organisations are not inherently publicly accountable via democratic mechanisms, as would be the policing decisions of public agencies. To surrender judgements about what comprises the public interest to private and unaccountable groups may be seen as a dangerous development that needs to be curtailed if the freedom of online expression is to be effectively safeguarded.

The problem of unaccountable private action can veer, and has veered, over into a kind of virtual vigilantism. Since the late 1990s, a number of self-styled hackers against child pornography have been active on the Internet. While some undertake their own private investigations into online child pornography and present their findings to the police (Radcliffe 1998), others have gone considerably further. For example, there have been reports of hacker vigilantes who break into the computers of those they suspect of hosting or distributing child pornography, and then erase the content of computer hard drives (Penenburg 1998). In a recent case, a Californian judge was convicted of possession of child pornographic images after a vigilante hacker had infiltrated his computer using malicious software in order to collect evidence (Gaudin 2007). Such cases raise significant ethical and legal problems: is it ethically acceptable to use illegal means (unauthorised computer intrusion and deployment of malicious code) for laudable ends? Can or should evidence obtained illegally be accepted as part of the prosecution process? And, finally, who decides when people are guilty of an offence and deserve to have their computer trashed in retribution? The phenomenon of vigilante hacking inevitably raises the possibility that the rule of law and due legal process will be thrown to the winds in the search for online child sex offenders.

A third issue to be considered concerns not the specific provisions for preventing or punishing online child sex offences, but the wider climate of suspicion that the threat of paedophilia has evoked in British culture. The attention devoted to child sex offences in recent decades is undoubtedly a necessary corrective to what must be seen as a shameful neglect of child sex abuse, exploitation and victimisation. However, numerous commentators have voiced of late the view that contemporary British culture has developed an ultimately unhealthy fixation with child sex offences, in both the off-line and online environments. Sociologist and cultural critic Frank Furedi (2001) argues that in such a cultural context, children as well as their parents are coming to increasingly view all contact with strangers as a potential overture to sexual abuse or worse. Some child welfare agencies have expressed serious concerns over the effects on children's health and development wrought by over-protective parents who isolate their children to keep them safe from predation (Furedi 2005). I'm reminded here of a discussion some years ago with a well-known legal expert on Internet crime, who calmly revealed to an audience that while he allows his young daughters to surf the Internet in their bedroom, he has equipped the room with a CCTV camera so that he can monitor their activities from a screen in his living room! One must wonder just what kind of long-term effects such an intrusive form of distrust might have on the long-term psychological and emotional development of these children. More reasonable assessments might point out that the risk of stranger abuse is statistically far less likely than current levels of concern warrant. Furedi (2005) points out that in the ten years between 1983 and 1993, 57 children were murdered by strangers in the UK, an average of five per year. In contrast, more than 4,000 children are killed or seriously injured every year in road traffic accidents (Royal Automobile Club 2003). Yet child murder at the hand of paedophiles has attracted far greater media attention, public anxiety, and political action than issues relating to road safety, despite the fact that it is the latter that presents by far the greater threat to children's safety. Consequently, critics such as Furedi call for a balanced reassessment of the risks that children actually face, rather than surrendering to a wave of cultural panic that will inevitably further erode people's ability to establish relationships of openness, trust and social bonds with their fellow citizens. The over-estimation of the dangers of online victimisation might simply serve to create a generation of adults who view the Internet as a dangerous no-go territory, rather than embracing it as an invaluable opportunity for fostering social communication, interaction and exchange.

Conclusion

Only the most obtuse of observers would suggest that online child sex exploitation is a non-problem that can be conveniently dismissed as just another moral panic. Indeed, experts who heretofore tended to deconstruct crime problems as social constructions have been compelled to admit that online child pornography and paedophilia are not only real but appear to be widespread (e.g. Jenkins 2001). Yet, furnishing a viable and balanced response to these problems is far from easy. I have discussed here the many definitional, legal and practical challenges presented by online child sex offending, alongside some of the current attempts to tackle it. What is perhaps most urgently needed is an ongoing public and policy discussion based upon empirical evidence and expert assessment, one that seeks to balance the welfare of children, the rights of Internet users, and the use of rehabilitative and educational as well as punitive responses in addressing the problems at hand.

References

Akdeniz, Y. (2000) 'Child Pornography', in Y. Akdeniz, C. Walker and D. Wall (eds), *The Internet, Law and Society*. Harlow: Longman.

Akdeniz, Y. (2001a) *Governing Pornography and Child Pornography on the Internet: The UK Approach* [online]. Available at: http://www.cyber-rights.org/yamancv.htm (accessed 4 January 2009).

Akdeniz, Y. (2001b) *International Developments Section of Regulation of Child Pornography on the Internet* [online]. Available at: http://www.cyber-rights.org/reports/child.htm (accessed 4 January 2009).

Association of Sites Advocating Child Protection (2005) *About ASACP?* [online]. Available at: http://www.asacp.org/page.php?content=aboutus (accessed 13 December 2008).

BBC News (2008a) *Sex Offenders Face Website Bans*, 4 April [online]. Available at: http://news.bbc.co.uk/2/hi/uk_news/7328170.stm (accessed on 11 December 2008).

BBC News (2008b) *Wikipedia Child Image Censored*, 8 December [online]. Available at: http://news.bbc.co.uk/1/hi/uk/7770456.stm (accessed 13 December 2008).

BBC News (2008c) *IWF Backs Down in Wiki Censorship*, 9 December [online]. Available at: http://news.bbc.co.uk/1/hi/technology/7774102.stm (accessed on 13 December 2008).

Bennion, F. (2003) 'The UK Sexual Offences Bill: A Victorian Spinster's View of Sex', *Commonwealth Lawyer*, 12(1): 61–66.

Child Exploitation and Online Protection Centre (2009) *Think You Know?* [online]. Available at: http://www.thinkuknow.co.uk/11_16/ (accessed on 8 January 2009).

Creighton, S. (2003) 'Child Pornography: Images of the Abuse of Children', *NSPCC Information Briefings*. London: NSPCC.

End Child Prostitution, Child Pornography and Trafficking of Children for Sexual Purposes (1997) *Child Pornography: An International Perspective* [online]. Available at: http://www.csecworldcongress.org/PDF/en/Stockholm/Background_reading/Theme_papers/Theme%20paper%Pornography%201996_EN.pdf (accessed 2 December 2008).

Feather, M. (1999) 'Internet and Child Victimisation', *Children and Crime: Victims and Offenders Conference*, Brisbane, Australia, 17–18 June.

Forde, P. and Patterson, A. (1998) 'Paedophile Internet Activity', *Trends and Issues in Criminal Justice No. 97*. Canberra: Australian Institute of Criminology.

Furedi, F. (2001) *Paranoid Parenting*. London: Penguin/Allen Lane.

Furedi, F. (2005) *Culture of Fear: Risk Taking and the Morality of Low Expectation* (rev. edn). London: Continuum.

Gaudin, S. (2007) *Vigilante Hacker's Evidence Puts Judge Behind Bars*, 23 February [online]. Available at: http://www.safernet.org.br/site/noticias/vigilante-hackers-evidence-puts-judge-behind-bars (accessed 4 January 2009).

Graham, W. (2000) 'Uncovering and Eliminating Child Pornography Rings on the Internet: Issues Regarding and Avenues Facilitating Law Enforcement's Access to "Wonderland"', *Law Review of Michigan State University-Detroit College of Law*, 2: 457–484.

Home Office (2004) *Protecting the Public: Strengthening Protection Against Sex Offenders and Reforming the Law on Sexual Offences*. CM 5668. London: Home Office.

Internet Filter Review (2004) *Internet Pornography Statistics* [online]. Available at: http://internet-filter-review.toptenreviews.com/internet-pornography-statistics.html (accessed 3 June 2007).

Internet Watch Foundation (IWF) (2008) *Trends 2007* Available at: http://www.iwf.org.uk/media/page.195.524.htm (accessed 12 December 2008).

Jenkins, P. (2001) *Beyond Tolerance: Child Pornography Online*. New York: New York University Press.

Jewkes, Y. and Yar, M. (2008) 'Policing Cybercrime: Emerging Trends and Future Challenges', in T. Newburn (ed.), *Handbook of Policing* (2nd edn). Cullompton: Willan.

Loader, I. (1997) 'Thinking Normatively About Private Security', *Journal of Law and Society*, 24(3): 377–394.

Loader, I. (2000) 'Plural Policing and Democratic Governance', *Social and Legal Studies*, 9(3): 323–345.

Loader, I. and Walker, N. (2004) 'State of Denial? Rethinking the Governance of Security', *Punishment and Society*, 6(2): 221–228.

Loader, I. and Walker, N. (2006) 'Necessary Virtues: The Legitimate Place of the State in the Production of Security', in J. Wood and B. Dupont (eds), *Democracy, Society and the Governance of Security*. Cambridge: Cambridge University Press.

Mota, S. (2002) 'The U.S. Supreme Court Addresses the Child Pornography Prevention Act and Child Online Protection Act in *Ashcroft* v. *Free Speech Coalition* and *Ashcroft* v. *American Civil Liberties Union*', *Federal Communications Law Journal*, 55(1): 85–98.

National Criminal Intelligence Service (1999) *Project Trawler: Crime on the Information Highways* [online]. Available at: http://www.cyber-rights.org/documents/trawler.htm (accessed 13 December 2008).

O'Connell, R. (2003) *A Typology of Cybersexploitation and On-Line Grooming Practices*. Preston: Cyberspace Research Unit.

O'Connell, R., Price, J. and Barrow, C. (2004) *Cyber Stalking, Abusive Cyber Sex and Online Grooming: A Programme of Education for Teenagers*. Preston: Cyberspace Research Unit.

Ofcom (2008) *Social Networking: A Quantitative and Qualitative Research Report into Attitudes, Behaviours and Use* [online]. Available at: http://news.bbc.co.uk/1/shared/bsp/hi/pdfs/02_04_08_ofcom.pdf (accessed 5 January 2009).

Penenburg, A. (1998) *Vigilante Hacker*, 17 April [online]. Available at: http://www.forbes.com/1998/04/17/feat.html (accessed 5 January 2009).

Radcliffe, D. (1998) *Hacking Away at Kiddie Porn*, 18 August [online]. Available at: http://www.cnn.com/TECH/computing/9808/18/childporn.idg/index.html (accessed 5 January 2009).

Richmond, S. (2008) *The Internet Watch Foundation Must Learn from the Wikipedia Debacle, Daily Telegraph*, Wednesday, 10 December [online]. Available at: http://blogs.telegraph.co.uk/shane_richmond/blog/2008/12/10/the_internet_watch_foundation_must_learn_from_the_wikipedia_debacle (accessed 13 December 2008).

Royal Automobile Club (2003) *Road Traffic Accident Statistics* [online]. Available at: http://www.rac.co.uk/web/personalinjuryclaims/claim_categories/road_traffic_accidents/statistics (accessed 3 September 2007).

Stanley, J. (2002) 'Child Abuse and the Internet', *Journal of the Health Education Institute of Australia*, 9(1): 5–27.

Sutter, G. (2003) '"Don't Shoot the Messenger?" The UK and Online Intermediary Liability', *International Review of Law, Computers and Technology*, 17(1): 73–84.

Quayle, E. and Taylor, M. (2003) *Child Pornography: An Internet Crime*. London: Routledge.

The Register (2008) *Social Networking Site Bans Oldies Over Sex Offender Fears*, 22 May [online]. Available at: http://www.theregister.co.uk/2008/05/22/faceparty_bans_oldies/ (accessed 13 December 2008).

Telofono Arcobaleno (2004) *Monitoring Paedophilia on the Internet: 2004 Annual Report* [online]. Available at: http://www.telefonoarcobaleno.org/en/pdf/ANNUAL_REPORT_2007.pdf (accessed 10 December 2008).

Wallop, H. (2008) *MySpace Bars 29,000 Sex Offenders, Daily Telegraph*, 19 April [online]. Available at: http://www.telegraph.co.uk/news/uknews/1558560/MySpace-bars-29000-sex-offenders.html (accessed 13 December 2008).

Wikipedia (2008) Internet Watch Foundation and Wikipedia [online]. Available at: http://en.wikipedia.org/wiki/Internet_Watch_Foundation_and_Wikipedia (accessed 13 December 2008).

Williams, N. (1999) *The Contribution of Hotlines to Combating Child Pornography on the Internet*. London: Childnet International.

Chapter 13

Media constructions of, and reactions to, paedophilia in society

Kieran McCartan

Introduction

This chapter will address media constructions and representations of paedophilia in modern society, based on the existing literature and current reporting. It will first examine what the media actually is, and this will allow for a discussion of the role and impact of the media on the public. In doing so, the psychology of media influence will be addressed, therefore examining why the media has the impact it does on public opinion and how it can help shape individual attitudes. This will then tie into ideas around the social construction of reality, particularly with regard to social issues, examining paedophilia as a socially sensitive and traumatic topic. The chapter will then address how the media, especially the press, has reported and discussed paedophilia, looking at the language and ideas used with regard to paedophiles and dangerous child sexual offenders, and asking how close to reality these practices are. This will finally lead into a discussion of the social responsibility, morality and ethics of the media, and whether they achieve this in their reporting and presentation of stories concerning paedophilia. In discussing the UK press coverage of paedophilia, the chapter will focus on *The News of the World*'s Sarah Payne campaign; this will not only demonstrate how the press used this case to raise the profile of paedophilia, cementing it as a moral panic, but will also allow for a discussion concerning media sensitivity and ethics. In closing, the chapter will bring these various strands together to demonstrate the impact of the media's representation of paedophilia on the public and how by changing their approach the media could help change the public perception and social construction of paedophilia towards a more realistic representation that could help in child protection.

What is the media?

Prior to discussing the role and function of the media in depth, it is first important to understand what the media actually is. Although the media is often discussed in monolithic and homogeneous terms, it is anything but. Rather it is a variety of different formats, with different purposes, focusing on different issues all with different agendas (McQuail 2007). As such, the different aspects of the media can be, and often are, at odds with one another. This means that the media in contemporary society is a complex and multi-faceted industry, which is continually adapting in light of modernisation, technological developments, changing social norms and globalisation (McQuail 2007). Consequently, the majority of people living in our global society, not just Westernised countries, will come into contact with multiple media formats as well as various media perspectives and agendas every day. Understanding the complex and multifaceted nature of the modern media is important as it affects the stories being told, the way that they are told, who accesses them, and the impact that these stories have. This is salient, as the media plays an increasingly important role in modern society (Giddens 1991), with regard to crime and criminal justice matters (Howitt 1998; Brown 2003; Gray 2009), particularly in the UK, which has become a media-centred society (Howitt 1998; Cohen 2002). As such, it would be impossible and irresponsible to portray the media as one homogeneous sector. With this in mind, this chapter will focus upon the news and current affairs sector of the media, particularly in the form of the press (i.e., the press and broadcast media).

There are many potential explanations of what the role and the function of the media should be in society; these fluctuate both between and within the various types of media. However, in general, the media is seen as the main method for the dissemination of information, the shaping of public perception and the reinforcement of societal attitudes (Greer 2003). Potentially, the media has a great deal of power and influence in society, in that it can shape and influence public opinion, while at the same time inform society in a quick in-depth fashion that legitimises the subject, thereby re-establishing the creditability of the story (McQuail 2007). Howitt (1998) argues that the media can affect public opinion by utilising one of three potential models, either the cause-and-effect model, the uses and gratification model, or the cultural ratification model. As such, the media helps shape individual attitudes through a series of psychological and sociological processes including, but not limited to, stereotyping, group processes and norm reinforcement. Research indicates that attitude formation and opinion making are based on many premises, including active and inactive processing, the attitude of the processor, the story being told, and the expertise/reliability of the person telling it (Bohner and Wanke 2009). All of these are relevant with regard to the media, as we come into contact with it on a daily basis and we have very individualised attitudes to it, with research indicating that the general public are invested in and trust their preferred media sources (McCartan forthcoming). Consequently, there seems to be a symbiotic relationship between the media and the public, with the public selecting its media based upon its content and approach and the media producing stories and voicing opinions that the public, or certainly specific sections of the public, want to engage with (Cohen and Young 1981; Gamson *et al.* 1992; Howitt 1998; Greer 2003). This leads to the suggestion that the media has a dual function of reporting and creating the news (Cohen and Young 1981); however, the degree to which the media would agree with this is a hotly debated issue. Despite this, the media does play some role in the shaping of public opinion (Bohner and Wanke 2009; Gray 2009), societal attitudes (McQuail 2007) and current debates (Silverman and Wilson 2002; Cross 2005; McCartan 2008a; Gray 2009), and thus it would be inappropriate to suggest that it has no impact, although the question has to be, of what extent is this influence? Is it just limited to individual receptors or can the media help form/change social attitudes wholesale?

Media, social constructionism and moral panics

The media helps shape societal attitudes through a series of sociological processes including, but not limited to, reflexivity modernisation and social constructionism, which can have a lasting and significant impact (i.e., social attitudes and government legislation). Social constructionism is the idea that society is a socially constructed reality that adapts and changes depending on the cognition of the individuals involved (Gergen 1973; Burr 1995); this is why society adapts over time and space (Giddens 1991). Social constructionism is shaped by the twin concepts of meaning (the act of defining) and power (the motives for the definition), and is rooted in ideas around language and communication. Social constructionalism places an emphasis on contextualisation and social interaction (Burr 1995), arguing that all concepts are transitory and specific, meaning that society is constructed through the individuals and culture that shape it and, as such, can change over time, with regard to the meaning and power attributed to it by its members' attitudes, beliefs and opinions. This suggests that social constructionism is closely related to modernisation, because in both processes, society and the individual constantly re-evaluate life in relation to new information being produced. This is particularly important with regard to media influence because the media argues that it produces relevant news that is in the public interest (McQuail 2007), meaning that new information is continually being produced and social attitudes are always changing. This can be seen very clearly in certain social issues, especially socially sensitive topics such as paedophilia (McCartan 2009) and child protection (Scott *et al.* 1998).

Paedophilia is in part a social construction, specifically the labelling and definition of it (for more information on this see Chapter 1 of this volume), which has partly occurred through the media coverage and representation of paedophilia. There has been a vast amount of media coverage of paedophilia in recent years through a multitude of media formats (print, television, radio, film, etc.) and styles (news reporting, documentaries, opinion pieces, soap operas, etc.); however, the print media, especially particular sections of it (the tabloid newspapers), have focused completely on paedophilia, contributing to its status as a high-profile public interest issue. Hence, paedophilia has become a prominent social issue, a popular social risk, and a modern moral panic (Kitzinger 1999; Cohen 2002; McAlinden 2006). Moral panics, the media and social constructionism are a series of notions that tie together quite well, with the media being one of the main mechanisms in the development and maintenance of moral panics (Goode and Ben-Yehuda 1994; Thompson 1998), which can lead either directly or indirectly to the changing of social attitudes and social norms, as clearly seen in the example of paedophilia. Hence, the moral panic is one of the clearest examples of the influence of the media on society.

The concept of the moral panic was first developed and then expanded in more detail by Cohen (1971, 1972, 2002), who argued that a moral panic is an overblown social concern relating to the negative or anti-societal actions and/or ideologies of a certain event, group or subculture by society, which sees the actions as being destructive to modern life. Moral panics tend to focus on specific groups of 'folk devils', such as paedophiles, young males and drug users (Cohen 2002), who are vilified and branded as deviant by society and suffer from a form of offender apartheid (whereby society excludes and morally rejects them) (Kleinhaus 2002). This is then reinforced though deviancy amplification (that the issue is so salient in society that anything that is related to it is seen as it) (Cohen 2002), leading to an extreme social response that often overshadows the threat of the actual problem (Silverman and Wilson 2002). This in turn creates a need for a solution, generally an emotional response that is not always well conceived and usually with severe repercussions for the current folk devils (Kleinhaus 2002; Silverman and Wilson 2002; Soothill and Francis 2002).

However, this is not the only interpretation of the construction of moral panics. Goode and Ben-Yehuda (1994) indicate three different theoretical perspectives, of which Cohen's thesis is only one. Cohen's theory is closely linked to Goode and Ben-Yehuda's concept of the interest group model of moral panics, which perceives moral panics as unintended and unplanned outcomes of crusades pursued by moral groups. The second theoretical perspective is the elite-engineered model where the moral panic is a conscious/deliberate outcome of manufactured campaigns designed to divert attention away from the actual crisis. This is closely linked to the work of Hall *et al.* (1978), who argued that moral panics are mechanisms employed by the ruling classes to mystify the existing crisis in society, and, as such, the media disseminates these panics, but does not create them. The third definition of moral panic that Goode and Ben-Yehuda discuss is the grass-roots model, in which the moral panic is created though the anxieties of the normal public, and these are reinforced and/or perpetuated by the media or government. According to the grass-roots model, the media and government cannot create moral panics; these panics have to be based on public anxieties that already exist. Although all the models suggested by Goode and Ben-Yehuda, as well as Cohen, have validity, moral panics are complex, and it is difficult to pin down why one social concern becomes a moral panic and another does not. Therefore, it seems likely that a more integrated theory would be better, especially with regard to paedophilia, which has arisen out of the fears of the general public (grass-roots model), in conjunction with a series of media and government campaigns (interest group model). Moral panics therefore seem to be created

253

from and perpetuated through the interactions between the media, the government and the public.

Media coverage, moral panics and paedophilia

Paedophilia has become one of the, if not the, most prevalent moral panic of recent years (Kitzinger 1999; Cohen 2002; Silverman and Wilson 2002; Cross 2005), with the UK media, especially the press, discussing paedophilia almost on a daily basis (Critcher 2002; Greer 2003; Davidson 2008). The UK press tends to discuss paedophilia in an inappropriate, generalised, fearful and negative light; this is especially the case with the language and sentiment used to discuss paedophilia, especially by the tabloids (Thomas 2005). UK tabloid headlines have included: 'Vile sickos skulking in high places' (Parsons 2003), 'Paedo caught by perv site' (Flynn 2006), 'Lonely heart sicko was a paedo' (Patrick 2009), 'My brave girl caged a monster' (Coles 2007), 'Paedos have dodgy wiring' (*The Sun* 2007a), and 'Pervs on the loose' (*Daily Star* 2007). However, this emotive and reactionary language is not just limited to the tabloid press; the broadsheets often follow suit, albeit in a toned-down fashion: 'Don't betray Sarah now' (*The Guardian* 2000), 'Mobs and monsters' (Younge 2000), and 'Child-killers on the loose' (McKie 2000). In conjunction with headlines, this language continues in the articles, with paedophiles being described as perverts, monsters and beasts (Greer 2003; Thomas 2005). The media further complicates the reporting of paedophilia by not distinguishing between the different types of sex offenders (i.e., paedophile, hebophile, child sexual abuser), with all being labelled as paedophiles (Thomas 2005), contributing to a further escalation of the moral panic. This slanted media reporting contributes to the social construction of paedophiles and child sexual offenders as threatening and inhuman, therefore reinforcing the myth of stranger danger (Silverman and Wilson 2002), and promoting the negative social reactions in modern society (Critcher 2002; Silverman and Wilson 2002; Cross 2005). The clearest example of the media significantly contributing to the moral panic of paedophilia can be seen in *The News of the World* campaigns surrounding Sarah Payne.

The News of the World ran a series of anti-paedophile campaigns, arguing for stricter government procedures, including the introduction of the public disclosure of sex offender information, in the wake of the abduction, sexual abuse and murder of Sarah Payne in 2000. During the police investigation, the Paynes were approached by

Rebekah Wade, then editor of *The News of The World* and now editor of *The Sun* (Wade 2009), who befriended the family and helped to spearhead an anti-paedophile campaign. *The News of the World* wanted to see the introduction of 'Sarah's Charter', which contained 13 policy changes in relation to sex offenders, the last of which was Sarah's Law (Critcher 2002). Sarah's Law is based on the USA's Megan's Law (Silverman and Wilson 2002), and calls for the full public disclosure of all registered sex offender information in the UK (Critcher 2002). *The News of the World* ran its 'Name and Shame' campaign to convince the government to implement Sarah's Law. The main argument behind Sarah's law, which is also its Achilles heel, is the premise that public disclosure would have saved Sarah Payne, but this is, unfortunately, untrue. The murder of Sarah Payne happened at her grandparents' home where the family were on holiday. Roy Whiting was not actually from Kingston Gorse, where the grandparents lived, and would not have been registered there; thus, the abduction of Sarah Payne was a crime of opportunity. Public disclosure of Roy Whiting's information would therefore not have alerted the Paynes to his whereabouts and enabled them to prevent the unfortunate events that unfolded.

The News of the World's 'Name and Shame' campaign ran for two consecutive Sundays, 23 and 30 July 2000, and published the details, including photographs, of some of the UK's most prolific paedophiles and child sexual abusers, the paper arguing that public disclosure was the most effective mechanism to allow parents to protect their children, appropriately and successfully, from sexual abuse. Whether the campaign led to parents feeling safer and better able to protect their children is debatable, but it did seem to be a causal factor in the Paulsgrove riots of the same year (Critcher 2002). During the campaign, the newspaper received mixed reactions, with condemnation by policymakers and the government (Dodd 2000; Morris 2000) and mixed reactions from the media, who, while it supported Sarah's Charter, condemned public disclosure (Hodgson 2001; Critcher 2002). The Payne family, however, were positive about the campaigns (Day 2001), and seemingly widespread public support (Critcher 2002) allowed the newspaper to justify its actions (Hodgson 2001). The campaign was successful in the implementation of 12 of its 13 conditions in Sarah's Charter, excluding a full Sarah's Law (Critcher 2002).

The British government's reaction to Sarah's Law was interesting, as it fluctuated quite significantly. The government initially rejected Sarah's Law, claiming it would drive paedophiles underground, off the register, and make them a greater potential threat to children (Plotnikoff and Woolfson 2000). These concerns were reinforced, as Sarah's Law is in direct opposition to the Human Rights Act 1998, which guarantees people, among other things, a right to privacy (for more information on this, see Chapters 4 and 14 of this volume). However, the government's opinion on the viability of this controversial law has changed in recent years, becoming complex, confusing and worryingly inconsistent. Although the government initially rejected Sarah's Law (Dodd 2000; Morris 2000), it then reconsidered its position (Assinder 2006; BBC 2006), agreed to implement it (*The Sun* 2007b), and then quickly backtracked, rejecting the entire premise (Travis 2007). The government then agreed to pilot partial public disclosure, whereby parents, carers and guardians are allowed to ask whether anyone with access to their children has a history of sexual offending, and single mothers are allowed to check on the past histories of new partners. The police provide relevant information, using due care and attention, and all material revealed is done so with the greatest of confidentiality in mind (Home Office 2007; BBC 2009). It has recently been decided that, following this successful pilot, which saw no public disorder or vigilantism, but also did not seem to evidence a high enquiry rate, the procedure will be extended within the police forces involved. Full evaluation will take place at the end of 2009, at which point a decision will be made as to whether to roll the scheme out nationally (Home Office 2009).

The News of the World's campaign was, therefore, partly responsible for the moral panic surrounding paedophilia that swept Britain at the start of the twenty-first century, and which is still in existence today. At the time, few could have known that the death of one little girl (Sarah Payne) and the actions of one newspaper editor (Rebekah Wade) would have had such an inflammatory effect on the public (Critcher 2002; Silverman and Wilson 2002). The development of the name and shame campaign shows how *The News of the World* seized on public concern and reinforced social boundaries, while at the same time promoting a level of unrealistic fear and paranoia over an already sensitive issue (Silverman and Wilson 2002). The newspaper played on the irrational fear of parents, warning of stranger danger, and the corruption of the nation's children as a result of the sexual practices of a number of harmful deviants. However, it must be asked whether the paper manipulated and exploited the Paynes' tragedy for its own commercial gain. Both the Paynes (Day 2001) and Rebekah Wade (Wade 2009) have denied this. This has not, however, been true in all high-profile cases of media influence; for example, in the Madeleine McCann case, the parents here felt betrayed and used by sections of the press (*Leicester Mercury* 2009), with whom they had initially had a good relationship and who had initially helped to publicise their case.

Despite this, moral panics are important, as they are thought to reinforce popular ideas and stabilise social order (Hier 2003), by emphasising the core social beliefs (Thompson 1998) and reinforcing social norms. This means that the moral panic of paedophilia works to reinforce current social and cultural attitudes with regard to childhood, public protection and social order.

Media coverage of paedophilia versus the realities of paedophilia

Despite the high-profile nature of paedophilia in the UK media, the realities and complexities of paedophilia are not fully discussed. This is especially true of the tabloid press; for instance, *The News of the World* and *The Sun* do not discuss the reality of threats of abuse to children from within the home (incest, domestic violence, and neglect), which are far more prevalent in society than the threats from solitary, sexual predators (Howitt 1995; Briere and Elliott 2003). Consequently, it is important to highlight the realities of paedophilia, especially as research indicates that, despite the current high-profile nature of paedophilia, there is no easily accessible or widely accepted definition or explanation of the causes, the behaviour, or the most effective treatments available (McCartan 2008a). This complexity and ambiguity are exacerbated when paedophilia is considered in tandem with other forms of childhood sexual abuse, especially child sexual abuse, which is often used as a blanket term to cover all childhood abuse and all child sexual offenders (Rind *et al.* 1998).

Hence, the complexity of paedophilia, especially the heterogeneous nature of its offenders (Taylor 1981; Wilson and Cox 1983; La Fontaine 1990; Dobash *et al.* 1996; Blanchette and Coleman 2002; Cantor *et al.* 2005), the potential aetiologies of their paedophilic offending (Bagley *et al.* 1994; Howitt 1995; Blanchard *et al.* 1999; Lee *et al.* 2002; Cantor *et al.* 2008), their victims (O'Carroll 1980; Howitt 1995; Silverman and Wilson 2002; Taylor and Quayle 2003), their offending behaviours (O'Carroll 1980; La Fontaine 1990; Taylor and Quayle 2003), and their treatments (Howitt 1995; Brooks-Gordon *et al.* 2006; Harrison 2007). All this is never really examined by the media, especially the print media, and therefore this may affect the public's understanding of paedophilia. Research indicates that child sexual abuse and paedophilia are one of the most misunderstood crimes in modern society, particularly as society denies the occurrence of, underestimates the frequency of (O'Grady 1994), and under-reports paedophilia (West 2000; Simmons *et al.* 2002). The public, therefore, tend to see paedophiles as a homogeneous group who have fixed personality traits that are unchangeable, and so do not advocate treatment, but rather castration or incarceration (McCartan 2004, forthcoming). This seems reasonable given the public's relative lack of exposure to paedophiles and informed opinion/literature. This has led professionals who work in and around the field of child sexual abuse to suggest that the public have a poor understanding of paedophilia and that this poor comprehension was developed through their exposure to the media (McCartan 2007).

Social responsibility, the media and paedophilia

As we have previously discussed, the media has a degree of influence on individual and social attitudes, contributing to the formation as well as maintenance of moral panics and social risks. This is particularly true of paedophilia, where the media's seemingly slanted reporting appears to have affected the public perception and attitude to paedophilia, on occasion leading to socially unacceptable behaviour (Bell 2002; Silverman and Wilson 2002; Cross 2005; Breen 2008). Hence, how socially responsible, moral and ethical has the media been in its coverage of paedophilia?

Notions around morality, responsibility, professionalism and ethics are very individualistic, with different people having different beliefs of what is and what is not acceptable. This links with the type of media that people expose themselves to, the degree to which they accept the media's interpretation of stories, and the extent to which they believe the media to be socially responsible (McCartan 2007, forthcoming). The media in the UK, and in any free society, is seen as the fourth estate (i.e., the idea developed by Burke in late eighteenth-century England to discuss the power of the press; he likened it to the other 'estates' of power and social control that existed at the time, and to a degree still exist today: the Lords, the Commons and the Church), which results in their believing that they can, and generally do, report what they wish with no real obligations (McQuail 2007). Despite this sense of autonomy, the media is confined to a certain degree by the social norms of the society and culture within which they operate, reinforcing the socially constructed nature of the media and the symbolic relationship that they have with the public. There are certain expectations placed on the press in society, for they have both internal (editorial, corporate ownership, etc.) and external pressures (the government and the public), which help shape the social and moral responsibility of what they should and should not produce (McQuail 2007). The media argues that it has a responsibility to produce stories which have a social purpose and are relevant (McQuail 2007), providing justification for it to focus on certain sensitive and controversial stories, such as child sexual abuse, terrorism and political scandal. However, in doing so, the media has a dual public interest, in that they have roles and responsibilities that are in the public interest, and as such the public are interested in the way that the media conducts itself. This means that the press must maintain a high degree of accountability and impartiality, always presenting themselves and their stories in the best light. These notions of best practice tie in neatly with the social responsibility theory of the press, which states that the media has obligations to society and in achieving these obligations it has to be truthful, fair and relevant; and although the media has the right to self-regulate, it must adhere to professional codes of ethics. These ethical guidelines have become more professional and coherent, with the media, and especially the press, having to account to the public and government for their stories and stance; particularly with the creation of the Press Complaints Commission.

Despite this proposed idea of media civic duty, social responsibility and self-directed regulation, does the media always act responsibly and morally when dealing with sensitive issues? The media has been criticised for its handling of sensitive and traumatic issues, particularly paedophilia and child sexual abuse with *The News of the World*'s 'Name and Shame' campaign, as highlighted earlier, receiving widespread condemnation. Furthermore, there has been speculation that the media, especially the press, sacrifices its core responsibilities in how it reports crime, especially socially sensitive crimes, in an attempt to boost sales and make profits (Friendly and Goldfarb 1968; Reiner 2002). However, the media would counter this, arguing that it has acted morally, ethically and responsibly by providing relevant stories that are in the public interest, and suggesting that if the public does not want to read the stories it produces, then the public would not support it (Cohen and Young 1981; Howitt 1998; Greer 2003). This reinforces the link between the media and the public, emphasising that both are involved in the selection and promotion of certain stories and social campaigns, as the public continually invest in the stories they are interested in and the media only covers those issues which support the public's interests (Gamson *et al.* 1992; Howitt 1998).

The media's coverage of socially sensitive and traumatic stories can also be criticised, particularly with regard to paedophilia, through the language used and the discussion provided. This is more of an issue for the tabloid press, who skim over complex issues, providing simplistic and generalised coverage (Thomas 2005). As already highlighted in this chapter, the language used to discuss paedophilia, as well as the approach to understanding paedophilia, has contributed to an increase in the public perception of stranger danger, the promotion of paedophile myths, and a lack of real insight into the issue. Hence, is the media really acting in a socially responsible way? Does such behaviour by certain sections of the media promote an unrealistic and inappropriate understanding of a complex issue and are they really informing the public of threats to their children as they claim (Wade 2009)? Consequently, are they being relevant, honest, impartial and acting in the public interest or just reinforcing as well as promoting socially constructed fears?

Hence, questions must be asked about the media's culpability in the stories it reports and way that it does so. Thus, is the media responsible for the social, political and personal outcomes of its stories? *The News of the World*'s 'Name and Shame' campaign was linked to vigilante action (Bell 2002; Thomas 2005; McCartan 2008a), so were they responsible for this social unrest? On one level, it can be argued that they were, as their story provided the incitement and directed the public's outrage (Bell 2002; Silverman and Wilson 2002); however, on the other hand, we cannot hold the media responsible for the actions of a few who would have engaged in deviant behaviour in any event and consequently jumped upon a bandwagon (Williams 2004; McCartan 2007). While the media would argue that it is their responsibility to produce socially relevant material and not to sanction, promote or encourage public reaction, they would also say that they are not responsible for individual and social reactions. However, is this merely shifting the blame and downplaying their social responsibility? Does this cognitive distortion mean that the media is absolved of all guilt?

The social and ethical responsibility of the media in dealing with socially sensitive, traumatic and difficult stories is important, because it can contribute to both individual and social reactions to these stories, helping to socially construct attitudes and possibly creating further moral panics. This is what has happened with paedophilia in modern society, and we must ask whether the media has acted responsibly, and, if not, why not?

Conclusions

This chapter has discussed the role of the media in the creation and maintenance of the current crisis of paedophilia in modern society, suggesting that the media, especially the press, has played a central role in the current phenomenon of paedophilia, helping to shape individual attitudes, public opinion and government strategy. However, the media representation of paedophilia has been problematic, possibly socially irresponsible, and has contributed to the unrealistic social construction of the realities of paedophilia that exist in modern society. The main conclusion that this chapter comes to is that if the media, especially the tabloid press, took a more responsible, socially conscious and informed approach to the discussion as well as to the reporting of paedophilia, this could lead to a more appropriate social construction and a better informed public. Public education through the media is not a recent phenomenon (McQuail 2007), but in the case of paedophilia it may be the best strategy to get the public to engage with a difficult and sensitive issue. In order to improve public education, it is suggested that the media should adapt its coverage of paedophilia in the following ways:

- The media should change its approach to discussing and presenting paedophilia. Some have started to do this, especially the visual media, by producing a mixed bag of approaches, including a more rounded and thought-provoking perception of paedophilia through films such as *Secret Life* (2008) and *The Woodsman* (2005), and the portrayal of paedophilic activities in the television soap opera *EastEnders*, during 2008–9, a more controversial perception (the television programme *Brass Eye Special – Paedophilia* (2001)), or a more factual insight (the television programmes *The Hunt for Britain's Paedophiles* (2002) and *Exposed: The Bail Hostel Scandal* (2006). However, this has only occurred in certain sections of the media, with portions of the print media, especially the tabloids, sticking to the traditional, reactive and emotional approaches to reporting paedophilia.

- The media would have to question its social and civic responsibility with regard to paedophilia; for instance, whether it is socially, morally and professionally responsible to print the names and addresses of child sexual abusers (Critcher 2002; *Belfast Telegraph* 2009), especially when this can result in vigilante action (Bell 2002; Silverman and Wilson 2002; Cross 2005; Breen 2008)?

- In discussing and reporting upon paedophilia, the media, especially the tabloid press, needs to use non-emotive, sensible and more realistic language. This would enable the media to realistically discuss the realities of paedophilia and its potential impact upon society; this would also allow it to become more impartial.

- The media needs to present the issues and debates around paedophilia in a balanced light, suggesting the possible explanations for the offenders' behaviour, possible treatments and resolutions, and socially positive reintegration strategies; it is not enough to label these people as sick, mad or otherwise and then socially disregard them.

- The media should, as some sections already do, continue to engage with professionals when discussing the realities of paedophilia in an attempt to give a more realistic understanding. Although this can be problematic, as professionals do not necessarily have a consistent perception and understanding of paedophilia (McCartan 2008b, 2009), and media representatives are often pressurised by deadlines and space (i.e., copy space, recording time or air time). However, it is still not too much to ask that a more realistic approach be taken. If it were, it would mean that the public were able to get the most informative as well as most sensible advice on paedophilia and child sexual abuse, hopefully leading to a reduction in the current moral panic.

- The media, specifically the press, needs to decide what its standpoint on paedophilia is – are they enforcing social guardianship or popular punitiveness? *The News of the World* claimed that it was doing the former, although it seems more likely that it was enforcing the latter.

In conclusion, it is important to realise that although the media construction and representation of paedophilia have played an important role in the current moral panic surrounding paedophilia in the UK it is not the only factor; the public and government also play a pivotal role. The social construction of reality that is aided by the media can help promote an understanding of paedophilia in modern society and as such allow us to deal with this prevalent social issue in a more realistic and level-headed fashion.

References

Assinder, N. (2006) 'Why is Reid Looking at New Law?', *BBC News* [online]. Available at: http://news.bbc.co.uk/1/hi/uk_politics/5094186. stm (accessed 29 January 2006).

Bagley, C., Wood, M. and Young, L. (1994) 'Victim to Abuser: Mental Health and Behavioural Sequels of Child Sexual Abuse in a Community Survey of Young Adult Males', *Child Abuse and Neglect*, 18: 683–697.

BBC (2006) 'No 10 Admits Megan's Law Problems', *BBC News* [online]. Available at: http://news.bbc.co.uk/1/hi/uk_politics/5093804. stm (accessed 19 June 2006).

BBC (2009) 'Child Sex Warning Scheme Expanded', *BBC News* [online]. Available at: http://news.bbc.co.uk/1/hi/uk/7945364.stm (accessed 18 March 2009).

Belfast Telegraph (2009) 'Indecent Assault Accused Says Boy was Spying on Him' [online]. Available at: http://www.belfasttelegraph.co.uk/news/ local-national/in.htmlnt-assault-accused-says-boy-was-spying-on-him-14176776.html (accessed 18 March 2009).

Bell, V. (2002) 'The Vigilant(e) Parent and the Paedophile: The *News of the World* Campaign 2000 and the Contemporary Governmentality of Child Sexual Abuse', *Feminist Theory*, 3: 83–102.

Blanchard, R., Watson, M.S., Choy, A. *et al.* (1999) 'Paedophiles: Mental Retardation, Maternal Age, and Sexual Orientation', *Archives of Sexual Behavior,* 28: 111–127.

Blanchette, M. C. and Coleman, G. D. (2002) 'Priest Paedophiles: Paedophiles and Ephebophiles Have No Capacity for Authentic Sexual Relationships', *America*, 186(13): 18.

Bohner, G. and Wanke, M. (2009) 'The Psychology of Attitudes and Persuasion', in J. Wood and T. Gannon (eds), *Public Opinion and Criminal Justice*. Cullompton: Willan.

Brass Eye Special – Paedophilia (2001) TV programme, Channel 4, 26 July 2001.

Breen, S. (2008) *Machete Attackers Thought I Was a Perv. Sunday Life* [online]. Available at: http://www.belfasttelegraph.co.uk/sunday-life/ machete-attackers-thought-i-was-perv-14028226.html (accessed 18 March 2009).

Briere, J. and Elliott, D. M. (2003) 'Prevalence and Psychological Sequelae of Self-Reported Childhood Physical and Sexual Abuse in a General Population Sample of Men and Women', *Child Abuse and Neglect*, 27: 1205–1222.

Brooks-Gordon, B., Adams, C., Bilby, C. *et al.* (2006) *A Systematic Review of Psychological Treatments for Adults Who Have Sexually Offended or Are at Risk of Sexually Offending.* Final report for NHS National Programme on Forensic Mental Health Research and Development.

Brown, S. (2003) *Crime and Law in Media Culture.* Buckingham–Philadelphia: Open University Press.

Burr, V. (1995) *An Introduction to Social Construction.* London: Routledge.

Cantor, J. M., Blanchard, R., Robichaud, L. K. and Christensen, B. K. (2005) 'Quantitative Reanalysis of Aggregate Data on IQ in Sexual Offenders', *Psychological Bulletin*, 131: 555–568.

Cantor, J. M., Kabani, N., Christen, B. K. *et al.* (2008) 'Cerebral White Matter Deficiencies in Paedophilic Men', *Journal of Psychiatric Research*, 42: 167–183.

Cohen, S. (1972) *Folk Devils and Moral Panics: The Creation of Mods and Rockers.* London: MacGibbon and Kee.

Cohen, S. (2003) *Folk Devils and Moral Panics: The Creation of Mods and Rockers* (3rd edn). London: MacGibbon and Kee.

Cohen, S. and Young, J. (1981) *The Manufacture of News: Social Problems, Deviance and the Mass Media.* Beverly Hills, CA: Sage.

Coles, J. (2007) 'My Brave Girl Caged a Monster', *The Sun* [online]. Available at: http://www.thesun.co.uk/sol/homepage/news/article28138. ece (accessed 22 September 2007).

Critcher, C. (2002) 'Media, Government and Moral Panic: The Politics of Paedophilia in Britain 2000–1', *Journalism Studies*, 3: 521–535.

Cross, S. (2005) 'Paedophiles in the Community: Inter-agency Conflict, News Leaks and the Local Press', *Crime, Media and Culture*, 1: 284–300.

The Daily Star (2007) 'Pervs on the loose', [online]. Available at: http://www.dailystar.co.uk/posts/view/10766/Pervs-on-the-loose-/ (accessed 23 September 2007).

Davidson, J. C. (2008) *Child Sexual Abuse: Media Representations and Government Reactions.* New York: Glasshouse.

Day, J. (2001) 'Paynes Pay Tribute to the Media', *The Guardian* [online]. Available at: http://www.guardian.co.uk/media/2001/dec/12/ pressandpublishing2 (accessed 18 March 2009).

Dobash, R., Carnie, J. and Waterhouse, L. (1996) 'Child Sexual Abusers: Recognition and Response', in L. Waterhouse (ed.), *Child Abuse and Child Abusers: Protection and Prevention.* London: Jessica Kingsley Publishers.

Dodd, V. (2000) 'Tabloid's Naming of Paedophiles Condemned by Police Chief', *The Guardian* [online]. Available at: http://www.guardian.co.uk/ Archive/Article/0,4273,4043689,0.html (accessed 24 June 2002).

Exposed: The Bail Hostel Scandal (2006) TV programme, BBC1, *Panorama*, November 2006.

Flynn, B. (2006) 'Paedo Caught by Perv Site', *The Sun* [online]. Available at: http://www.thesun.co.uk/sol/homepage/news/article72054.ece (accessed 23 September 2007).

Friendly, A. and Goldfarb, R. L. (1968) *Crime and Publicity: The Impact of the News on the Administration of Justice.* New York: Twentieth Century Fund.

Gamson, W. A., Croteau, D., Hoynes, W. and Sasson, T. (1992) 'Media Images and the Construction of Reality', *Annual Review of Sociology*, 18: 373–393.

Gergen, K. J. (1973) 'Social Psychology as History', *Journal of Personality and Social Psychology*, 26, 309–320.

Giddens, A. (1991) *Modernity and Self-Identity; Self and Society in the Late Modern Age.* Cambridge: Polity Press.

Goode, E. and Ben-Yehuda, N. (1994) *Moral Panics: The Social Construction of Deviance.* Oxford: Blackwell.

Gray, J. M. (2009) 'What Shapes Public Opinion of the Criminal Justice System?', in J. Wood and T. Gannon (eds), *Public Opinion and Criminal Justice.* Cullompton: Willan.

Greer, C. (2003) *Sex Crime and the Media: Sex Offending and the Press in a Divided Society.* Cullompton: Willan.

The Guardian (2000) 'Don't Betray Sarah Now', [online]. Available at: http://www.guardian.co.uk/child/story/0,,351101,00.html (accessed 22 September 2007).

Hall, S., Critcher, C., Jefferson, T., Clarke, J. and Robert, B. (1978) *Policing the Crisis: Mugging, the State and Law and Order.* London: Macmillan.

Harrison, K. (2007) 'The High-Risk Sex Offender Strategy in England and Wales: Is Chemical Castration an Option?', *Howard Journal*, 46: 16–31.

Hier, S. P. (2003) 'Risk and Panic in Late Modernity: Implications of the Converging Sites of Social Anxiety', *British Journal of Sociology*, 54: 3–20.

Hodgson, J. (2001) 'Sun challenges *News of the World* Over Paedophile Law', *The Guardian* [online]. Available at: http://www.guardian.co.uk/archive/article/0,4273,4325992,00.html (accessed 24 July 2002).

Home Office (2007) *Review of the Protection of Children from Sex Offenders.* London: Home Office.

Home Office (2009) 'Protecting Children from Sexual Abuse'. Press Release [online]. Available at: http://press.homeoffice.gov.uk/press-releases/Child-sex-offenders-disclousre (accessed 18 March 2009).

Howitt, D. (1995) *Paedophiles and Sexual Offences Against Children.* Chichester: Wiley.

Howitt, D. (1998) *Crime, the Media and the Law.* Chichester: Wiley.

The Hunt for Britain's Paedophiles (2002) TV programme, BBC2, June 2002.

Kitzinger, J. (1999) 'The Ultimate Neighbour from Hell? Stranger Danger and the Media Framing of Paedophilia', in C. Critcher (ed.), *Critical Readings: Moral Panics and the Media.* Maidenhead: Open University Press.

Kleinhaus, M. M. (2002) 'Criminal Justice Approaches to Paedophilic Offenders', *Social and Legal Studies*, 11: 233–255.

La Fontaine, J. (1990) *Child Sexual Abuse.* Cambridge: Polity Press.

Lee, J. K., Jackson, H. J. and Ward, T. (2002) 'Developmental Risk Factors for Sexual Offending', *Child Abuse and Neglect*, 26: 73–92.

Leicester Mercury (2009) 'Madeleine Search was "Hampered by the Media"', 11 March 2009, p. 2.

McAlinden, A. (2006) 'Managing Risk: From Regulation to the Reintegration of Sexual Offenders', *Criminology and Criminal Justice*, 6: 197–218.

McCartan, K. F. (2004) '"HERE THERE BE MONSTERS"; The Public's Perception of Paedophiles with Particular Reference to Belfast and Leicester', *Medicine, Science and the Law*, 44: 327–342.

McCartan, K. F. (2007) *Implicit Theories of Paedophilia: Professional and Trainee/Non-Professional Understandings of Paedophilia in Modern Society*. PhD dissertation, University of Leicester.

McCartan, K. F. (2008a) 'Current Understandings of Paedophilia and the Resulting Crisis in Modern Society', in J. M. Caroll and M. K. Alena (eds), *Psychological Sexual Dysfunctions*. New York: Nova.

McCartan, K. F. (2008b) *'Professionals' Implicit Theories of Paedophilia'*, *Association for the Treatment of Sexual Abusers Conference*, Atlanta, Georgia, October 2008.

McCartan, K. F. (2009) 'Paedophilia: The Actual vs. the Constructed? Is a Change of Terminology Needed?', *ATSA Forum*, 21(2): 16–20.

McCartan, K. F. (forthcoming) 'Student/Trainee-Professional Implicit Theories of Paedophilia', *Psychology, Crime and Law*.

McDonald Wilson Bradford, J. (2000) 'The Treatment of Sexual Deviation Using a Pharmacological Approach', *Journal of Sex Research*, 37: 248.

McKie, D. (2000) 'Child Killers on the Loose', *The Guardian* [online]. Available at: http://www.guardian.co.uk/Columnists/Column/0,,365294,00.html (accessed 23 September 2007).

McQuail, D. (2007) *Mass Communication Theory* (5th edn). London: Sage.

Morris. S. (2000) '"Name and Shame" Court Threat', *The Guardian* [online]. Available at: http://www.guardian.co.uk/Archive/Article/0,4273,4046033,00.html (accessed 24 July 2002).

Nurcombe, B. (2000) 'Child Sexual Abuse 1: Psychopathology', *Australian and New Zealand Journal of Psychiatry*, 34: 85–91.

O'Carroll, T. (1980) *Paedophilia: The Radical Case*. London: Peter Owen.

O'Grady, R. (1994). *The Rape of the Innocent: One Million Children Trapped in the Slavery of Prostitution*. Bangkok: ECPAT.

Parsons, T. (2003) 'Vile Sickos Skulking in High Places', *The Mirror* [online]. Available at: http://www.mirror.co.uk/news/columnists/parsons/2003/01/20/vile-sickos-skulking-in-high-places-89520-12551595/ (accessed 24 September 2007).

Patrick, G. (2009) 'Lonely Heart Sicko Was a Paedo', *The Sun* [online]. Available at: http://www.thesun.co.uk/sol/homepage/news/article2313271.ece (accessed 18 March 2009).

Plotnikoff, J. and Woolfson, R. (2000) *Where Are They Now?: An Evaluation of Sex Offender Registration in England and Wales*. Police Research Series, Paper 126. London: Home Office.

Reiner, R. (2002) 'Media Made Criminality: The Representation of Crime in the Mass Media', in M. Maguire, R. Morgan and R. Reiner (eds), *The Oxford Handbook of Criminology* (3rd edn). Oxford: Oxford University Press.

Rind, B., Tromovitch, P. and Bauserman, R. (1998) 'A Meta-Analytic Examination of Assumed Properties of Child Sexual Abuse Using College Samples', *Psychological Bulletin*, 124: 22–53.

Scott, S., Jackson, S. and Backett-Milburn, K. (1998) 'Swings and Roundabouts: Risk Anxiety and the Everyday Worlds of Children', *Sociology*, 32: 689–705.

Secret Life (2008) TV programme. Channel 4, 19 April.

Silverman, J., and Wilson, D. (2002) *Innocence Betrayed: Paedophilia, the Media and Society*. Cambridge: Polity.

Simmons, J., Allen, J., Aust, R. *et al.* (2002) *Crime in England and Wales 2001/2002*. London: Home Office.

Soothill, K. and Francis, B. (2002) 'Moral Panics and the Aftermath: A Study of Incest', *Journal of Social Welfare and Family Law*, 24: 1–17.

Stone, T. H., Winsdale, W. J. and Klugman, C. M. (2000) 'Sex Offenders, Sentencing Laws and Pharmaceutical Treatment: A Prescription for Failure', *Behavioural, Sciences and the Law*, 18: 83–110.

The Sun (2007a) 'Paedos Have Dodgy Wiring' [online]. Available at: http://www.thesun.co.uk/sol/homepage/news/article519145.ece (accessed 18 March 2009).

The Sun (2007b) 'Sarah's Law to Start in Months' [online]. Available at: http://www.thesun.co.uk/article/0,,2-2007160278,00.html (accessed 9 April 2007).

Taylor, B. (1981) *Perspectives on Paedophilia*. London: Batsford Academic and Educational Ltd.

Taylor, M., and Quayle, E. (2003) *Child Pornography: An Internet Crime*. Hove and New York: Brunner-Routledge.

Thomas, T. (2005) *Sex Crime: Sex Offending and Society* (2nd edn). Cullompton: Willan.

Thompson, K. (1998) *Moral Panics*. London: Routledge.

Travis, A. (2007) 'Home Office Disowns Plan for UK Version of Megan's Law', *The Guardian* [online]. Available at: http://politics.guardian.co.uk/homeaffairs/story/0,,2054229,00.html (accessed 11 April 2007).

Wade, R. (2009) 'Cudlipp Lecture', *The Guardian* [online]. Available at: http://www.guardian.co.uk/media/2009/jan/27/rebekahwade-sun (accessed 18 March 2009).

West, D. (2000) 'Paedophilia: Panic or Plague?', *Journal of Forensic Psychiatry*, 11: 511–531.

Williams, A. (2004) *"There Ain't No Peds in Paulsgrove": Social Control, Vigilantes and the Misapplication of Moral Panic Theory*. PhD dissertation, University of Bristol.

Wilson, G. D. and Cox, D. N. (1983) 'Personality of Paedophile Club Members', *Personality and Individual Differences*, 4: 323–329.

The Woodsman (2005) Film directed by Nicole Kasell. USA: Dash Films.

Young, J. (1971) 'The Role of the Police as Amplifiers of Deviance, Negotiators of Drug Control as Seen in Notting Hill', in S. Cohen (ed.), *Images of Deviance*. Harmondsworth: Penguin.

Younge, G. (2000) 'Mobs and Monsters', *The Guardian* [online]. Available at: http://www.guardian.co.uk/child/story/0,,354018,00.html (accessed on 24 September 2007).

Chapter 14

Dignity and dangerousness: sex offenders and the community – human rights in the balance?

Bernadette Rainey

Introduction

In 1997, the Labour government proposed the incorporation of the European Convention of Human Rights (ECHR) into domestic law, with the slogan 'bringing rights home' (Human Rights Bill 1997). The rationale for the new Act included the creation of a human rights culture, recognised by both government and the public as integral to civil society. At the same time, governmental penal policy was prioritising community protection, with risk being the primary driver of policy. This chapter will examine the impact of rights protection on penal policy and community protection in three areas: indeterminate sentencing, the sex offender register, and the use of pharmacotherapy. The examples illustrate the role rights protection premised on dignity can play in penal policy even where sex offenders pose a risk to others.

Human dignity and human rights

The concept of human dignity is a central tenet of liberal human rights law and is enshrined in state constitutions and international human rights instruments. The concept has become increasingly important in UK lawmaking since the incorporation of the ECHR by the Human Rights Act (HRA) 1998 (Feldman 2000). Gearty argues that the principle of respect for human dignity is one of three principles that underpin the adjudication of human rights law (Gearty 2004: 4).[1]

However, the meaning of dignity is not straightforward (Feldman 1999). Respect for human dignity is not an immutable concept, and it is open to cultural and temporal reinterpretation (Donnelly 2003). However, as Feldman notes, we must strive for a consensus as a basis for mutual respect in society. He describes dignity as 'an expression of an attitude to life which we humans should value when we see it in others as an expression of something which gives particular point and poignancy to the human condition' (Feldman 1999: 686). The role of law is to provide rights to help preserve the opportunity for a dignified life (Feldman 2000). The ECHR provides a list of such rights. A dignified life includes the right to self-determination, autonomy and integrity. However, the idea of subjective dignity encompassing autonomy can clash with the concept of objective dignity with the emphasis placed on the dignity of the human collective. It may be justifiable for the state to interfere with a person's autonomy if that measure is shown to protect the dignity of humanity as a whole (Feldman 2000). The ECHR does not refer in its text to respect for dignity. However, the jurisprudence of the European Court of Human Rights (ECtHR) has used the concept to illustrate its reasoning. These rights and their application to sex offenders will be examined below.

Dangerousness as justification for limiting rights

If dignity is accepted as the basis for rights protection, then sex offenders are entitled as human beings to a similar minimum level of protection as others. However, in some circumstances, the state has attempted to justify the limitation of offender rights on the grounds of dangerousness. The state is under an obligation to protect the rights of all within the community, an obligation that has been recognised as a positive obligation on the state by the ECtHR. For example, under Article 2 on the right to life, the state has obligations to provide protection where there is a real and immediate risk of death and the state can take reasonable steps to protect as laid down by the European Court in *Osman* v *UK* ((2000) 29 E.H.R.R. 245). Similar obligations apply under Article 3 and Article 8. However, the permissibility of limitations on rights is dependent on the right involved and the justifications used. Any breach of Article 3 cannot be justified, whereas the qualified rights such as Article 8 allow the state to limit rights as long as any limitation meets a legitimate aim, is in accordance with law, and is proportionate. The safety of others is recognised as a legitimate aim of public policy when considering qualified rights. However, a question arises as to the legitimacy of claims of dangerousness and risk when law and policy limit rights.

Dangerousness and the concomitant idea of risk are concepts that have increasingly been used in social, criminological and legal literature. Both terms have been used interchangeably to justify the imposition of restrictions and longer sentences on sex offenders. The defining of high-risk offenders is complex and, like the concept of dignity, is open to interpretation across the political, social and legal spectrum as well as between policymakers, practitioners and law enforcement (Kemshall 2008). The term 'risk' is value laden and reflects the context in which, and by whom, it is used (Douglas 1992). The concept of risk in social theory is now being used as a descriptor for the postmodern or late modern age; we are living in a risk society and in a world at risk (Beck 2007). Traditional notions of risk have been transformed from being measurable and predictable to being indeterminate. This leads to demands for a risk-averse society driven by the precautionary principle (Beck 2007). This defensive approach to risk impacts on the law: 'Security is displacing freedom and equality from the highest position on the scale of values. The result is a tightening of laws, a seemingly rational totalitarianism of defence against threats' (Beck 2007: 8-9).

The emphasis on risk has led to a shift from treating the offender as a moral agent who can be transformed (Garland 1985) to the management of risk classified by dangerousness (Feely and Simon 1992). This new risk penalism has been driven not only by a focus on risk by policymakers and theorists but also by the perception and fear of risk held by the public. Sex offenders are the new folk devils, and moral panic has heightened the fear of paedophiles following high-profile murders such as that of Sarah Payne (Kemshall and McIvor 2004). The cultural understanding of risk (Kemshall and McGuire 2003) has led to legislative and policy changes that focus on regulating the perceived dangerousness of sex offenders.

If risk has become the predominant driver of penal policy, then there has to be a method to assess the risk that offenders pose. Public protection dictates that risks should be measurable. Assessment tools have been developed in order to manage and differentiate risk. Different methods have been used, including clinical assessment tools which focus entirely on the individual and actuarial methods of assessment focusing solely on the context and statistical data available (Grubin 2004). In actuarial methods, focus on the individual is removed. The failure to take individual characteristics into account has been criticised as being flawed (Grubin 2004) and

271

would compromise the rights protection of the individual. Removing individual characteristics objectifies the offender and so removes him from the sphere of humanity, undermining his dignity. Recent risk assessment tools use dynamic methods of assessment, which combine actuarial methods of assessment with the individual circumstances and characteristics of the offender. These third-generation tools are arguably more effective and do consider the needs of the offender (Kemshall 2003). However, there are still difficulties with assessing high-risk offenders (Kemshall 2003). The use of risk moves the penal system further from traditional notions of proportionate punishment and deterrence focused on what a person has done, to prevention of acts that may occur.

The applicable rights

Alongside the rise of the risk penology, the UK has developed human rights protection within its jurisdiction by passing the HRA 1998. As mentioned above, the Act incorporates the ECHR into domestic law. All public authorities are bound by the Act and must act in a way that is compatible with the ECHR (s. 6 HRA 1998). The criminal justice system must not undermine the essence of the rights in the convention.

Article 3 – torture, degrading and inhuman treatment

Article 3 of the ECHR[2] prohibits the use of torture, and inhuman or degrading treatment. This right has been interpreted by the ECtHR as imposing both negative and positive obligations on states. The state must not be responsible for, or fail to take measures to prevent, a person within its jurisdiction being ill-treated. The fundamental importance of this right is illustrated by its absolute, non-derogable nature. Once an interference of the right has been found, the state cannot justify an interference by reference to a legitimate aim. Ill-treatment deals directly with the idea of an attack on the human dignity. How dangerous the person may be is irrelevant to the protection afforded by the Article. The ECtHR has reiterated this by stating that 'the Convention prohibits in absolute terms torture or inhuman or degrading treatment or punishment, irrespective of the victim's conduct' (*Chahal* v *UK* (1997) 23 E.H.R.R. 413, para 80).

The ECtHR has defined torture, inhuman and degrading treatment on a hierarchical scale with the most egregious acts of suffering inflicted on a person being defined as torture though there is not necessarily a clear delineation between them. Degrading treatment or punishment is described as 'degrading if it grossly humiliates him before others or drives him to act against his will or conscience' (*Greek case* (1969) 12 Yearbook 186–510). The ECtHR has further defined degrading treatment as 'treatment which arouses in the victim feelings of fear, anguish and inferiority capable of humiliation and debasement and possibly breaking physical or moral resistance' (*Ireland* v *UK* (1979–1980) 2 EHRR 25 para 197). The difference between each is a matter of degree. In each case the punishment or treatment has to reach a minimum level of severity for the Article to be engaged, and it is for the court to decide whether this threshold has been met. In making its decision, the court will assess a number of factors, including the nature and duration of the punishment or treatment; the age, sex, and health of the victim; and the physical and mental effects (*Ireland* v *UK* (1979–1980) 2 EHRR 25 para 162). The threshold for degrading treatment would appear to be high though the treatment does not have to be deliberate. In *Tyrer* v *UK* it was held that 'it is enough if the victim's treatment amounts to humiliation only in his eyes' (*Tyrer* v *UK* (1979–1980) 2 EHRR 1, para 23).

Article 5 – arbitrary detention

Although Article 5 can be derogated from in times of state emergency under the convention, the state is limited by the Article as to when it can deprive persons of their liberty within a state. The Article states that persons can only be deprived of their liberty for specified reasons such as criminal sanction, health and deportation and in accordance with law (Ovey and White 2006). Article 5 also guarantees a review of detention to be held speedily by a judicial body under Article 5(4). 'Speedily' is not defined but has been held by the court to be dependent on the issue before the court and type of detention in question (*Bezicheri* v *Italy* (1990) 12 EHRR 210).

Article 8 – family and private life

Under Article 8 of the ECHR, the state is prohibited from interfering in a person's private and family life, home and correspondence.[3] Unlike Article 3, Article 8 is not absolute. It is a qualified right in that the state may justify interference if it is in accordance with law, meets a legitimate aim, and is necessary in a democratic society.[4]

Article 8(1) does not define what private and family life means. Family life covers most familial relationships, while private life has been interpreted expansively by the court to include 'a person's physical and psychological integrity' for which respect is due in order to 'ensure the development, without outside interference, of the personality of each individual in his relations with other human beings' (*Botta* v *Italy* (1998) 26 EHRR 241). This wide basis for the right covers not only integrity but also sexual relations (*Dudgeon* v *UK* (1983) 5 EHRR 573). The concept of dignity is prevalent in the jurisprudence concerning Article 8 (*Pretty* v *UK* (2002) 35 EHRR 1 para 65). The idea of developing relationships with others is closely linked to that of living a dignified life (Dupre 2006).

As even a minor intrusion can constitute interference, many cases are decided under Article 8(2). A measure has to be 'in accordance with law', meaning that there should be some legislative basis for the treatment. Any such legislation should be accessible and predictable and its application foreseeable (*Malone* v *UK* 7 EHHR 14). The state will then have to demonstrate a legitimate aim when implementing the measure. These include public safety, crime prevention and protection of others.

The issue upon which most of the ECHR jurisprudence on Article 8 is decisive, is that of the necessity for such a measure in a democratic society. For a measure to be necessary it has to be proportionate; does it strike a 'fair balance' between the right of the individual and the needs of society as a whole? Criteria that the court will examine to decide whether a balance has been struck include whether there is a link between the measure and the legitimate aim, whether it is the least intrusive measure that could have been taken, and whether it defeats the essence of the right in question (*Hatton* v *UK* (2003) ECHR 338). The decision maker will carry out a balancing exercise where the right of the individual is weighed against the public interest. In this balancing exercise, the clash of the differing forms of dignity is illustrated; the dignity of the individual against the need to maintain the dignity of mankind as a whole by protecting society from dangerous offenders.

As noted above, Article 8 places positive obligations on states to ensure respect of the right. Victims of sex offenders have potentially a claim for protection in order to fulfil their rights to protection under Article 8.[5] Where a court decides the balance should be struck may depend on the margin of appreciation it gives to the states. This is the amount of discretion the ECtHR will give to the states as best placed to decide on certain issues due to 'their direct and continuous contact with the vital forces of their countries' (*Handyside* v *UK* (1976) 1 EHRR 737). Various factors influence the amount of discretion given to a state, including the nature of the right, the nature of the public interest, or where there is a lack of European consensus on the issue.

Article 12 – the right to found a family

The right to marry and a found a family under Article 12[6] does not contain the qualifications found in Article 8(2). However, it is limited by the reference to men and women and by the reference to national laws governing the exercise of the right. Again, this right also involves the concept of human dignity. If dignity does involve the development of personality and relationships, then it also includes the potential ability to procreate. Proportionality and the margin of appreciation also play important roles in decision making under Article 12.

Applying the principles and rights

Sex offenders in detention

The shift in the criminal justice system from welfarism to risk is illustrated in the increased sentencing for serious sex offenders. This includes indeterminate sentencing. This type of sentencing goes beyond traditional rationale for sentencing, such as just deserts based on proportionality (von Hirsch 1985). Indeterminate sentencing is increasingly being used to keep dangerous sex offenders in detention and has been introduced in various jurisdictions (Fish 2008).

In England and Wales, the sentencing of offenders beyond fixed-term sentences is governed by ss 225–230, Criminal Justice Act 2003 (as amended by the Criminal Justice and Immigration Act 2008). Under the legislation there are three types of sentences involving detention beyond a fixed sentence: life, imprisonment for public protection (IPP) and extended sentences, with decisions on release made by the Parole Board. Under s. 225, IPPs may be made if there is a 'significant risk to members of the public of serious harm' and the offence is a listed serious offence with a determinate sentence of 10 years or the notional minimum term of the offence is two years. Extended sentences under s. 227 can be given for less serious offences where there is a similar risk to the public as above. As noted, the rationale for this sentencing structure is dangerousness, which is set out in s. 229. When assessing future risk of harm, the court must take into account the nature and circumstances of the offence and may take into account the nature and circumstances of any other offences of which the offender has been convicted, information on patterns of behaviour, and any information about the offender before it. The criteria are open to subjective interpretation by the courts. The courts have attempted to clarify the criteria. In *R v Lang and Others* ((2005) EWCA Crim 2864), the Court of Appeal adopted the dictionary definition of significant meaning 'of considerable importance' (para 17). The court stated that it should be guided by the assessment of risk in reports put before it but should also consider the circumstances of the offences, including socio-economic factors, employability, relationships, etc. The decision indicated that the judiciary should take a 'restrained and careful approach' to sentencing (Thomas 2006: 179). However, when the provisions came into force in 2005, the number of IPPs increased as judges 'loyally followed the unequivocal terms of the statute' (Per Lord Brown, *Wells v Secretary of State for Justice (Parole Board Intervening)* [2009] UKHL 22 para 119). The amendments in the 2008 Act reflected the judicial concerns over the complexity of the indeterminate sentencing scheme. The presumption of risk for those who had committed a previous offence under s. 229 was removed and the mandatory nature of sentencing under s. 225 and s. 227 has also been removed to allow more discretion to the judiciary.

Human rights challenges

The ECtHR has consistently held that indeterminate sentencing schemes are compatible with Article 5 as long as there is a nexus between the sentence passed by the court and the reason for continuing detention (*Weeks v UK* (Application No: 9787/82)). The detention cannot be arbitrary under Art 5(1) as long as the nexus exists, though the ECtHR has recognised that the reasons for continuing detention may change (*Stafford v UK* (2002) 35 EHRR 1121). The need for a speedy review under Article 5(4) is important once the minimum tariff is fulfilled to ensure that the link between the reason for deprivation of liberty and continuing detention still exists. The indeterminate sentence scheme has been challenged under the HRA, focusing on the assessment of risk and the determination of risk when the indeterminate sentence has begun.

First, fears have been expressed that assessment tools may be applied arbitrarily, depending on their use by professionals in the system (Kemshall 2008). Unpredictability may undermine the legal certainty needed to satisfy rights concerns. When applying 'accordance with law' and 'lawful' under Articles 5 and 8, the law must be predictable (Harris *et al.* 2009). As noted, the legislation has laid down criteria which the court should follow when determining dangerousness. In *R v Pedley and Ors* ([2009] EWCA Crim 840), the claimants argued that IPP sentences violated their convention rights based on the vagueness of the assessment of risk. Significant risk should mean more likely than not or should be a numerical possibility (35–50 per cent). Without this standard, 'significant' has an arbitrary and disproportionate threshold, meaning the legislation would be incompatible with Article 5(1), as any detention would be based on arbitrary grounds, and Article 3, as arbitrary detention based on disproportionate sentencing may amount to degrading treatment. The court rejected this argument, emphasising the interpretation given in *Lang* and the controls put on judicial discretion by statute. It rejected the proposition that a numerical value could be put on risk assessment. Given the interpretation of *Lang*, it is unlikely that the significant risk test would be found to violate the convention unless a claimant can clearly demonstrate a judge has failed to apply the statutory scheme. As noted, the ECtHR has accepted dangerousness and risk as reasons for detention (*Stafford v UK* (2002) 35 EHRR 1121), though there has been no definitive case on how risk should be assessed. In deportation/removal cases, the ECtHR has found that the real risk of ill-treatment to the claimant could violate Article 3. Whether a risk is real is based on the circumstances of the case (*Chahal v UK* ((22414/93) [1996] ECHR 54). It is likely that the ECtHR would examine the compliance of a domestic decision with the statutory scheme. It may be prepared to consider the domestic assessment of 'real' risk, but it is suggested that unless there was evidence of a failure to assess relevant material, the ECtHR would be reluctant to intervene.

Secondly, several cases have challenged the indeterminate detention, as the offenders had not been provided with the means to demonstrate they were no longer a risk. In *Walker v Secretary of State for Home Department* ([2008] 3 All ER 104), the Court of Appeal found that the Secretary of State had failed in his public law duty to provide the necessary resources. The court stated that the subsequent delay before the offender could put his case to the parole board would not automatically contravene convention rights but may lead to a violation of Article 5(4) as a review by the parole board may become meaningless. This seems a cautious approach. The House of

Lords in *Wells* v *Secretary of State for Justice (Parole Board Intervening)* ([2009] UKHL 22) went further in restricting the application of Article 5. The court found no violation of Article 5(1), as the nexus had not been broken between the reason for the indeterminate sentence and continuing detention. When considering Article 5(4), the court took a functional and minimalist approach. It noted that although it was difficult for a prisoner to demonstrate that he was no longer a risk, he had access to the review process and the parole board had information on which to base a decision with a further review at reasonable intervals. Lord Brown had some sympathy for the argument that the review could become an empty exercise but found that Article 5(4) required the procedural obligations to be met and no more. Article 5(4) could in theory be breached by a lack of resources to demonstrate lack of risk, but only in circumstances where the board could not carry out its functions and any delay was for a lengthy period of time, described as years (para. 126 per Lord Mance).

Although highly critical of the complexity of the IPP scheme before the 2008 amendments, the House of Lords has taken a functional and cautious approach to the application of Article 5. It has shown a reluctance to go beyond present ECtHR jurisprudence and provide substantive protection for offenders' rights while under the indeterminate sentencing regime. This conservative approach may be a result of a reluctance to interfere in state resource allocation. It may also be a result of unwillingness by the courts to interfere in substantive penal policy (Londono 2008) as long as the procedures are compatible. However, a failure to provide an opportunity for rehabilitation leading to an extended sentence can undermine the dignity of the offender. It is also unclear how this promotes public protection, as the continuing risk from the offender goes unmeasured and the offender does not get recourse to tools that could prevent him from reoffending.

Sex offenders in the community

The public protection agenda has also led to restrictions on sex offenders in the community, usually after a conviction for a sexual offence. These include supervision requirements, registers and notification requirements. Two major issues that affect the rights of the offender will be examined: sex offender restrictions and registers and the disclosure of information to the public.

Registers and human rights challenges

As Thomas notes (see Chapter 4 of this volume), the use of sex offender registration in the UK was influenced by US federal law. The premise for establishing a register was public protection and crime prevention. The requirements for the register were first legislated for by the Sex Offenders Act 1997 and later updated by the Sexual Offences (SOA) Act 2003. Thomas outlines the increasingly draconian additions to the register since 1997. The register requires registration for designated sexual offences: registration is indefinite for sentences of more than 30 months; for a period of 6–30 months, registration is for 10 years; for less than 6 months, registration is for 7 years; and a police caution means registration for two years (ss 81–82 SOA 2003). As well as being on the register, an offender must report to the police station within three days, be photographed, give fingerprints, give notification of trips abroad, have annual verification visits, give notification of changes within three days, and be subjected to the use of polygraphs (Thomas 2006). These measures are motivated by protectionism and public pressure (Thomas 2006; Kemshall 2008). However, the offender's rights are engaged when placed under the register regime.

The register itself is an administrative requirement as a result of a criminal sentence rather than a stand-alone punitive measure and has been recognised as such by the ECtHR. In *Adamson* v *UK* (Application No. 42293/98), the applicant argued that not only was the register a violation of Articles 3 and 8 due to the register's effects but also that it was a penalty separate from his conviction and so violated Article 7, as a penalty heavier than the one applicable for his offence. The ECtHR rejected this, finding that the requirements at the time of the case were not onerous enough to constitute a penalty. However, the more draconian the requirements of the register become, the more likely that it may be seen as a penalty. This has been noted as a potential problem by government (Home Office/Scottish Executive 2001). *Adamson* v *UK* also recognised that the register engaged Article 8. As noted above, even a minor interference with an individual's personal integrity can amount to an interference with the right to privacy under Article 8. In *Adamson*, the measure was not held to be disproportionate or reaching the threshold for degrading treatment under Article 3. However, the more onerous the interference, the less likely that it will be found to be proportionate under Article 8(2), and it may also amount to degradation. There have been several challenges to the register, which were dismissed. However, recent case law has challenged the compatibility of the register regime with convention rights.

A series of cases challenged the automatic nature of the register regime. Those placed on the register indefinitely have no right to seek a review of the decision. In *Re Gallagher* ([2003] NIQB 26), the applicant used Article 8 to challenge the automatic nature of the register requirements, which failed to consider the individual circumstances of the claimant and denied him the right to review of the indefinite registration. The judge, Kerr J., underlined the need for the state to justify interferences with individual rights (para 24) but noted that Parliament had determined the necessity of the scheme and that 'the gravity of sex offences and the serious harm … must weigh heavily in favour of a scheme designed to protect potential victims of such crime' (para 24), and that individuals 'must be of secondary importance' (para 23). Kerr J. was placing dangerousness above individual rights, deferring to Parliament, and reflecting governmental and public attitudes. Subsequent case law followed this reasoning, such as *Forbes* v *Secretary of State for Home Department* ([2006] 1 WLR 3075) and *H* v *The Queen* ([2007] EWCA Crim 2622). In both cases, arguments based on Article 8 failed, as the register was found to be proportionate. The Scottish case of *A* v *Scottish Ministers* ([2007] CSOH 189) was equally reluctant to find Article 8 disproportionate. The latter two cases dealt with minors. The argument that, as children, their circumstances should have been open to greater scrutiny was rejected. However, in both cases, the court did seem to consider individual circumstances in finding that the seriousness of the offences in question meant the indefinite registration period was not disproportionate.

However, the courts now seem prepared to show less deference to Parliament. In *F and Thompson* v *Secretary of State for Justice* ([2008] EWHC 3170), the Divisional Court declared the indefinite nature of registration incompatible with Article 8. F was 11 years old when the offence was committed. The court found that juveniles should have a right to review indefinite registration, and an inability to do so was disproportionate given that the general approach of the courts to juvenile sentencing was to consider the maturity of the offender (para 19). In Thompson's case, the court disagreed with the *Gallagher* decision. It noted that indefinite registration may be necessary, but where an offender believes he is no longer a risk, in principle he should be able to seek to establish the fact (para 33). As the statutory scheme made no provision for review, it was declared incompatible. The case may reflect concerns that the legislation fails to consider juvenile characteristics. The courts have been aware of the necessity of considering maturity and age in sentencing, and recent ECtHR case law has criticised the UK for blanket penal policies that fail to consider children (*S and Marper* v *UK* (2008) Application No. 30562/04). The decision in *F and Thompson* does not go as far as interfering with the actual requirements of the register but lays down a minimum safeguard of access to review. How a review should be framed is a matter of debate and may be circumscribed in the public interest (*F and Thompson* v *Secretary of State for Justice* ([2008] EWHC 3170, para 27). This reflects the cautious approach discussed above with regard to indeterminate sentences and the emphasis on procedural rather than substantive protection, but it also demonstrates that the judiciary is prepared to find that a scheme excluding any consideration of the individual undermines convention rights.

Disclosure and challenges

The question of disclosure of information on the sex offender register has been controversial. Following Megan's Law in the USA, there has been public pressure for the release of information and notification to the public of the whereabouts of registered sex offenders. The UK government has resisted the public pressure to do so (for more information on this, see Chapter 4 of this volume; Kemshall 2008). There is no general duty on the police to disclose the whereabouts of registered sex offenders, though there has been a discretionary disclosure policy in practice which is circumscribed and controlled (Kemshall 2008). However, disclosure is now legislated for in limited circumstances. S. 327A Criminal Justice Act 2003 (as amended by s. 140 of the Criminal Justice and Immigration Act 2008) allows a public authority to disclose to a relevant member of the public if a sex offender poses a risk of serious harm to a child and it is necessary to protect the child. The authority may impose conditions on the relevant person as to further disclosure. There is a presumption that disclosure should be made.

The case law on public disclosures has tended to uphold the right to disclose in particular circumstances, but the courts have been clear that any disclosure does engage Article 8(1) and must be justified under Article 8(2). For example, in *Re C* (unreported, 15 February 2002), the High Court allowed a disclosure concerning the dangerousness of C but it carefully weighed the need to protect others with the right to privacy, the danger to C from vigilantes, and dangers in controlling sensitive information (Power 2003). One of the problems facing the new presumption to disclose may be the difficulty in restricting information to those deemed in need of protection. Based on previous case law, any challenge to a disclosure may lead to careful scrutiny of the necessity and effect of such disclosure. The court has demonstrated greater vigour when scrutinising disclosures to the public than in indeterminate sentencing or the register requirements. This may be because of the fear of vigilantism or that offenders would be forced underground. It may also be an awareness that the state is under a positive obligation to protect. This applies to Articles 2 and 3 as well as 8. As noted above, the ruling in *Osman* v *UK* ((2000) 29 EHRR 245) found that the state can be held responsible for a death if it knew or ought to have known of a real and immediate threat and did not take reasonable steps to protect. This applies both to offenders and to the potential victims. A registered sex offender could be put in danger if information is made public and measures were not in place to protect him, a consideration noted in *Re C*. However, a potential victim may claim a real and immediate threat against him/her if an offender is in the area and the police know about it. This may be more difficult to argue, as the claimant would have to demonstrate he/she was a specific target for the offender and that the requirements of the register, etc., did not provide reasonable protection. Nevertheless, these hypothetical situations may come before the court. In decisions based on *Osman*, the courts have shown a reluctance to find against the police (*Van Colle* v *Chief Constable of Hertfordshire Police* [2008 UKHL 50]), but the potential for challenges still remains if an offender or victim is killed or injured. There is also an argument that there may be a positive obligation under Article 8 to provide information where members of the public may be in danger. The ECtHR has held that where claimants' health was affected by a failure to disclose information, a state may be liable (*Guerra* v *Italy* [1998] 26 EHRR 357). However, as Power (2003) notes, register disclosure involves competing rights of the offender and the potential victim whereas *Guerra* did not, as the rights of the factory owners were not an issue. Non-disclosure of the register details can also enhance public protection by allowing continued monitoring of the offender, unlike in *Guerra*, where the threat came from factory fumes and threatened only the claimants.

Sex offender treatment: pharmacotherapy

As discussed in Chapter 6 of this volume, pharmacotherapy is the use of drugs to lower the testosterone levels in male sex offenders. Anti-libidinal suppressants are emotively known as a form of chemical castration, though the drugs are not supposed to cause the permanent castration of the offender (Harrison and Rainey 2009). Pharmacotherapy has been used in several states in the USA as well as several European countries. The type of drug used and the method and length of administration of the drug vary in different jurisdictions. In several states in the USA, the drug medroxyprogesterone (MPA) is used, often on a mandatory basis as part of a sentence or a condition of prison release. In contrast, European countries administer the drug cyproterone acetate (CPA) on a voluntary basis as part of a treatment programme (Harrison 2007; Chapter 6, this volume). There is some debate on the effectiveness of drug therapy for sex offenders, though the research suggests that positive results are only likely to occur with preferential paedophiles (Harrison and Rainey 2009). The use of the drugs also produces side effects. MPA has been reported to have caused side effects such as migraine headaches, blood clotting, serious allergic reactions, diabetes, depression and irreversible feminisation (Spalding 1998). Reportedly, CPA has fewer side effects and any effects are reversible (Cooper 1981).

In England and Wales, the government has been trialling the use of pharmacotherapy since 2007 following a Home Office review of child protection (Home Office 2007). The trial administers treatment on a voluntary basis. Referral is based on either mental health issues or sexual urges or fantasies that the offender finds difficult to control (Harrison and Rainey 2009).

Human rights challenges
The use of pharmacotherapy has not yet been directly challenged in England and Wales or at the ECtHR, but it does raise potential issues of conflict with the dignity of the offender. If an offender consents to treatment, then it could arguably be difficult to raise objections based on rights arguments. However, the nature of consent is important. Consent should be valid and given by someone who has the capacity to do so. Valid consent consists of understanding the nature and effects of treatment and not being coerced into making decisions he would not otherwise have made. Consent should be free and informed. If consent is conditional, then it may be difficult to define such consent as free. This is the case when treatment is linked to sentencing or prison release. Although it has been argued that conditional consent can still be a free choice (Miller 2003), it is still a choice between two evils. The Council of Europe has emphasised the need for any offender treatment to be free and fully informed (Council of Europe 2006). Those receiving treatment should also have the capacity to consent. If an offender does not have the competence to consent, then

he could be forcibly medicated. One common method of treating sex offenders without consent is under mental health legislation (Mental Health Act 1983 as amended by the Mental Health Act 2007), which now includes sexual deviancy in the definition of mental disorder and allows forced medication under s. 58. The state no longer has to demonstrate treatability, and the reformed Act has been criticised as been predicated on social control rather than individual treatment. The reformed Act raises human rights concerns given the vagueness of the wider definition, and the three-month delay before forcible treatment is reviewed under s. 58 of the Act (Harrison and Rainey 2009).

If consent is free and informed, then the use of pharmacotherapy may be rights compliant, but if this is not the case or the state decides to have a compulsory regime on competent (or incompetent) persons, then issues may arise under the ECHR. Would pharmacotherapy meet the threshold necessary for degrading treatment under Article 3? There is no doubt pharmacotherapy is better than surgical castration which has been found to be cruel and unusual punishment by the US Supreme Court (*State* v *Brown* 326 S.E2d 410). However, the side effects of the drugs may be enough to humiliate an offender and therefore be degrading. CPA seems a better alternative than MPA, as the effects of this drug can be irreversible. The length and appropriateness of the treatment may also be a factor. Drug therapy should have a temporal limitation and be suitable for the offender. Some US programmes have broad definitions of sex offenders and lack clear procedures for suitability (Spalding 1998). It should be noted that ECtHR jurisprudence may limit the possibility of finding a breach of the convention. The court has found that even quite severe side effects of coercive drug therapy do not meet the threshold for Article 3 (*Grare* v *France* (Application No 18835/91)). Furthermore, in *Herczegfalvy* v *Austria* ((1992) 15 EHRR 437), the ECtHR held that 'as a general rule, a measure which is a therapeutic necessity cannot be regarded as inhuman or degrading' (para 82). It may be the case that only treatment which is not medically necessary will be considered by the court. It makes it even more important to ensure that the offender is medically suitable and also that the medication is effective; if this is not the case, then it is not therapeutically necessary. Consequently, any excessive use of force or treatment beyond that which is necessary may violate Article 3. In *Jalloh* v *Germany* ((2006) ECHR 721), the ECtHR held that the use of medication to remove drugs from a suspect's stomach was in breach of Article 3. In *Nevmerzhitsky* v *Ukraine* ((2005) ECHR 21), it was held that the primary purpose of force feeding a prisoner was not for medical reasons but as a means of preventing legitimate protest. If the use of anti-libidinal treatment is primarily to offer public protection, with the 'medical' needs of the offender as a secondary aim, then the ECtHR may find it is not medically necessary. However, whether the ECtHR would consider the use of pharmacotherapy as medically necessary is yet to be tested, but it is assumed that the court would have to take into account the seriousness of the side effects and the *Herczegfalvy* test. This might suggest that it would be difficult to find a state in violation of Article 3 unless the side effects were severe and long-term (possibly akin to surgical castration), and where the treatment was clearly beyond what was considered to be therapeutically necessary.

It may also be possible to bring a case under Article 8, as any coercive treatment would clearly be an interference with the right to private life. The outcome would depend on whether treatment is justifiable. Any programme of drug therapy would have to be in accordance with law. Legal guidelines would have to be in place and meet a legitimate aim such as health, public order or protection. Drug therapy should be necessary in a democratic society, meaning that the treatment would have to be proportionate. A court may put great weight in the public interest, given that vulnerable groups such as children may be the target of sex offenders. The court would also consider whether there is a less intrusive measure that could be taken to achieve the aim. It could be argued that treatment is actually less intrusive than prison if the drugs were offered in lieu of prison (Harrison and Rainey 2009). The court will also examine the side effects, etc., when balancing the rights of the offender against the interests of the community. A similar balancing exercise would take place if Article 12 was found to be applicable. If the treatment did cause irreversible sterilisation, then a claimant may have a case for arguing that his right to found a family had been violated. The right to found a family is limited (Harrison and Rainey 2009). However, it should be noted that when deciding whether a measure is proportionate under Article 12, the court may consider the concomitant right of the partner of the claimant to found a family (*Dickson* v *UK* (2007) 34 EHRR 21).

If pharmacotherapy is to be used, then it should be operated within a human rights framework so that the dignity of the offender is maintained while meeting policy goals of managing risk. It is suggested that all programmes should be voluntary, should have published protocols and procedures which are publicly available, should ensure that the offender is medically suitable and treatment is medically necessary, should monitor the offender's health throughout the programme so as to check on potential negative side effects, should allow for independent reviews of individual treatment and treatment programmes, and should permit the offender to freeze sperm before programme commencement in case of irreversible side effects.

Conclusion: finding a balance?

Running parallel to the risk penology in governmental policy has been the increasingly transparent role of dignity and rights in law. In the areas described, it is apparent that the state has placed community protection above the individual rights of the offender (Kemshall 2008). The government has argued that the balance of the criminal justice system should be tipped in favour of the community, with public protection as a 'top priority' when considering cases involving sex offenders (Kemshall 2008: 110).

However, it is suggested that the idea of balance can be a misnomer when discussing rights protection. In some instances, a balancing act does take place between the rights of the individual and the community. This is most obvious when discussing Article 8. The focus is still on dignity, as it is a balancing of subjective and objective dignity (Feldman 1999). This allows for limitations on an individual's rights, but the essence of the right itself should not be undermined (Fenwick 2002). It could be argued that indeterminate sentencing without the ability to challenge the efficacy of continuing detention could amount to undermining the right to a private life to such an extent that the right itself becomes meaningless. Furthermore, the idea of balance seems misplaced in relation to due process and ill-treatment. The basic procedural rights in the criminal justice system apply to all, irrespective of conduct, in the same way as the right not to be tortured or degraded is universal. Can access to a review procedure mean the offender's rights trump the victim or potential victim? Having access to a review does not mean that sex offenders are more likely than not to be released or removed from a register. Indeed, it could be argued that the system will be enhanced by a review of risks and a continuing examination of risk with the chance of rehabilitation. Case law has provided some limited protection for offender rights, and legal reasoning in the areas described suggests that determinations should be subjective and not depend upon objective measurements of risk.

Sex offenders should have, as a minimum, the right to demonstrate they are no longer a risk and disclosure of information should be carefully weighed. If pharmacotherapy is to be used, it should be within a transparent and accessible human rights framework. The state has a duty to protect all within its jurisdiction. However, public protection should not allow the objectifying of offenders within the system. To do so would undermine the humanity of all. As Baroness Hale noted when referring to Article 3, human rights reflect

> the fundamental values of a decent society, which respects the dignity of each individual human being, no matter how unpopular or unworthy she may be. (*R (Adam and Others)* v *Secretary of State for Home Department* (2005) UKHL 66).

Notes

1 The other two principles are the principle of respect for civil liberties and the principle of legality.
2 'No one shall be subjected to torture or to inhuman or degrading treatment or punishment.'
3 '(1) Everyone has the right to respect for his private and family life, his home and his correspondence.'
4 '(2) There shall be no interference by a public authority with the exercise of this right except such as is in accordance with the law and is necessary in a democratic society in the interests of national security, public safety ... or the economic well-being of the country, for the prevention of disorder or crime ... for the protection of health or morals, or for the protection of rights and freedoms of others.'
5 Where the state fails to prevent a violation of Article 8 either by its own agents or by non-state actors: see *X and Y* v *Netherlands* (1986) 8 EHRR 235.
6 'Men and women of marriageable age have the right to marry and to found a family, according to the national laws governing the exercise of this right.'

References

Beck, U. (2007) *World at Risk*. Cambridge: Polity Press.
Cooper, A. J. (1981) 'A Placebo-Controlled Trial of the Antiandrogen Cyproterone Acetate in Deviant Hypersexuality', *Comprehensive Psychiatry*, 22(5): 458–465.
Council of Europe (2006) *European Committee on Crime Problems. The State of Work on the text of 'A Draft Recommendation on the Treatment of Sex Offenders in Penal Institutions and the Community'*. CDPC-BU, 02 E.

Donnelly, J. (2003) *Universal Human Rights in Theory and Practice* (3rd edn). Cornell, NY: Cornell University Press.

Douglas, M. (1992) *Risk and Blame*. London: Routledge.

Dupre, C. (2006) 'Human Dignity and the Withdrawal of Medical Treatment: A Missed Opportunity?', *European Human Rights Law Review*, 6: 678.

Feely, M. and Simon, J. (1992) 'The New Penology: Notes on the Emerging Strategy for Corrections', *Criminology*, 30(4): 449–475.

Feldman, D. (1999) 'Human Dignity as a Legal Value: Part 1', *Public Law*, Winter: 682.

Feldman, D. (2000) 'Human Dignity as a Legal Value: Part 2', *Public Law*, Spring: 61.

Fenwick, H. (2002) *Civil Liberties and Human Rights* (3rd edn). London: Cavendish Publishing.

Fish, M. J. (2008) 'Proportionality as a Moral Principle of Punishment', *Oxford Journal of Legal Studies*, 28(1): 57–71.

Garland, D. (1985) *Punishment and Welfare: A History of Penal Strategies*. Aldershot: Gower.

Gearty, C. (2004) *Principles of Human Rights Adjudication*. Oxford: Oxford University Press.

Grubin, D. (2004) 'The Risk Assessment of Sex Offenders', in H. Kemshall and G. McIvor (eds), *Managing Sex Offender Risk*. London: Jessica Kingsley.

Harris, D. J., O'Boyle, M. and Warbrick, C. (2009) *Law of the European Convention on Human Rights* (2nd edn). Oxford: Oxford University Press.

Harrison, K. (2007) 'The High-Risk Sex Offender Strategy in England and Wales: Is Chemical Castration an Option?', *Howard Journal* 46(1): 16–31.

Harrison, K. and Rainey, B. (2009) 'Suppressing Human Rights? A Rights-Based Approach to the Use of Pharmacotherapy with Sex Offenders', *Legal Studies*, 29(1): 47–74.

Home Office/Scottish Executive (2001) *Consultation Paper on the Review of Part 1 of the Sex Offenders Act 1997*, July. London: Home Office.

Home Office (2007) *Review of the Protection of Children from Sex Offenders*. London: Home Office.

Kemshall, H. (2003) *Understanding Risk in Criminal Justice*. Maidenhead: Open University Press.

Kemshall, H. (2008) *Understanding the Community Management of High Risk Offenders*. Maidenhead: Open University Press

Kemshall, H. and McGuire, M. (2003) 'Sex Offenders, Risk Penality and the Problem of Disclosure in the Community', in A. Matravers (ed.), *Sex Offenders in the Community*. Cullompton: Willan.

Kemshall, H. and McIvor, G. (2004) 'Sex Offenders: Policy and Legislative developments', in H. Kemshall and G. McIvor (eds), *Managing Sex Offender Risk*. London: Jessica Kingsley.

Londono, P. (2008) 'The Executive, the Parole Board and Article 5 ECHR: Progress Within an "Unhappy State of Affairs"?', *Cambridge Law Journal*, 67(2): 230–233.

Miller, R. (2003) 'Chemical Castration of Sex Offenders: Treatment or Punishment', in B. J. Winick and J. Q. LaFond (eds), *Protecting Society from Sexually Dangerous Offenders. Law, Justice and Therapy*. Washington, DC: American Psychological Association.

Ovey, C. and White, R. (2006) *The European Convention on Human Rights*. Oxford: Oxford University Press.

Power, H. (2003) 'Disclosing Information on Sex Offenders: The Human Rights Implications', in A. Matravers (ed.), *Sex Offenders in the Community*. Cullompton: Willan.

Spalding, L. (1998) 'Florida's 1997 Chemical Castration Law: A Return to the Dark Ages', *Florida State University Law Review*, 25: 117.

Thomas, D. A. (2006) 'Case Comment: Sentencing Dangerous Offenders – Criminal Justice Act 2003', *Criminal Law Review*, February: 174–179.

von Hirsch, A. (1985) *Past or Future Crimes: Deservedness and Dangerousness in the Sentencing of Criminals*. Manchester: Manchester University Press.

Index

Added to a page number 'f' denotes a figure, 't' denotes a table and 'n' denotes notes.

A v Scottish Ministers [2007] 280
abuse *see* physical abuse; sexual abuse; substance abuse; virtual abuse
'accordance with law' 273, 277, 285
accountability 211, 242, 259
acetylcholinesterase inhibitors 205
actuarial justice 41
actuarial risk assessment 20, 21, 30, 271–2
actus reus 211
Adamson v UK (1999) 71, 279
adaptive dysfunctions 210
adolescence 24
adolescent offenders *see* juvenile sex offenders
adult, problems concerning meaning of 6
adult abusers, use of Internet to disguise identity 235
adult ADHD 203–4
adult-child interactions (online) 235

adult-child sex, variations in understanding of 12
adulthood/childhood boundary 12
age
    legal problems concerning 6
    of paedophiles 5, 8
    and sexual activity 6–7
    of victims 5, 215
age-appropriate relationships 10, 118, 123
aggression 24, 113, 115, 220
alcohol abuse 215
alcohol dependence 195
alienation 23, 24
Alzheimer's dementia 204
American Psychiatric Association (APA) 9
Androcur (cyproterone acetate) 111–12, 113, 115, 116, 120, 125, 126, 213, 283, 284
androgen antagonists 28, 108, 205
androgen receptors 108, 213
anger management 88, 196
anime 233
anti-libidinal medication 107–8, 126, 282–3
    comparison 115–16

cyproterone acetate 111–12, 113, 115, 116, 120, 125, 126, 213, 283, 284
LHRH inhibitors/GnrH agonists 112–15, 116, 120, 125, 126, 127n
medroxyprogesterone acetate 109–11, 113, 115, 121, 125, 283, 284
antipsychotic medications 193, 199
antisocial attitudes 165, 167
antisocial cognitions 25
antisocial personality disorder 170, 195, 215, 220, 221
anxiety disorders 117, 195, 198, 202–3
arbitrary detention 273, 277
arrests 161, 215
assertiveness 84, 88, 166
Association of Chief Police Officers (ACPO) 74
Association of Sites Advocating Child Protection (ASACP) 238
Association for the Treatment of Sexual Abusers' Collaborative Data Committee 100
asylums 193
atomoxetine 204
attachment 24, 27, 87, 88
attention deficit hyperactivity disorder 195, 198, 203–4, 215, 220
attitudes
   antisocial 165, 167
   condoning abuse 166, 168
   effective collaboration 185
   hardening of 33
   impeding reintegration 134
   inhibiting prevention and intervention 174
   media shaping of 251
   moral panic of paedophilia 257
   negative 25
   non-judgemental 183
   review of, in treatment 87
auditory hallucinations 199
Australia 138, 139, 142, 160, 161, 162

'automatic approach' style 222
autonomy 270
aversion therapy 83, 84

Bebo 238, 241
behaviour
   MAPPA role in changing 54
   see also criminal behaviour; deviancy; normal behaviour; sexual behaviour
behaviour skills, impaired 25
behavioural programmes
   traditional 83, 84
   see also cognitive behavioural programmes
benperidol 120
Bezicheri v Italy (1990) 273
bias, against intellectually disabled 211
bilateral orchiectomy see surgical interventions, castration
biological regulatory system 124
bipolar disorder 193, 195, 201
Blunkett, David 66, 67
bone demineralisation 114, 115
borderline intellectual functioning 211, 221, 223n
borderline personality disorder 170
Botta v Italy (1998) 274
boundary confusion, risk management failures 45
boys, sexual aggression 24
brain
   sexual behaviour 116
   see also neurosurgery
British culture, fixation with child sex offences 244
Brown, Lord 276, 278
bupropion 204

Canada 82, 141, 149n, 160, 162, 164, 196, 198
case law 286
case-based audits 51

castration *see* chemical castration;
  surgical interventions, castration
cause-and-effect model 251
cautions 49, 67
censorship 232
Center for Sex Offender
  Management 177, 178
Chahal v UK [1996] 277
Chahal v UK (1997) 272
chat-room grooming 229–30, 234–5,
  236
chat-rooms 229
chemical castration 28, 107
child, problems concerning meaning
  of 6
Child Benefit Act (2005) 6
Child Exploitation and Online
  Protection Centre (CEOP) 239
Child Line research 160
child murder, media attention 244
child pornography
  age of consent 8
  and child sexual abuse 234
  criminal charges against ISPs 237
  difficulty of definition 230
  image classification 231–2
  legal definitions 231
  see also Internet, child
    pornography
Child Pornography Prevention Act
  (US, 1996) 233
child protection 44, 140
child sexual abuse
  arrests, ID offenders 215
  British culture and fixation with
    244
  and child pornography 234
  commencement and continuation
    of 11
  long-term effects 22
  as misunderstood in modern
    society 258
  paedophilia distinguished from 5
  pathway model of 25–6
  prevalent forms 11

Stop It Now! programme 140–1
  see also cyber-sex offences
childhood 10, 12, 24, 33
childhood ADHD 203
children
  abuse *see* child sexual abuse;
    physical abuse
  competence assessment 6, 7
  early intervention for vulnerable
    26
  female maltreatment of 170
  over-protectiveness of parents 244
  reassessment of risk posed to 245
  recidivism and proximity to 48–9
  sexual activities with 7–8, 12
  sexual behaviour problems 175
  vulnerability to online sexual
    predation 229–30
  see also adult-child interactions;
    adult-child sex; juvenile sex
    offenders
Children Act (1989) 6, 8
children's rights 6–7
children's services 174, 178
Circles of Support and
  Accountability (COSA) 11, 11–12,
  29, 133, 139, 141–2, 149n
citalopram (Cipramil) 117
civil rights movement 193–4
clinical definitions, paedophilia 4–6,
  7, 11–12
co-morbid psychiatric disorders 176,
  195, 198, 201, 215, 220
co-offenders, female sex offending
  165, 168
Coaker, Vernon 70
coerced female offenders 165–6
coercive treatment 285
cognitive behavioural programmes
  11, 27, 82–3, 83–8
  cognitive component 86–7
  efficacy studies 88–99
  incorporation of relapse
    prevention 85–6
  origins 83

and pharmacotherapy 27
shift from traditional
    programmes to 84–5
social phobia 202
cognitive distortions 11, 25, 168,
    169
cognitive impairment/deficits 25,
    199
communitarian societies 136–7, 141
community, sex offenders in 278–82
community care programmes 11
community collaboration, to stop
    sexual harm by youth 177–9
community management 46, 47
community notification 62, 67, 71–2,
    74, 76n
community protection approach 43
Community Rehabilitation Orders
    29–30
community reintegration 48, 54, 133,
    134, 137, 147, 194
community restorative justice 147
community safety 142, 143, 180
community support 200
community treatment 30, 197
Community-Based Standards for
    Addressing Sexual Harm by Youth
    181, 183–4
competence
    assessment of children's 6, 7
    development, juvenile offenders
        181–2, 183, 185
    to consent to medication 283–4
compliance rates, voluntary vs.
    mandatory treatment 122
concentration, poor 200
conferencing, restorative 138, 139
consensual participation, restorative
    justice 147
consensual sexual activity 8
consent
    legislation and age of 7, 8
    to medication 121, 122, 283–4
contracts, with offenders 53
convictions 49

coping mechanisms 25, 137, 167,
    169, 212
court orders 46, 49
court-referred offenders 122
Crime and Disorder Act (1998)
    149n
criminal behaviour 167, 211–12, 222
    see also sexual offending
criminal history, recidivism 164–5,
    176, 215–16, 217–20
criminal justice
    agencies 41, 45
    definition of an offence 211
    recognition of potential of RJ
        133
    vilification of MDSOs 200
Criminal Justice Act (1991) 39
Criminal Justice Act (2003) 42, 68,
    275, 281
Criminal Justice and Court Services
    Act (2000) 23, 42, 68, 72, 75
Criminal Justice and Immigration
    Act (2008) 70, 72, 75, 275, 281
Criminal Justice and Public Order
    Act (1994) 233
criminal records 210
criminality v pathology 9, 10
critical few 42
Crown Prosecution Service (CPS)
    178
cultural ratification model 251
cultural variation, understanding of
    adult-child sex 12
culture of control 30
curfews 43, 53, 68
curiosity, online (sexual) interactions
    235
cyber-rape 235
cyber-sex offences 229–45
    child sex offences
        challenges for policing and
            protection 241–5
        from policing to prevention
            237–41
    treatment programmes 29, 82

see also Internet child
pornography; online sexual
predation
cybersexploitation 234
Cyberspace Research Unit (CRU)
234, 235
cyproterone acetate (CPA) 111–12,
113, 115, 116, 120, 125, 126, 213,
283, 284

dangerousness
cycle of offending 10
detention 277
extended sentences 275
justification for limiting rights
270–2
MAPPA contribution to
management of 46
public discourse 40
De Waag Study, ID offender
treatment 212
analysis 216–17
criminal history and recidivism
215–16
discussion 220–1
future research 222
implications for treatment
221–2
instruments 216
intensive outpatient group
therapy 212–13, 221–2
intraclass correlation coefficients
216–17
population sample 213–15
results 217
criminal history and
recidivism 217–19
demographic characteristics
and family background 219
treatment and co-morbidity
220
Decapeptyl (triptorelin) 115
decision making, in RJ 138
degrading treatment 272–3, 277, 279,
284, 286

deinstitutionalisation 193
Delatestryl 114–15
delirium 205
delusions/delusional disorders 198,
199
dementia/dementing disorders 195,
198, 204–5
denial 168, 222
dependence/dependencies 166, 168,
195
Depo-Provero (medroxyprogesterone
acetate) 109–11, 113, 115, 121, 125,
283, 284
deportation 277
depression 10, 22, 117, 170, 195, 200,
201, 203
Derwent Initiative 55
desipramine 118
desistance 86, 143, 149n
detention 9, 273, 275–6, 277
deterrence 30, 32, 148
development perspective, of
inappropriate sexual behaviour
24
developmental disorders 176, 195,
199, 215
deviancy 48
see also sexual deviancy
deviancy amplification spiral 137,
211, 253
deviant fantasies 108, 166, 167
*The Diagnostic and Statistical Manual
of Mental Disorders* (DSM) 5–6, 8,
9, 210
Dickson v UK (2007) 285
difference 31
disclosure 23, 70, 72, 256, 281–2, 286
discretionary disclosure 72, 75
discrimination 200
disintegrative shaming 31, 33, 136,
137
disorganised family systems 10
dissociation 202
distorted beliefs 166, 167
distraction techniques 54

diversion 159–60
documentation, community
  collaboration 180
dopamine 116
drug treatments *see*
  pharmacotherapy
Dudgeon v UK (1983) 274
duty to cooperate 39, 45
dynamic risk factors 27, 165–7, 176
dysfunctional schemas 25, 26
dysfunctional self-regulation 222
dysthymia 195, 200

early intervention 26
eating disorders 195
education, about online sexual
  predation 238–9
Effective Supervision Inspections 47,
  48t
ejaculation 113, 115, 116
electroconvulsive therapy (ECT) 201
elite-engineered model, moral panics
  253
emotional dysregulation 25, 165,
  167
emotive language, UK press 254
empathy 25, 84, 87
empirically supported risk factors
  177
employment agencies 44
empowerment 138, 145
endocrine system 124
enforcement pyramid 148
England and Wales
  age of consent law 7
  appropriate age for sexual
    activity 6
  mental health law 9
  restorative justice 138, 141, 143,
    147
  sentencing in 275–6
  treatment
    current practices 29–30
    increasing use of medical 28,
      30

pharmacotherapy 120–1, 125,
  283
  programmes 81–2, 85
environmental factors, inhibitory
  controls 24
ephebophilia 7
erotic fantasies 106, 108
erotica web pages 231
escapism 10
ethical duty, to evaluate treatment
  programmes 89
etidronate 114
European Convention on Human
  Rights (ECHR) 70–1, 106, 269,
  270, 272, 273, 284
European Court of Human Rights
  (ECtHR) 71, 270, 272–3, 274,
  276, 277, 278, 279, 282, 284,
  285
evidence-based risk factors 21, 27
exclusion 19, 41
exclusion zones 48, 49, 53
exhibitionists/exhibitionism 109,
  110, 118, 199, 215, 218
extended sentences 275
external controls 32, 53

*F and Thompson v Secretary of State
  for Justice* [2008] 71, 280–1
Facebook 238
Faceparty 240
family
  human rights 273–5, 285
  rejection by friends and 28
family conferencing 139
family-sensitive services 182, 183
fantasies *see* sexual fantasies
Faverin (fluvoxamine) 117, 118
female sex offenders 159–71
  assessment 159
  contexts of offence 171
  juvenile 176
  prevalence 159–61
  recidivism 161–7
  treatment 159, 167–70

females
  anger towards 24
  see also women
feminist engagement, new forms of
  justice 144
film censorship 232
filtering packages 240
'flare-up' effect 113, 115
fluoxetine (Prozac) 117, 118
fluvoxamine (Faverin) 117, 118
folk devils 253, 271
follicle-stimulating hormone 112–11
*Forbes v Secretary of State for Home
  Department* [2006] 280
force feeding 284–5
forced medication 284
forensic psychiatric research 222
forgiveness 137
fourth estate 258
frontal lobe disinhibition 204

Gadd, Paul (Gary Glitter) 229
gender role behaviour 84
generalised anxiety disorder 202,
  203
generalist ID offenders, De Waag
  study 219, 220, 221
Gillick competent 7, 14n
girl-related child pornography 231
gonadotrophin-releasing hormones
  (GnRH) agonists 112–15, 116, 126,
  127n
Good Lives Model 53, 86
gosorelin 116
Grare v France (Application No.
  18835/91) 284
grass-roots model, moral panics 253
grooming 10, 221
  see also chat-room grooming
group homes 200
group therapy 198, 199, 200, 201,
  202, 203
  see also intensive outpatient
    group therapy
Guerra v Italy [1998] 282

guilt 10, 200, 244
gynaecomastia 108, 114, 120, 123

H v The Queen [2007] 280
hacker vigilantism 243–4
hallucinations 199
Handyside v UK (1976) 275
harm 8, 21–2, 54, 138, 170, 275–6
Hatton v UK (2003) 274
health services 44, 45
hentai 233
Herczegfalvy v Austria (1992) 284,
  285
hierarchy of medication 119
high-profile cases 40, 44, 73, 229,
  256–7
high-risk prisoners, understanding
  of risk assessment 54
high-risk sex offenders 18
  consensus in issues relating to 3
  defining 271
  lack of social support 48
  policy and legislative
    developments 19
    problem with national
      initiatives 23
    see also interventions;
      treatment
  restorative justice 133–49
  targeting of resources to 21
historical variation, understanding
  of adult-child sex 12
Home Detention Curfew 68
Home Office 23, 61, 70, 74
Home Office Consultation
  Document 62–3
homelessness 49
homes *see* sex offender homes
hopelessness 201
hormonal treatments 83, 124
hotlines, for reporting Internet
  abuse 237–8, 239
housing agencies 44
human dignity 269–70, 274, 275,
  278, 286

human rights
   applicable
      Article 3 – torture, degrading
         and inhuman treatment
         272–3, 277, 279, 287
      Article 5 – arbitrary detention
         273, 276, 277, 278
      Article 8 – family and private
         life 71, 107, 273–5, 277, 279,
         280, 281, 286
      Article 12 – right to found a
         family 107, 275, 285
   applying 275–86
   balance between public
      protection 286–7
   challenges to SOA 70–1
   curtailment or forfeiture of 23
   dangerousness and justification
      for limiting 270–2
   and human dignity 269–70
   surgical castration 83, 106–7
Human Rights Act (1998) 256, 269,
   272
Human Rights Bill (1997) 269
humiliation 165, 273, 284
hyper-arousal 120
hyperactivity 203
hypercholesterolaemia 205
hypersexuality 113, 201
hypertension 205
hypomania 201

identity disguise, Internet and 235
imprisonment for public protection
   (IPP) 275, 276, 277, 278
impulse-control disorder 195
impulsiveness 27, 203, 212, 221
inappropriate sexual behaviour 24,
   25, 113, 210
incapacitation 30, 148
incest 8
indecent photographs 8, 232
indefinite registration 280–1
indeterminate sentencing 275, 276–8,
   282, 286

indifference 24
informed consent 122, 284
inhibitory controls 24
inhuman treatment 272–3, 284
insecurity 30, 41
integrity 274
intellectual dysfunction/disability
   210, 211–12
intellectually disabled sex offenders
   209–23
   prevalence estimates 209–10
   recidivism and risk factors
      210–12
   treatment study see De Waag
      study
intensive outpatient group therapy
   (IOG) 212–13, 221–2
intention 7
inter-agency working 40, 55
   see also partnerships
interdependence 136, 186
interest group model, moral panics
   13, 253
interference, with individual rights
   273–5, 279, 280, 285
internal controls 32
Internet
   child pornography
      concerns about 229
      developments and legal
         responses 230–3
      efforts to eradicate 238
      see also cyber-sex offences
   and identity disguise 235
   service providers (ISPs) 237, 242
Internet Hotline Providers in Europe
   (INHOPE) 238
Internet Watch Foundation (IWF)
   231, 237–8, 242–3
interpersonal violence 25
interventions
   intensity of 21
   providers of 32
   rehabilitative 24–30
   restrictive 22–3, 32, 43, 47–8

see also treatment
intimacy deficits 25, 165, 168
intimate abuse circles 139
intoxication 25
intrusive fantasies 120
IQ 10, 211
Ireland v UK (1979–80) 273

Jalloh v Germany (2006) 284
Japan, child pornography legislation 232, 233
Judicial Documentation System (JDS) 215
just deserts 30, 32
juvenile justice 182
juvenile sex offenders
    competence development 181–2, 183, 185
    defined 174–5
    diversity of group 176
    prosecution 8
    and registration
        penalties for non-compliance 68–9
        review of indefinite 280–1
    restorative justice 138
    treatment 82, 182–5
    see also sexual harm by youth

Kanka, Megan 71, 234
    see also Megan's Law
Kaplan-Meier survival analysis 217
Keeping Track? Observations on Sex Offender Registers in the US 72
Kerr J 280
KidsWatch 240
known sex offenders 18, 19, 148

labelling 137
late modernity 18, 30
learning difficulties, treatment programmes 82
legal perspective, paedophilia 6–8, 11–12

legal responses, Internet child pornography 232–3
leuprolide acetate (Lupron) 113, 125
leuprorelin 114
libido see sexual desire; sexual drive; sexual urges
lie-detector tests 23
likelihood dimension 19–21
liver damage 123
local inter-agency risk management 42
Local Safeguarding Children Boards 178, 185
loneliness 10, 24
Long Squeeze 47
long-term effects, of abuse 22, 33
low risk offenders 22, 148, 217–18, 219, 220
    see also De Waag study
low self-esteem 22, 117
Lupron (leuprolide acetate) 113, 125
Lustral (sertraline) 117, 118
luteinising hormone (LH) 112
luteinising-hormone-releasing hormone (LHRH) inhibitors 112–15, 116, 120, 125, 126, 127n

Madeleine McCann case 257
maladaptive beliefs/desires 25
male domination 25
male offenders see sex offenders
males
    over-reliance of women on 168
    propensity/capacity for sexual behaviour and aggression 24
    static risk factors 162–3
Malone v UK (7 EHHR 14) 274
management of offenders see interventions; treatment
mandatory self-notification 135
mandatory vs. voluntary treatment 121–3
mania 201
Mann, Sally 231
MAPPA – The First Five Years 46, 49

marriage, human rights 275
Maryland Scale of Scientific Rigor
    90–1
masculinity, dysfunctional view of
    25
master status 31
masturbation 83, 113, 114, 115
media 249–63
    coverage
        of abuse and heightened sense
            of children's vulnerability
            233–4
        child murder 244
        of paedophilia see paedophilia
    defined 250–1
    hardening of attitudes 33
    impeding of reintegration 134
    interest in MAPPA 46–7
    relationship between public and
        251, 259–60
    sex offender descriptions 31
    social constructionism and moral
        panics 251–4
mediation 138, 139
medical perspective, paedophilia 9
'medical problem' excuse 124
medical treatment 27
    efforts to increase uptake of 30
    passive nature of 83
    see also pharmacotherapy; surgical
        interventions
medroxyprogesterone acetate (MPA)
    109–11, 113, 115, 121, 125, 283,
    284
Megan's Law 62, 67, 71, 76n, 240,
    281
memory deficits 205
mens rea 211
mental disorder 9, 12
mental health
    examinations, prior to medication
        122
    legislation, England and Wales
        9
Mental Health Act (1983) 9, 284

Mental Health Act (2007) 9, 284
mental illness 10, 170, 193
    see also specific disorders
mental institutions 9, 193–4
mental retardation 195, 198, 221
mental states, impaired 25
mentally disordered sex offenders
    193–206
    rate of illness 195
    role of disorders 195–6
    specific populations 198–205
    trans-institutionalisation 193–5
    treatment 196, 199
        diagnosis 197, 204
        examining role of disorder in
            offending 198
        prioritisation of needs 197
        vilification in criminal justice
            system 200
meta-analyses, treatment
    programmes 27–8, 92–9
methylphenidate 203–4
Michael, Alun 63
minimisation of offending behaviour
    168
misregulation 222
mission statements, community
    safety 180
mood disorders 195, 198, 200–1
    see also anxiety disorders;
        depression
moral outrage 31
moral panics 13, 245
    concept and theoretical
        perspectives 252–4
    paedophilia and media coverage
        254–7
motivation
    engagement with treatment 122
    female sex offending 166–7
Multi-Agency Public Protection
    Arrangements (MAPPA) 39–57
    audits: process and outcome
        49–56
    effectiveness

difficulties in measuring 45–9, 56–7
evaluations of 49
as a reduction in reconviction 55
history and context 39–43
high-profile cases and the punitive turn 40–1
risk management 42–3
involvement of lay people 68
partnerships
development of formal 41–2
evaluating 55–6
issues 44–5
research evaluations 43, 57
success of, as a beacon for management of offenders 23
multi-agency working 23, 147
multi-faceted theories, of offending 24–5, 26
multi-infarct dementia 204
multi-modal treatment, youth violence 183
multiple dysfunctional mechanisms 26
MySpace 238, 240

'name and shame' campaigns 31–2, 133, 136, 137, 255, 256, 259, 260
National Offender Management Service (NOMS) 120, 121, 126
negative emotional states 167, 169, 222
negative life cycle 169, 170
negative reinforcement 86
Netherlands, ID offender study *see* De Waag study
neurosurgery 105–6
neurotransmitters 116
Nevmerzhitsky v Ukraine (2005) 284–5
new penology 19, 41, 271
New Zealand 138, 160, 161, 162
News of the World 249, 254–7, 259
non-compliance
with court conditions 200

with medication 199
with registration 67, 68–9
non-physical sexual abuse 11
non-sexual aggression 115
norm reinforcement 251
normal behaviour 7, 48
Northern Ireland, restorative justice 141, 147
'not criminally responsible' 198, 204
'not guilty by reason of insanity' 198, 204
Notification Orders 64
NSPCC 74, 76n
nutritional deficits 205

Obscene Publications Act (1959) 232
obsessive compulsive disorder (OCD) 117, 202, 203
oestrogen 108
off-line-contact abuse 236
Offender Management Act (2007) 70
online sexual predation
children's vulnerability to 229–30
virtual abuse and chat-room grooming 233–6
Operation Ore 229, 237
Operation Starburst 234
ordinary risk management 42
Oregon Depo-Provera programme 110
Osman v UK (2000) 270, 282
other/othering 31, 40, 41
outcome audits 49
outreach programmes 200

paedophile rings 229
paedophile websites 231
paedophiles
aetiology 10–11
child murder 244
clinical classification 5
legal perspective 7
pure 26
treatment 11, 109, 110, 113, 118

paedophilia
  addressing variations in
    understanding of 11–13
  analysis and risk management
    202
  definitions 4–9
    clinical 4–6, 7, 11–12
    legal 6–8, 11–12
    medical 9
    as a public health problem 4,
      12
  media coverage
    increased 4, 40
    moral panics 254–7
    social responsibility 258–61
    suggested ways of adapting
      261–2
    versus realities of paedophilia
      257–8
  social constructionism 13, 252
  treatment 113
  visual media 261
  in women 159
paedophilic fantasies 118
panic disorder 202
paraphilia 5, 113, 195, 201, 203
paraphiliac fantasies 116
parents
  Internet advice 239
  over-protectiveness 244
parole licences 46, 49
parole officers 197, 200
paroxetine (Seroxat) 117
partial public disclosure 256
partnerships
  MAPPA *see* Multi-Agency Public
    Protection Arrangements
  police and probation 23
passive avoidance 222
pathology v criminality 9, 10
pathway models 25–6
Payne, Sarah 67, 71, 73, 136, 234
  News of the World campaigns 249,
    254–7
  see also Sarah's Law

penal policy 41, 269, 278
penal practice 29
penalty(ies)
  non-compliance with registration
    68–9
  registristration as an additional
    279
penile erection 106, 113, 114, 115,
  116, 123
personality disorders 170, 195, 198,
  215, 220, 221
pessimism 201
pharmacotherapy 11, 27, 107
  anti-libidinals *see* anti-libidinal
    medication
  attention deficit disorders 203–4
  dementing disorders 205
  evidence for use of 126
  hierarchy of medication 119–20
  legal and ethical issues
    costs 125
    human rights 282–6, 287
    treatment or punishment
      123–5
    voluntary or mandatory 121–3
  psychotropic medication 116–17
  selective serotonin reuptake
    inhibitors (SSRIs) 28, 113,
    117–19, 120, 125, 126, 201, 203,
    205
  use in England and Wales 120–1
physical abuse 11, 234
physical assaults, on MDSOs 200
'polibation' officer 45
police
  bias against intellectually
    disabled 211
  investigations of online
    paedophile rings 229
  and probation partnerships 23,
    44, 45, 56
  registration of offenders with
    22–3
  risk assessment responsibility
    42

sex offender homes, entering/
    accessing 69, 75
Police National Computer (PNC)
    19, 61
Police and Probation Inspectorate
    report (2005) 47
policing
    cyber-sex offences 237–41
    challenges 241–5
political anxiety, regarding MAPPA
    46
populist punitiveness 32, 74, 124,
    135–6, 262
positive reinforcement 86
possible risk factors 177
post-release schemes 141
post-traumatic stress disorder
    (PTSD) 170, 202–3
power 24
pre-release work 52
precautionary principle 271
prepubescent children, sexual
    activity with 12
prescription charges 125
'presumption to disclose' 72
Pretty v UK (2002) 274
prevention/preventive initiatives
    26–8, 238–41
primary prevention 26
prison(s) 28, 30, 45, 85, 200, 202
privacy/private life, human rights
    273–5, 279
private policing 242–3
pro-offending behaviour/attitudes
    143, 167
probation 23, 28, 29, 40, 42, 44, 45,
    56, 135
probation officers 52–3, 197, 200
problem-solving 24, 27, 87, 88
problematic relationships 165–6, 168,
    170
procedural rights 286
process audits 49, 50
professional practice 12
promising risk factors 177

property offences 212, 218
proportionality 275, 285
prosecution, of children 8
Protection of Children Act (1978)
    232
protocols, community collaboration
    180
Prozac (fluoxetine) 117, 118
pseudo-photographs 230, 233
psychological damage, long-term 22
psychological integrity 274
psychological treatments 30
psychosocial deficits 170
psychotherapy 105, 108, 118, 183
psychotic disorders 195, 198–200
psychotropic medication 116–17
puberty 12, 24
public
    acceptance of treatment as
        sentencing option 124
    access to sex offender register 71
    anxiety regarding MAPPA 46
    attitudes see attitudes
    attunement of government to
        concerns of 75
    discourse, dangerousness 40
    education about sexual offending
        147
    relationship between media 251,
        259–60
public health problem, paedophilia
    as 4, 12
public opinion 31, 32, 251
public protection
    human rights 278, 286–7
    industry 41
    justification for continued
        sanctions 32
    non-disclosure 282
    sex offender registration 72
    shame penalties 135
    see also Multi-Agency Public
        Protection Arrangements
punishment 86, 123–5, 273
    see also self-punishment

punitiveness 32, 41, 74, 124, 134, 135–6
pure paedophiles 26

quantitative evaluation, treatment programmes 92–3

R (Adam and Others) v Secretary of State for Home Department (2005) 287
R v Chief Constable of North Wales Police ex p. AB (1997) 72
R v Lang and Others (2005) 276, 277
R v Pedley and Ors [2009] 277
randomized control trials, cognitive behavioural programmes 88–9
rapists 109, 110
Re C (unreported– 15 February 2002) 281, 282
Re Gallagher [2003] 280
Re Kevin Gallagher [2003] 71
re-arrests 164, 210, 218f, 219
reactionary language, UK press 254
reactive initiatives, cyber-sex offences 238
recidivism
    criminal history 164–5, 215–16, 217–19
    female sex offenders 161–7, 170
    intellectually disabled offenders 210–12
    juvenile sex offenders 176
    mental disorder and 195
    programme efficacy studies 91, 93, 94, 95, 96, 97, 98, 99, 100
    and proximity to children 48–9
    restorative justice 133, 143
    surgical castration 106
Recognition Service System (RSS) 215
reconviction rates 19–21, 143
referral, for medication 120
registration see Sex Offender Register
rehabilitative responses 24–30, 30

Reid, John 72
reinforcement 86
reintegration 48, 54, 133, 134, 137, 147, 194
reintegrative shaming 31, 33, 137, 141–2
rejection 28
relapse prevention 27, 52, 85–6, 95
relationships 29, 87, 88, 274
    between media and the public 251, 259–60
    of paedophiles 10
    see also age-appropriate relationships; problematic relationships; sexual relationships
reoffending
    female sex offenders 162
    ID offenders 210
    marginalisation and increased risk of 133
    reconviction rates as a measure of 19–21
    research into 19
    restorative justice 142
    treatment and 27, 109–10, 122
repetitive retribution 41
resettlement 28
residual psychosis 199
resources
    supervision and impact of low 47
    targeting towards higher risk groups 21
respect 138, 274
responsibility, for deviant behaviour 168
restorative conferencing 138, 139
restorative justice 105, 133–49
    addressing the critics 144–6
    case for 134–7
    contemporary policy context 138–9
    effectiveness 133, 142–4, 148
    need for recognition of potential 133–4

and risk management 146–8
sexual offending 139–42
RESTORE 139
restrictive interventions/conditions 22–3, 32, 43, 47–8
retributive justice, RJ and 146–7
retributive responses 30, 41
revenge 165
right(s)
    to appeal, against registration for life 71
    see also children's rights; civil rights movement; human rights; procedural rights
rioting 32, 67, 255
risk
    adolescent offenders and manageable level of 175
    defensive approach to 271
    institutionalisation 194
    justification of restrictions 271
    meaning of 19–22
    multi-agency approaches to 147
    psychotic disorders and decreased 195
    RJ and addressing levels of 147–8
    significant 277
    situational factors and heightened 25
risk agenda, impact on penal policy 41
risk assessment
    actuarial 20, 21, 30, 271–2
    of harm 275–6
    of MDSOs 196
    offender involvement in 54
    prisoners understanding of 54
    responsibility 42
    strategies 41
    tools 20, 21, 30, 40, 271–2, 276–7
risk aversion 40, 271
risk factors 162–7
    dynamic 27, 165–7, 176
    evidence-based 21, 27
    ID offending 210–12, 216

sexual harm by youth 176–7
static 163–5, 176
risk management
    agency cooperation 42–3
    allocation of offenders to appropriate level of 50
    balance, external/internal controls 53
    exclusion zones 49
    failures 45
    MDSOs 199–200, 202, 205
    partnerships 44
    pharmacotherapy as 124–5
    precedence over rehabilitation 41
    preoccupation with 30
    restorative justice 146–8
    self reporting 54
Risk Matrix (RM2000) 20, 21, 30
'risk, need and responsivity' principles 27, 29, 81, 211
risk penology 41, 271, 286
risk principle 21
risk society 18, 30, 271
rites of passage 12
role confusion, risk management failures 45
Royal Ottawa Hospital study 118

S and Marper v UK (2008) 281
safety 40, 141, 142, 143, 180, 270–1
Safety Button 239
Sarah's Charter 255
Sarah's Law 73, 135, 240, 255–6
scapegoating, of MDSOs 200
schizoaffective disorder 198
schizophrenia 120, 193, 197, 198, 199
secondary prevention 26–8
security 30, 40, 271
selective serotonin reuptake inhibitors (SSRIs) 28, 113, 117–19, 120, 125, 126, 201, 203, 205
self-efficacy 87, 88
self-esteem 22, 87, 88
self-hate, voluntary treatment 122
self-punishment 122

self-referred offenders 122
self-regulation 222
self-regulation programmes 199
self-rejection 10
self-risk management 54
self-worth, poor 10
sensitivity 10
sentencing
  acceptance of treatment as 124
  and detention 275–6
  deterrent 30
  human rights challenges 276–8
  indeterminate 275, 276–8, 282,
    286
  Internet grooming 236
Sentencing Circles 149n
serious crime, RJ as a trivialisation
  of 145
seriousness dimension 21–2
serotonin 116–17
Seroxat (paroxetine) 117
sertraline (Lustral) 117, 118
sex 8, 124, 167
sex education 84, 88
sex hormone production 113
Sex Offender Act (1997) 22–3, 63–4,
  70, 279
Sex Offender Bill 63, 65
sex offender homes
  MDSOs with dementia 205
  planned unannounced visits to 50
  police entering/accessing 69, 75
  see also group homes
Sex Offender Register, UK 61–76
  action to enforce 46
  community notification 71–2
  discussion 72–5
  evaluations 73
  government response to media,
    lobbyists and practitioners
    74–5
  human rights challenges 279–81
  information collection 69
  introduction of 61
  lack of research studies 73

legal challenges 70–1
legislation 63–4
non-compliance 67, 68–9
notification requirements 22–3,
  61, 64, 72
origins 62–3
purpose and aims 61, 62–3
registration periods 64t
reviews, right/access to 280–1,
  286
right to appeal 71
toughening and strengthening of
  65–70
Sex Offender Risk Appraisal Guide
  195
sex offenders
  in the community 278–82
  community management 47
  continued sanctions against
    unconvicted/released 32
  hardening of attitudes towards 33
  high level of interest in 3
  increased sentencing 275–6
  marginalisation and increased
    offending 133
  media descriptions 31
  other/othering 31, 40, 41
  public opinion of 31
  rights see human rights
  social networking sites 240–1
  supervision 46–7, 48t, 53–4
  treatment see treatment; treatment
    programmes
  unhelpfulness of term 20
  value and benefit of personal
    attention 53
  see also adult abusers; co-
    offenders; female sex
    offenders; high-risk sex
    offenders; intellectually
    disabled sex offenders;
    juvenile sex offenders; low
    risk offenders; mentally
    disordered sex offenders;
    paedophiles

sexual, problems concerning
meaning of 6
sexual ability 106
sexual abuse
attitudes condoning 166, 168
distorted beliefs 167
long-term effects 33
sexual gratification 168
see also child sexual abuse
sexual activity
age and 6–7
with children 7–8, 12
consensual 8
normality and acceptability 12
sexual aggression 24, 113
sexual arousal 11, 83, 84, 105, 108,
124, 167
sexual assaults, on MDSOs 200
sexual behaviour
and the brain 116
changes in understandings of 12
inappropriate 24, 25, 113, 210
Sexual Behaviour Unit (Newcastle)
121
sexual desire 106, 108, 117, 124
sexual development, female
offending 167
sexual deviancy 9, 25, 27, 83, 105,
113, 115, 119f, 124, 168–9, 284
sexual deviation, paedophilia as 5
sexual drive, inhibitors 108, 213
sexual fantasies 10, 24, 27, 28, 31,
113, 114, 115, 120
see also deviant fantasies; erotic
fantasies; paedophilic fantasies;
paraphiliac fantasies
sexual frustration 108
sexual gratification 165, 168
sexual harm by youth
challenge of addressing 174
collaboration to stop 177–9
barriers to effective 179
difficulties 178
effective 179, 185–6
multidisciplinary 178

recommendations 186–8
standardized approach 179–81
eliminating 181–5
prevalence 175
risk factors 176–7
see also juvenile sex offenders
sexual history, female offending 167
sexual intercourse 11
sexual offences
children under 16 years of age
14n
exclusion from RJ agenda 144
involvement of children and
reporting of 211
see also cyber-sex offences;
paedophilia; sexual abuse
Sexual Offences Act (2003) 7–8, 46,
64, 68, 69, 232, 235, 236, 279
Part II 134–5, 149n
Sexual Offences Prevention Orders
(SOPOs) 46, 149n
sexual offending
cycle of behaviour 10–11
denial and minimisation of 168
extending RJ to 148
growing awareness of 40
popular responses 135–6, 145–6
public education and awareness
147
restorative justice 139–42
effectiveness 142–4
risk *see* risk; risk assessment; risk
factors; risk management
state-led responses 134–5
theories, research and attitudes
13
understanding 24–6
see also sex offenders; sexual
offences
sexual orientation 124
sexual paraphilia 5
sexual predation *see* online sexual
predation
sexual predators, female offenders
committed as 163

sexual preoccupation 27
sexual relationships 84
sexual sadism 120
sexual scripts, deviant 25, 26
sexual stimuli 25
sexual urges 28, 106, 109, 110, 114, 120
sexual victimisation
    female sex offending 160, 161, 166–7
    of MDSOs in prison 202
sexual violence 211–12
Sexual Violence Risk-20 (SVR-20) 216
sexuality 8, 25, 167
sexually explicit conversations 235
shame/shaming 31, 33, 135, 136–7
side effects
    medication 108, 111, 112, 114, 115, 117–18, 123, 126, 283, 285
    surgical castration 107
'significant other(s)' 31, 168
'significant risk' 277
situational factors 25
sleep disorders 202
Smith, Jacqui 66, 67
social approaches 28–9
social class, and paedophilia 10
social constructionism 12–13, 251–4
social control 31
social dysfunctions 210
social introversion 10
social isolation 10, 48, 137
social learning 48
social networking sites 229, 238, 239, 240–1
social phobia 202
social policy 12
social responsibility 258–61, 262
social services/agencies 44, 45
social skills deficits 10, 25, 176
social skills training 27, 84, 87
social support, lack of 48
social welfare approach 26
socially sensitive stories, media coverage of 260

sociopathic condition, paedophilia as 5
South Africa 139
South Australia 139, 142
specialist ID offenders, De Waag study 218–19, 220, 221
Stafford v UK (2002) 276, 277
standards, community collaboration 180
State v Brown (1985) 107, 284
state-led responses, sexual crime 134–5
static risk factors 163–5, 176
static risk scales 20, 21
statistical analyses, treatment programmes 92
stereotaxic hypothalamotomy 105–6
stereotyping 251
sterilisation, irreversible 285
stigma/stigmatisation 136, 137, 200, 203, 205
stilboestrol 108
Stop It Now! 140–1, 142–3
stranger danger 40
stress 25
Structured Assessment of Risk and Need (SARN) 30
substance abuse 165, 168, 170, 204, 215
substance dependence 195
substance use disorders 195, 196, 198
The Sun 257
supervision, of offenders 46–7, 48t, 53–4
support
    lack of social 48
    post-release schemes 141
    see also Circles of Support and Accountability; community support
Sure Start 26
surgical interventions
    castration 27–8, 83, 106–7, 123
    neurosurgery 105–6

Sutcliffe, Gerry 72
systems approach, to treatment 29

Task Force Report on Children with
    Sexual Behavior Problems 175
technological innovations,
    prevention of Internet abuse
    239–40
tertiary syphilis 205
testosterone 108, 116, 205
testosterone enanthate 114–15
testosterone injections 107
testosterone reduction 27, 106, 108,
    109, 110, 111, 112–13, 113–14, 116,
    123
theory-driven research 222
torture 272–3, 286
Townsend, Pete 229
tracking outcomes, juveniles
    offenders 185–6
training, probation and parole
    officers 200
trans-institutionalisation 193–5
trauma
    histories, MDSOs 202
    juvenile sex offending 176
    see also post-traumatic stress
        disorder
trauma-sensitive foundation, youth
    development 183
traumatic stories, media coverage
    of 260
treatability 284
treated offenders, compared with
    treatment refusers 90–1
treatment
    early need identification and
        referral 52
    effective 22
    female sex offenders 167–70
    intellectually disabled offenders
        see De Waag study
    justification on mental health
        grounds 9
    juvenile sex offenders 182–5

known sex offenders 18, 19
low risk offenders 22
mentally disordered sex offenders
    196–8, 199
paedophiles 11
systems approach 29
see also interventions; medical
    treatment
treatment programmes
    accreditation 81–2
    construction of significant other
        31
    development and expansion 27,
        81
    effectiveness 27
    mandatory 29–30
    meta-analyses 27–8, 92–9
    see also cognitive behavioural
        programmes
Trelstar (triptorelin) 114
Trenantone 113–14
triptorelin 114, 115, 116
Truth and Reconciliation
    Commissions 139
Tyrer v UK (1979–80) 273

United Kingdom
    female sex offenders 160, 162
    government reaction to Sarah's
        Law 255–6
    press coverage of paedophilia
        254–7
    see also British culture; England
        and Wales
United Nations Convention on the
    Rights of the Child 6
United States
    child pornography legislation 233
    difficulty of evaluating restrictive
        laws 23
    exclusion zones 48
    female sex offenders 160, 161, 163
    mandatory medical treatment 121
    mandatory self-notification 135
    paedophile websites 231

rates of institutionalisation 194
sex offender registers 62, 71, 72, 76n
sex offender treatment 82, 84–5
victim-offender mediation 139
unlikely risk factors 177
unmet needs, female sexual offending 169
uses and gratification model 251

Van Colle v Chief Constable of Hertfordshire Police [2008] 282
vandalism 218
victim issues, offender articulation of 54
victim liaison 52
victim–offender mediation 139
victims
  age of 5, 215
  long-term effects of abuse 22, 33
  right to claim for protection 274
  and RJ 145, 147
vigilantism 67, 243–4, 282
Violent Crime Reduction Act (2006) 69, 75
violent offenders 40
Virgin Killer 242–3
virtual abuse 234–5
virtual pornography 233
virtual vigilantism 243–4
visual media, paedophilia 261
vitamin D 114
voluntary participation, restorative justice 147
voluntary vs. mandatory treatment 121–3
volunteers (COSA) 29
vulnerability(ies)
  media coverage and heightened sense of children's 229–30

pathway model, child sexual abuse 25–6, 33
vulnerable children, early intervention 26

Wade, Rebekah 255
Wales *see* England and Wales
Walker v Secretary of State for Home Department [2008] 277
Wechsler Adult Intelligence Scale (WAIS) 210, 216
Weeks v UK (Application No: 9787/82) 276
Weems v United States (1910) 106
Wells v Secretary of State for Justice (Parole Board Interviewing) [2009] 276, 278
What Works 27, 82, 85
Whiting, Roy 73, 255
Wikipedia 242, 243
willpower 124
withdrawal 10
women
  dependence on men 168
  negative attitudes towards 25
  see also female sex offenders; females
Wonderland Club 229
working class, paedophiles as 10
Wormwood Scrubs, pharmacotherapy study 120

Young People Who Sexually Abuse 179, 181
Youth Justice Board 176, 179
Youth Justice and Criminal Evidence Act (1999) 149n
youth offending teams 178, 185
youth violence, prevention 183, 188